*Financial
Decision Making
in the
Process Industry*

AMUNDSON *Mathematical Methods in Chemical Engineering: Matrices and Their Application*
AMUNDSON AND ARIS *Mathematical Methods in Chemical Engineering: Vol. II, First Order Partial Differential Equations with Applications*
ARIS *Elementary Chemical Reactor Analysis*
ARIS *Introduction to the Analysis of Chemical Reactors*
ARIS *Vectors, Tensors, and the Basic Equations of Fluid Mechanics*
BALZHISER, SAMUELS, AND ELIASSEN *Chemical Engineering Thermodynamics*
BRIAN *Staged Cascades in Chemical Processing*
CROWE et al. *Chemical Plant Stimulaion*
DENN *Stability of Reaction and Transport Processes*
DOUGLAS *Process Dynamics and Control: Vol. I, Analysis of Dynamic Systems*
DOUGLAS *Process Dynamics and Control: Vol. II, Control System Synthesis*
FOGLER *The Elements of Chemical Kinetics and Reactor Calculations: A Self-Paced Approach*
FREDRICKSON *Principles and Applications of Rheology*
FRIEDLY *Dynamic Behavior of Processes*
HAPPEL AND BRENNER *Low Reynolds Number Hydrodynamics with Special Applications to Particulate Media*
HIMMELBLAU *Basic Principles and Calculations in Chemical Engineering,* 3rd edition

HOLLAND *Fundamentals and Modeling of Separation Processes:*
  Absorption, Distillation, Evaporation, and Extraction
HOLLAND *Multicomponent Distillation*
HOLLAND *Unsteady State Processes with Applications in*
  Multicomponent Distillation
KOPPEL *Introduction to Control Theory with Applications to Process Control*
LEVICH *Physicochemical Hydrodynamics*
MEISSNER *Processes and Systems in Industrial Chemistry*
MODELL AND REID *Thermodynamics and its Applications*
NEWMAN *Electrochemical Systems*
OHARA AND REID *Modeling Crystal Growth Rates from Solution*
PERLMUTTER *Stability of Chemical Reactors*
PETERSEN *Chemical Reaction Analysis*
PRAUSNITZ *Molecular Thermodynamics of Fluid-Phase Equilibria*
PRAUSNITZ, ECKERT, ORYE, AND O'CONNELL *Computer Calculations for*
  Multicomponent Vapor-Liquid Equilibria
RUDD et al. *Process Synthesis*
SCHULTZ *Polymer Materials Science*
SEINFELD AND LAPIDUS *Mathematical Methods in Chemical Engineering:*
  Vol. III, Process Modeling, Estimation, and Identification
WHITAKER *Introduction to Fluid Mechanics*
WILDE *Optimum Seeking Methods*
WILLIAMS *Polymer Science and Engineering*
WOODS *Financial Decision Making in the Process Industry*

PRENTICE-HALL, INC.
PRENTICE-HALL INTERNATIONAL, INC.,
  UNITED KINGDOM AND EIRE
PRENTICE-HALL OF CANADA, LTD., CANADA

Financial
Decision Making
in the
Process Industry

DONALD R. WOODS

Department of Chemical Engineering
McMaster University

PRENTICE-HALL, INC.
Englewood Cliffs, New Jersey

Library of Congress Cataloging in Publication Data

WOODS, DONALD R
    Financial decision making in the process industry.

    Bibliography: p.
    1. Corporations—Finance. 2. Costs, Industrial.
I. Title.
HG4026.W65   658.1′5   74-14570
ISBN 0-13-314849-1

© 1975 by Prentice-Hall, Inc.
Englewood Cliffs, New Jersey

10 9 8 7 6 5 4 3 2 1

Printed in the United States of America

PRENTICE-HALL INTERNATIONAL, INC., *London*
PRENTICE-HALL OF AUSTRALIA, PTY. LTD., *Sydney*
PRENTICE-HALL OF JAPAN, INC., *Tokyo*
PRENTICE-HALL OF CANADA, LTD., *Toronto*
PRENTICE-HALL OF INDIA PRIVATE LTD., *New Delhi*

Contents

Preface   x

1.   The Decision Makers   1

1.1 Process Feasibility, 5   1.2 Impact Feasibility, 6   1.3 Resource Feasibility, 16   1.4 Making Decisions, 27   1.5 The Objectives and Plan of the Book, 31   1.6 Summary, 33   Problems, 33.

2.   Qualitative View of the Economy   35

2.1 The Model Market, 36   2.2 The Individual Company in Real Life, 39 2.3 Costs, Selling Price, and Profits, 40   2.4 Value, 45   2.5 Summary, 46   Problems, 46.

3.   Overall Company Financial Decisions and Cash Flow   47

3.1 A Sample Company and the Overall Decisions, 47   3.2 An Individual Company in Real Life, 53   3.3 Background for Decisions about Operations, 57   3.4 Background for Decisions About Profit Distribution, 61   3.5 Summary, 67   Problems, 67.

4. Background for Financing and Financial Feasibility   69

4.1 Time Value of Money: Interest, 69   4.2 Time Value of Assets: Depreciation, 77   4.3 Financial Feasibility, 91   4.4 Summary, 95 Problems, 95.

5. Financial Attractiveness of Alternatives   97

5.1 Financial Characteristics of Alternatives, 99   5.2 Time Available and the Financial Attractiveness Criteria, 102   5.3 Payback Time and Simple Return on Investment, 105   5.4 Venture Profit, 111   5.5 Equivalent Maximum Investment Period and the Interest Recovery Period, 113   5.6 Present Value and Internal Rate of Return, 115   5.7 Special Methods for Selecting Among Alternatives Satisfying One Objective, 130   5.8 Interrelationships Among the Methods, 134   5.9 Comparison and Evaluation of the Methods, 141   5.10 Summary, 148   Problems, 148.

6. Estimation of the Capital Investment   150

6.1 Time Available and the Principle of Successive Approximation, 152 6.2 Universal Factor Method, 154   6.3 Cost Correlations for Fixed Capital Investments, 159   6.4 Factor Methods of Cost Estimation, 175 6.5 Detailed Estimation for Each Component, 204   6.6 Estimating Additional Capital Expenditures, 204   6.7 Overall Summary and Recommendations, 205   Problems, 207.

7. Estimation of the Cost and Selling Price of a Product   210

7.1 Estimation of the Product Cost at a Fixed Production Rate, 211   7.2 Estimation of the Product Cost at Reduced Rates of Production, 224   7.3 Estimating the Selling Price, 228   7.4 Summary, 229   Problems, 229.

8. Using Costs to Generate Ideas for Screening Studies and Process Improvement   234

8.1 The Cost Per Function of Equipment in the Process Flow Diagram, 236 8.2 Cost Per Function of Utilities and Effluents, 237   8.3 Raw Material Costs: Cost Per Mole or Cost Per Property, 238   8.4 Product Specifications and Costs Per Property or Comparisons Per Attribute, 238   8.5 Summary, 239   Problems, 241.

9.   Financial Decision Making : Summary   242

      Bibliography   244

      Nomenclature   257

      Glossary   260

      Appendix A   Discrete Rate-of-Return Factors   271
              B   Cost Correlations for Processes   288
              C   Cost Correlations for Equipment   291
              D   Cost Correlations for Auxiliaries   304
              E   Unit Usages for Different Processes   307

      Author Index   313

      Subject Index   316

Preface

Interwoven in the fabric of the process industry are technical and financial threads. Without both technical and financial expertise the industry or company will collapse. In most educational institutions the emphasis for engineers and technicians is on technical expertise, and rightly so. However, some consideration must also be given to the financial aspects of the process industry if engineers and technicians are to function effectively.

The financial concepts are broad in scope. The spectrum includes basic economic concepts, the allocation of financial resources among the different company activities, the challenge of raising capital, interest and depreciation, financial attractiveness criteria, how to estimate the capital requirements for different proposals, estimation of product and production costs, and the use of costs to identify areas in the process for plant improvement. Said in other words, an appreciation of the financial framework plus an ability to calculate certain financial parameters combine to provide the thrust for the fruitful application of technical skills. Without these skills, the young professionals spend too much time working on technical problems that are academic and a waste of valuable resources.

A second need is for a better delineation of some aspects of professionalism: how professional engineers behave; their obligations to society, their company, and themselves; how they develop engineering judgment; how they make decisions.

Many books have been written to satisfy some of these needs, but they have been written for a different level of reader and have emphasized one or two but not most of the topics.

Some books that illustrate different aspects of the subject include *The Chemical Business Handbook*, Conrad Berenson's *The Administration of the Chemical Enterprise*, Barish's *Economic Analysis for Engineering and Managerial Decision Making*, F. C. Jelen's *Cost and Optimization Engineering*, C. M. Thatchers' *Fundamentals of Chemical Engineering*, M. Peters and K. Timmerhaus' *Plant Design and Economics for Chemical Engineers*, C. H. Chilton's *Cost Engineering in the Process Industry*, H. Popper's *Modern Cost Estimation Techniques*, C. Bauman's *Fundamentals of Cost Engineering in the Chemical Industry*, L. D. Miles' *Techniques of Value Analysis and Engineering*, and J. L. Riggs' *Economic Decision Models for Engineers and Managers.*

The many diverse topics have not been integrated into a continuous spectrum. Furthermore, because the topic is money, the books tend to be written for one particular country. The challenge is that the concepts are the same regardless of the country. With the greater mobility of engineers and with the growth of international business, there is a need to appreciate financial conditions in countries other than the United States. The reader needs to be encouraged to take a less parochial view and to realize the universality of many of the concepts.

This book is unique because of its integration of the diverse topics into a spectrum. It combines the development of mature decision-making ability and engineering judgment with financial considerations. The importance of solving a problem in the time available is emphasized and superimposed on calculating the financial attractiveness, the capital investment, and the product cost. The initial chapters discuss concepts in general to provide an overall appreciation of decision making and the financial aspects of an enterprise. The business game "Venture," available from Procter & Gamble Co., is an extremely stimulating, but not necessary, complement to this portion of the text.

The later chapters give practical experience in calculating the financial attractiveness, the capital investment, and the product cost. Extensive tables of data are given in the appendices. Examples and data are drawn from the chemical, metallurgical, hydrometallurgical, and sanitary engineering disciplines. Attempts have been made to provide background on Canadian and U.S. conditions and to encourage the reader to acquire a less parochial viewpoint.

It is extremely important that the young professional learn to communicate and work with his accounting colleagues, therefore accounting terminology and procedures have been used where applicable.

The book is written for a variety of readers. Primarily it is written for first- or second-year students for a separate course or as a complement to a design synthesis course or mass and energy balance course. The material is needed and complements subsequent courses in equipment design, unit operations, and senior design and optimization courses.

I feel that the sooner most of these concepts are introduced, the better appreciation the student has of the relationships of his other courses and what professional life will be like. Furthermore, most of the concepts are not difficult, but I have found that many students undergo a long induction period before they appreciate some of the concepts.

The book can also be used to complement unit operations or design courses, for young professionals in industry who have not had sufficient exposure to the financial aspects of industry and for professional engineers who have not had a chance to learn some of the latest methods of financial analysis.

I am grateful to my students, who have made extensive suggestions to improve the various versions of this book. My colleagues in the faculty of Business, Professors L. G. Eckel, G. W. Torrance, and A. Z. Szendrovits and Dean W. J. Schlatter and Dr. J. A. Johnson of the Department of Economics have helped me immensely. From industry, C. A. Miller of Canadian Industries Ltd. influenced the work significantly. The text benefited from the comments and suggestions of Howard W. Martin, Monsanto Co.; William H. Gauvin and A. A. Condy, Noranda Research Centre, Pointe Claire, Quebec; Stephen Dunn and Emil H. Nenniger, Hatch Associates Ltd., Toronto; Carl W. Hopp and Fred Cooper of Stevens, Thompson and Runyon Consulting Engineers, Portland Oregon; Gord M. Robb, Union Carbide Canada Ltd., Toronto; Roger M. Butler and Jack Pasternak of Imperial Oil Ltd., Sarnia; Andy Blair, The Lummus Co., Toronto; E. R. Acton of Phillips Cables Ltd., Brockville, and Dale F. Rudd, of the University of Wisconsin.

I thank Miss Charlotte M. Traplin for patiently typing the many different versions of this book and Miss Susan J. Anderson, who helped compile the material in the appendices. The cost data have been collected from published and private sources. I am grateful to the many who assisted me in evaluating the cost data. In particular, I thank P. A. Loucks, Trane Co. of Canada Ltd.; D. Flathmann, SiHi Co. Ltd.; A. Cunningham, Arthur S. Leitch Co. Ltd.; Margaret Peppler, Smart Turner Hayward Pumps Ltd.; P. Langsetmo, the Strong Scott Manufacturing Co.; R. H. J. Ritchie, Tenace Tools Ltd., and Indiana General Ltd.; J. Townsend, Sharples-Stokes; F. C. Ho and J. W. Nelson, Toronto Coppersmithing Ltd.; D. Jones, RAB Engineering; W. C. Goman and Carl Ljungberg, Canada Pumps; R. J. Laidlaw, Gatx Fuller; G. Panthel, Denver Equipment; T. Sullivan of Sullivan Mills Ltd.; R. J. Schramm, J. Newell and G. J. Hoolboom, Westinghouse Canada Ltd.; Brian Minns, P. R. Donahue Ltd.; M. H. Pickfield, Vickers Warnick Ltd.; J. Dimitroff, Canadian Bearings Co. Ltd.; and E. M. Cook, Bowen Engineering Inc; A. D. Boothroyd, Atomic Energy of Canada Ltd.; and R. Frederick, Norton Co.

Hamilton, Ontario, Canada DONALD R. WOODS

The Decision Makers 1

Engineers are expected to make good decisions: good decisions for society, good decisions for their company, and good decisions for themselves.

"Good decisions for society" means that natural resources are not squandered, that the quality of the environment remains unchanged or is improved, that the product is safe, and that the product is needed and beneficial.

"Good decisions for the company" means that the product will provide sufficient financial return on the investment to satisfy present owners or investors and to attract investment for future company activities; that the projects recommended by the engineer are those that make the best use of the limited money available within the company; that the decisions are timely, i.e., the new processes are new and are introduced before competitors introduce them; that the processes are technically possible to construct and are safe for the operators to run; and that the product will sell. Naturally, the company wants the decisions to be good decisions for society and for their employees.

"Good decisions for the individual" means that the individual is pleased with the decisions made, that they fit within the individual's sense of values or ethics, and that the individual feels that the decisions are good for the company and for society.

Figure 1.1 shows the plane of all possible ideas, good and bad. Since an engineer has to decide whether an idea is good or bad, acceptable or unacceptable, each idea can be identified as a decision. If the idea is to build a device

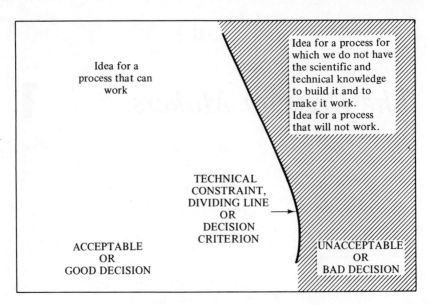

Figure 1.1. The plane of ideas showing the technical constraint.

that is impossible to build, the idea represents a bad decision. Figure 1.2 shows an idea for a new candlestick. To accept this idea would be a bad decision because it cannot be built. Similarly, some complex plants or processes cannot be built because we lack scientific and engineering knowledge.

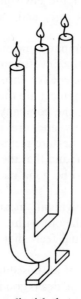

Figure 1.2. A candlestick that cannot be built.

Hence, we can divide the plane of ideas into two regions: those processes that are technically possible to build and those that are not. The dividing line is called the constraint or the criterion for making the technical decision.

Similarly, decisions are good or bad depending on the following criteria:

> Benefits-to-society feasibility: The product is not just a frill.
>
> Safety feasibility: The process is safe to operate, and the products are safe.
>
> Environmental feasibility: The environment suffers no harmful effects.
>
> Economic feasibility: The effects on the nation's economy are acceptable.
>
> Market feasibility: Consumers will buy the product in the volume supplied.
>
> Natural resource feasibility: The resources are available and are not squandered.
>
> Originality feasibility: The idea does not infringe on a patent.
>
> Time feasibility: The project can be completed in the time available.
>
> Social feasibility or the political criterion: The product is socially acceptable and is in tune with the political climate of the times.
>
> Financial feasibility: The money is available to finance the project.
>
> Financial attractiveness feasibility: The reward for investing in the project is attractive relative to the risk involved.

These criteria are shown on the decision plane in Fig. 1.3. For each criterion there is an acceptable region and an unacceptable region. The central region represents good decisions that bring valuable products or services to benefit society. Professional engineers must consider all these criteria, and the criteria are not easy to apply. Often these criteria conflict with each other; they overlap, and many cannot be quantitatively predicted reliably. For discussion purposes, the criteria are classified into three general areas. These areas are not mutually exclusive, and, indeed, many of the criteria can be included in more than one grouping. For discussion purposes the classification is

> *Process feasibility:*
> > Technical
> > Safety
> > Environmental
> > Originality
>
> *Impact feasibility:*
> > Benefits to society

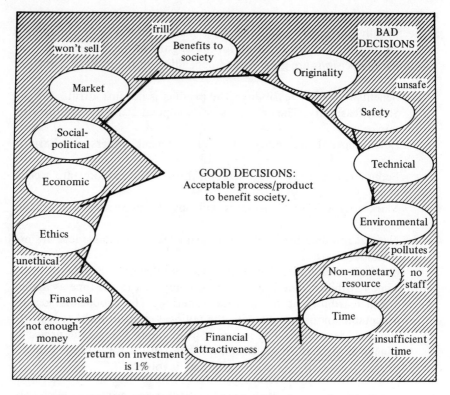

Figure 1.3. The plane of ideas or decisions showing good and bad decisions and the criteria.

       Market
       Social, or the political criterion
       Economic
       Ethical

Resource feasibility:
       Nonmonetary resource
       Time
       Financial
       Financial attractiveness

In this chapter we shall discuss these criteria briefly. The theme of the book is the financial and the financial attractiveness feasibilities. Some of the implications of time feasibility are emphasized.

1.1 Process Feasibility

A process must work safely for the people running it and safely for the environment. The process may be an innovation that will bring the company future patents and a definite edge over the competition.

Technical feasibility

There are many reasons something will not work. Perhaps the process violates a law of nature, such as fluids do not flow uphill on their own, gravity acts downward, we cannot push on a rope, entropy increases but never decreases spontaneously, and the laws of conservation of species and of energy. Perhaps we require materials of construction that have not yet been developed. For example, for a process to work we may need a thin glass vessel that withstands a pressure of 50,000 psi, and glass cannot withstand this high pressure. Perhaps the equipment is similar to that shown in Fig. 1.2 and simply cannot be built. Perhaps we require that a given piece of machinery be available immediately off the shelf, and such equipment is not so manufactured. Perhaps we just do not know enough about the science and technology of the process to make it work. For example, it is scientifically possible to produce ketene from acetic acid:

acetic acid (vapor) $\rightleftharpoons$ ketene (vapor) + water (vapor)

However, the reaction is reversible. Once the ketene is formed it is important that it be separated from the water quickly. One separation process might be to condense the water and separate the ketene vapor from the liquid water. However, the rate of the reverse reaction increases if ketene dissolves in liquid water. On a laboratory scale, we have been able to condense and separate the water fast enough to minimize the reversion. Question: Can we successfully do this as a large-scale industrial process? If this cannot be done successfully, then acetic acid goes into the process and acetic acid comes out.

With a firm understanding of the laws of nature and the properties of materials and an appreciation of practical equipment, the technical criterion is not too difficult to understand or to apply to yield a good decision.

Safety feasibility

The process must be safe to operate and the products must be safe to transport and to use.

Environmental feasibility

Many processes interact with the environment. For example, each ton of paper requires about 400 tons of water; chemical plants use large quantities of air; solid wastes must be discarded safely. Noise, odor, and esthetic appearance should not affront the surrounding community. The weather should be appropriate for the process being considered.

It is not sufficient to satisfy present-day conditions and legal requirements; the processes that we design and the decisions that we make are for the future. Future trends and needs should be anticipated.

Originality feasibility

Some ideas lead to inventions and innovations that are patentable. Some decisions are acceptable but unoriginal; that is, the decision is to duplicate the process we presently use. Alternatively, we may purchase process technology from someone else. An unacceptable decision is one that illegally uses an idea or process under patent protection.

1.2 Impact Feasibility

In the past engineers have brought society just about all the material benefits that surround us; refrigerators, drugs, synthetic clothing, automobiles, fuels to heat our homes, highways and bridges, electricity, our homes, telephone, radio, television, artificial kidneys, newsprint and the printing presses. For more details of the contribution to and the impact on society, see *Man-Made World* (1971), Toffler (1970), and Commoner (1971).

Today, engineers try to apply the findings of science to help society. We are looking at how we have done things in the past to see if they can be done less expensively without sacrificing quality. For example, engineers are developing new materials for artificial organs that will be accepted, not rejected, by human bodies; new instruments are being developed for measuring concentrations, blood flow, and breathing rates so that researchers can develop a better understanding of man and nature; new machines are being built to help machinists do precision work more easily—machines that will remove the drudgery from our daily work. In the future, engineers will continue to try to bring an ever-increasing and amazing array of material benefits, yet there will be a challenging difference. We realize today how much technology affects our daily life; technology may make us less self-reliant and may rob us of our self-confidence, our pride of personal accomplishment, and our dignity. The challenge, then, is to bring benefits and devices that aid society yet ensure that any sacrifice in human dignity is small or that human dignity is built up elsewhere. In our decision making, we need to assess the short- and long-range impact on society of some of the engineering innovations before the innovation is released. We need to look at the total picture—our total environment, our total available resources, and our total society. We do not prevent air pollution only to have water pollution; we do not build larger and larger energy-consuming devices knowing that there is a limit to the amount of energy available in this world; we do not build larger and larger concrete cities only to realize that there are insufficient recreation forests close at hand; we do not concentrate our efforts to develop devices to aid the affluent and neglect the needs of any one segment of society.

In summary, the engineer decision makers must include impact feasibility in their decisions. This includes the benefits to society, the market, the social or political issues, and the economic and ethical considerations; Lear (1970) and Branscomb (1971) elaborate on the assessment of the future impact of technology on society.

Benefits-to-society feasibility

Little is known about the benefits-to-society criterion, yet we need to keep reminding ourselves that our role in society is to provide beneficial products.

One approach might be to produce every type of product and let the user decide whether it is used for the benefit or to the detriment of society. In other words, the responsibility rests with the user. Indeed, every product can be used or abused, as Albert Nobel found with his discovery of explosives. However, I believe that responsibility also rests with the engineer, for he is part of that society. The responsibility includes making products that are not just frills but that satisfy a basic need, products that benefit many and not just a few, products and services that do not unwittingly cause individuals to lose their sense of human worth or their dignity or personal freedoms. Furthermore, the engineer has a responsibility to provide information to the users about the beneficial uses.

Starr (1969) discusses the dilemma of social benefit versus technological risk with examples mainly in safety and transportation; Hull (1971) analyzes the environmental risks from power plants.

Market feasibility

The proposed consumers must buy the product in the quantity, in the quality, and for the price suggested. For example, it would be unwise to offer black, foul-smelling soap on the market at 2 cents a bar if the consumer wanted white, fragrant soap "no matter what." There are some products that the consumer just does not want. People traveling in aircraft or by sea associate travel sickness with the color yellow. Therefore, it would be unwise to try to sell large quantities of corn to the aircraft industry. Other factors to consider are discussed by Fiegel (1972) and O'Meara (1961).

Social feasibility or the political criterion

We may have a very good product and the resources to produce it but find that politically the project should be dropped. We may not agree with the politics, but we cannot neglect them.

In general, a political decision is based on a need for acceptance by others—on a willingness to forego logic to make a decision based on emotion. The decision is not the best, but it is acceptable to others at this particular time.

Engineers encounter politics in two ways: the politics in others and in themselves. For example, the politics in the early 1970s was such that air pollution was a major concern. This would mean that processes that released steam plumes into the atmosphere (with no particulate or chemical contamination) would be viewed with a jaundiced eye. It was not what we were doing; it was what it looked like we were doing. It could be that research on test-tube babies would be stopped because of the politics of the times.

Turning now to the situation within ourselves, usually people tell us what they think we want to hear and not necessarily what they think. Thus, a project that we initiate may be reported to us as being attractive, whereas a better project that contradicts our views is not reported to us. To combat this, we must try to identify our own emotions and to encourage others to express themselves freely without fear of being judged harshly.

Economic feasibility

The decisions within one part of a company affect the other company activities, the industry as a whole, and to some extent the economy of the nation. While this may seem too idealized, the total is nevertheless the sum of the parts, and the impact of our decisions on the total economy at least should be considered.

Ethical feasibility

Ethics refers to our personal system of values—our view of what is good and bad behavior. Each person has a personal set of ethics, moral principles, or rules of conduct. Engineers, because of their responsibility to society, have a code of ethics which delineates the conduct of the individual professional engineers. Thus, individuals have a *microethical* responsibility to ensure that their decisions satisfy their personal and professional ethics. On the other hand, engineers are, by and large, the decision makers in industry and technology, and so we need to ensure that the industrial impact on society is ethical. This macroethical responsibility is to ensure that the *company* that purchases our talent and services assumes an ethical responsibility to society. Hodgins (1970) describes this as a responsibility to ensure that our legacy to future generations is not one of starvation or suffocation. Consider first the microethics. We cannot memorize someone else's set of ethics; ethics are personal. We need to learn different alternatives of behavior, to accept and/or reject certain attitudes, to integrate those that we accept into our value system, and eventually to behave according to that personal system of values [Krathwohl et al. (1964) clearly defines the stages in developing a system of ethics]. Some attitudes that are important for engineers are summarized in Table 1.1.

The purpose of this section is to provide an opportunity to explore some alternatives in behavior open to us, to introduce the professional code of ethics, and to introduce through examples some ideas of its interpretation. It rests with each of us to develop ethics for ourselves.

TABLE 1.1
SOME ATTITUDES IMPORTANT TO ENGINEERS

Use of all resources:

What products and services are useful and needed by mankind?
Does this represent the optimum long-term use of natural resources?
Sense of urgency of man's needs.
Willingness to compromise theory with reality in satisfying man's needs.

Values of human worth: Plant safety, safe products, salary and job security, human relations, and effect of present operations and products on future health of society.

Esthetic values.

Moral and ethic values:

Micro- and macroscale:
Employment (seeking and hiring and firing those working for you).
Environment.
Use of natural resources.
Use of intellectual human talent.
Information.
Honesty.

Interaction with other professionals:

Willingness to actively participate in the professional organization.
Loyalty to colleagues.
Confidence in one's own abilities.
Initiative to start programs based on one's own and maturity of outlook.
Reliability.

As professional engineers we have an obligation to understand, accept, and behave according to the professional code of ethics expected by the general public. This code guarantees to the clients and the public that competent engineering services are supplied for the fees received by the engineer. Teller (1966) elaborates on the need for the observance of the code of ethics by the individual practitioners. We need to study this code carefully because although it may be "someone else's set of ethics" we must agree to accept it as professionals. Each state, provincial, or national profession has

TABLE 1.2

CODE OF ETHICS OF THE ASSOCIATION OF PROFESSIONAL ENGINEERS OF ONTARIO*

GENERAL
1. A professional engineer owes certain duties to the public, his employers, other members of his profession and to himself and shall act at all times with,
    (a) fairness and loyalty to his associates, employers, subordinates and employees;
    (b) fidelity to public needs; and
    (c) devotion to high ideals of personal honour and professional integrity.

DUTY OF PROFESSIONAL ENGINEER TO THE PUBLIC
2. A professional engineer shall,
    (a) regard his duty to public welfare as paramount;
    (b) endeavour at all times to enhance the public regard for his profession by extending the public knowledge thereof and discouraging untrue, unfair or exaggerated statements with respect to professional engineering;
    (c) not give opinions or make statements on professional engineering projects of public interest that are inspired or paid for by private interests unless he clearly discloses on whose behalf he is giving the opinions or making the statements;
    (d) not express publicly or while he is serving as a witness before a court, commission, or other tribunal, opinions on professional engineering matters that are not founded on adequate knowledge and honest conviction;
    (e) make effective provisions for the safety of life and health of a person who may be affected by the work for which he is responsible; and at all times shall act to correct or report any situation which he feels may endanger the safety or welfare of the public; and
    (f) sign or seal only those plans, specifications and reports actually made by him or under his personal supervision and direction.

Article Two of The Code of Ethics is to be interpreted to include responsibility for meeting all lawful standards for environmental control in all engineering work; and

That failure knowingly or unknowingly to meet such standards is cause for disciplinary procedures to be instituted by the Association against such Member; and

That any Member who is prevented by any employer, governmental agency, or other person or party from meeting such standards in the course of his work, or who suffers personal loss or harm from insisting on such standards being met, is to be supported by the Association through all available channels until redress is obtained; and

That the Association is to police and enforce this interpretation of the Code of Ethics in a vigorous and determined manner; and

That employers, governmental agencies, the public and the press are to be fully and regularly informed on this stand of the Association.

DUTY OF PROFESSIONAL ENGINEER TO EMPLOYER
3. A professional engineer shall,
    (a) act in professional engineering matters for each employer as a faithful agent or trustee and shall regard as confidential any information obtained by him as to the business affairs, technical methods or processes of an employer and avoid or disclose any conflict of interest which might influence his actions or judgment;
    (b) present clearly to his employers the consequences to be expected from any deviations proposed in the work if his professional engineering judgment is overruled by non-technical authority in cases where he is responsible for the technical adequacy of professional engineering work;
    (c) have no interest, direct or indirect, in any materials, supplies to equipment used by his employer or in any persons or firms receiving contracts from his employer unless he informs his employer in advance of the nature of the interest;
    (d) not tender on competitive work upon which he may be acting as a professional engineer unless he first advises his employer;
    (e) not act as consulting engineer in respect of any work upon which he may be the contractor unless he first advises his employer, and
    (f) not accept compensation, financial or otherwise, for a particular service, from more than one person except with the full knowledge of all interested parties.

DUTY OF PROFESSIONAL ENGINEER TO OTHER PROFESSIONAL ENGINEERS
4. A professional engineer shall,
    (a) conduct himself towards other professional engineers with courtesy and good faith;
    (b) not accept any engagement to review the work of another professional engineer for the same employer except with the knowledge of that engineer, or except where the connection of that engineer with the work has been terminated;
    (c) not maliciously injure the reputation or business of another professional engineer;
    (d) not attempt to gain an advantage over other members of his profession by paying or accepting a commission in securing professional engineering work;
    (e) not advertise in a misleading manner or in a manner injurious to the dignity of his profession, but shall seek to advertise by establishing a well-merited reputation for personal capacity; and
    (f) give proper credit for engineering work, uphold the principle of adequate compensation for engineering work, provide opportunity for professional development and advancement of his associates and subordinates; and extend the effectiveness of the profession through the interchange of engineering information and experience.

DUTY OF PROFESSIONAL ENGINEER TO HIMSELF
5. A professional engineer shall,
    (a) maintain the honour and integrity of his profession and without fear or favour expose before the proper tribunals unprofessional or dishonest conduct by any other member of the profession; and
    (b) undertake only such work as he is competent to perform by virtue of his training and experience, and shall, where advisable, retain and co-operate with other professional engineers or specialists.

---

*Courtesy of the Association of Professional Engineers of Ontario.

its own code. As an example, the code of the Professional Engineers of the Province of Ontario is summarized in Table 1.2. In scrutinizing it, we see that the code is not precise for every situation. Furthermore, it applies to the individual and not to corporate behavior. Individuals, using their best judgment, must interpret the code. To provide an example of how one professional interprets a situation, consider the following cases:

Example:* Disclosure of the Technical Processes of a Former Employer

Fact: An engineer employed by the ABC Company is assigned by his supervisor to develop processing equipment for the manufacture of certain chemical products. In his previous employment with the XYZ Company, the engineer had participated in the development of similar equipment. The technical information concerning the equipment has not been published in the technical press, or otherwise released. By virtue of his previous involvement in its development the engineer is familiar with the equipment and the principles of its design. His superiors in the ABC Company suggest that this knowledge will be useful in developing similar equipment for their use and expect him to make his knowledge concerning the particular equipment available to the ABC Company to aid in the development of the similar equipment.

Question: May the engineer ethically apply his knowledge to the development of equipment for his employer based on experience and information gained in similar work for a previous employer, without the consent of the latter?

Reference: Code of Ethics, Section 3(a)—Table 1.2.

Discussion: General professional knowledge gained by experience accrues to the individual and is carried with him in the course of his career to be used by him in the performance of his work for any client or employer. The situation here, however, refers not to general professional knowledge, but to a specific process or equipment of a former employer. The facts indicate that the particular equipment of the XYZ Company is in the nature of a "trade secret" and hence may not be disclosed to other persons without consent.

The courts have often been called upon to distinguish between general knowledge and trade secrets. The guiding principles in drawing the line have been stated as follows:

"While it has been said that an exact definition of a trade secret is not possible, the courts nevertheless define a trade secret to be a plan or process, tool, mechanism or compound, known only to its owner and those of his employees to whom it is necessary to confide it in order to apply it to the uses for which it is intended. Like any

*Supplied courtesy of L. C. Sentance.

other secret, a trade secret is nothing more than a private matter; something known only to one or a few and kept from the general public, and not susceptible to general knowledge. There must exist a substantial element of secrecy, and the term 'trade secret' is not applied to matters of public knowledge, or of common knowledge to a trade, or of general knowledge in an industry, or to matters which are completely disclosed by the goods which are marketed."

Conclusions: Most employers of engineers accept the obligation of permitting their engineers to decide for themselves what information they can carry and use from job to job, recognizing the ethical duty of the engineer not to disclose confidential information of a former employer.

Inasmuch as the equipment developed for the XYZ Company had not been made known to the public or the industry, it is in the nature of a "trade secret" and the engineer who participated in its development may not ethically use or impart that particular knowledge to another employer without the consent of his former employer, although he may ethically apply general knowledge and general engineering principles gained in his former employment to solving the problems of his present employer.

Example:*   QUALITY OF PRODUCT

Facts: For many years the ABC Company has manufactured a product which enjoys a high quality rating in the industry and among the public. Competing manufacturers have now introduced a similar product of lower quality at lower cost, and this competition has caused a serious decline in the sales of the product manufactured by the ABC Company. To meet this competition the ABC Company instructs its engineers to redesign its product in order that it may be made available to the market at lower cost. Upon receiving these instructions some of the engineers question whether such an action would be consistent with the Code of Ethics because a lower quality product under the same brand name would mislead the public into accepting a product of lesser quality in the mistaken belief that it meets the high quality standards with which the product has been associated in the public mind for many years.

Question: Do the engineers have a proper interest and ethical obligation to protest the company's decision, or to refuse to design a lower quality product?

Reference: Code of Ethics, Sections 2(a), 2(d), 3(a), 5(a)—Table 1.2.

Discussion: The primary thrust of the Code of Ethics is to protect and serve the public safety, health and welfare by the application of engineering knowledge and to protect and defend the high standing of the

*Supplied courtesy of L. C. Sentance.

engineering profession's integrity and public confidence in it. If the engineers believe that the lower quality product would jeopardize safety or health, Section 2(d) clearly indicates their ethical responsibility to advise management.

However, the Code of Ethics does *not* deal with business decisions of companies, and should be restricted to situations which clearly raise questions of the ethical conduct of individual engineers.

Here, the decision to offer a lower quality product is exclusively a matter for management determination, based on the company's evaluation of its commercial operations. The engineers are not requested to engage in an activity which collides with their duty to advise management. They may feel that the decision is not a wise one, that it may reflect adversely upon the public acceptance of the Company's product, or even that the public may be misled. These are risks for management evaluation, but there is no reason for the engineers to refrain from offering the company their opinions and comments through normal communication channels within the company. It would be a disservice to the engineering profession to attempt to extend the Code of Ethics to the point of interference in business decisions of the commercial world.

Conclusion: The engineers assigned to the re-design of a commercial product of lower quality should not question the company's business decision, but have an obligation to point out any safety hazards in the new design, and may offer their personal opinions and comments to management.

Other examples of opinions about ethics are given by Aries (1966), Alger et al. (1965), Chemical Engineering Editorial Staff (1963), and Popper and Hughson (1970).

Some cases that you might discuss with your friends that concern microethics are listed below; for each case, try to play the role of the individual involved:

Case 1:   I am a fourth-year student seeking employment. In January I am offered a job by company X for $400/month and am given 10 days to accept their offer. I accept their offer. Two weeks later I receive an offer of $700/month and a more exciting position from company Y. What do I do?

Case 2:   I am a third-year student. Last summer I had an excellent job designing a new type of heat exchanger that the company was developing. When I returned to school my professor asked me to give a lecture in the heat transfer course on how to design heat exchangers. I really feel I have something exciting to share with my fellow classmates. Is it ethical for me to present this lecture?

Case 3:   I am a fourth-year student, and I plan to go on to medical school, although I have not been accepted as yet. I want a good summer job, yet if my application for medical school is turned down, I would want the job to be permanent. Jobs are hard to get, and the interviewers with whom I have talked so far will offer me permanent employment but not summer employment. I have three interviews left. What do I tell these interviewers?

Case 4:   I am a first-year student. None of my classmates has a summer job. Jobs are hard to get, and I need money to pay for school next year. I have been offered a good-paying job with lots of engineering experience to work on the production of napalm (or fill in your personal answer to Problem 1.6 given at the end of this chapter). Personally, I strongly believe that this product should not be manufactured. Do I accept the job? Do I tell the company of my personal beliefs?

Case 5:   I accept a summer job for staff day work in a research laboratory. I turn down other job opportunities with other companies. When I start my summer job I find that they plan to use me on the afternoon and midnight shifts to run the pilot plant. I had already joined the tennis club and two evening clubs and have met a number of girls who work days only. What do I do?

It is useful if you pose your own cases of microethics and discuss them with your friends. It helps if you have an older engineer present just so that you can hear his viewpoint.

Macroethics offers quite a challenge to the individuals because we must identify our own position on the microethic level and then find effective means within the company for translating a personal view into a corporate view. If we cannot find such effective means or if the others in the department or the company will not accept our view, then we have to decide what to do as an individual. Finding effective means within the company depends on the structure of the company, the personalities of our colleagues, and our own ability to persuade. However, identifying the problem is worthy of discussion, and exploring possible avenues of procedure is beneficial. Discuss the following cases with your friends:

Case 6:   I am permanently employed by a toaster manufacturer. Today I received a memo saying that our toasters are lasting too long and that I am to design a below-capacity connecting link in the heater circuit so that the toaster will fail after about 3 years of use. The weak link is to be in such a location that the labor cost of repair will be within 80% of the cost of a new toaster. Last week, three of my colleagues were prematurely retired because of the tight economic situation in the industry. What do I do?

Case 7:   Our company needs to dispose of waste acids from the mines. I have just been assigned the job of selecting the site within 50 miles of the mine and designing the necessary piping arrangement for deep well disposal [see Sheldrick (1969), for example]. The previous occupant of my desk was fired because he believed that this was unethical and he quit rather than design the system. I am told that if I don't design it I will be transferred to Siberia and the company will hire a local deep well disposal contractor. What do I do?

Case 8:   I am a project engineer in charge of land fill operations reclaiming portions of a nearby lake. A legal dispute has arisen between a local conservation authority and my company as to the legality of the land fill operations. My employer ignores the conservation authority and has instructed me to continue land fill operations. What do I do?

Case 9:   I am the process engineer in charge of margarine production. By mistake I dropped a mercury thermometer into a 30-ton processing tank of finished product. The glass and mercury are now finely dispersed throughout this $10,000 quantity of product. What do I do?

If we are unsatisfied by the response of our supervisors and the response of the company, then the code of ethics usually provides an avenue for bringing the macroethical problem to the attention of the profession for further action. Other avenues have been suggested, such as through pressure brought to bear from groups outside the profession [see, for example, Nader (1971), Nader et al. (1972) and Boffey (1971)], but I believe that working through the professional organization is best for the individual, society, and the profession.

1.3 Resource Feasibility

Any process requires resources: raw materials, machinery, manpower, money. Hence, any decision concerning a process must consider the availability and utilization of these resources. Furthermore, we must have the ideas and time necessary to successfully implement the decision. Hence, we need to consider nonmonetary resource feasibility, time feasibility, financial feasibility, and financial attractiveness feasibility.

Nonmonetary resource feasibility

For any project we must ensure that the resources are available and that they are not squandered.

Consider availability first. No company can start a project if it lacks the resources. The most important resource is people: people to carry out the projects and people to generate ideas and to successfully innovate them. The company also must have access to the required raw materials.

Next the utilization of the resources should be considered. While it may be easy to view this resource utilization from a parochial viewpoint, it is important to account for local, national, and worldwide implications.

Consider people first. Are we making the most effective use of the people in our company? Have we created an environment that encourages the development of good ideas? From a national viewpoint, are we making the most effective use of the trained personnel, and how do we as a company encourage the training of these people?

With regard to natural raw materials, some are nonrenewable, for example, oil and mineral reserves. We must use these resources carefully to ensure that society will be well served both now and in the future. Other resources are renewable, such as plants and animals. Some resources have alternative uses today; for example, a forested area can be protected as a recreational area or it can be strip-mined to yield cheap access to the minerals beneath the ground. Which alternative is in the best interest of society?

This criterion is difficult to apply, although some consideration must be given to these concerns when decisions are made.

Time feasibility

Time is one of our most precious commodities. No amount of money will buy us a 25-hr day. We cannot board an airplane that has just taken off. What each of us is called upon to do is to make the best use of the time available.

Within the process industry, there are pressures of time. If the market will support the installation of one and only one large-sized plant to produce margarine, then one company designs and gets the process into operation first, and the rest of the companies are sitting with the plans on the drawing boards. The latter companies must absorb the expenses incurred in the abortive attempt to produce margarine elsewhere in the company's operation. As another example, for every minute a process produces product of unacceptable quality money is lost. Thus, an important decision criterion is the time feasibility. For any problem to solve or decision to be made, we need to identify the time available. For a technical or financial decision, an accuracy can be attributed to the answer that reflects the time available. That is, if an answer is expected in 5 min, the accuracy is usually within $\pm 200\%$, whereas if a month is allowed, the accuracy may be within $\pm 10\%$.

As an example, consider the problem "What is the temperature of the room in which you are now sitting?" You can usually estimate the temperature to within $\pm 3°C$. This takes about 30 sec. If we want the answer to within

$\pm 1°C$, we can locate a thermometer and measure the temperature. This might take 30 min, depending on the availability of the thermometer. To increase the accuracy to $\pm 0.1°C$, we could calibrate the thermometer. This might take a day. More sophisticated instruments could be devised or purchased to measure the temperature to $\pm 0.0001°C$, but this might take several years to perfect. Thus, there are many answers to any question, the accuracy of the answer depends on the local circumstances and the time available.

We can learn a strategy for solving problems in the time available. The principles we could use are either

> *"The law of optimum sloppiness":* For any problem, there is any optimum amount of sloppiness we can use to solve the problem.
>
> *Corollary:* There are occasions when we must be sloppy or imprecise in our calculations, and there are times when we must be precise. Gushee (1965) describes the essence of engineering as being only as complicated as you have to be, but you must also be able to get as complicated as the problem demands.
>
> *"The principle of successive approximation":* According to this principle, we start simply and get a feel for the order of magnitude of the answer at the beginning and then solve the problem successively with increased accuracy at each step.

These principles are slightly different in their approach; with the law of optimum sloppiness, one set of calculations is done; the calculation procedure and the accuracy are chosen to match the time available. With the principle of successive approximation, a series of calculations is done starting with the sloppiest and gradually increasing in accuracy. Between each successive calculation the question "Are we still interested?" is asked. For different situations, one or the other or a mixture of approaches can be used. Each of us needs to acquire proficiency in using these strategies and in evolving a personal strategy for solving problems. The overall strategy for solving problems where the resources are limited is shown in Fig. 1.4. In most instances, the sloppiest calculation takes such a short period of time that there is very little difference between the hybrid and the strategy based on the law of optimum sloppiness.

The major challenges in implementing the strategies are to collect the information needed (as part of the "define" step) and to develop the plan. Collecting the necessary information is a complex mixture of background experience in the subject area, one's ability to search the literature, and the resources available. To assist us in developing plans in the future, for every problem we solve we can prepare algorithms of how we solve the problem

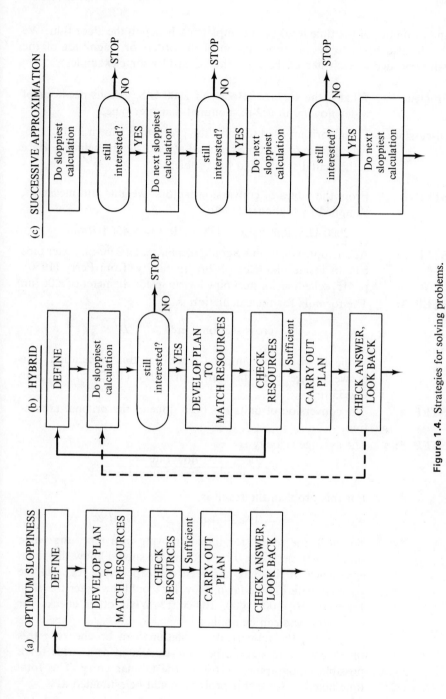

Figure 1.4. Strategies for solving problems.

19

and estimates of the time it takes to complete each step in the algorithm. We should also begin to get an appreciation of the orders of magnitude of the values needed at each step of the algorithm. Consider some examples:

Problem: What is the average velocity of 2000 U.S. gallons per hour of water flowing in a 2-in.-nominal-diameter pipe?

Discussion: The algorithm used to solve the problem is shown in Fig. 1.5. An estimate of the time required at each step is included. Here is the actual solution to the problem:

STEP 1:   From the tables of conversion factors: weights and measures, compiled by Gaboury (1949),

$$2000 \text{ U.S. gph/hr} \times 2.228 \times 10^{-3} = 4.456 \text{ ft}^3/\text{min}$$

STEP 2:   As an approximation we could *assume* that a 2 in.-diameter pipe has an inside diameter of 2in. In reality, from Perry (1950), p. 415, schedule 40, steel pipe has an inside diameter of 2.067in.

STEP 3:   The formula for the calculation is

$$\text{cross-sectional area} = \frac{\pi}{4} D^2$$

While it would be simple to perform this calculation, the answers have been tabulated in Perry (1950), p. 415, as 0.0233 ft^2.

STEP 4:   The conversion of units has been done in the original tabulation.

STEP 5:   The average velocity is

$$\langle v \rangle = \frac{\text{flow rate}}{\text{inside cross-sectional area}}$$

For this problem the result is

$$\langle v \rangle = 191.24 \text{ ft/min} \quad \text{or} \quad 3.19 \text{ ft/sec}$$

To check the result, for liquids flowing in a pipe, the value should be in the range 0.1–20 ft/sec. We should know this from experience. If this has not been our experience yet, imagine yourself watering the lawn. How far would the water travel in 1 sec: 1, 10, 100, 1000, 10,000 ft? What other checks for reasonableness can be applied?

Second, the numerical calculations can be checked; this time steps 3 and 4 could be hand-calculated as a check for a possible typographical error in the tabular entry. The total time taken to solve this problem could be estimated as

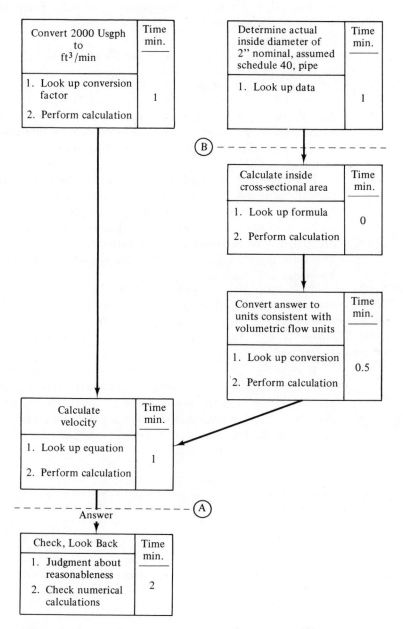

Figure 1.5. Algorithm or plan for calculating the average velocity of liquid flowing in a pipe.

1. Definition: 5 min, including gathering reference books you know you will need.
2. Develop plan: 2 min.
3. Carry out the plan: 3 min, 30 sec (from Fig. 1.5).
4. Look back: 2 min.
   Total: 12 min, 30 sec.

This seems like a long time, but part of the time was spent locating books and in developing a detailed plan for future use. Normally, we do not spend the time writing out the plan; the plan is in our heads.

For the future, we need to see how we can be sloppy with this type of problem and to estimate the error and the time.

The quickest estimate would be to start at A and assume, on Fig. 1.5, that the answer is 6 ft/sec. The answer might be 0.1 or 20 ft/sec; so the error is, in the extreme, $+600\%$, -70%. This estimation takes about 20 sec for definition and recall. No books are required.

The next quickest approach would be to locate for future use a nomograph that shows this calculation graphically. Some examples are given by Crane (1957) and by Kharbanda (1958), p. 164. This accuracy depends on the format of the nomograph and is probably $\pm5\%$.

If a nomograph is not available, the next quickest approach is to bypass the need for a book listing the exact inside diameter and to assume that the inside diameter equals the nominal diameter. This is at level B in the calculation, but the real time saving is in the definition step. The result is 6% in error. Table 1.3 summarizes this example.

TABLE 1.3
SUMMARY OF ACCURACY & TIME FOR DIFFERENT METHODS
OF CALCULATING THE AVERAGE VELOCITY IN PIPE

Method	Error	Time taken (min)
Estimate 6 ft/sec	$+600$ -70	0.3
Use nomograph (if available)	±5	3
Assume that the nominal diameter equals the inside diameter	±6	8.5
Detailed calculation	Depends on calculation technique	12.5

Problem: What is the density of methane gas at 385°R and 1075 psia?

Discussion: For these temperature and pressures, the gas is not likely to be ideal. Hence, an equation of state such as the compressibility factor is reasonable:

$$z = \frac{p\tilde{V}}{RT} = 1 + \frac{B}{\tilde{V}} + \frac{C}{\tilde{V}^2} + \frac{D}{\tilde{V}^3} + \cdots \tag{1.1}$$

$$= f(z_c, p_r, t_r) \tag{1.2}$$

where B, C, D = second, third, and fourth virial coefficients, respectively

$\tilde{V}$ = molar volume

p_r = reduced pressure = p/p_c

T_r = reduced temperature = t/t_c

c = values at the critical point

The algorithm to use to solve the problem based on the empirical correlation approach and based on Eq. (1.2) is given in Fig. 1.6. The actual solution to the problem is as follows:

STEP 1: On the basis of 1 lb of gas, from Perry (1950), p. 142, the molecular weight is 16.04; from Perry (1950), p. 290, $R = 0.7302$ ft³-atm/lb mole-°R; and the pressure is 1075 psia/14.7 = 73.34 atm.

STEP 2: From Perry (1950), p. 204, the critical constants for methane are $t_c = -82.5$°C, $p_c = 45.8$ atm, and $d_c = 0.162$ g/cc. Converting the temperature to °K yields

$$T_c = -82.5 + 273.16$$

$$= 190.7°K$$

Therefore,

$$p_r = \frac{p}{p_c} = \frac{1075}{(458)(14.7)} = 1.6$$

$$T_r = \frac{T}{T_c} = \frac{385}{1.8(190.7)} = 1.12$$

An analysis of Table 49 in Hougen et al. (1959), p. 591, indicates that for these values of p_r and T_r the results are independent of z_c. Hence, a calculation of z_c from d_c is unnecessary.

STEP 3: From Hougen et al. (1959), p. 591, the value of z is 0.505.

STEP 4: The density is

$$\left(\frac{W}{V}\right) = \frac{pM}{zRT}$$

$$= \frac{(73.3)(16.04)}{0.505(0.7302)385}$$

$$= 8.28 \text{ lb}_m/\text{ft}^3$$

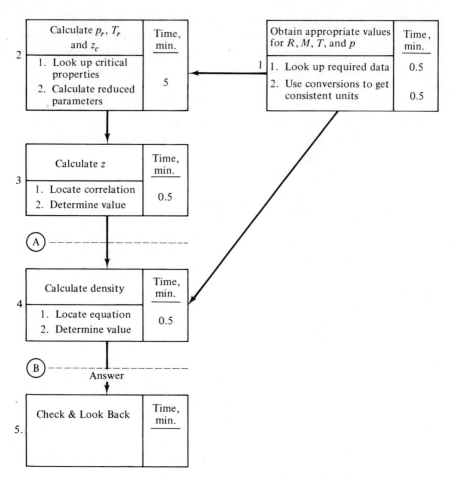

Figure 1.6. Algorithm for calculating gas density. (Basis: 1 lb$_m$ of gas).

STEP 5:   Checking the reasonableness: The density of air at STP
(1 atm and 520°R) is about 0.075 lb$_m$/ft³. The density of
methane, assuming the ideal gas law, would be about

$$0.075 \times \frac{73 \text{ atm}}{1 \text{ atm}} \times \left(\frac{16 \text{ moles}}{29 \text{ moles}}\right)\left(\frac{520}{385}\right) = 4.1 \text{ lb}_m/\text{ft}^3$$

Thus, for a compressibility factor of 0.5, the density would be
double. Hence, this value seems reasonable. A rough check on
the value of the compressibility factor can be made from the
graphical display on p. 353 of Perry (1950). Note, however,
that the later-published data of Hougen et al. (1959) differ from

the 1936 graph. This check does, however, illustrate that the compressibility factor is in the correct order of magnitude.

The total time taken to solve this problem could be estimated as

1. Definition: 5 min, including gathering reference books.
2. Develop plan: 2 min.
3. Carry out the plan: 6 min.
4. Look back: 3 min.
   Total: 16 min.

The major portion of time was spent defining the problem and locating the appropriate information resources. We may have had to review the material because we had forgotten some details. The major calculational step was in determining the compressibility factor.

The quickest estimate, taking about 20 sec total and shown at location B in Fig. 1.6, is to recall the density of some gas or the range of gas densities. I remember the density of air at STP as being about 0.075 lb_m/ft^3. In this example the error is -100%.

The next quickest estimate is based on the assumption that the gas is ideal, level A in Fig. 1.6. How the calculation is performed depends on whether we can recall the appropriate value of the gas constant R or the density of air at STP as being about 0.075 lb_m/ft^3. As students, we usually remember R; as practicing engineers we usually remember the properties of common materials such as air, water, steam, "typical" organic liquid, etc. It is ideal, of course, if we can remember both. The total time for the calculations is about 1.5 min because we do not have to look up the conversion factors for pressure and for temperature and we can quickly estimate or look up the molecular weights. Thus, we estimate the density as about 4 lb_m/ft^3, and this is -50%. We could use a nomograph if it were available for the above calculation.

These two examples illustrate the technique of preparing algorithms and using them to gain an appreciation of the time distribution among the various steps required to solve problems. Armed with this experience, we can identify where to start in the algorithm to solve the problem in the time available. This provides a strategy for solving problems when time is limited.

Too often the answer was expected "yesterday." Sometimes this demand for an immediate answer reflects poor organization and planning by our supervisors. At other times, events move so quickly and are so difficult to anticipate that quick decisions need to be made; for example, White (1970), p. 521, suggests that the pace of change forces us to a decision faster than our ideas can sort out right from wrong. To attempt to remedy this we can learn to anticipate and forecast decisions to be made in the future and to plan ahead. Anticipation and forecasting require that we take time now to draw back from our immediate concerns and think about where we and our company are going. We can use developments within the company, in the technical world, and in the scientific world. But the developments in politics and in society are equally important. Consider some examples:

> Rachel Carson's *The Silent Spring* was published in 1962. About 8 years later society arose in a cry to stop pollution and to stop the use of pesticides. Thus, Carson's book pointed to future events.
>
> As another example, an integrated company is developing a revolutionary method of making acetic acid extremely cheaply. The engineers in this company should be looking for other processes to develop that use acetic acid as a raw material. In this way, they could anticipate future projects.

Financial feasibility

For any decision, we must have access to the total amount of money or capital required to finance the project. For example, we may have a brilliant idea to rent canoes to tourists, but if we cannot buy (or provide enough collateral to rent the fleet of canoes) the canoes, we would be foolish to decide to accept this project. In this book we shall elaborate on the financial needs of a company and on the sources of money to finance a project.

Financial attractiveness feasibility

Money is a resource. One who has it can exchange it, for example, for material goods or for pleasure or can loan it to someone else. If the money is loaned, the one loaning the money expects to be paid, at some future date, the original loan plus an additional monetary reward commensurate to the risk. Thus, if you have $100, you could put it in your sock (and have no future reward), you could put it in the bank and draw the 2–5% interest reward, or Tom may wish to borrow it to set up a dating service. He will not guarantee you any definite amount. Indeed, he may go broke whereby you lose everything. He *thinks* he will be able to pay you $110 in a year. Jack wants to borrow the money to start a computer information storage and retrieval service. Jack *thinks* that he will be able to repay you $125 in a year if business is good. He will not guarantee anything. What do you do?

The more money that is returned to you at the end of the year, the more financially attractive the alternative. The challenge is to be able to identify the risk in the alternatives, to translate this into different expected levels of return, and to translate the terms *think* and *if business is good* into quantitative terms if possible. This project is the major emphasis of this book.

1.4 Making Decisions

In the previous sections, the general criteria used in making decisions were briefly reviewed. The main theme of this book centers on the financial and financial attractiveness criteria; nevertheless, some brief comments are worth making now about how these criteria might be used in making a decision.

In most discussions about the financial attractiveness criterion it is assumed that a net profit, measured in money terms, can be identified. This can be visualized as being generated from the sale of goods. A monkey wrench is sold for $12; it cost $7 to make and the manufacturer had a net profit of $2.50 after paying $2.50 in tax. This occurs in the privately-owned process industries seeking a profit. However, decisions have to be made concerning the installation of an air and water treatment plant and, in general, in the public sector of the economy where no "product" is for sale. A benefit results but no product is sold. For these cases, a monetary value is often assigned to the benefit and that value is used as the inflow of money in the financial-attractiveness criterion.

Details on the discussion of how this work can be applied to the public sector of the economy are given by Marglin, (1967), Harberger (1973), and Dasgupta and Pearce (1972).

There are two challenges:

1. How to predict and account for the future.
2. How to account for all the criteria.

These are discussed in turn.

Accounting for the future

One of the major sets of criteria considered the impact on the future of society. From this viewpoint, we shall follow the *product* and its use by the consumer in succeeding years. This might be as shown in Fig. 1.7. A new product is made out of our resources; the product has a high value to the user or to society. The product is used, with various periods of repair or upgrading, until the product is obsolete, as judged by the user. The product may be used as an alternative use of some small value, say a broken iron used as a child's toy or a broken lamp used as a paperweight. Eventually, it is discarded and has a negative value to society because we must find a place to

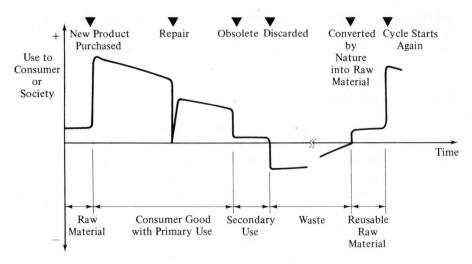

Figure 1.7. Consumer's view of the life cycle of a good or product.

get rid of it. Eventually, it is converted by nature into a new, valuable raw material that is used to make a new product. Money could be used as the unit of measurement of the value or usefulness to the user.

A second viewpoint is to follow the *product* line from the manufacturer's viewpoint. This might be as shown in Fig. 1.8. It all starts with an idea, an idea to produce something. The idea grows through calculations, research and development, and market surveys until a decision is made to produce the product. The plans are implemented at significant expense through detailed calculations complemented with the required gathering of information, plant construction, and startup. At last, the product is available for sale. As time passes the product sales pass through stages of introduction, growth, maturity, saturation, and decline until the product is abandoned and the plant shut down. The value to the company is usually expressed with money as the unit of measurement. These two examples, from the viewpoint of the product-consumer and the product-producer, illustrate how the value or usefulness changes in the future. Any decision making should attempt to account for the future.

Using all the criteria

To analyze any complex problem we break it into its component parts. We have identified and discussed most of the components that affect decision making. How can these be used to make a decision?

First, for each criterion the alternatives have different values or worth that make one alternative better than others. Some possible variations are

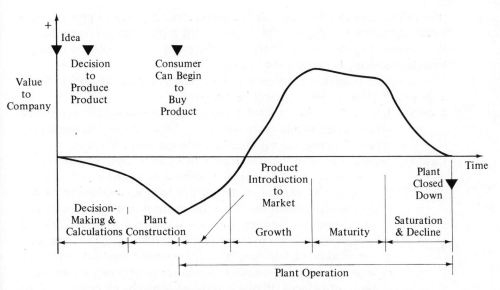

Figure 1.8. Producer's view of the life cycle of a good or product.

given in Fig. 1.9. In Fig. 1.9(a) there is only either good or bad, acceptable or unacceptable alternatives. There is no shading in the alternatives. With regard to the technical criterion, for example, the alternatives either work or do not work, and the line separating the two is well defined. In Fig. 1.9(b) there is a clearly defined unaccepted region, but within the acceptable range there are better and poorer alternatives. Regarding the technical criterion, for example, the alternatives work or do not work, but some processes still have some uncertainty as to the design procedures. At A the process is a purchased turnkey plant; at B we know we can make it work eventually (there is no fundamental reason it will not work), but it may take some experimentation. As another example—the environment criterion—the

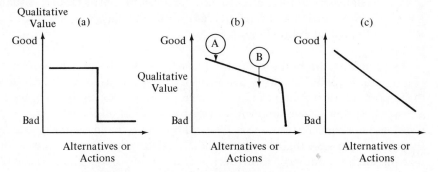

Figure 1.9. Variation in value for different alternatives.

present law identifies the acceptable emission standards, say 10 ppm of oil in
water. Alternative A might yield 2 ppm and B 8 ppm. Most criteria follow
this pattern. Figure 1.9(c) indicates that there is no clearly defined decision
basis for selecting between good and bad.

With these possible characteristics, how can the criteria be used to make
a decision? Three possibilities will be discussed:

Case 1: If all the criteria (except financial attractiveness) are acceptable
versus unacceptable as shown in Fig. 1.9(a), the best decision is to
accept the proposal with the best financial attractiveness.

Case 2: Money is a unit of measurement which can be used for most of the
criteria. Here, one alternative is selected as the base case, and we
estimate the amount of money needed to bring all the alternatives
to the base case condition. Thus, for the technical criterion, we add
as an expense, the amount of money necessary for the research and
development program to bring all the alternatives to the same level
of technical feasibility. Similarly, for environmental feasibility, the
expense is added for the waste treatment facility to give the same
quantity of effluent. If this is possible, whereby all criteria can be
expressed in terms of money, then again the financial attractiveness
criterion is the one used for decision making.

Case 3: When all the criteria cannot be simply related to money, then a
decision matrix approach combined with opinion analysis is
appropriate. In this method, all the criteria are listed and assigned
relative weightings by soliciting the opinions of others and using
statistical techniques to represent the distribution of opinions. In a
similar manner, the relative weighting of all the alternatives are
estimated. The resultant summary for the attractiveness of each
alternative is a distribution. The best decision is to select the
alternative with the highest weighting and the smallest standard
deviation. A sample decision matrix, showing only the mean value
of the weightings, is shown in Table 1.4. Other examples where the
relative weightings are assigned are given by Harris (1961); Jordan
(1968), p. 18; and Kiefer (1964). Opinion analysis is described by
Reilly and Johri (1969).

In summary, the purpose of this section was to illustrate how all the
criteria are or could be used in decision making. Furthermore, it illustrated
the importance of the financial attractiveness criterion. Given that money is
a reasonable unit of measurement of relative worth of all the criteria, good
decisions are financially attractive. It would be incorrect and inappropriate to
leave the impression that decision making with multiple criteria is easy or
that the methods outlined in this section are the only ones. The purpose of
this section has been to provide some idea of how attempts can be made to

TABLE 1.4
SAMPLE DECISION MATRIX SHOWING MEAN VALUES ONLY

Criterion	Relative import-ance	Alternatives				
		1	2	3	4	5
Process						
Technical	15	14	3	10	7	11
Safety	10	8	5	3	9	7
Environmental	5	3	5	3	2	4
Originality	5	1	5	2	3	1
Impact						
Benefits to Society	10	3	4	8	4	6
Market	15	10	13	11	9	13
Social/political	5	5	4	5	2	3
Economic	2	0	0	1	2	1
Ethical	10	7	8	4	7	3
Resource						
Nonmonetary	10	9	5	3	7	5
Time	5	4	3	3	2	4
Financial	10	9	9	2	5	6
Financial attractiveness	10	4	10	2	7	5
Total		77	74	57	66	69

incorporate multiple criteria into decision making. The interested reader can study this further by reading, for example, Kazanowski (1968a and b) Keeney (1973) and Fishburn (1968).

1.5 The Objectives and Plan of the Book

In this book you will learn about the overall economy and about the financial needs and uses of money within the process industry or within a company. This provides an overall appreciation of the importance and use made of financial and financial attractiveness criteria for decision making. In general, young engineers will not make decisions about how to raise capital, how to allocate the money available, the amount of dividends that should be paid to the stockholders, or the method of depreciation the company should use. Nevertheless, the engineers should appreciate the overall environment in which they function, the alternatives available, and the requirements these place on them and should have a general understanding of how their professional ability contributes to the health of the company. Besides, while they may not be making the decisions when they first join the company, they should know what lies ahead and start preparing for their future roles.

The main objective is to describe the methods of calculating different financial attractiveness criteria and to provide sufficient data so that such calculations can be done for most problems in the process industry. In particular, a knowledge of the capital investment and the product cost must be known; details are provided for these calculations.

The overall organization of the book is shown in Fig. 1.10. The central theme is the financial attractiveness criterion (Chapter 5).

As background information Chapter 2 describes overall economic

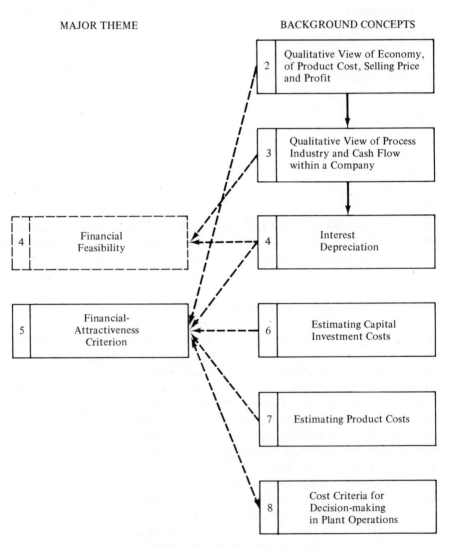

Figure 1.10. Overall plan of the book.

principles and provides a qualitative view of product costs, selling price, and profit. A qualitative view of the process industry and the need for money in the different phases of the industry are given in Chapter 3. Chapter 4 supplies some background about financing, interest, and depreciation and introduces a qualitative view of financial feasibility.

Chapter 5 discusses the methods of expressing the financial attractiveness of alternatives. Needed in these calculations are estimates of the capital investment (Chapter 6) and of the cost price (Chapter 7). Chapter 8 discusses other uses of the cost criteria for decision making in improving plant operations. Many problems are given at the end of each chapter. They are used to highlight, elaborate, and make the material in the chapter specific. All of them should be perused, if not solved.

1.6 Summary

Engineers make decisions that affect everyone in society. The making of these decisions is complicated because of the apparent host of complicating factors that should be taken into account: the process, the impact, and the resource feasibilities. In this chapter, we identified and discussed these factors. Sometimes, they can be expressed quantitatively and incorporated into a single criterion, the financial attractiveness of the alternative.

PROBLEMS

1.1. List some of the laws of nature. Describe processes or equipment that violate some of these laws and that are thus technically unfeasible.

1.2. Determine the maximum design pressure and fabrication diameter for cylindrical reactors as a function of temperature for carbon steel, stainless steel 316, and Monel.

1.3. Listed below is some processing equipment. Find the minimum and maximum commercial sizes or capacities for this equipment. (*Hint: Chemical Equipment Catalog*, an annual publication of Van Nostrand Reinhold Company, New York, is a useful place to start.)

Fans, blowers, reciprocating compressors
Crushers, grinders, ball mills, hammer mills
Trommels, screens, plate and frame filters, rotary vacuum filters
Centrifugal pumps
Spray driers

1.4. For the industrial production of ketene from acetic acid, determine the steps taken to minimize the reversion after the exit of the reactor.

1.5. Draw a sketch of a piece of equipment that is impossible to build. In the covering letter, explain why you think it is impossible. The reason why it cannot be built should not be because the sketch failed to communicate.

1.6. List the benefits and detriments of your company producing the following products. For each make a personal decision as to whether you think your company should make the product. Prepare a press release explaining your decision.

napalm, bugs and listening devices, nerve gas, barbiturates, beer, cigarettes, supercloth that will last 50 years and that is unstainable and uncreasable, TV-telephone, 3-D smellivision, and an artificial body that plugs into a human head and runs on an atomic pacer

1.7. The writer is often called society's conscience. What are the 10 fiction and nonfiction books on the current list of best sellers? What are their messages, and how do you think they will affect you and your company in the future?

1.8. What do you think are the present major scientific breakthroughs that will be used by technology in the next 10 years? What does this say about the company for which you should be working?

1.9. Write a 600-word report on what society will be like when you are 40—the time when you as a professional will have a key decision-making role.

1.10. Describe a case you encountered where ethics became very important. Clearly state both sides of the case, and indicate what you would do as a professional.

1.11. Kardos (1969) describes the incidents leading up to and surrounding the collapse of the Heron Road Bridge. Answer the "think" questions in Parts A, B, C, and D in this Engineering Case Library report.

1.12. In an attempt to forecast the impact of technology on the future, Forrester (1970) has developed a simulation of the future. Comment on the appropriateness of the factors he included, identify other factors you believe should have been included, and comment on the predictions of the simulations and the effect they have on the engineering profession.

Qualitative View of the Economy   **2**

Economics is the study of man's activities and exchange in satisfying his wants by using scarce resources which have alternatives uses. If a scarce resource has only one *use*, the problem is not an economic problem in an economist's way of thinking; it is a problem of design and technique. It is not an exact science; the principles are generalizations about human behavior.

Just as we do in engineering, the economist sets up models of how man behaves economically. Figure 2.1 shows two such simple models. The assumptions in Fig. 2.1(a) are

1. Man is driven by the profit motive.
2. There is no legal interference by the government.
3. There are no trade unions or organizations of the *factors of production* against the entrepreneur.
4. There is no organization of the entrepreneurs together (combines, agreements not to increase prices, etc.).

Despite these limitations, the simplified model of Fig. 2.1(a) is helpful in understanding some principles of economics.

(a)   GOODS & SERVICES   (b) INCOME, GOODS & SERVICES

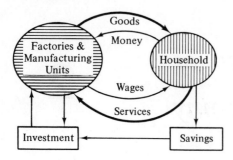   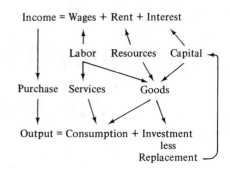

Figure 2.1. Simplified models of society to illustrate economist's approach.

2.1 The Model Market

Now, let us go one step further and describe the arena where goods and services are bought and sold. In the first instance we assume that there is perfect competition. That is, there are a large number of buyers and sellers so that no one is big enough to influence the price, there is no differentiation in the *minds* of the buyers between commodities, there is freedom to buy and sell as a response to price alone, there is no restriction on the number of vendors, and, finally, there is a reasonable knowledge of the market. The market is where the suppliers meet those who demand or want to buy a commodity.

Consider first the demand for a product. The quantity of any commodity that one individual purchases (an actual willingness to buy) depends on

1. Price of commodity and prices of others.
2. Personal taste.
3. Income.
4. Law of diminishing utility. If he buys one pair of shoes, he is less anxious to buy a second pair.

The general assumptions are that people buy more at a cheaper price and that the buyer must choose what he wants from a limited income.

The market demand curve is the sum of the individual demands and resembles Fig. 2.2. The total demand rarely intersects the abscissa, the total demand curve will be less steep than the individual curves, and the demand curves for a material used to produce a consumer product will be similar to the demand curve for the consumer product. That is, if wood pulp is needed to

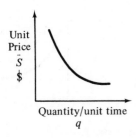

Figure 2.2. Market demand curve.   **Figure 2.3.** Shifts in demand.

make newsprint, the demand curve for pulp is similar to that for newsprint. By convention a positive shift in demand means the curve moves away from the origin, as shown in Fig. 2.3.

There are other characteristics of demand curves, depending on whether the commodity is a luxury or a necessity. This is represented by *elasticity*, which is how much a change in price will affect the change in quantity demanded; mathematically it is the ratio

$$\epsilon = \frac{\Delta q/q}{\Delta \ddot{S}/\ddot{S}}$$

The symbol ϵ is often called the coefficient of elasticity. It measures the responsiveness of the quantity demanded to changes in price.

A quick way to see how the *total revenue* changes depending on the elasticity is shown in Fig. 2.4. It should be noted that unless the demand curve is hyperbolic the elasticity will vary from point to point. In particular the straight lines in Fig. 2.4 have varying elasticity at different points. On the other hand, just because a curve is hyperbolic does not mean that the demand curve necessarily has unit elasticity. It does mean that the elasticity is *constant*. Examples are shown in Fig. 2.5.

Next consider the supply of a product. A typical total supply curve is

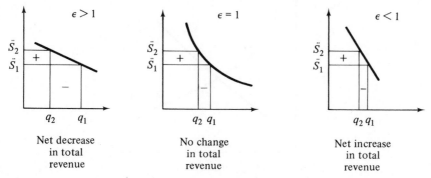

Figure 2.4. How elasticity affects total revenue.

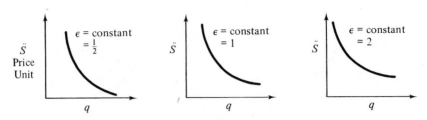

Figure 2.5. Curves of constant elasticity.

shown in Fig. 2.6. The price and the quantity supplied per unit time are directly related because producers will decide that it is more profitable to substitute the production of more expensive products for less expensive products. We can describe supply curves by elasticity (as shown in Fig. 2.7). Different products have different supply curves. The shape depends on the relative perishability of the product and on the technical difficulties of expansion and contraction. For a given product, the shape changes because of technological advance and because of changes in the cost of productive resources.

Finally, the total demand and supply curves can be superimposed to give the market conditions. This is shown in Fig. 2.8, with the market price being established at $7, where supply equals demand.

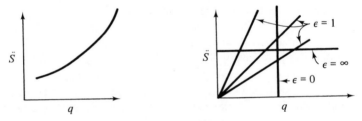

Figure 2.6. Supply curve.   **Figure 2.7.** Supply and elasticity.

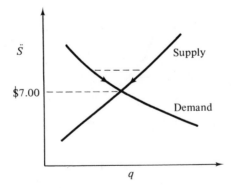

Figure 2.8. Market conditions of supply and demand.

2.2 The Individual Company in Real Life

The market and total demand-supply curves are interesting, but what about the conditions within a real company? What influences output and price, and how does reality differ from the model described in Section 2.1?

For a few products, such as wheat, the market does behave like pure competition. However, for many other products a monopolistic competition, oligopoly, or monopoly exists. Pure competition, we recall, means that the supplier cannot affect the market price. A supplier's individual demand curve is shown in Fig. 2.9(a). Monopoly, on the other extreme, means that the supplier can affect the selling price of his own product. The demand curve for his product appears in Fig. 2.9(b). A monopoly can arise because of

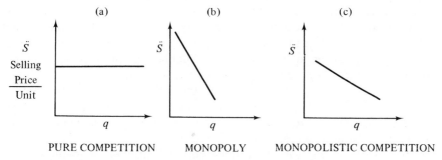

Figure 2.9. Demand curves for a commodity in different market conditions.

patents, because only very large businesses can produce it efficiently (electricity, telephone, atomic energy), and because of a government franchise. In monopolistic competition the individual supplier has some but very little control over the price. Their individual supply curves are shown in Fig. 2.9(c). An oligopoly has a small number of suppliers, for example, the car industry.

Every supplier is trying to have his demand curve shift over to a monopoly or inelastic situation so that he can raise his price without any buyer shifting products or suppliers. This arises because of location, brand names, trademarks, and reputation of the company and because the supplier has, through extensive advertising, established product differentiation in the mind of the buyer. Packard's (1957) *Hidden Persuaders* provides interesting reading on these activities. Product *value* is related to this discussion; it is considered in Section 2.4.

2.3 Costs, Selling Price, and Profits

To produce any product, a company needs manpower, materials, machinery, and money. The variety is shown in Table 2.1. All cost money. The cost is what is spent to make the product, the price is what the product sells for, and the profit is the price less the cost. The costs can be classified many different ways; the two most common ways are how they originate or how they vary with production rate. The costs are usually reported as costs per unit or as annual costs. Figure 2.10 is an example of a classification of costs per unit classified according to how they originate. When costs are classified according to how they vary with production rate, the broadest classification is into fixed and variable. Fixed costs are those that do not change with the production rate if the amount of manpower and machinery is kept fixed. The latter condition is called the short run and means that the time period is so short that the producer can change the rate of production, the amount of raw materials, and the hourly labor but he cannot build new plants or hire new staff. In the long run (when the supplier can produce new commodities, build new plants, etc.), the fixed costs can change.

Variable costs vary with production rate. Table 2.2 gives some examples of fixed and variable costs. The total cost is the sum of the fixed and variable costs, and a graphical representation of the unit cost as a function of production rate, q, is shown in Fig. 2.11.

It is worth noting why the variable costs go through a minimum in Fig. 2.11(b). In the short run, the machinery cannot be expanded. For any given piece of equipment, there is a limit to how much can be produced, and as we approach the extreme limit the efficiency usually is decreased. Consider a typical pump curve, shown in Fig. 2.12. The pump should be operated at 1800 U.S. gpm for a maximum mechanical efficiency of about 74%. Nevertheless, it could be operated at 2800 U.S. gpm at a mechanical efficiency of 50%, or at about 800 U.S. gpm for a similar efficiency. This indicates that the efficiency passes through an optimum as the flow rate or throughput increases. This behavior can be generalized and is referred to as the law of diminishing returns. Stated formally, the law says that as we increase the quantity of any one variable factor of production (in this example, flow rate) which is combined with a fixed quantity of other factors of production, the marginal productivity of the variable factor will decline after a certain point. Expressed in simpler terms, a point is reached beyond which an increase in the variable factors will produce a less than proportionate increase in output. As we increase the input to a process, the output goes through an optimum. Returning to Fig. 2.11(b), we see that variable costs increase beyond a production rate of q_1 because of the law of diminishing returns.

The marginal or incremental concept is very useful for studying financial

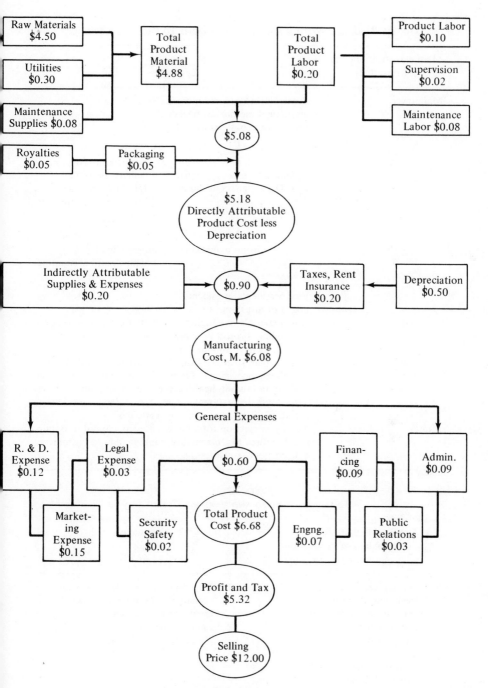

Figure 2.10. Distribution of costs.

TABLE 2.1
THE 4M RESOURCES WITHIN A COMPANY UTILIZED TO PRODUCE A PRODUCT

Main classification: the 4M resources	Examples
Manpower	Process operators, maintenance and instrument mechanics, packers, restaurant cooks, waitresses
	Technicians, process engineers,— Security, health centers, personnel R & D., design, consultants typists, secretaries, librarians, receptionists
	Group managers —— Market research, sales, advertising, legal, financial, and accounting
	Vice presidents, president, board of directors
Materials	Raw materials, packaging, maintenance supplies, process supplies, protective clothing, uniforms, ink, pencils, food, medical supplies, paper
Machinery	Process plants, utilities supplies, warehouse and storage, maintenance shops, fire-fighting equipment, printing shop, restaurant, health center, operator's office, offices for staff, recreational center, typewriters, desks, computers, VIP house, company cars, land
Money	To pay interest on total money needed, capital to obtain other three Ms, hospitality, supply credit to customers, keep stock, royalties

TABLE 2.2
EXAMPLES OF FIXED AND VARIABLE COSTS

Fixed costs that are independent of production rate, C_F	Variable costs, C_V
Rent, insurance, land taxes, depreciation, interest. Medical, payroll, restaurant, recreation, storage facilities, safety, security, engineering, library Administration, legal, sales and research expenses	1. Raw materials, utilities, packing containers, shipping, royalties, credit for by-products 2. Labor, supervision, maintenance, plant supplies, laboratory

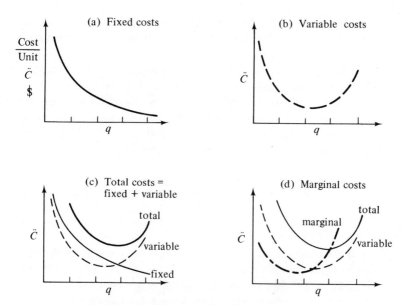

Figure 2.11. Cost curves for the short run.

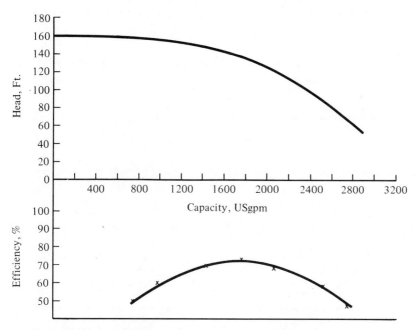

Figure 2.12. A typical head-capacity curve for a pump to illustrate the law of diminishing returns.

behavior. Marginal costs, ΔC, are the addition to the total cost associated with an increase in production by one unit. It is the first derivative of the total cost with respect to q. A typical marginal cost curve is shown in Fig. 2.11(d). Note that it passes through the minimum of the cost curve and that the minimum of marginal cost curve occurs at a production rate less than for the minimum of the cost curve. Similarly, marginal revenue, ΔS, is the addition to the total revenue (selling price times quantity sold) resulting from the sale of an additional unit of the commodity. This is also the first derivative of the total revenue. In mathematical terms, for a fixed selling price per unit of $\ddot{S}$,

$$\Delta S = \ddot{S}q_n - \ddot{S}q_{n-1} = \frac{d(\ddot{S}q)}{dq} = \ddot{S}\left(1 - \frac{1}{\epsilon}\right) \tag{2.1}$$

In graphical terms, the marginal revenue relative to the demand curves is shown in Fig. 2.13.

Every enterprise wants to maximize profits. One might think that profit is a maximum when the cost is a minimum. However, in Table 2.3 the minimum total cost, C, is \$33.30 for the production of six units with a total loss of \$8. The maximum profit of \$25 occurs for a total cost of \$40.85. This occurs when marginal revenue equals marginal cost. Graphically the various curves are shown in Fig. 2.14 for both competition and monopolistic competition.

It should be emphasized that the maximum profit occurs when marginal

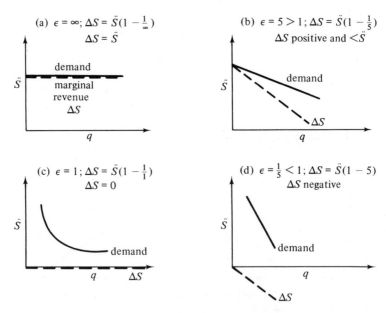

Figure 2.13. Demand curves and marginal revenue.

TABLE 2.3
COST-REVENUE RELATIONSHIPS

Quantity, q	Price, $\ddot{S}$	Total revenue, $S = \ddot{S}q$	Marginal revenue, ΔS	Fixed costs, C_F	Variable costs, C_V	Total cost, C	Marginal cost, ΔC	Unit cost, $\ddot{C}$	Profit, P
2	70	140		70	65	135		67.50	5
			34				14		
3	58	174	(14)	70	79	149	(14)	49.66	25
4	47	188		70	93	163		40.85	25
			7				19		
5	39	195		70	112	182		37.40	13
			−3				18		
6	32	192		70	130	200		33.30	−8

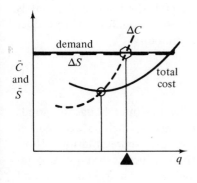
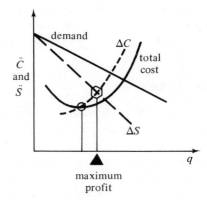

Figure 2.14.

revenue equals marginal cost and not normally when the unit cost is a minimum.

2.4 Value

In reality, customers do not purchase goods and services based solely on the price. In fact, Packard (1957) suggests that people buy images and symbols rather than the actual product. This, then, leads to the concept that the value or price that customers are willing to pay consists of two parts: a functional or use cost and an esteem cost. That is, we can make a bar soap that satisfies the function of separating dirt and grease from our hands, but customers are willing to pay x cents/bar more to have the soap scented and white or pastel-colored rather than have it foul smelling and black. Hence, we should temper decisions based on the mathematical concepts presented in Sections 2.1–2.3 with an appreciation that customers are also interested in the esteem or image that they acquire with the commodity. Indeed, the value of a commodity can be classified into

> Cost value: what it costs to make the commodity,
> Use value: the lowest cost of reliably obtaining a function. This can be less than the cost value.
> Exchange value: what we could gain through exchange.
> Esteem value: what we would be willing to pay for the image the article has.

For example, a "diplomat" automobile might have an esteem value of $60,000 and a cost value of $40,000; as an automobile, its use value may be $1500, and its exchange value may be $80,000 because Prince Igor once owned this car. While these distinctions are useful, the important point is that *value* has many meanings and that cost and esteem qualities of a product both combine to entice people to purchase a commodity.

2.5 Summary

Economists have developed models to describe the interchange of goods and services within society. The important concepts include the market where supply equals demand. Elasticity is a convenient representation of how supply or demand changes with unit price. The product cost and cost components and the very important marginal concepts of marginal costs and revenues were introduced. The profit is a maximum when marginal cost equals marginal revenue. In the short run, the law of diminishing returns requires that the total unit cost curve first decrease and then increase with increasing production rate.

    Advertising and the creation of product value in the minds of the consumer have a significant effect on the behavior of consumers in real life.

PROBLEMS

2.1. a. List commodities you believe would have elastic, unit elastic, and inelastic demand curves, for example, automobiles, glue, house paint, and bread.
     b. Repeat the classification in part a for chemical commodities or products from the chemical industry or in the process industry of your choice.

2.2. In your country, identify which companies might be operating under monopoly, oligopoly, or pure competition conditions. (Does the answer to this problem help with the answer to Problem 2.1b?)

2.3. Cite two examples other than the pump example used in this chapter to illustrate the law of diminishing returns.

Overall Company Financial Decisions and Cash Flow **3**

Chapter 2 provided some background for the overall business environment. Here we shall consider a single company's viewpoint and discuss the main financial decisions. First, we shall consider the financial operations and profit distribution activities of a company. Then we shall study the annual reports and some details on operation and profit distribution.

3.1 A Sample Company and the Overall Decisions

A typical company organizational chart and the interaction of decisions are given in Figs. 3.1 and 3.2. Although these decisions are not ones normally made by a young engineer, an appreciation of them helps us understand our role. In general the major decisions are in two categories: decisions about the operations and decisions about distribution of profits.

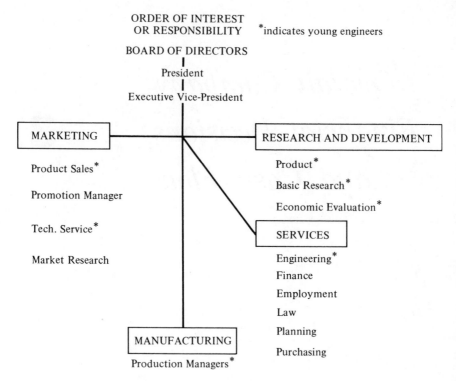

Figure 3.1. Typical company organizational chart and associated responsibilities.

Decisions about operations

Concerning operations, we have four main resources: money, manpower, materials, and machinery. These resources are used to produce a product to be sold on the market, and this, in turn, is expected to yield a financial profit.

A summary illustrating a typical allocation of the resources is shown in Table 3.1 for the "every company" faced with a "normal" business outlook.* The starting resources include the results of previous operation: an inventory (A^1), a capital plant and the associated manpower to give a given capacity (A^2), some cash on hand (B^1), general business information that is available to all (C^3), specific market information from previous expenditures in market

---

*A business game, called "Venture," is available from Procter & Gamble Co., Director of Educational services, P.O. Box 599, Cincinnati, Ohio 45201. Other business games have been developed [see Szendrovits (1971), for example], but the "Venture" game is simple to run yet adequately provides an appreciation of the overall company financial decisions.

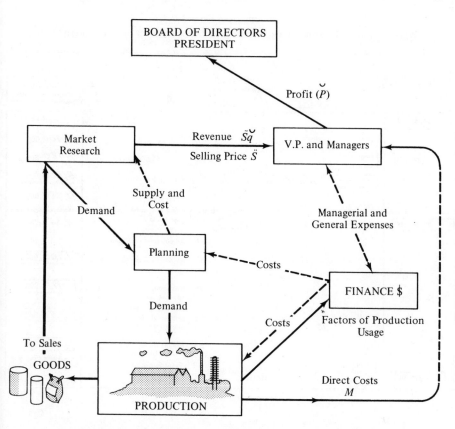

Figure 3.2. Generalized flow of information and organizational chart: company structure and financial interest in the short run.

research (C^1 and C^2), and cost data for production based on the present efficiency of the plant (A^7).

The decisions to be made for the next period of operation include

How many cases to produce for the next business period (A^3).
How much to spend on marketing and advertising (B^7).
  On research and development operations (B^8).
  On maintenance (B^9).
  On market research (B^{10}).
How much, if any, should be left as a buffer between the cash on hand (B^1) and the total expenditure (B^{11}).
What the selling price should be (B^{12}).

Three things influence these decisions: the starting resources (which mainly place constraints on operations), the overall general policies, and a knowledge of the consequences of different results.

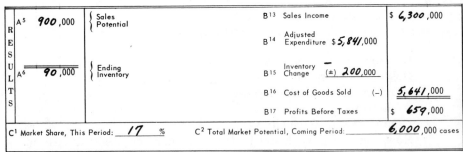

FORM G243 9/66
VENTURE BUSINESS SIMULATION EXERCISE
© The PROCTER & GAMBLE CO.

VENTURE
OPERATIONS FORM

C^3

BUSINESS OUTLOOK

POOR — (NORMAL) — BOOM

EVERY CO. YEAR _0_ , _2_ HALF

RESOURCES	A CASES			B DOLLARS
	A^1 **40** ,000	Beginning Inventory	B^1 Cash on hand	$ **6,100** ,000
			B^2 Value @ \$4.50/ case	**180** ,000
		A^2 Capacity **1,100** ,000 cases	B^3 Plant & Equipment	**5,500** ,000
			B^4 Total Assets	$**11,780** ,000

OPERATIONS	A^3 **950** ,000	Cases Produced Cost Schedule # **10** A^7	B^5 @ $ **4.58** / case (From current cost schedule)	$ **4,351** ,000
			B^6 Administrative Expense	2 0 0 ,000
			B^7 Marketing & Advertising	**1,100** ,000
			B^8 Research & Development (Maximum: \$250,000 each period)	**115** ,000
		B^{12} Sales Price **1.00**	B^9 Depreciation (Option: O or 1% of B^3)	**55** ,000
			B^{10} Market Research (Option: O or purchase C^1, C^2 at \$10,000 each)	**20** ,000
	A^4 **990** ,000	Total Available for Sale $(A^1 + A^3)$	B^{11} Total Expenditure (Cannot exceed B^1)	$ **5,841** ,000

RESULTING INCOME

RESULTS	A^5 **900** ,000	Sales Potential	B^{13} Sales Income	$ **6,300** ,000
			B^{14} Adjusted Expenditure $ **5,841**,000	
	A^6 **90** ,000	Ending Inventory	B^{15} Inventory Change (±) **200**,000	
			B^{16} Cost of Goods Sold (−)	**5,641** ,000
			B^{17} Profits Before Taxes	$ **659** ,000

C^1 Market Share, This Period: **17** % C^2 Total Market Potential, Coming Period: **6,000** ,000 cases

Notes for review of decisions:

*Courtesy of the Procter & Gamble Co.

The overall general policies are represented by the dollar distributions shown in Fig. 2.10 and in the example given in Table 3.1 and from overall and typical industrial averages [reported, for example, by Perry (1954) and Berenson (1963a) and in later sections of this book].

The consequences of the decisions can be that we ran out of product because we sold more than we produced, we built up inventory, or we sold but did not make a profit.

If we sell more than we make, we incur a penalty because customers are dissatisfied. This is difficult to assess, but for the example in Table 3.1 this might be assessed at about 6 % of sales or approximately $40,000.

If we build up inventory, we tie up capital that cannot be used elsewhere in the operations, incur a cost to move the material in and out of storage, and incur a cost of operating the storage facility. In the example in Table 3.1, this could amount to an average of $1/case. For accounting convenience this might be charged as $4 for each case built up in storage and as $5 for each case sold from storage and hence a net charge of $1/case. This accounting for inventory can drastically inflate profits for one term of operation, but it is a wise manager who realizes the actual source of this profit.

Finally, if we price the product too low, the profit per case sold is so small that when all is considered, we end up with no profit, yet we have great sales. For example, in Table 3.2 are given some annual reports of companies competing under the general conditions outlined in Table 3.1. We see that the total sales are similar, yet the profits are drastically different.

An alternative view of the decisions about operations is to consider the flow of money or cash at any one instant in time. The sales income (B^{13}) flows into the operations; part flows out as the cost of goods sold (B^{16}) and part is the profit before tax (B^{17}). This can be represented on a cash

TABLE 3.2
ABBREVIATED ANNUAL REPORTS OF COMPETING COMPANIES OVER A THREE-YEAR PERIOD
(All entries expressed as thousands)

Year		Smiley Co.	S.A.M. Co.	Grigo Co.	Unirek Co.	Jodadi Co.
1	Total cases sold	1,885	1,910	1,995	1,850	1,845
	Total sales income ($)	12,818	13,370	13,965	13,120	12,928
	Net profit ($)	635	1,758	1,770	1,453	1,270
2	Total cases sold	1,600	1,880	2,065	2,060	1,580
	Total sales income ($)	11,504	13,160	14,351	14,121	11,535
	Net profit ($)	717	1,350	1,331	1,328	220
3	Total cases sold	1,815	1,995	2,070	2,180	1,765
	Total sales income ($)	12,068	13,766	14,697	15,260	12,876
	Net profit ($)	1,171	1,445	1,857	1,976	111

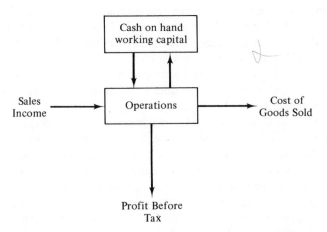

Figure 3.3. Cash flow for model company during operations.

flow diagram (Fig 3.3), which is similar to the way material flows are shown on a process flow diagram. One feature that might not be apparent from Table 3.1 is the reservoir of money, the cash on hand (B^1), that is needed to get the company started. This is also needed to allow for the fluctuations in inventory and in plant operations. This reservoir is called the working capital and has approximately equal inflows and outflows of cash into the plant operations.

Decisions about the distribution of profit

The financial profit is distributed, in general, in four different ways: taxes to the government, profits to those who have risked capital or money by investing it in the company, plowback into the operations and future health of the company, and payment of financial debt. Often the federal taxes can be averaged at 50% of the gross profit. Some of the profits can be distributed to the investors according to the magnitude of the dollars invested. The plowback into operations can go to the improvement of the present operations, to the expansion of facilities to produce greater quantities of existing products or to produce new products, to purchase fixed assets for research and development, and to changes in the cash on hand or working capital. The distribution of funds to pay financial debt is mainly determined by previous commitments made when the debt was incurred. The cash flow for the distribution of profit is shown in Fig. 3.4 for the complete operations of the whole plant. The dotted lines do not show cash flows; they represent influences that affect the cash flows elsewhere.

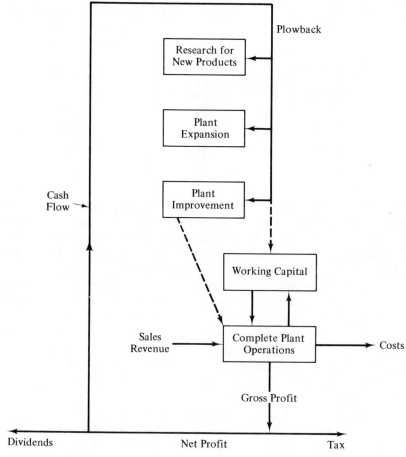

Figure 3.4. Cash flow for model company: operations and profit distribution.

3.2 An Individual Company in Real Life

In Section 3.1, with regard to a model company, the decisions made for one product and the general factors were described. In reality, a company has many products and has the problem of financing, paying off debts, and gaining more capital. Depreciation was not included in the discussion. In this and the next sections we shall consider briefly some of these factors that influence the operation of a company in real life.

In calculating the profit, some financial allowance should be made for the gradual wear, tear, and obsolescence the equipment suffered, over and above maintenance, while making the product. This allowance is called depreciation. Depreciation can be calculated from the following equality:

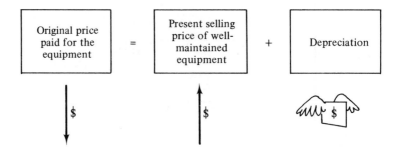

In this equation, only two items involve the actual exchange of money; depreciation is an idea to represent the disappearance of value of the equipment as time passes. Thus, the value of the equipment has decreased, and to be realistic in estimating the profit accrued from the use of the equipment, depreciation must be included as an expense (even though no money is actually paid out of the company bank). In a sense, the depreciation allowance is temporarily set aside while the profit is calculated and the taxes and dividends on profit are distributed. Then what money remains from the profit is combined with that set aside as depreciation, and the total is used as plowback into the company. This is shown on the cash flow diagram in Fig 3.5. More details about depreciation are given in Chapter 4. A numerical example that illustrates the effect of depreciation on the tax, dividends, and plowback is shown in Fig 3.6.

The material resources of a company include fixed assets and, in some cases, reserves of raw material resources necessary for the successful future operations of the company. The latter could include oil and gas reserves, minerals, and forests. Just as depreciation is an allowance for equipment, depletion is an allowance for the consumption of exhaustible reserves of natural resources. A comparison of the cash flow diagrams for the model and the real company shows the added features of depreciation and depletion and the more complicated financial activities related to the raising and investing of money.

Typical ratios and operations of chemical companies are given in Table 3.3. Such information can be obtained from the annual reports of companies, although the data given in Table 3.3 have been simplified to minimize the complexities of taxes and deferred taxes, multiple investments, etc.

Annual reports usually include two financial statements that provide the financial information needed to evaluate the company's operation. They are the balance sheet, which lists the assets and liabilities of the company at one specific time, and the income statement, which summarizes the annual revenue and expenditures. The income statement summarizes all the cash

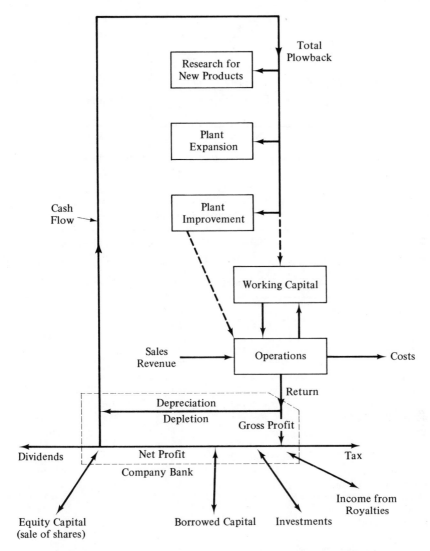

Figure 3.5. Cash flow for real company adapted from Uhl and Hawkins (1971).

flows that have occurred between two successive balance sheets. Other useful statistics include the statement of retained earnings and the summary of the source and application of funds. More details on how to read a financial report can be obtained from Merrill Lynch, Pierce, Fenner and Smith (1971) and Myer (1968).

Although some of the detailed breakdown is not given, general trends

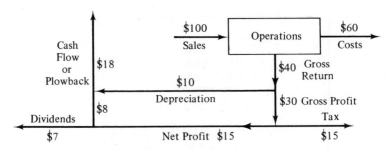

Figure 3.6. Example of cash flows neglecting problem of financing.

TABLE 3.3

TYPICAL OPERATING AND PROFIT DISTRIBUTIONS FOR REAL COMPANIES COMPARED
WITH THE "MODEL" COMPANY

	Table 3.1 "model" (consumer-oriented)	Company, millions of $		
		A	B	C
Cash on hand or working capital	6.1	88	42	113
Fixed assets	5.5	248	228	288
Starting inventory	0.180	27	27	46
Net sales	6.3	208	120	241
Costs directly attributed	4.90		80	
Selling and administration	1.32	167	10	174
R & D	0.115		1.6	
Depreciation	—	15	9.3	20.8
Miscellaneous	—	1	3.3	
Profit $\langle \breve{P} \rangle$*	0.659	25	15.8	46.5
Tax	0.330	13	6.9	16.4
Net profit $\langle \breve{P} \rangle$	0.329	12	8.9	30.1
Depreciation allowance	—	15	9.3	20.8
Net return for distribution $\langle \breve{R} \rangle$	0.329	27	18.2	50.9
Dividends		8	4.6	23.4
Debt repayment		8	3.2	1.0
Investments		—	5.4	3.0
Plowback (efficiency, expansion, R & D facilities)		12	5.3	53
Change in working capital		−1	−0.3	−29.9

are apparent. The same trends are apparent for all companies. In general,
gross profit is 10–13% of net sales. The net sales for the real companies
studied are between 50 and 85% of the fixed assets; the model shows sales
greater than the fixed assets. The inventory levels vary from 13 to 22% of
net sales for the companies to as high as 33% in the model. The dividend

TABLE 3.4

PERFORMANCE RATIOS

$$\text{Turnover ratio} = \frac{\text{annual revenue (sales)}}{\text{total assets}} \simeq 1$$

$$\text{Current ratio} = \frac{\text{current assets}}{\text{current liabilities}} \simeq 3\tfrac{1}{2}$$

$$\text{Liquidity ratio} = \frac{\text{current assets minus inventories}}{\text{current liabilities}}$$

$$\text{Profits-worth ratio} = \frac{\text{net income}}{\text{shareholder's equity}} \simeq 0.17$$

$$\text{Rate of dividends} = \frac{\text{common stock dividends}}{\text{shareholder's equity}}$$

$$\text{Operating ratio} = \frac{\text{operating charges}}{\text{operating revenue}}$$

policy of the real companies varies and is difficult to idealize in the model because in real life the net profit, which is the basis for dividend distribution, is a complex result of depreciation policy. This effect is discussed in Section 5.1.

Some order-of-magnitude factors used to qualitatively illustrate the performance of a company are listed in Table 3.4. More information is given, for example, by Osburn and Kammermeyer (1958), and corporate information is listed annually in *Chemical Engineering News*.

3.3 Background for Decisions About Operations

Each company must identify its overall financial goal. Kapfer (1967) lists some of these as

1. To maximize the short-range profit
2. To maximize the long-range profits
3. To maximize the rate of earnings for existing operations, based on an arbitrarily selected reference datum
4. To realize some arbitrary rate of earnings for existing operations
5. To break even but supply a desirable service to the consumer
6. To minimize cost to a consumer
7. To exceed some minimum acceptable profit subject to the constraint of minimum risk
8. To operate in high-risk or short-lived projects
9. To maximize profits with a minimum capital outlay
10. To maximize short-range profit subject to the constraint of being able to attract sufficient capital for future projects and to satisfy stockholders.

Then, the specific decisions are made to achieve this goal. In this section specific decisions about operations and the availability of background information pertinent to the decisions are surveyed.

Business outlook

In Table 3.1 the outlook was classified as poor, average, or boom. Forecasting of future economic conditions is based on developing reasonable relationships between the past and the future. Three types of short-range forecasting techniques are the Gross National Product model, mathematical simulations of the economy called econometric models, and the use of indicators. More details are given by the National Bureau of Economic Research (1954) and Doody (1965). An example of an economic forecast is the Gordon Commission (1958).

For our purpose, three indicators have been suggested as being indicative of the economic trends in the chemical process industry. They are an output index, the value of output, and the operating rate [McGraw-Hill Department of Economics (1967)] and are reported for the U.S. economic conditions in each issue of *Chemical Engineering*. The indices are about 4 months behind the times. Figure 3.7 shows values of these indices. The output index relates the volume of products produced by the chemical industry relative to the volume produced in 1957–1959. This is taken as a base year with an index value of 100.

The value of the output is the U.S. dollar value of goods shipped during the month prorated to an annual basis by multiplying by 12.

The operating rate is the percentage of full capacity at which plants operated during the the month. The operating rate preferred by management to yield optimum operating conditions is 95% [McGraw-Hill Department of Economics (1967)]. Details on how to calculate these indices for your own conditions are given by the McGraw-Hill Department of Economics (1967).

Interpretation is made based on all three indices considered together. For example, if the output index remains constant and the value increases, then prices are rising. If the operating rate decreases at the same time, then this would indicate new increased capacity that is not utilized as yet.

Inventory policies

The level and control of inventory is extremely important to the financial success of a company. With insufficent raw materials or operating supplies, production is slowed down unnecessarily. With insufficient finished product, orders cannot be filled. Yet money tied up in inventory is not generating a

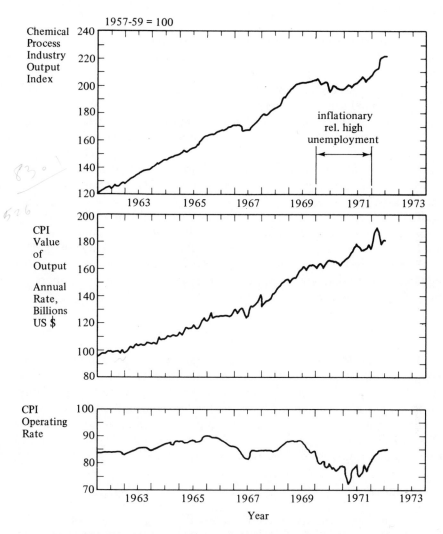

Figure 3.7. Three economic indicators for U.S. chemical industry. (Data courtesy of McGraw-Hill Dept. of Economics. Reprinted by permission of "Chemical Engineering", a McGraw-Hill publication.)

return on investment. Indeed, stored material requires storage space and protection to maintain quality and hence incurs additional expense. Thus, there is an optimum level and mix of inventory, and, once established, this should be carefully controlled. For more discussion, see Mueller (1963), Magee and Boodman (1967), Brown (1967), Ali (1970), Riggs (1968), and Rudd and Watson (1968).

Marketing and advertising

Many marketing policies can be used. The usual components are technical services, advertising, and public relations. Technical services are a major characteristic of chemical industries' marketing policies. Although the expenditure depends on the company and the products, the expenditure is often 1–2% of annual sales. For more details, see Berenson (1963b).

Although we normally think of advertising as being important for direct consumer products, chemical companies also advertise their image and their products to both the public and their industrial consumers. The topic may be pollution control or a new synthetic fiber; it could be advertised in *Newsweek*, on television, or in *Chemical Week*. The average expenditure on advertising is about 1% of annual sales for most chemical companies, with this increasing to about 6% for beverage companies, about 8% for soap and detergent manufacturers, about 10% for drug companies and about 14% for perfume and cosmetic firms [Ganis and Jordan (1963)]. This method of correlating advertising expenses with sales is not recommended by Ganis and Jordan (1963), but for our purposes it provides some appreciation of the expenditure.

R & D operations

The overall R & D activity in a company embraces the fixed assets devoted to R & D and operating expenses incurred because of salaries and supplies. The annual operating expenses, which may include depreciation on R & D assets, is about 2–5% of the total revenue, although the amount varies dramatically from company to company. The annual expenditure for R & D fixed assets is dependent on the company's policy regarding retained earnings and is discussed in Section 3.4.

Maintenance

Maintenance costs are usually expressed as a percentage of the fixed capital investment, I_F. The amount ranges from about 1 to 15% of I_F depending on the corrosive and mechanical wear conditions.

Selling price

Determination of the selling price is difficult. First, it is not likely to remain fixed over the life of the product. In general, the price decreases as competitors come into the market place. At the same time, we expect the costs to decrease because we are continually learning about and improving the process. The general trends are illustrated in Fig. 3.8.

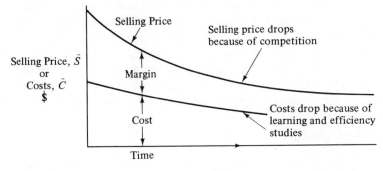

Figure 3.8.

Berenson (1963b) suggests that there are three pricing policies. In the policy *meet the competitor's price*, the selling price is shifted close to that of the competitor because the proponents claim that competition is so keen that the price is determined in the market place. The second policy employed is *cost-plus*. Here the price is set to yield an acceptable return on the investment. For example, the net profit should yield between an 8 to 20% return. A third method is *pricing the uniqueness*. Here, the price is set high enough to reflect the contribution to society yet low enough to prevent competitors from being overanxious to enter the market place. Here an attempt is made to financially evaluate the market, resource, financial, and technical feasibilities of others who may wish to produce the new product.

The method many use is cost-plus. For example, Malloy (1969) and Twaddle and Malloy (1966) set the cost or floor price to recover the costs plus a return sufficient to cover the cost of capital for the plant both at the beginning and at the end of the project life. These authors report data for two typical chemicals experiencing rapid growth. Their margin is decaying at about 18% per year. Decay rates of the cost through improvements are on the order of 1–4% per year. These trends are shown in Fig. 3.8.

If the selling price is unknown, it can be estimated from cost-plus methods based on a positive present value calculation (excluding book depreciation and opportunity costs) or on an internal rate of return calculation. Details of these methods are given in Chapter 5 and Section 7.3.

3.4 Background for Decisions About Profit Distribution

The gross profit is taxed. The taxation rates vary slightly from year to year, and each country has its own subtleties. For example, Canada has its Program for the Advancement of Industrial Technology (1956) and the Industrial Research and Development Incentives Act (1967); in the United Kingdom there are the *number 2 repairs*. In general, however, the tax rate in Canada and the United States can be approximated as 50% of gross profit. Some of the gross profit is used to pay the interest and perhaps part of the principal on the debt. The debt is analogous to a bank loan because the rate of interest and the timing of the payments are specified. The cost of the debt is deductible before taxes. Payments against the principal are not deductible.

Dividends and debt

Some of the profit after tax or net profit is distributed as dividends to the shareholders. Dividends and shareholders are analogous to a partnership whereby all invest money in an enterprise and anticipate a financial reward. Thus, some decision needs to be made by the managers concerning the amount of dividends that should be paid to the shareholders. Policies vary from company to company.

In general, shares in a company are purchased by investors because they want income (in the form of dividends) or because they anticipate that the value of their share in the company will increase with time. Thus, they can sell their share at a future time for a reward. The dividend policy can be considered from several viewpoints: the yield on money invested in a share and the relative percentage of the net profit or earnings that is distributed as dividends. These can be calculated easily from the annual reports and the stock exchange quotations.

The earning per share is the net profit after tax divided by the number of shares. The price to earning ratio is the value of the share at market value divided by the corporate earnings per share. The yield is the ratio of the dividends to the market value. The yields range from 0.2 to 6% with 4 to 6% being considered by many investors as being attractive. The payout of the dividend as a percentage of earnings per share is about 50% for many companies. The earnings and dividends for shares in some chemical companies are summarized in Table 3.5.

Total plowback

The retained earnings or retained net profit is the net profit after tax less the amounts paid on the debt and as dividends. The total amount of money to be plowed back or invested for the future health of the company is the sum of the retained net profit and the book depreciation. This can be invested in improving the efficiency, in expanding the facilities, for research and development, or as increased working capital.

Thus, if the gross profit is $400,000, the debt payment on principal is $10,000, and the depreciation allowance is $275,000 for a company with a

TABLE 3.5
SAMPLE DIVIDEND HISTORIES OF SOME COMPANIES

Company	Year	Earnings per share ($)	Dividends per share ($)
Cominco	1968	1.93	1.40
	1967	2.31	1.50
	1966	2.95	1.80
	1965	3.18	1.80
	1964	2.37	1.60
	1963	1.82	1.30
	1962	1.42	1.10
	1961	1.31	1.00
	1960	1.43	1.00
DuPont of	1968	1.57	1.00
Canada Ltd.	1967	1.30	1.00
	1966	1.73	1.00
	1965	1.57	1.00
	1964	2.11	1.00
	1963	1.89	0.90
	1962	1.60	0.80
	1961	1.20	0.60
	1960	0.92	0.50
Stelco	1968	2.79	1.00
	1967	1.94	0.85
	1966	1.77	0.85
	1965	1.80	0.85
	1964	1.91	0.85
	1963	1.82	0.775
	1962	1.50	0.625
	1961	1.43	0.60
	1960	1.23	0.60
Chemcell	1968	0.61	0.29
	1967	0.46	0.36
	1966	0.735	0.40
	1965	0.735	0.40
	1964	0.74	0.32
	1963	0.60	0.30
	1962	0.49	0.24
	1961	0.37	0.17
	1960	0.38	0.11

policy to supply 50% of net profit as dividend, the total plowback is

$$\text{net profit after tax} = \$400{,}000\ (1 - t)$$
$$= \$400{,}000\ (0.50)$$
$$= \$200{,}000$$

$$\text{the dividends} = 0.50 \times \$200,000$$
$$= \$100,000$$

$$\text{the retained earnings} = \text{net profit} - \text{dividends} - \text{debt payment}$$
$$= \$200,000 - \$100,000 - \$10,000$$
$$= \$90,000$$

Hence,

$$\text{the total plowback} = \text{retained earnings} + \text{depreciation}$$
$$= \$90,000 + \$275,000$$
$$= \$365,000$$

This is to be distributed among efficiency, expansion, invention, and working capital.

Improving efficiency of existing processes

The efficiency of a process can be improved with relatively little financial risk to the company; it should also be relatively easy to do, but the opportunities to improve processes are relatively few by the time the young professional reaches an established process. Nevertheless, because the constraints and technology change drastically over relatively short periods of time, sources of improvement can always be found. No general ratios are available to indicate corporate policies regarding the fraction of money invested in improving efficiency.

Expanding facilities of existing processes

The financial risk in expanding known processes is moderate. It should be appreciated, though, that expansion is normally a stepwise process with incentives to build large plants in order to decrease the unit costs of manufacture. Simmonds (1969) indicates that plant sizes increase in steps of 150–250%, whereas the general petrochemical markets increase on the order of 7–15% per year. Therefore, decisions to expand should be tempered by the realization that the expansion will probably be followed by a supply that exceeds demand and hence fierce price competition. Simmonds (1969) provides more details and examples.

The ease with which the new facilities can be designed depends on the problems of scaling up the process and the impact of radically different technology on the existing process. In one sense, expansion is extremely simple because we can purchase a turnkey facility; however, this discussion assumes that the engineers within the company will handle the complete project.

Invention and innovation

The overall activity whereby established products are produced by new processes and/or new products are produced is called invention and innovation. By definition, invention is the conception of ideas, whereas innovation is the translation of the invention into the economy. Innovation is the practical implementation of the results of research and development to provide new or improved goods or services. Innovation is often a capital-intensive activity since new facilities are often required [Science Council of Canada (1968) and U.S. Department of Commerce (1967)]. Innovation consists of invention, design construction, startup and marketing.

The term R & D refers to the invention stage, which accounts for about 10% of the cost of the overall innovation costs, with the other 90% being accounted for through engineering and design, 15%; getting ready to manufacture, 50%; startup expense, 10%; and marketing startup expense, 15% [U.S. Department of Commerce (1967)]. However, since all the activities except R & D are so closely associated with other activities within established companies, only the R & D expenditures are reported separately by most companies. Hence, our discussion here centers around the R & D or invention stage of the overall innovation activities.

The chemical industry is known as an invention-intensive industry. Yet, the invention or R & D activity within a company offers the most risk for capital invested. The innovation is extremely difficult to nurture through all the stages from conception to realization yet is a wide-open subject area in any industry. To illustrate the risk and challenges, the Commercial Chemical Development Association [Berenson (1963a)] cites a typical example where of the 540 ideas proposed for new industrial chemicals only one chemical actually reached the commercial basis after a 6-year program of innovation.

Within any company the questions to be answered from an administrative viewpoint are how much money should be spent on R & D, and how should money be distributed among the different phases of invention?

The chemical, aircraft, and electrical industries are classified as research-intensive industries because these industries spend a relatively large percentage of their capital on "invention." Table 3.6 summarizes the national average values for R & D expenditures. For the chemical industry in Canada, for example, the gross expenditure on R & D (GERD) is about 1% of the Gross National Product. A relatively small percentage of GERD is contributed by industry as compared to the percentage contribution in other countries. In other words, the R & D activities in government and universities are major components of the Canadian national GERD. This gives some appreciation of the total expenditure in R & D.

The total expenditure in a company for invention is the sum of the capital expenditures for assets needed for this activity and the annual operating or

TABLE 3.6
NATIONAL AND CORPORATE EXPENDITURES ON R & D*

Country	National (GERD) gross expenditure R & D as % of GNP (1964)	Industry, Total industries as % of GERD	Chemical % of total industry	Chemical % of total chemical sales
Canada	1.1	35	24	3.3
United States	3.4	61	13	3.2
Japan	1.4	59	27	
United Kingdom		61	14	
Germany		60	35	
Netherlands	1.5	55	—	
Italy		54	28	
France		46.5	19	

*From Dominion Bureau of Statistics of Canada, and OECD and U.S. Department of Commerce (1967).

current expenditures. The percentage of the total industrial R & D that is spent on capital expenditures (as opposed to current operating expenditures) is between 12 and 17% in Canada [Canadian Research and Development (1969)].

The expenditure also needs to be distributed among the different phases of the overall invention activity. Many subactivities contribute to the overall activity of thinking up a feasible new process or new products. These have been described by the Science Council of Canada [(1968), *Report 4*] as

1. Basic or fundamental research: the generalized search for new knowledge without specific application in mind. Basic research is judged on the contribution it makes to the conceptual development of science.
2. Applied research: the search for new knowledge to provide a solution to a specific problem which is defined at the onset of the research program. It does not differ radically from basic research in methods or scope but in motivation. Applied research programs must be judged by their relevance to the preselected objective.
3. Development: really a final stage of applied research which is most clearly seen in the evolution of new goods or services.

All these activities are referred to as the invention activities in a company, although the term R & D is often used. Typical overall averages for the distribution among these activities are given in Table 3.7. These overall percentages are guidelines; in practice the amount spent naturally depends on the company, the money available, and the outlook.

TABLE 3.7
DISTRIBUTION OF TOTAL R & D EXPENDITURES AMONG PHASES IN INDUSTRY

Country		Basic research	Applied research	Development
Canada*	Industrial	5	27	68
(1967)	National	22	41	37
United	Industrial	3	—	—
States	Petroleum refining†	15	45	39
(1964–1965)	National	12	22	66

*Fom Science Council of Canada (1968), *Report 4.*
†From National Science Foundation Review of Data on Science Resources (1966).

3.5 Summary

The key decision is how to best allocate the resources within a company. From the discussion of or from playing a business game, we learn that what we want to do is limited by the amount of money available and that the major challenge is to do the best with the resources available. A cash flow diagram is a convenient representation of the distribution of money within a company at any one time. An analysis of the allocation of resources among different activities has been given for a variety of companies.

PROBLEMS

3.1. For the process industry that interests you, write a brief report on the financial and technical characteristics. [For example, you might start with *The Economics of the Chemical Industry* by Backman (1970) for the chemical industry.]

3.2. From the annual reports of a company that you are interested in,
   a. Prepare an abbreviated table similar to Table 3.3.
   b. Compare your data with those in Table 3.3, calculate appropriate ratios, and explain, where possible, any differences or significant features.

3.3. a. For your country, would you describe the present economic outlook as poor, average, or boom?

   b. How did you reach this decision?

   c. The set of indicators developed by the McGraw-Hill Department of Economics is oriented toward U.S. conditions. If you work in the United States, are these indicators useful? If so, why? If not, why not, and what alternative do you suggest? If you do not work in the United States, what set of indicators can you find to help predict the economic outlook in your location?

3.4. a. Collect a series of advertisements or a description of the TV or radio programs sponsored by the company that interests you. What appeal or image
is being presented?

   b. Is the image consistent with the impression gained from your analysis of
the annual report in Problem 3.2?

3.5. a. What are the federal and state tax laws in your country?

   b. What governmental programs of direct financial assistance are available to
your company?

   c. What indirect financial assistance through tax adjustments is available to
your company or in your country?

3.6. From the annual reports of a company and from information about new construction, estimate the distribution of the plowback funds among efficiency,
expansion, and R & D.

3.7. a. Carefully study the breakdown of the national expenditures on R & D.
These are usually made up of university, governmental, and industrial
components. Which components dominate in your country? How can a professional in industry gain the most from this R & D effort?

   b. For your particular location in the country, what is your access to R & D
information from all three sources? How can you improve on this?

3.8. Prepare a simple computer-aided simulation of the cash flow diagram for
the purpose of generating an annual report and for checking some important
ratios (such as in Table 3.4 and those described in this chapter). An executive
computer program such as GEMCS, PACER, CHESS, or U.P. PACER can
be useful. For more information about simulation, see Crowe et al. (1971) or
Myers and Sieder (1973). See Gershefski (1972), for example, for a discussion
of business models.

3.9. Prepare two monthly budgets for yourself, one based on your present financial
situation and one based on an assumed starting salary of $8000/year. Summa-
rize your cash flow for both situations on a cash flow diagram similar to Fig.
3.8, with salary replacing sales revenue (unless you plan to go into business for
yourself).

Background for
Financing and
Financial Feasibility

4

Every venture needs money at one time or another. "Is the money available in the amount and at the time it is needed?" is a vital question. Because time plays such an important role in the decision making, the effect of time on the value of money will be discussed first. Second, since money can be in the form of cash or in fixed assets such as machinery or buildings, the effect of time on the value of fixed assets needs to be considered. Some general impressions will be given as to the amount of money needed for different projects, and finally some methods of financing will be discussed briefly.

4.1 Time Value of Money: Interest

Money is a resource. One who has it can exchange it, for example, for material goods or for pleasure. If he foregoes these exchanges and lends the money (now called the *principal* in a lender-borrower situation) to a borrower, he does so because he will receive compensation. *Interest* is the compensation paid by the borrower for each unit of capital borrowed for a unit of time. Since the amount of compensation should depend on the risk assumed by the lender, higher interest rates are demanded by lenders when the risk increases.

The conditions agreed upon for the interest require a specification of the *rate of interest*, the unit of time, and what happens if the interest is not paid at the end of each time period. The rate of interest may be nominal, effective, or exact. Common choices of the unit of time are annually, semiannually, quarterly, and continuously. If the interest is not paid at the end of each period, it can be merely added to the total debt (this is called simple interest) or the unpaid interest can be added to the outstanding principal and the subsequent interest rates can be calculated on the sum of the unpaid interest and principal (this is called compounded interest). The definitions and implications will become apparent as we proceed.

Simple interest and the future value of the money

For an interest rate of i per period and for n interest periods, the interest on a principal $\mathcal{P}$ is

$$\mathcal{I} = i\mathcal{P}n \tag{4.1}$$

Hence, the total future sum of money that is owed to the lender, $\mathcal{S}$, at the end of n periods is

$$\mathcal{S} = \mathcal{P} + \mathcal{I} \tag{4.2}$$
$$= \mathcal{P}(1 + in) \tag{4.3}$$

This assumes that no interest was paid until the end of the n periods. Table 4.1(a) is a dollar-time chart for simple interest. In this sketch, a principal $\mathcal{P}$ accumulates interest $\mathcal{I}$ for n time periods after which the future sum, $\mathcal{S}$, consists of the original principal plus the interest that has been generated. The interest is represented by the shaded section of Table 4.1(a).

Compound interest and the future value of money

For an interest rate per period of i compounded for n interest periods, the future sum, $\mathcal{S}$, that is owed to the lender at the end of n periods is

$$\mathcal{S} = \mathcal{P}(1 + i)^n \tag{4.4}$$

That is, the sum at the end of the

> First year is $\mathcal{S}_1 = \mathcal{P}(1 + i)$.
> Second year is $\mathcal{S}_2 = \mathcal{S}_1(1 + i)$.
> Third year is $\mathcal{S}_3 = \mathcal{S}_2(1 + i)$.
> nth year $\mathcal{S}_n = \mathcal{S}_{n-1}(1 + i)$.

TABLE 4.1
SUMMARY OF INTEREST RELATIONSHIPS

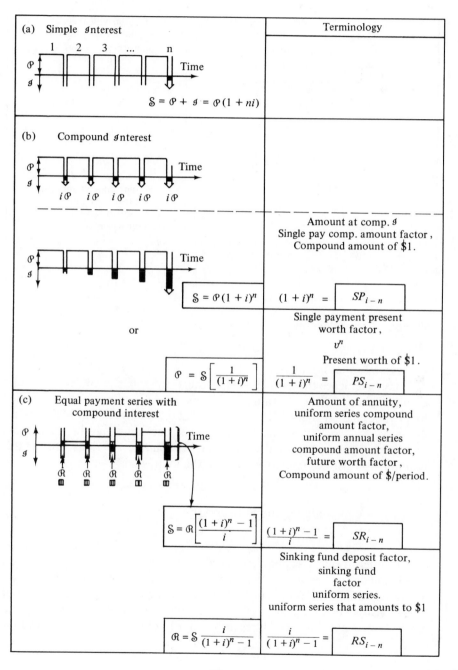

	Terminology
(a) Simple interest	
$S = P + g = P(1 + ni)$	
(b) Compound interest	
	Amount at comp. g Single pay comp. amount factor, Compound amount of \$1.
$S = P(1 + i)^n$ $(1 + i)^n = \boxed{SP_{i-n}}$	
or	Single payment present worth factor, v^n Present worth of \$1.
$P = S\left[\dfrac{1}{(1 + i)^n}\right]$ $\dfrac{1}{(1 + i)^n} = \boxed{PS_{i-n}}$	
(c) Equal payment series with compound interest	Amount of annuity, uniform series compound amount factor, uniform annual series compound amount factor, future worth factor, Compound amount of \$/period.
$S = R\left[\dfrac{(1 + i)^n - 1}{i}\right]$ $\dfrac{(1 + i)^n - 1}{i} = \boxed{SR_{i-n}}$	
	Sinking fund deposit factor, sinking fund factor uniform series. uniform series that amounts to \$1
$R = S\dfrac{i}{(1 + i)^n - 1}$ $\dfrac{i}{(1 + i)^n - 1} = \boxed{RS_{i-n}}$	

TABLE 4.1 (Continued)

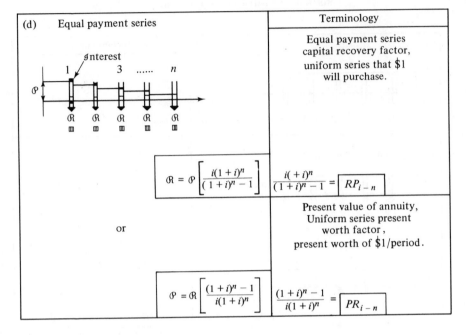

(d) Equal payment series	Terminology
interest 1 3 ...... n $\mathcal{P}$ $\mathcal{R}$ $\mathcal{R}$ $\mathcal{R}$ $\mathcal{R}$ $\mathcal{R}$	Equal payment series capital recovery factor, uniform series that $1 will purchase.
$\mathcal{R} = \mathcal{P}\left[\dfrac{i(1+i)^n}{(1+i)^n - 1}\right]$	$\dfrac{i(+i)^n}{(1+i)^n - 1} = \boxed{RP_{i-n}}$
or	Present value of annuity, Uniform series present worth factor, present worth of $1/period.
$\mathcal{P} = \mathcal{R}\left[\dfrac{(1+i)^n - 1}{i(1+i)^n}\right]$	$\dfrac{(1+i)^n - 1}{i(1+i)^n} = \boxed{PR_{i-n}}$

Simplification yields

$$S_n = \mathcal{P}(1+i)^n$$

This assumes that no interest has been paid before the end of the nth year.

For convenience the term $(1+i)^n$ is called the single-payment compound amount factor $(S\mathcal{P}_{i-n})$. Its values are given in Appendix A. The simplified dollar-time chart, Table 4.1(b), illustrates that for an investment of $\mathcal{P}$, interest $i\mathcal{P}$ can be recovered at the end of each interest period or that the interest can accumulate with the principal until the end of n interest periods. During this accumulation period, interest is paid on the interest.

Interest compounded quarterly and the future value of money

The interest rate, i, is nominally based on 1 year. Thus, when an interest rate is quoted as being 8% we expect that at the end of 1 year the interest would be $8 on a $100 principal. However, if the interest is calculated four times a year so that the year has four time periods, the interest rate per period is $8\% \div 4 = 2\%$. The overall result for four interest periods, or 1 year, is

Nominal 8% compounded quarterly		8% compounded annually
$S = \$100(1 + 0.02)^4$	$\neq$	$\$100(1 + 0.08)$
$= \$108.24$	$\neq$	$\$108.00$

In this example, the nominal interest rate, φ, is 8%. But since the interest is compounded quarterly, the effective annual interest rate is one that by definition will yield the same annual future sum S_1. That is, in general terms for 1 year,

$$S_1 = \mathcal{P}\left(1 + \frac{\varphi}{m}\right)^m = \mathcal{P}(1 + i)$$

where m is the number of time periods per year. Thus, the interrelationship is

$$i = \left(1 + \frac{\varphi}{m}\right)^m - 1 \qquad (4.5)$$

In this example, the nominal rate, φ, is 8% and the effective rate, i, is 8.24%.

Problem: Calculate the future sum at the end of the second year if $\mathcal{P} = \$100$ and the interest is 8% compounded quarterly.

Sample solution: The relationship is

$$S = \mathcal{P}\left(1 + \frac{\varphi}{m}\right)^{mn}$$

since $\mathcal{P} = \$100$, $\varphi = 8\%$, $m = 4$, and $n = 2$, the result is

$$S = \$100(1 + 0.02)^8$$
$$= \$117.20$$

Continuously compounded interest and the future value of money

If the number of interest periods per year, m, approaches infinity, the future sum is the limit as $m \to \infty$. Hence,

$$S_n = \mathcal{P}\left[\lim_{m\to\infty}\left(1 + \frac{\varphi}{m}\right)^{mn}\right]$$

$$= \mathcal{P}\left[\lim_{m\to\infty}\left(1 + \frac{\varphi}{m}\right)^{(m/\varphi)(\varphi n)}\right]$$

$$= \mathcal{P}\exp(\varphi n) \qquad (4.6)$$

Alternatively, if the effective interest rate i is used, then

$$S_n = \mathcal{P}(1 + i)^n$$

where $i = [\exp(\varphi)] - 1$.

(4.7)

Present worth relationships or discounting
the future to the present

All the preceding relationships were developed to calculate the future worth, $\mathcal{S}$, of a present amount $\mathcal{P}$. Alternatively, we can calculate backwards in time by rearranging all these relationships to calculate $\mathcal{P}$ given $\mathcal{S}$. Thus,

$$\mathcal{P} = \mathcal{S}\left[\frac{1}{(1 + i)^n}\right]$$

The term $(1 + i)^{-n}$ is called the single-payment present worth factor or $\mathcal{PS}_{i-n}$. Values are given in Appendix A. It is the reciprocal of $\mathcal{SP}_{i-n}$.

Equal payment series

Another common method of lending or borrowing money over a period of time is a series of uniform payments or withdrawals. In Table 4.1(c) is shown the dollar-time results of a series of uniform payments each valued at $\mathcal{R}$ made starting at the end of year 1 and continuing until a final payment is made at the end of year n. In this diagram the payment is represented by $\boxed{\text{III}}$ and the interest by $\blacksquare$. Since $\mathcal{R}$ is considered to be principal, it is shown above the time axis and the interest is shown below the time axis.

The future sum $\mathcal{S}$ of n equal payments of $\mathcal{R}$ is

$$\mathcal{S} = \mathcal{R}\left[\frac{(1 + i)^n - 1}{i}\right] \tag{4.8}$$

where the bracketed term is called the uniform series compound amount factor ($\mathcal{SR}_{i-n}$). Values are tabulated in Appendix A.

The amount $\mathcal{R}$ that must be set aside each time period to generate a future sum $\mathcal{S}$ is

$$\mathcal{R} = \mathcal{S}\left[\frac{i}{(1 + i)^n - 1}\right] \tag{4.9}$$

The bracketed term is called the sinking fund deposit factor ($\mathcal{RS}_{i-n}$). Values are given in Appendix A.

An alternative equal payment situation occurs when n equal payments of value $\mathcal{R}$ are each to be withdrawn from a starting principal $\mathcal{P}$ such that the last withdrawal at the end of the nth period removes all the money. This is shown schematically on Table 4.1(d). The relationships are

$$\mathcal{R} = \mathcal{P}\left[\frac{i(1 + i)^n}{(1 + i)^n - 1}\right] \tag{4.10}$$

where the factor is called the uniform series capital recovery factor ($\mathcal{RP}_{i-n}$), and

$$\mathcal{P} = \mathcal{R}\left[\frac{(1 + i)^n - 1}{i(1 + i)^n}\right] \tag{4.11}$$

where the factor is called the uniform series present worth factor ($\mathcal{PR}_{i-n}$). Tabulated values are given in Appendix A.

Detailed derivations of these equations are given, for example, by Olsen (1968) in Appendix K, Taylor (1964), de Garmo (1967), and Thuesen and Fabrycky (1964). Interrelationships among these concepts are summarized in Table 4.2.

TABLE 4.2
CONVENIENT INTEREST RELATIONSHIPS

$$\mathcal{PS}_{i-n} = \frac{1}{\mathcal{SP}_{i-n}}$$

$$\mathcal{SR}_{i-n} = \frac{1}{\mathcal{RS}_{i-n}}$$

$$\mathcal{RP}_{i-n} = \frac{1}{\mathcal{PR}_{i-n}}$$

$$\mathcal{RP}_{i-n} = i + \mathcal{RS}_{i-n}$$

$$1 + \sum_{k=1}^{k=g-1} (1+i)^k = \frac{(1+i)^g - 1}{i} = \mathcal{SR}_{i-g}$$

$$\sum_{k=1}^{k=g} \frac{1}{(1+i)^k} = \frac{(1+i)^g - 1}{i(1+i)^g} = \mathcal{PS}_{i-g}$$

Continuous compounding

The preceding discrete compounding concepts describe what happens when interest is calculated periodically, i.e., compounded annually or quarterly. This approach is appropriate for financial transactions where money flows into or out of the company discretely. Alternatively, it applies if the interest or return is determined, say, on the minimum balance in the account for the period of interest. However, money flows into and out of a company almost continuously as the product is sold, the excess cash is invested, and bills are paid. Hence, to account for either discrete or continuous cash flows, both discrete and continuous methods of accounting for the time value of money need to be developed. Consider the concept of continuous compounding of interest.

Previously, as the number of interest periods per year approached infinity, it was shown that

$$S_n = \mathcal{P} \exp(\varphi n) \tag{4.6}$$

where φ is the nominal interest rate. Thus, the interest factor $\mathcal{SP}_{i-n}$ becomes

$$\mathcal{SP}_{\varphi-n} = \exp(\varphi n) \tag{4.12}$$

It is important to note that the interest rate in Eq. (4.12) is the nominal annual rate and not the effective rate. Continuously compounded interest tables could be developed based on either the nominal rate, φ, or on the effective rate, i. Use of the nominal rate means that all the formulas summarized in Table 4.1 can be rewritten with $\exp(\varphi)$ replacing i and $\exp(n\varphi)$ replacing $(1+i)^n$. These are summarized in Table 4.3. The advantage to using interest tables based on the effective rate [as given by Grant and Ireson (1970) and

Taylor (1964)] is that the present worths calculated by effective continuous interest equals that calculated from the discrete interest rate. Care must be taken to ensure that the basis of the table is clearly understood before it is used.

From the viewpoint of financial attractiveness, the major use made of the time value of money is to express all cash flows in terms of the present value of all such flows. Thus, a computational advantage, besides the merit of the realism about the continuous nature of some of the cash flows, is gained by using continuous compounding.

If the cash flow is continuous at a rate of $\$\mathcal{R}$/year for n years, the present value is

$$\mathcal{P} = \int_0^n \mathcal{R} \exp{(-\varphi n)} \, dn \tag{4.13}$$

If the rate is assumed to be uniform each year, then integration of Eq. (4.13) yields

$$\mathcal{P} = n\mathcal{R}\left[\frac{1 - \exp{(-\varphi n)}}{\varphi n}\right] \tag{4.14}$$

If the rate of cash flow changes, say because of improved performance in the plant, because of increasing competition, or because of the product experiencing the growth-decline phases indicated in Figs. 1.8 and 3.8, then the appropriate expression for $\mathcal{R}$ can be included in Eq. (4.13) and the results calculated. More details are given by Hirschmann and Brauweiler (1970). Tables, based on the nominal rate, for discounting various cash flow patterns are given by Hirschmann and Brauweiler (1970) and Gregory (1946). The latter are presented by Weaver et al. (1963).

TABLE 4.3
COMPARISON BETWEEN DISCRETE AND CONTINUOUS
INTEREST FORMULAS BASED ON NOMINAL RATES

	Discrete	Continuous based on nominal rate, φ
Single payment compound amount factor	$\mathcal{SP}_{i-n} = (1 + i)^n$	$\mathcal{SP}_{\varphi-n} = e^{n\varphi}$
Single payment present worth factor	$\mathcal{PS}_{i-n} = \dfrac{1}{(1 + i)^n}$	$\mathcal{PS}_{\varphi-n} = e^{-n\varphi}$
Uniform series compound amount factor	$\mathcal{SR}_{i-n} = \dfrac{(1 + i)^n - 1}{i}$	$\mathcal{SR}_{\varphi-n} = \dfrac{e^{n\varphi} - 1}{e^{\varphi} - 1}$
Uniform series sinking fund deposit factor	$\mathcal{RS}_{i-n} = \dfrac{i}{(1 + i)^n - 1}$	$\mathcal{RS}_{\varphi-n} = \dfrac{e^{\varphi} - 1}{e^{n\varphi} - 1}$
Capital recovery factor	$\mathcal{RP}_{i-n} = \dfrac{i(1 + i)^n}{(1 + i)^n - 1}$	$\mathcal{RP}_{\varphi-n} = \dfrac{e^{\varphi} - 1}{1 - e^{-n\varphi}}$
Uniform series present worth factor	$\mathcal{PR}_{i-n} = \dfrac{(1 + i)^n - 1}{i(1 + i)^n}$	$\mathcal{PR}_{\varphi-n} = \dfrac{1 - e^{-n\varphi}}{e^{\varphi} - 1}$

In this book, discrete compounding techniques are used; nevertheless, an understanding of continuous compounding is necessary in case your company uses it.

4.2 Time Value of Assets : Depreciation

Fixed assets can increase or decrease in value as time progresses. For example, the value of Rembrandt's painting "The Night Watch" has increased greatly in value since 1642 when it was painted. Nevertheless, the majority of assets decrease in value with time because the assets wear out or become obsolete. In this text, we shall consider only assets whose value decreases or depreciates with time.

An example of such depreciation in value of an asset, a car, is shown in Fig. 4.1. The depreciation in value is the decrease in value of the asset. The annual depreciation of the car is summarized in Table 4.4. The rate of depreciation is high in the early life of the car and becomes almost constant in later life. Not all assets depreciate in this manner.

An important point about depreciation is that we know only the actual amount of depreciation when we buy and sell. That is, the data in Fig. 4.1 are opinion; inferred is a certain make of car, a certain condition of the car, and that the used car is being sold in a given market situation. The only way we know the actual depreciation is to take the car out onto the lot and sell it. Second, between the time we buy and eventually sell the asset we must use our best judgment to estimate the annual depreciation rate on the asset, and, even though no money is actually paid out of the company bank, this

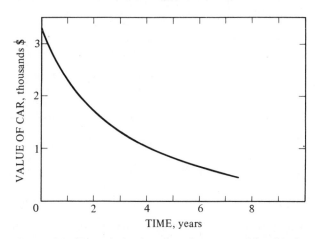

Figure 4.1. Depreciation in value of an automobile with time.

TABLE 4.4
VALUE AND DEPRECIATION OF AUTOMOBILE A*

Time (yr)	Resale value ($), start of year	Annual Depreciation ($), during year
0	3300	
		1100
1	2200	
		450
2	1750	
		450
3	1300	
		300
4	1100	
		300
5	800	
		155
6	645	
		145
7	500	

*From *The Globe and Mail*, Sept. 1, 1969, p. 25; or *Popular Mechanics* (1970).

depreciation must be subtracted as an expense so that we obtain a realistic estimate of the profit. To emphasize and illustrate the importance of depreciation in estimating profit, consider the following situation:

Harry has $3250 to invest. He can invest it in the bank at 4% interest compounded annually for the next 2 years. Alternatively, he can buy a car and go into the cab business. Assuming that he has the necessary working capital to get the cab business going, at the end of the 2 years the results of the two alternatives might be

	Cab business		Invest in bank	
	Outflow ($)	Inflow ($)	Outflow ($)	Inflow ($)
Fees, licences	800		Interest calculated from the table in	
Gas, oil, maintenance	6400		Appendix A =	
Income		8800	$3250 × 1.082	
	7200	8800	3250	3516.50
Actual money generated	1600		265.50	

Harry withdraws the interest and compares the actual money he has in in his pocket from these two alternatives: $1600

from the cab business and $265.50 from the banking venture.
Insofar as money in his pocket is concerned, he gets more
from the cab business. But someone has to point out that the
cab is now worth, from Fig. 4.1, about $1500 less than his
original investment in the car of $3250. (That is, if we forced
Harry to recover his invested money, he would have to sell
the car for $1750 and withdraw his $3250 from the bank
account.) Thus, the calculation of the profit would be

	Cab business	Bank
Actual money generated	1600	265.50
Reasonable estimate of depreciation of asset, ($)	1500	—
Profit	100	265.50

Hence, an unrealistic estimate of profit is obtained unless an
estimate of the depreciation is included as an expense.

In estimating the depreciation an estimate is needed of the length of time
the asset is useful to us and of how the rate of depreciation changes with
time.

The life of the asset

The length of time over which we are interested in the depreciation is
called the life of the asset. Since the life depends on our interest or purpose,
there are many different kinds of life.

For a car, for example, we may hang onto the car until we have driven it
into the ground; the life might be 8 years. Alternatively, we might view our
car as a prestige symbol; the life of the car might be 1 year. Or, from an
economic viewpoint, we have the least overall cost if the car is traded in
every 4 years. The life depends on the purpose of calculating the profit: 8
years when we think we will be able to afford the out-of-pocket repairs and
upkeep but will not have the amount of money necessary to buy a new car
(a financial feasibility constraint), 1 year when we express profit in terms of
prestige instead of money, and 4 years when profit is expressed in terms of
money.

For calculating profit in a company, the life of the asset is the company
estimate of the length of time the asset will actually be kept in operation
considering both obsolescence and changing competition, which could be 5
years for a process that will become obsolete rather quickly. It is called the
economic life. When the plant is being designed, the economic life is called

the design life because there is uncertainty as to the life of the asset in the marketplace. After the process is in operation, better information is available for estimating the economic life and so the term is relabeled. For example, at the design stage the design life might be 12 years; however, 2 years after the plant is actually in operation a new development by competitors indicates that the economic life should be reduced to 5 years. In general, design life and economic life are synonymous, and in this book this is given the symbol g years.

For calculating the profit for the purpose of taxation, the taxation agencies by law have defined the life of different types of equipment or assets. This definition by law was a necessary compromise between the economic life and the actual physical life of an asset when the asset had to be shut down because of physical deterioration. In this book the tax life is given the symbol of y years.

As an example, a pump may have an economic life of 8 years, a tax life of 12 years, and a physical life of 24 years.

The change in asset value

Once the life that is of interest has been established, the change in value of the asset between the start and finish of the life needs to be estimated. The value at the beginning is easy to establish, and methods of estimating the value are given in Chapter 6. The net salvage or scrap value (after the expenses of removal and sale have been subtracted) is more difficult to estimate. Often we assume for most engineering calculations that the scrap value at the end of the life is zero.

Methods of representing the rate of depreciation

Four different methods are commonly used to represent the rate of depreciation. These are straight line, declining balance, sinking fund, and sum of the year's digits methods. In general, the annual amount of depreciation, $\check{D}$, is given as

$$\check{D} = eI_F \tag{4.15}$$

where e = rate of depreciation for company purposes of calculating profit; this is sometimes called the book rate of depreciation

I_F = initial fixed capital investment in the asset

The straight line method uses a constant rate. Thus, the annual depreciation is constant, and the relationship is

$$e = \frac{1}{g} \tag{4.16}$$

where g is the economic or book life of the asset. This definition assumes that the scrap value $V_S = 0$.

In the declining balance method, the rate gradually decreases. In this method the annual depreciation is a fixed percentage of the asset value at the beginning of the year under study. Unfortunately, the fixed percentage, c, is defined in terms of the salvage value. Thus,

$$c = 1 - \left[\frac{V_S}{I_F}\right]^{1/g} \tag{4.17}$$

The method cannot be used if $V_S = 0$. The depreciation during the jth year is

$$\check{D}_j = cI_F(1 - c)^{j-1} \tag{4.18}$$

Hence, in the jth year the value of e is

$$\check{D}_j = e_j I_F$$
$$e_j = c(1 - c)^{j-1} \tag{4.19}$$

Values are given in Table 4.5 to illustrate the approach. However, this method is seldom used because it cannot be used when $V_S = 0$.

The principles of this method are used, however, in the double declining balance method. In this method the value of c is set equal to two times the reciprocal of the book life, g. Thus, the rate of depreciation in the jth year is

$$e_j = \frac{2}{g}\left[1 - \frac{2}{g}\right]^{j-1} \tag{4.20}$$

This approach is applicable when $V_S = 0$, but the mathematics is such that at the end of year g the predicted scrap value is not zero. The value of the asset at the end of the gth year is

$$V_S = I_F\left(1 - \frac{2}{g}\right)^g$$

Hence, if $g = 10$ years,

$$V_S = I_F\left(1 - \frac{2}{10}\right)^{10}$$
$$= I_F(0.8)^{10}$$
$$= 0.107 I_F$$

To force the scrap value to zero at the end of the gth year, straight line depreciation is used in the latter years with the economic life, with the double declining balance method being used during the first years. More details are given by Happel (1958).

Consider now the sinking fund method of depreciation. In the most idealized sense, depreciation can be visualized as a sum of the money set aside each year such that at the end of g years the capital invested initially is recovered. Thus, if we bought a car for $3300, we would set aside enough money so that at the end of the fifth year we would have set aside $3300.

This could be made up of the used car sale value of $645 and five payments totaling $2655. We note that no allowance is made for anticipated inflation in the price.

TABLE 4.5
SOME DECLINING BALANCE CALCULATIONS

Year	Asset value at beginning	Depreciation during the year	Asset value at end of year
1	I_F	cI_F	$[I_F - cI_F] = I_F(1 - c)$
2	$I_F(1 - c)$	$cI_F(1 - c)$	$I_F(1 - c) - cI_F(1 - c)$ $= I_F(1 - c)(1 - c)$ $= I_F(1 - c)^2$
3	$I_F(1 - c)^2$	$cI_F(1 - c)^2$	$I_F(1 - c)^2 - cI_F(1 - c)$ $= I_F(1 - c)^3$

Several things could be done with the depreciation money set aside each year. It could just be set aside to accumulate; it could be invested at interest rate i; it could be combined with the retained earnings and used as plowback in the financial operation. The sinking fund method is based on the principle that the money is set aside in an imaginary sinking fund to generate interest for g years at rate i. Thus, if the scrap value is zero, the annual sinking fund depreciation is

$$e = \frac{i}{(1 + i)^g - 1} \tag{4.21}$$

This idealized viewpoint is recommended by de Garmo (1967) for use in comparing the financial attractiveness of alternative investments. This is an idealization because a sinking fund is very rarely set up in practice.

In the sum of the year's digits method of depreciation, the annual depreciation for year j is the number of years left in the economic life $g - j + 1$ divided by the sum of the arithmetic series from 1 to g. This mathematical correlation is similar to the double declining balance method in that large annual depreciations occur during the first years. However, the scrap value can become zero, if desired, at the end of the gth year, whereas in the double declining balance method this has to be forced by resorting to straight line depreciation. The relationship for the depreciation rate, e, in the jth year is

$$e_j = \frac{2(g - j + 1)}{g(g + 1)} \tag{4.22}$$

To summarize, the overall depreciation relationships are given in Table 4.6 and Fig. 4.2.

Example: The present value of an ethylbenzene plant is $1 million. The design life is 10 years.

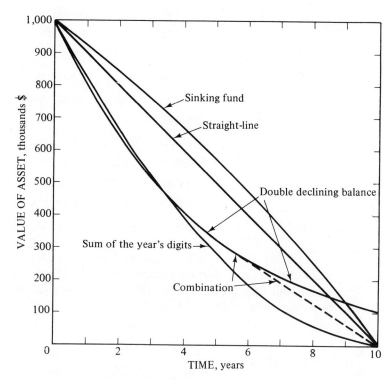

Figure 4.2. Changes in asset value with time for different methods of depreciation.

Problem: Estimate the value of the plant as a function of time using straight line, double declining balance, double declining combined with linear, sinking fund, and sum of the year's digits (SYD) methods. Assume that the scrap value is zero.

Sample solution: In straight line depreciation, the annual depreciation $e = 1/g = \frac{1}{10} = 0.1$. Hence, each year the value of the asset decreases by

$$eI_F = 0.1(\$1 \times 10^6)$$
$$= \$100,000$$

This is shown in Fig. 4.2.

In the double declining balance, the annual depreciation is not constant. Indeed, the undepreciated reserve at the end of year j is $V_j = I_F(1 - c)^j$.

For the double declining rate, assume that $c = 2/g$. Hence, $c = 0.2$, and the asset values at the end of each year are, respectively, year 1: $\$1,000,000(1 - 0.2)^1 = \$800,000$

year 2: $\$1,000,000(1 - 0.2)^2 = \$640,000$

year 3: $\$1,000,000(1 - 0.2)^3 = \$512,000$

year 4: $\$1,000,000(1 - 0.2)^4 = \$409,600$

year 5: $\$1,000,000(1 - 0.2)^5 = \$327,680$

year 6: $\$1,000,000(1 - 0.2)^6 = \$262,144$

year 7: $\$1,000,000(1 - 0.2)^7 = \$209,715$

year 8: $\$1,000,000(1 - 0.2)^8 = \$167,772$

year 9: $\$1,000,000(1 - 0.2)^9 = \$134,218$

year 10: $\$1,000,000(1 - 0.2)^{10} = \$107,374$

In the combined method, straight line depreciation takes over as the method of depreciation when the annual depreciation rate for the straight line method exceeds the depreciation rate for the double declining balance method. Happel (1958), pp. 49 and 280, concludes that the year j^1 when straight line depreciation should be used for the first time is

$$j^1 = \frac{2g + \cos(\pi g) + 7}{4}$$

For $g = 10$

$$j^1 = \frac{20 + \cos(10\pi) + 7}{4}$$

$$= \frac{(20 + 1 + 7)}{4} = 7$$

Hence, the value of the asset at the beginning of the seventh year is $\$262,144$. This is to be depreciated to zero over the remaining $(g - j^1 + 1)$ years. Hence, the annual depreciation is $\$262,144/4 = \$65,536$.

In the sinking fund method assume that $i = 6\%$. Hence, for $g = 10$, from Appendix A, the value of $e = 0.07587$. The value of the plant at the end of each year is given by

$$V_j = I_F - \frac{(1 + i)^j - 1}{i} \frac{i}{(1 + i)^g - 1} I_F$$

$$= I_F \left[1 - \frac{\Re S_{i-g}}{\Re S_{i-j}}\right]$$

Hence, the asset value at the end of each year based on data from Appendix A is, respectively,

year 1: $\$10^6 \left(1 - \dfrac{0.0758}{1.00}\right) = \$924,200$

year 2: $\$10^6\left(1 - \dfrac{0.0758}{0.48544}\right) = \$844{,}000$

year 3: $\$10^6\left(1 - \dfrac{0.0758}{0.31411}\right) = \$759{,}000$

year 4: $\$10^6\left(1 - \dfrac{0.0758}{0.22859}\right) = \$669{,}000$

year 5: $\$10^6\left(1 - \dfrac{0.0758}{0.17740}\right) = \$573{,}000$

year 6: $\$10^6\left(1 - \dfrac{0.0758}{0.14336}\right) = \$471{,}000$

year 7: $\$10^6\left(1 - \dfrac{0.0758}{0.11914}\right) = \$364{,}000$

year 8: $\$10^6\left(1 - \dfrac{0.0758}{0.10104}\right) = \$250{,}000$

year 9: $\$10^6\left(1 - \dfrac{0.0758}{0.08702}\right) = \$130{,}000$

year 10: $\$10^6\left(1 - \dfrac{0.0758}{0.0758}\right) = \$0$

For the SYD calculations the undepreciated reserve at the end of each year j is given as

$$V_j = \frac{(g-j)(g-j+1)}{g(g+1)}I_F$$

For this example, the annual values are at the end of

year 1: $\$10^6\left[\dfrac{9(10)}{110}\right] = \$820{,}000$

year 2: $\$10^6\dfrac{8 \times 9}{110} = \$658{,}000$

year 3: $\$10^6\dfrac{7 \times 8}{110} = \$510{,}000$

year 4: $\$10^6\dfrac{42}{110} = \$382{,}000$

year 5: $\$10^6\dfrac{30}{110} = \$274{,}000$

year 6: $\$10^6\dfrac{20}{110} = \$182{,}000$

year 7: $\$10^6\dfrac{12}{110} = \$109{,}000$

$$\text{year 8:} \qquad \$10^6 \frac{6}{110} = \$54,600$$

$$\text{year 9:} \qquad \$10^6 \frac{2}{110} = \$18,200$$

$$\text{year 10:} \qquad \$10^6 \frac{0}{110} = \$0$$

*This example illustrates the different values of the undepreciated reserve for the different methods of depreciation.

So far, the different methods of calculating depreciation have been described. Since the purpose of depreciation is to offer a realistic view of profit from the taxation and the company viewpoints, the company usually keeps two different sets of records to satisfy these two purposes.

TABLE 4.6
SUMMARY OF DEPRECIATION CONCEPTS

Name	Annual rate, $\breve{D} = e I_F$	Undepreciated reserve at end of year j, $(I_F)_j$	Comments
Straight line	$e = \dfrac{1}{g}$	$I_F\left(1 - \dfrac{j}{g}\right)$	
Declining balance Single	$e_j = c(1 - c)^{j-1}$ $c = 1 - \left(\dfrac{V_S}{I_F}\right)^{1/g}$	$I_F(1 - c)^j$	Seldom used because of incompatibility if $V_S = 0$
Double rate	$e_j = \dfrac{2}{g}\left(1 - \dfrac{2}{g}\right)^{j-1}$	$I_F\left(1 - \dfrac{2}{g}\right)^j$	Need to combine with straight line for later years
Sinking fund	$e = \dfrac{i}{(1 + i)^g - 1}$	$I_F\left(1 - \dfrac{\mathfrak{RS}_{i-g}}{\mathfrak{RS}_{i-j}}\right)$	
Sum of the year's digits	$e = \dfrac{2(g - j + 1)}{g(g + 1)}$	$I_F \dfrac{(g - j)(g - j + 1)}{g(g + 1)}$	

TABLE 4.7
TAX REGULATIONS CONCERNING DEPRECIATION

Country	
Canada (1970)	Must use double declining balance method; the maximum rate acceptable is double rate with a tax life = 10 years
United States (1969)	Any method can be used provided the depreciation over the first two-thirds of the tax life does not exceed the total calculated by the double declining balance method
Australia (1971)	Straight line or declining balance with salvage value not considered

From the company viewpoint the annual depreciation is $\check{D} = eI_F$ while from the taxation viewpoint the annual depreciation is $\check{D} = dI_F$. The numerical value of e and d depend on the life and the rate. The rate that can be used for tax purposes is listed in Table 4.7. Most companies use the same method for the calculation of both depreciations. However, because the economic life is usually shorter than the tax life, the book depreciation will be larger than the tax depreciation. This slight complication is shown in the revised cash flow diagram in Fig. 4.3, which shows a book depreciation greater than the tax depreciation. From this diagram we note that there is an important

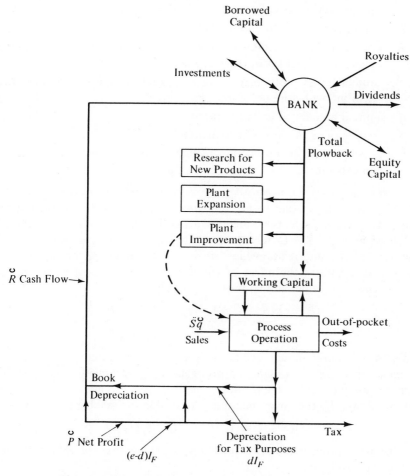

Figure 4.3. Revised cash flow diagram to illustrate use of book and tax depreciation. Bank is relocated so that cash flow refers to a specific process operation.

difference between cash flow, or net return $\check{R}$, and the net profit from a company viewpoint, $\check{P}$, and that the correct depreciation needs to be used in the appropriate place. In studying cash flow it is useful to define and use a convenient set of terms and nomenclature. The concepts are simple; the difficulty is in keeping the definitions clear. Some important symbols and definitions are

dI_F = annual depreciation for taxation purposes based on rate d

eI_F = annual depreciation for company or book purposes based on rate e

t = annual tax rate to be applied to the annual gross profits with the allowable annual depreciation, dI_F; usually about 50%

$\check{P}$ = annual net profit after tax

$\check{P}*$ = annual gross profit before tax

$\check{R}*$ = annual net profit after tax plus book depreciation eI_F; called the cash inflow after tax or the net return.

$\check{R}$ = annual gross profit before tax plus book depreciation; called the cash inflow before tax or the gross return

$\check{q}$ = annual number of units produced

$\ddot{S}$ = selling price per unit of production

$\ddot{C}$ = cost per unit of production including book depreciation, $eI_F/\check{q}$, as an expense

The interrelationships among all these concepts are summarized in Table 4.8. In general, it is usual to use *after tax* concepts and for mathematical simplicity to use R concepts for financial attractiveness calculations (discussed in Chapter 5) or $\ddot{S} - \ddot{C}$ relationships for product costing (discussed in Chapter 7). The interrelationships are also represented pictorially in Fig. 4.4, which illustrates the effect of the different depreciation rates on the results. The average net annual profit is given by

$$\langle \check{P} \rangle = \langle \underbrace{(\ddot{S} - \ddot{C})\check{q}(1 - t)}_{\text{net income if } e=d} - \underbrace{tI_F(e - d)}_{\substack{\text{depreciation} \\ \text{adjustment}}} \rangle \qquad (4.23)$$

In Fig. 4.4 the total annual income is $\ddot{S}\check{q}$ and the total annual cost including depreciation is $\ddot{C}\check{q}$. To obtain the profit as the government sees it for tax purposes we must add to the profit our depreciation, eI_F, and subtract depreciation allowed by the government, dI_F, to obtain the taxable profit. Hence,

$$[(\ddot{S} - \ddot{C})\check{q} + eI_F - dI_F]t = \text{tax} \qquad (4.24)$$

The company profit is the gross profit $(\ddot{S} - \ddot{C})\check{q}$ less tax. Hence, the annual average net profit $\langle \check{P} \rangle$ is

$$\langle \check{P} \rangle = (\ddot{S} - \ddot{C})\check{q} - (\ddot{S} - \ddot{C})\check{q}t - teI_F + tdI_F$$
$$= (\ddot{S} - \ddot{C})\check{q}(1 - t) - tI_F(e - d)$$

TABLE 4.8

TABLE 4.8
(a) TERMINOLOGY FOR ANNUAL PROFITS

Tax	Book depreciation, eI_F	
	Include as expense	Exclude as expense
Before	$\check{P}*$	$\check{R}*$
After	$\check{P}$	$\check{R}$
		$\check{R} = \check{P} + eI_F$

(b) INTERRELATIONSHIPS AMONG DEFINITIONS

$$\check{P} = \check{q}\check{P} \qquad\qquad \check{R} = \check{q}\check{R}$$
$$\check{P}* = \check{q}(\check{S} - \check{C})$$
$$\quad\; = \check{R}* - eI_F$$
$$\check{P} = \check{q}(\check{S} - \check{C})(1 - t) - tI_F(e - d)$$
$$\quad = \check{P}*(1 - t) - tI_F(e - d)$$
$$\quad = \check{R}*(1 - t) + tdI_F - eI_F$$
$$\quad = \check{R} - eI_F$$
$$\check{R}* = \check{q}(\check{S} - \check{C}) + eI_F$$
$$\quad\; = \check{P}* + eI_F$$
$$\check{R} = \check{q}(\check{S} - \check{C})(1 - t) + tI_Fd + eI_F(1 - t)$$
$$\quad = \check{P}*(1 - t) - tI_F(e - d) + eI_F$$
$$\quad = \check{P} + eI_F$$
$$\quad = \check{R}*(1 - t) + tdI_F$$

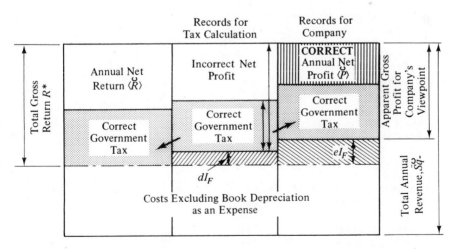

Figure 4.4. Annual net profit and the two different rates of depreciation, d and e. (Exaggerated areas to illustrate differences.)

To illustrate the difference through a mathematical example, consider the production of $\check{q} = 10^4$ units/year of a product made to sell for \$12/unit. The cost components are those listed in Fig. 2.10 and are conveniently summarized in Table 4.9. Hence, the gross profit per unit, $\check{P}*$, is

$$\check{P}* = \check{S} - \ddot{C} = \$12 - \$6.68 = \$5.32$$

The annual gross profit would be

$$\check{q}\check{P}* = \check{P}* = \$5.32 \times 10^4$$

The net profit after tax, for tax rate $t = 0.50$, is (assuming that $e = d$) from Eq. 4.23:

$$\check{P} = \check{P}*(1 - t) = \$5.32 \times 10^4(1 - 0.50)$$
$$= \$2.66 \times 10^4$$

From Table 4.9, where $\ddot{D} = \$0.50$, the net and gross returns, $\check{R}$ and $\check{R}*$, are

$$\check{R} = \check{P} + eI_F$$
$$= (\$2.66 + 0.50) \times 10^4$$
$$= \$3.16 \times 10^4$$
$$\check{R}* = \check{P}* + eI_F$$
$$= (\$5.32 + 0.50) \times 10^4$$
$$= \$5.82 \times 10^4$$

This illustrates the difference between return or cash flow and profit.

TABLE 4.9
GENERALIZED CONTRIBUTIONS TO THE SELLING PRICE $\check{S}$
(\$/unit of production)

	Value from Fig. 2.10 (\$)	% of selling price		Usual % of selling price*
Raw materials	4.50	37		38–55
Utilities	0.30	2		5
Labor	0.20	1		1–11
Other	0.18	1		
Directly attributable cost less depreciation	5.18		41	
Depreciation based on company's method	0.50	4		6
Other	0.40	3		1–6
Total manufacturing cost, $\ddot{M}$	6.08		50	50
General expense	0.60	5		10
Product cost, $\ddot{C}$	6.68		55	
Approximate tax	2.66	22		8
Approximate net profit, $\check{P}$	2.66	22		8
Selling price, $\check{S}$	12.00	100		

*From Wessel (1953) and Schuman (1955).

In summary, all assets depreciate. To realistically estimate profit, a numerical allowance must be included as an expense to account for depreciation. While many different methods of calculating the annual depreciation were reviewed, usually a linear depreciation with negligible scrap value will be assumed in the illustrations in this book. For comparisons of financial attractiveness, the sinking fund method is often used in practice. Because profit is seen in a different light by the government and the stockholders, different annual values of depreciation are often recorded so that two sets of account books are kept.

4.3 Financial Feasibility

Money must be available before action can be taken. How much money does it take? Some idea of how much money is required for different activities is provided by the data in Table 4.10. More details of estimating the amount

TABLE 4.10
SOME ORDER-OF-MAGNITUDE FINANCIAL REQUIREMENTS

Topic	Generalizations	Southern Canada (1972)	Fill in for yourself
Food expenses for 2 adults		$100/month	
Housing for 2 adults (rent)		$200/month	
Purchase of automobile		$3000	
Purchase of house	2–3 times annual salary	$20,000	
Operating cost of purchased house: mortgage, heating, electricity, maintenance	$\sim 1\%$ of purchase cost per month	$200/month	
Term life insurance	3 times annual salary	$30,000	
Housing			
Bungalow, at 1200 ft^2	$17/ft^2	$20,000	
Split level, at 1200 ft^2	$17/ft^2	$20,000	
Two story, at 1800 ft^2	$15/ft^2	$27,000	
Office building	$25/ft^2		
Small shopping center (20 stores)		0.5×10^6	
Small oil refinery (50,000 barrels/day)		55×10^6	
Domestic waste treatment plant for a city of 200,000 (secondary treatment)		15×10^6	
Blast furnace for a steel mill		30×10^6	

of money needed to build different process units and to buy processing equipment are given in Chapter 6.

Sources of money

Money or capital can be invested to improve efficiency, to expand operations, or to innovate. As outlined in Chapter 3, the risk increases as we move from efficiency to expansion to innovation. For an established company or large company these three ways of using money are balanced so that the overall risk is less than if a company required capital for innovation only. Here we shall consider the source of risk capital for innovation only and the sources of capital for an established company.

Sources of risk capital for innovation

If a technological innovation is to be implemented in a small company or if an invention of an individual is to become a commercial reality based on one's own initiative, then the capital required will be invested in a high-risk venture. This type of capital is called *risk or venture* capital, and the order of magnitude requirement for an innovation is about $500,000 in its first couple years [U.S. Department of Commerce (1967), p. 21]. Since over 50% of society's innovations are the work of independent inventors or small companies [U.S. Department of Commerce (1967), p. 17], the need for risk capital is not a trivial matter.

The sources of risk capital are persons with personal wealth, insurance companies, investment funds and trusts, corporate sources, investment bankers and underwriters, small business investment companies, and government agencies. A sample list of sources of risk capital in Canada is given in Table 4.11.

One of the main problems in obtaining risk capital is that the inventors usually have little appreciation of the financial considerations and requirements and the investors of the risk capital may not have sufficient expertise in

TABLE 4.11
SOME SOURCES OF RISK CAPITAL IN CANADA*

Industrial Development Bank (1944) (federal government)
Area Development Incentive Program (federal government)
Canada Patents and Development Corporation (provincial government)
Canadian Enterprise Development Corp. Ltd.
Unas Investments Ltd.
The Charterhouse Group (Canada) Ltd.

*From Beam (1970) and Royal Commission on Banking and Finance (1964).

the technical field to evaluate that risk. More details on this subject are given by Beam (1970), U.S. Department of Commerce (1967), Canadian Patents and Development Ltd., and Otto (1963).

Sources of capital for an established company

In 1961 about 90% of the capital required for plant and equipment in established companies came from plowback (retained earnings plus depreciation) [Anderson (1963)]. Besides this internal source of income, companies use bank loans, long-term debt or bonds, preferred shares, and common shares as external sources of capital for the remaining 10%.

Common shares are sold to investors who anticipate dividends and an increase in value of their share in the company. These investors have the right to vote for directors of the company. The shares are traded on the stock exchange. More details on the role of the stock market and how to invest in stocks or shares are given by Crane (1964). Investing in shares in a company is a combination of timing and of the quality of the shares of stocks. From an investment viewpoint there is a "best" time to buy a share and a "best" time to sell a share. Second, shares should not be bought in just any company but in one whose anticipated performance will satisfy personal investment needs. Investors use a variety of methods to evaluate stocks. The sample given in Table 4.12 illustrates that the overall economic considerations discussed in Chapter 3 play a major role in this evaluation.

Preferred shares usually offer an investor a defined dividend that is paid from the net profit before any other considerations are made. Anderson (1963) elaborates on this.

Bonds offer another external source of capital. They are usually long-term (about 20 years) and require a series of equal interest payments paid at a specified time. Details are given by Anderson (1963) and Riggs (1968), Chapter 7.

Companies attempt to keep a balance between the external sources of financing, i.e., between the shareholders' equity and the bond debt. Some illustrative examples are given by Anderson (1963) and Riggs (1968), Chapter 7. In summary, one important criterion in decision making, illustrated in Figure 1.3, was the financial feasibility. The money must be available from somewhere and by some means. Some sources of money or capital have been described. In general, whatever the source of the capital, there is a cost associated with it. The cost of capital is usually expressed as an interest rate i.

In most discussions of the cost of capital, two rates are used i and i_m. The former, i, is the average cost of capital for all the investor-committed capital in the company and is averaged over all the corporate uses of capital

TABLE 4.12
SAMPLE SHARE OR STOCK EVALUATION GUIDE

Company_____Industry_____Date_____
Years in business_____Years dividends paid_____on the stock exchange
_____Common shares outstanding_____Products and distribution_____

A. Sales growth (minimum 10%/year; 20%/year if possible)
   1. What is the yearly average for the last 10 years?_____
   2. Should this rate continue at least 5 more years?_____
   3. Why?_____

B. Earnings growth (in line with sales growth)
   1. What is the yearly average for the last 10 years?_____
   2. Should this rate continue at least 5 more years?_____
   3. Why?_____

C. Yield (at least 4–6% for full advantage of compounding)
   1. Present market price_____
   2. Average dividend for the last 5 years_____% of earnings
   3. Estimated total dividend for the next 5 years_____
   4. Average estimated dividend for the next 5 years_____
   5. Yield_____%
D. Upside-downside ratio (try for ratio of 3 to 1)
   1. Highest price during the next 5 years_____
   2. Present market price_____
   3. Lowest price during the next 5 years_____
   4. Upside potential_____(D1 minus D2)
   5. Downside potential_____(D2 minus D3)
   6. Upside-downside ratio_____to_____1_____(D4 divided by D5)
E. Zoning (to avoid paying too much, restrict buying to lower range, or to middle
    range if growth is especially fast)
   1. Highest price (D1)_____less lowest price (D3)_____equals an estimated
     price range for the next 5 years of_____points (one-third of this range
     is_____points)
   2. Lower third is_____through_____(buy range)
   3. Middle third is_____through_____(may be bought—hold range)
   4. Upper third is_____through_____(do not buy—sell range)
   5. The present market price of_____is in the_____range
Comments and recommendation

_____
_____
_____
_____

including the working capital. The latter, i_m, is the minimum acceptable cost of capital for a specific project under consideration. This is a larger value than i to account for the risk associated with the specific project.

4.4 Summary

The value of money and of assets varies with time. These two concepts are very simple to understand and to include in decision making (as we shall see in Chapter 5). If we neglect these ideas, we shall arrive at naive and incorrect conclusions. This material is the basis of later work. The problem of obtaining money sufficient to finance a project was discussed briefly.

PROBLEMS

4.1. You could buy a Putput car now for $3000 or invest your money at 6% simple interest for 3 years and hope to buy a Dasher car for $3650. What trade-in allowance would you have to get for your roller skates on a trade-in for a Dasher car? What would be the answer if the interest were compounded quarterly?

4.2. For your twentieth birthday you receive $500 invested for you at 8% compounded annually. You can withdraw the money when it has doubled in value. How old will you be when you can withdraw the $1000?

4.3. You are buying a home for $20,000. If you make a down payment of $7000 and take out a mortgage on the rest at 12% compounded quarterly, what is your monthly payment to retire the mortgage in 10 years?

4.4. Starting on your tenth birthday and every month thereafter you invested $15/month at 6% interest compounded monthly for 5 years when you held a paper route. Then you gave up the paper route and just let the money accumulate interest in the bank until now on your twentieth birthday you throw a party that costs $200. It is so successful that you decide to have a similar party every month until your money runs out. How many parties can you have?

4.5. The magazine *Metallurgical Management* offers two types of subscriptions payable in advance: 1 year at $8 and 2 years at $15. If money can earn 4% interest compounded quarterly, which subscription should you take?

4.6. Determine which depreciation method most accurately describes the depreciation of the automobile given in Fig. 4.1.

4.7. The present value of a machine is $200,000. Its economic life is 8 years. Estimate the value of the machine as a function of time using straight line, double declining balance, double declining combined with linear, sinking fund, and sum of the year's digits methods. Assume that the scrap value is zero. Plot the results.

4.8. The machine in Problem 4.7 produces 2 million articles/year that sell for 10 cents each. The total cost excluding depreciation is 5.2 cents each. If the tax life is 20 years and the company uses double declining balance for both book and tax purposes, what is the tax for a tax rate of 50%? What are the cash flow and the net profit for the second year of operation?

4.9. Analyze the stock of a company for short-term profit on the stock market. Would you recommend the purchase of this stock? Use the guide given in Table 4.12.

4.10. Repeat Problem 4.9 for long-term investment.

4.11. For the school year, you have $2000 to invest.
  a. Determine how much you would obtain by investing your money in a savings account at the bank.
  b. Invest in a portfolio of stocks and bonds. Record the dates of imaginary purchase and sale, and the price for all investments. Neglect the brokerage fee and the advantages of buying and selling in board lots.
  c. Compare part a with part b at the end of the school year.

4.12. As an undergraduate you made a mistake in preparing a catalyst for a reaction kinetics experiment. To your amazement, the activity and selectivity of catalyst treated with the mistake method are superior to the commercial catalysts presently available.
  a. To whom does this patentable method of preparing the catalyst belong: You? The laboratory supervisor? The department? The university? The government?
  b. What procedure would you follow to patent this idea? How much would it cost?
  c. You obtain the patent for this catalyst preparation and decide to start a small company to sell know-how, to market the catalyst, and to develop other catalysts. Prepare estimates of the amount of money you would need for the first two years of operation. Prepare as detailed a budget as possible, with estimates for salaries, rent, equipment, sales, etc.

4.13. As an undergraduate you become extremely interested in and well versed in computer-aided analysis of business and chemical systems. Upon graduation you decide to become a consultant and market your talent. Estimate the amount of risk capital you would need for the first two years in business. Prepare as detailed a budget as possible, with an estimate of your consulting fees, the amount of business, rent, costs of computer time, travel, advertising, etc.

4.14. Many have difficulty understanding the concept of depreciation—in particular, why depreciation is considered an expense when calculating the profit yet appears as "income" when discussing the total plowback. For example, in Table 3.3 for Company C the net profit before tax is sales less direct costs less depreciation or $241 - 174 - 20.8 = 46.5$. Yet, the net return for redistribution is the net profit after tax plus depreciation or $30.1 + 20.8 = 50.9$. Explain why depreciation is handled this way.

4.15. Dividends paid are usually about 50% of the net profit. Why is this 50% of the net profit and not 50% of the net profit plus depreciation?

4.16. Do you think it is ethical for a company to use two different depreciation rates?

Financial Attractiveness of Alternatives

5

Money plowed back into the company is distributed among expansion, plant improvement, research and development, and working capital. The money is expected to provide a return on the investment that "justly rewards the risks incurred." Engineers within the company offer a multitude of projects competing for the available money. Only a few projects can be implemented. The question then arises, Which of the many alternative projects most handsomely rewards the investment? This question is not easy to answer because even when only financial attractiveness is considered, there is no single financial attractiveness *index* that has been accepted universally as being the best index to use. Each has advantages and disadvantages that should be understood and appreciated.

This chapter describes methods for calculating the financial attractiveness of a proposal. These methods can be applied to any project: replacing the present reactor with one of a novel design, insulating a steam line, or selecting the paint for the office.

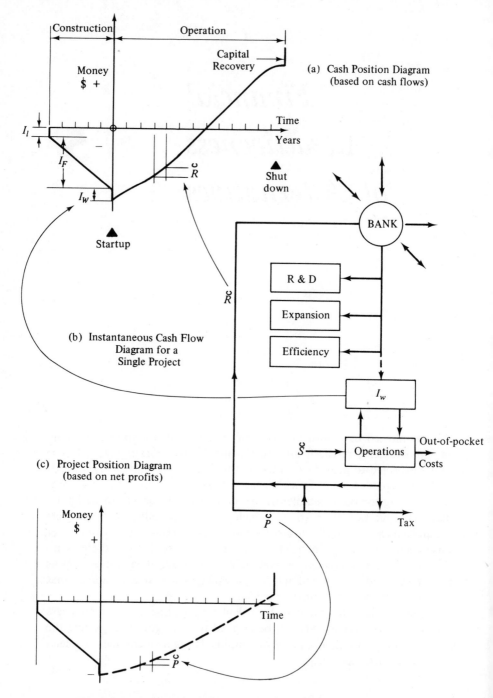

Figure 5.1. Development of cash and project diagrams from a series of instantaneous cash flow diagrams.

5.1 Financial Characteristics of Alternatives

Any proposal describes some action that will be in effect for a number of years in the future. In looking at the financial characteristics of any such proposal, account should be taken of the time value of money and of assets; the financial risk; the future variation in selling price, costs, sales volume, and tax rate; how long it takes to implement the project or install the equipment before it produces salable product; the total amount of money invested; the annual reinvestment or plowback of profits; and the economic life of the project. One way to visualize most of these characteristics and to force a careful consideration of the future is to use a cash position diagram. Previously, in Chapters 3 and 4, a cash flow diagram for any particular instance in time was described (Figs 3.5 and 4.3). A cash position diagram shows the results of consecutive annual cash flows as a function of time. This is illustrated in Fig. 5.1. In Fig. 5.1(a), money is plotted versus time. Zero time is when the plant starts to produce salable goods or services. For comparison, the instantaneous cash flow diagram for a specific project is shown in Fig 5.1(b). At negative times, the only cash flow is negative in that money is paid out for land, I_l, and for the fixed assets, I_F; the latter includes as expenses such overhead as engineering design. When the process is ready to start up, there is an additional outflow of cash for working capital, I_w. Once the process starts, money flows into the project through sales, S; the cash flows accumulate so that the cash position eventually shifts from negative to positive; and when the project terminates, the capital invested in working capital and land and recovered as scrap value is recovered and yields a terminal positive cash flow. An alternative (but not a common) way of showing the cumulative financial history of a project is to use the annual net profits, $\breve{P}$, instead of the annual cash flows or returns, $\breve{R}$, to yield what could be called the project position diagram. The difference between them is the annual book depreciation, as can be seen from Fig. 5.1(b).

These diagrams have the great advantage of showing all the financial characteristics except the risk*, the cost of capital to finance the project, the rate at which money is generated by the project, and the reinvestment of profits. The development of these diagrams forces a careful scrutiny of the future and the implications of competition, product life cycle, plant improvement through learning, and all other considerations necessary for wise decisions.

The cost of capital** can be accounted for by subtracting $i_m I$ from the

---

*Risk: the probable distribution of outcomes is known, whereas in uncertainty, the probable distribution of outcomes is *not* known.

**An alternative "wording" used by the economists is an opportunity cost. In public finance, as opposed to the process industry, it is sometimes difficult to identify the average

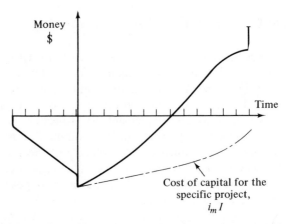

Figure 5.2. Cash position diagram with opportunity cost included to reflect risk.

cash or project flows. Normally, this is not shown as one resulting line but rather as two separate lines as shown in Fig. 5.2. Reasonable values for i_m should reflect the average cost of capital, i, for the company, as given in Table 5.1, and the risk associated with a specific project $(i_m - i)$ given in Table 5.2. The value of i_m chosen to reflect the risk should account for how

TABLE 5.1
VALUES OF RISK-FREE INTEREST OR AVERAGE COST OF CAPITAL
DEPEND ON THE INDUSTRY

Industry	i, 1967 (%)
This book	6
Public service electric and gas company	6.3*
American Telephone and Telegraph	6.8*
U.S. Steel	7.5*
General Motors	7.8*
Standard Oil of New Jersey	8.2*
Pulp and paper, rubber	8–10†
Synthetic fiber, chemical, and petrochem	11–13†
Drugs, extractive metallurgy	16–18†

*Blewitt (1967).
†Rudd and Watson (1968).

cost of capital and the relative risk. We often reflect on the lost opportunities in life. For any project, one attempts to visualize an imaginary investment opportunity that carries the same risk as the proposed venture. The income from the 'lost' opportunity, i_mI, is considered as an expense where i_m is the interest commensurate with the risk, and I is the total capital invested in the project. This appears on Fig. 5.2 as precisely the same line with the same numerical value. It differs only in terminology.

TABLE 5.2
ACCOUNTING FOR RISK $(i_m - i)^*$

Risk	$i_m - i$ (%)	Comment
None or negligible	0	Bonds, working capital, land
Low	1–5	Working capital; rented equipment; short-term projects; portable, general-purpose equipment; auxiliary equipment
Medium	5–20	Auxiliary equipment, specific processes requiring installed equipment, moderate-term projects, specialized equipment
High	20–100	Long-term projects, many unknowns about future market, specialized equipment

*Based on Rudd and Watson (1968).

easy it is to recover the money if the project folds after a few years, how long the money is tied up in the project, and what chances the project has of succeeding. The last is an indirect measure of the technical, market, environmental, resource, and other criteria discussed in Chapter 1. Qualitative explanations of the different risks are included in Table 5.2. For example, no interest is paid on money in a checking account where money flows in and out continuously with a negligible balance remaining in the account, 3% interest may be paid where a minimum balance of $2000 is maintained, 5% interest may be given when only one withdrawal is allowed per year and where 3-month notice of such is required, and 7% interest is paid on bonds where the money is essentially tied up for 10 years. This illustrates that if one is willing to let others use his money for increasing periods of time, then more interest is expected. In this example, the full amount of the initial investment was always guaranteed to be repaid. Another aspect of risk occurs if the amount and time period are fixed (say $50,000 and 10 years) but the alternatives are to invest in land or working capital, to rent equipment, or to buy a portable energy generator, a compressor, or a specialized snoggle pickle processor. The more specialized the asset purchased and the more firmly the money is tied up, say in buying equipment as opposed to renting or in working capital, then the more difficult it is to recover the initial $10,000 if the project flops. Who wants to buy a used snoggle pickle processor? This must be reflected in the risk.

The difference between i and i_m can be visualized, in Fig. 5.3(a), as a sloppy way of accounting for the actual calculated risk. As will be seen in section 5.9(c), there are mathematical methods for handling risk. In Fig. 5.3, a specific project is shown with a mean rate of return of i_p. There is risk associated with this project. The various probable rates of returns are represented by the distribution about the mean. Also shown is the average cost of capital for the company, i. From these data, we note that while the

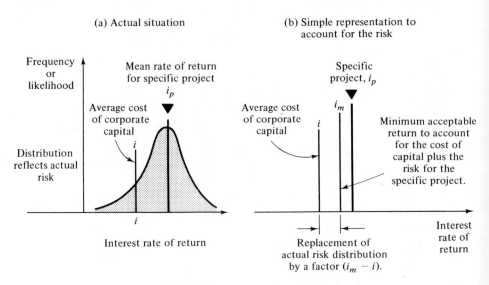

Figure 5.3. Accounting for risk in a specific project.

mean rate for the specific project, i_p, is greater than the corporate average cost of capital, there still is a probability that the actual project rate of return would be less than i. Hence a comparison between i and i_p is unrealistic. As a crude approximation, the distribution reflecting the risk can be replaced by a single value i_m. Then a more realistic comparison can be made between i_m and i_p.

In summary, the cash or project position diagrams show most of the financial characteristics of a project and can even indicate the risk through the cost of capital for the specific project.

5.2 Time Available and the Financial Attractiveness Criteria

Although the cash or project position diagrams are extremely useful to illustrate the financial characteristics of one project, they are difficult to use to compare alternative projects, as can be seen from Fig. 5.4, and impossible to use for optimization studies. Hence, the diagram is converted into a numerical index that, hopefully, summarizes adequately the information in the diagram. Many different indices can be developed: the slopes of the lines, the magnitude of the extremes, areas under the curves, etc. Which index or criterion should be used depends, to quite a large extent, on the time available. Although companies and supervisors may develop familiarity and confidence in using specific criteria and demand that everyone

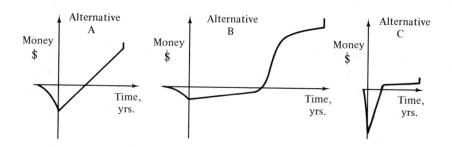

Which Alternative is the Best?

Figure 5.4. Comparison of the cash position diagrams for alternatives is difficult.

report answers accordingly, each individual should gain experience in working with all the methods and in using, for any given problem, the method appropriate to the time available.

In Chapter 1 it was emphasized that there is a trade-off between the time available to make a decision and the accuracy of the answer. The law of optimum sloppiness and the principle of successive approximation can be used to develop strategies for solving problems in the time available. These ideas can be applied to the calculation of financial attractiveness.

Basically, the difference between the criteria is in the data required before the criteria can be calculated. This, together with the actual calculation time, gives a qualitative indication of the time required. The key determining factor is whether or not a cash position diagram is needed. If it is, then this could take from 1 day to several years depending on the accuracy expected and on the cooperation and abilities of the marketing and technical groups. The time required is shown in these terms in Fig. 5.5. The accuracy cannot be expressed numerically, although a qualitative indication is given for the different methods by listing the different factors that are accounted for in the criterion, as also shown in Fig. 5.5. Thus, the simplest and least accurate criteria are payback time and the return on investment; the next level of accuracy, which accounts for risk, is venture profit. These methods rely on average values of the important information on the cash position diagram but do not require the diagram itself. A cash position diagram is needed for the equivalent maximum investment period (EMIP), interest recovery period (IRP), present value, and internal rate of return criteria.

In the next sections these methods are described and illustrated. They are not the only methods available, and some other methods will be discussed later for the special problem of selecting alternatives for *one* problem. None of the methods in Fig. 5.5 gives an indication of the amount of money re-

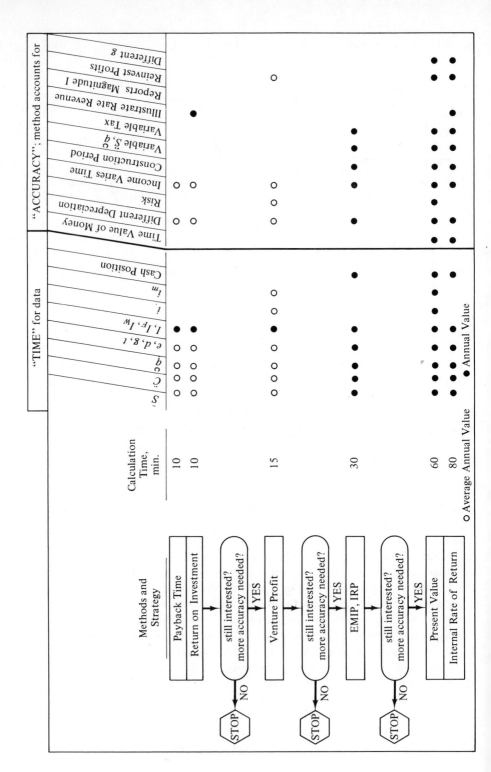

quired by the different alternatives; the column "Reports magnitude I" is empty in Fig. 5.5, and financial feasibility is a very important criterion in decision making, as was discussed in Chapter 4. To complete this chapter the methods are compared and evaluated.

All the methods are simple in concept, although care must be taken to ensure that the specific considerations and terms used by one individual are the same as those defined here. The major complications are the large number of synonyms for the methods, whether before or after tax values should be used, whether opportunity costs are included, and whether the total, fixed, or working capital is the reference expenditure. Upon first reading this chapter, the emphasis should be on the principles of the method. This can perhaps be most readily seen from the cash position diagrams presented with each method. Later perusal will clarify the specific details.

5.3 Payback Time and Simple Return on Investment

Payback time is based on the cash position diagram and is related to the intersection of the cash position line with the abscissa. Return on investment is related to the slope of the project position. These are shown in Figs. 5.6 and 5.7.

a. *Payback Time* (synonyms: payoff period, cash recovery period, payout time, payout period)	p

Payback time is usually the time required to recover the total depreciable investment, I_F, from the savings gained after taxes without considering depreciation as an expense. This is shown pictorially in Fig. 5.6.

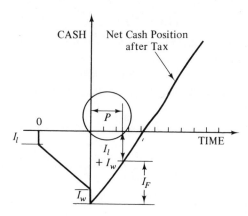

Figure 5.6. Payout or payback time on cash position diagram.

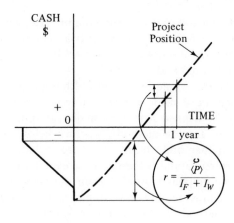

Figure 5.7. Simple rate of return on a project position diagram.

The mathematical relationship is

$$p = \frac{I_F}{\langle \breve{R} \rangle} \tag{5.1}$$

$$p = \frac{I_F}{\langle \breve{R}^*(1 - t) + tdI_F \rangle} \tag{5.2}$$

This expression applies whether or not the book and tax depreciation rates are the same. Alternative relationships expressed in terms of selling and cost prices are, for $d \neq e$ and $d = e$, respectively,

$$p = \frac{I_F}{\langle \breve{q}(\ddot{S} - \ddot{C})(1 - t) - tI_F(e - d) \rangle + \langle eI_F \rangle} \tag{5.3}$$

and

$$p = \frac{I_F}{\langle \breve{q}(\ddot{S} - \ddot{C})(1 - t) \rangle + \langle eI_F \rangle} \tag{5.4}$$

Some companies unrealistically use the total investment, I, and some prefer to report the result before taxes.

To use this criterion, we select the project with the shortest payout time. Order-of-magnitude values for p are given in Table 5.3.

TABLE 5.3
REASONABLE VALUES FOR p, EMIP, AND IRP

Project condition	Values of criterion for projects to be acceptable		
	Payback time (years)	EMIP (years)	IRP (years)
High risk	< 2		
Medium risk	< 5	< 3–3½	?
Low risk		< 6	?

Example 5.1:   The fixed capital investment for the plant to produce the product described in Table 4.9 is $80,000. The working capital is $10,000. The design and tax lives are estimated to be 16 years. Assume that demand and selling price are constant over this period of time. The construction and startup take 2 years. Assume that land costs $2,000. For simplicity neglect the startup costs and the annual retirements and replacement costs over and above the maintenance cost attributed to the product ($0.16/unit of production). The tax rate is 50%. Assume that the production rate is 10^4 lb/year and that the selling price was $7.35 instead of $12.00.

Problem: Calculate the payback time after tax. Assume that the annual depreciation is uniform,

$$\check{D} = eI_F = dI_F = \frac{I_F}{g} = \frac{I_F}{16 \text{ years}}$$

Sample solution: The payback time, from Eq. (5.4), is

$$p = \frac{I_F}{\langle \check{q}(\ddot{S} - \ddot{C})(1 - t) \rangle + \langle eI_F \rangle}$$

$$= \frac{80,000}{10^4(\$7.35 - \$6.68)0.50 + [\$0.50 \times 10^4]}$$

$$= 9.6 \text{ years}$$

Comment: The payback time on this project is far too long. The chance that this project is implemented is remote.

Problem: If the depreciation is increased to $1/unit so that the design life is approximately 8 years, what must the selling price of the product be to yield a payback time of 2 years? Neglect the difference because of taxation and book depreciations. Now the unit cost is $6.68 + $0.50 = $7.18.

Sample solution: The general equation is Eq. (5.4):

$$p = \frac{I_F}{\langle \check{q}(\ddot{S} - \ddot{C})(1 - t) \rangle + \langle eI_F \rangle}$$

Rearrangement yields

$$\ddot{S} = \ddot{C} + \left\{ \frac{I_F}{p} - \langle \check{D} \rangle \right\} \frac{1}{\check{q}(1 - t)}$$

$$= \$7.18 + \left\{ \frac{\$80,000}{2} - [\$1.00 \times 10^4] \right\} \frac{1}{0.5 \times 10^4}$$

$$= \$7.18 + \$6.00 = \$13.18$$

The selling price would have to be over $13.00 to yield a 2-year payback time.

Example 5.2:   The average unit cost per barrel (bbl) of alkylate is given in Table 5.4. Assume that the fixed capital cost is 2.9×10^6 and that the tax rate is 50%. Assume that the selling price is $8.00/bbl and that the capacity is 2000 bbl/day for a 320-day operating year. For this example, assume that the feed is high in n-paraffins.

Problem: Calculate the payback time assuming that the tax life and economic life are the same.

Sample solution: From Eq. (5.4) the payback time is

$$p = \frac{I_F}{2000 \times 320[(8.00 - 5.75)(1 - t) + \$0.45]}$$

$$= \frac{I_F}{1.44 \times 10^6(1 - t) + 0.288 \times 10^6}$$

$$= \frac{2.9 \times 10^6}{1.008 \times 10^6}$$

$$= 2.9 \text{ years}$$

Problem: Calculate the payback time for Example 5.2 if the depreciation rate for tax purposes, d, is constant and equals 0.0666 and that for internal book purposes, e, is constant and equals 0.10.

Sample solution: The equation for payback time when the company and government tax depreciations are not the same is

$$p = \frac{I_F}{\check{R}^*(1 - t) + tdI_F}$$

$$= \frac{I_F}{(1 - t)[\check{q}(\check{S} - \check{C}) + eI_F] + tdI_F} \qquad (5.3)$$

$$= \frac{2.9 \times 10^6}{0.5[2000 \times 320(\$8.00 - 5.75) + 0.10 \times 2.9 \times 10^6] + 0.066 \times 2.9 \times 10^6 \times 0.5}$$

$$= \frac{2.9 \times 10^6}{0.72 \times 10^6 + 0.145 \times 10^6 + 0.097 \times 10^6}$$

$$= 3.0 \text{ years}$$

b. *Simple Rate of Return* (synonyms: return on original investment, percentage return on investment, engineer's method, operator's method)	r

This very simple procedure has many limitations. It is the ratio of the average yearly profit after taxes to the total original investment excluding

TABLE 5.4

ESTIMATED COST FOR THE PRODUCTION OF ALKYLATE FOR TWO FEEDS*

Materials	Unit usage/bbl alkylate		Unit cost	Net cost/bbl alkylate	
	Low n-paraffin feed	High n-paraffin feed		Low n-paraffin feed	High n-paraffin feed
Raw materials					
Propylene ⎤	0.138 bbl	1.6 bbl	$1.20/bbl	$0.17	$5.68
Butylene ⎦ Olefin	0.445 bbl		$3.55/bbl	1.58	2.44
Isobutane	0.743 bbl	0.812	$3.00/bbl	2.23	0.33
Acid	0.054 bbl	0.038	$8.68/bbl	0.46	
Caustic	0.57 lb	neglect	—		
n-Butane for sale	—	0.44 bbl			−1.58
Propane for sale	—	0.81 bbl			−2.88
				4.54	3.99
Utilities					
Steam	150 lb	200 lb	$0.50/1000 lb	0.08	0.10
Process water	3.3 U.S. gal		$0.015/1000 U.S. gal	—	—
Electricity	15 kw	20 kw	$0.70/100 kw	0.11	0.14
Fuel gas	0.26 MM		$0.30/MM BTU	0.08	0.08
				4.81	4.31
Labor (L): 0.025 man hour/bbl			$4.00/mh	$0.10	
Maintenance: 0.03 I_F‡				0.14	
Supervision: 0.1 L				0.01	
Depreciation: 10 I_F‡				0.45	
Indirectly attributable: (0.75(1.1L + 0.03I_F))				0.19	
Total manufacturing cost: (M)				$5.70	$5.20
General expense: 0.1M				0.55	
Total cost/bbl of alkylate				$6.25	$5.75

*From Crowe et al. (1971).

‡Capital investment (I_F) in 1968 as estimated from Dryden and Furlow (1966) is $2.9 million for a 200 bbl/day plant. It is assumed that the plant operates 320 days/year.

land, $I = I_F + I_w$. This is shown in Fig. 5.7 and given by

$$r = \frac{\langle \check{P}\check{q} \rangle}{I} 100\% = \frac{\langle \check{P} \rangle}{I} 100\% = \frac{\check{R}^*(1 - t) + dI_F t - eI_F}{I} \qquad (5.5)$$

Some report the return before taxes:

$$r^* = \frac{\langle \check{q}(\ddot{S} - \ddot{C}) \rangle}{I} \times 100\% \qquad (5.6)$$

Note that the total investment should be used and not just the fixed capital investment.

To use this criterion, we select the project with the largest return. For the profits to be attractive the percentage return, r, should be greater than the minimum interest rate i_m. Values of i_m can be estimated from Tables 5.1 and 5.2.

Problem: From the data given in Example 5.1, calculate the simple rate of return.

Sample solution: The rate of return can be calculated from Eq. (5.5):

$$r = \frac{\langle \check{P} \rangle}{I} \times 100$$

The net profit is $(7.35 - 6.68)0.50$ or

$$\check{P} = \$0.33/\text{unit}$$

Hence, the return is

$$r = \frac{10^4 \text{ units/year} \times \$0.33/\text{unit}}{\$80,000 + \$10,000}$$

$$= \frac{0.33 \times 10^4}{9 \times 10^4}$$

$$= 3.7\%$$

Problem: From the data given in Example 5.2, calculate the simple rate of return, assuming that the working capital $= \$0.5 \times 10^6$, $e = 0.10$, and $d = 0.0666$.

Sample solution: From Eq. (5.5), the return is

$$r = \frac{\langle \check{P} \rangle}{I} \times 100 = \left\langle \frac{\check{R}^*(1 - t) + dI_F t - eI_F}{I} \right\rangle \times 100$$

$$= \left(\frac{1.73 \times 10^6(1 - t) + t \times 0.194 \times 10^6 - 0.29 \times 10^6}{(2.9 + 0.5) \times 10^6} \right) \times 100$$

$$= \left(\frac{0.865 + 0.097 - 0.29}{3.4} \right) \times 100$$

$$= 19.8\%$$

5.4 Venture Profit

The venture profit criterion is related to the average annual slope of the project position curve but uses the cost of capital as an expense. This is shown in Fig. 5.8.

Venture profit $\langle \breve{Q} \rangle$ is the average annual net profit in excess of a minimum acceptable return on the investment. This is usually averaged over the economic life of the project and is represented as

$$\langle \breve{Q} \rangle = \langle \breve{P} \rangle - i_m I_F - i I_w \tag{5.7}$$

In this equation the average annual net profit after tax, $\langle \breve{P} \rangle$, is decreased by the average annual money generated from interest paid on the fixed and working capital investments. Because the risk is greater in the money invested as fixed capital, often an interest rate, an i_m, is used that is larger than the corporate average minimum interest rate i.

When the company and governmental tax depreciation rates are not the same, the annual venture profit is given as

$$\langle \breve{Q} \rangle = \langle \breve{R}^*(1 - t) + d t I_F - e I_F \rangle - i_m I_F - i I_w \tag{5.8}$$

$$= \langle (\breve{S} - \breve{C}) \breve{q} (1 - t) - t I_F (e - d) \rangle - i_m I_F - i I_w \tag{5.9}$$

Although this relationship is generally applicable and although any method of depreciation can be used, a uniform series sinking fund is usually used to

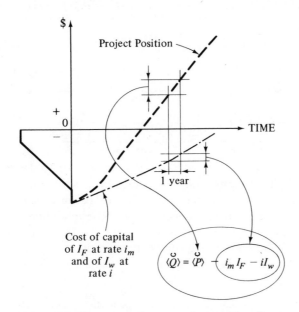

Figure 5.8. Venture profit on a project position diagram.

represent the depreciation.* Thus, we can assign a value for e if we elect to represent it by a series of uniform payments whose sum over the design life at compound interest rate i just equals the investment. This sinking fund deposit factor is

$$\mathcal{R}\mathcal{S}_{i-g} = \frac{i}{(1 + i)^g - 1}$$

as defined in Appendix A. Hence, we may substitute into Eq. (5.9) the relationship

$$e = \frac{i}{(1 + i)^g - 1}$$

Note that the design life is measured from the startup of the plant. If at the end of g years the capital investment that we have completely depreciated does indeed have a scrap value of V_s instead of the anticipated value of zero, then we could sell the scrap at the end of the gth year and receive a lump sum of V_s dollars at that time. This income would be taxed so that the net gain for the project would be $V_s(1 - t)$ dollars. To distribute this windfall equitably for each year of the project we can represent this as an annual credit to the project, given by a term

$$\text{annual scrap recovery allowance} = \left[\frac{i}{(1 + i)^g - 1}\right] V_s(1 - t)$$

In total, then, the average venture profit is

$$\langle \breve{Q} \rangle = \left\langle \breve{R}^*(1 - t) - \left[\frac{i}{(1 + i)^g - 1}\right] I_F + dI_F t \right\rangle - i_m I_F - i I_w$$

$$+ \left[\frac{i}{(1 + i)^g - 1}\right](1 - t)V_s \qquad (5.10)$$

$$= \underbrace{\left\langle (\ddot{S} - \breve{C})\breve{q}(1 - t) - \left[\frac{i}{(1 + i)^g - 1}\right] I_F t + (dI_F)t \right\rangle}_{\text{net profit}}$$

$$\underbrace{- i_m I_F - i I_w}_{\text{cost of capital}} + \underbrace{\left[\frac{i}{(1 + i)^g - 1}\right](1 - t)V_s}_{\text{scrap recovery}} \qquad (5.11)$$

Reasonable values for i_m and i are summarized in Tables 5.1 and 5.2. The overall graphical impression of this method is shown in Fig. 5.8. This impression can be little more than an impression because we are attempting to illustrate an average annual condition with the minimum acceptable return being withdrawn at the end of each year. To use this method, select the project with the highest average venture profit.

For more details, see Happel (1958), pp. 7 and 27, and Rudd and Watson (1968).

---

*We shall see in Section 5.6 that Eq. (5.17) simplifies to Eq. (5.15) only if this form of book depreciation is used.

Problem: Calculate the venture profit for Example 5.2. Assume that $i_m = 15\%$ and that $i = 6\%$. The working capital required is $\$0.5 \times 10^6$, $e = 0.10$, and $d = 0.0666$. Assume that $V_s = 0$.

Sample solution: The annual net profit, $\langle \breve{P} \rangle$, is

$$\$(0.865 + 0.097 - 0.29) \times 10^6 = \$0.674 \times 10^6$$

The opportunity cost or cost of capital is

$$\begin{aligned} i_m I_F + i I_w &= 0.15(\$2.9 \times 10^6) + 0.06(\$0.5 \times 10^6) \\ &= \$(0.435 + 0.30) \times 10^6 \\ &= \$0.465 \times 10^6 \end{aligned}$$

Hence, the venture profit is

$$\begin{aligned} \langle \breve{Q} \rangle &= \$(0.674 - 0.465) \times 10^6 \\ &= \$0.209 \times 10^6 \end{aligned}$$

This example illustrates the approach. Note that this definition is based on net profit and not on net return.

5.5 Equivalent Maximum Investment Period and the Interest Recovery Period

The use of this method requires that a cash position diagram be available; the principle is that the curve will be replaced by area. These two calculated times refer to the areas under the cash position diagrams. The EMIP considers the area between the start and the break-even point:

$$\text{EMIP} = \frac{\text{area between the start and the break-even point}}{\text{total capital investment } (I)}$$

To simplify the calculations, the dollar ordinate can be "normalized" by dividing the cash position by the total capital investment, I. Under these normalized conditions the EMIP is then the area between the zero cash position and the cash position of the project until the project break-even point.

The IRP is the time from the break-even point when simple interest charges on the total investment, I, can be recovered by investing the balance of profits at the same interest rate. Pictorially, this represents the time, from the break-even point, when the positive cash position area equals the negative cash position area. This is shown in Fig. 5.9.

To use these criteria, we select the project with the shortest EMIP or IRP. Orders of magnitude numbers are given in Table 5.3. For the amount of effort required to obtain a reliable cash position diagram, it is advisable to use the methods given in Section 5.6 to interpret the diagram rather than

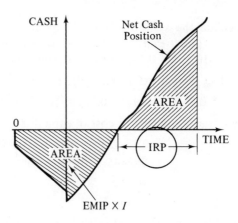

Figure 5.9. Interest recovery period on cash position diagram.

EMIP or IRP because of the increase in factors that can be accounted for for a very small increase in time. Hence, the EMIP and IRP methods are included more for completeness than as a recommendation.

Problem: Calcuate the EMIP and the IRP for the data in Example 5.2. Assume that the costs and selling prices do not vary from year to year. Assume also that $d = 0.0666$ and $e = 0.10$. The land costs $100,000, and a working capital of $500,000 is required. The construction period is 2 years, and the expenditure of money in fixed investment is assumed to be linear. Neglect replacement and retirement costs over and above maintenance.

Sample solution: The annual return after tax, net profit plus book depreciation, is 0.964×10^6. Hence, the EMIP can be calculated from Fig. 5.10. The area for the EMIP is given as

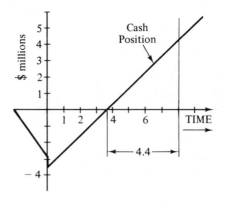

Figure 5.10. Cash position diagram for Example 5.2.

$$\text{area} = (\tfrac{1}{2} \times 3.5 \times 3.6\,\text{yr} + \tfrac{1}{2} \times 2.9 \times 2\,\text{yr}$$
$$+\ 0.1 \times 2\,\text{yr}) \times 10^6$$

Hence

$$\text{EMP} = \frac{9.4 \times 10^6\ \$\text{yr}}{3.5 \times 10^6\ \$}$$
$$= 2.68\ \text{years}$$

The IRP is calculated as

$$9.4 \times 10^6\ \$\text{yr} = \frac{0.964 \times 10^6}{2}(\text{IRP})^2$$

or

$$\text{IRP} = 4.4\ \text{years}$$

These calculations illustrate the procedure for this method. More details are given by Allen (1967).

5.6 Present Value and Internal Rate of Return

In reality, the annual sales and costs are not constant, and the variations can be represented on a cash position diagram, which is needed for these methods. The principle is that each element of the diagram is replaced by its present value so that the complete diagram is the net sum of the present values of the elements.

Thus, if the interest rate on invested capital is i and the "present" refers to the beginning of the production of salable product, and then if the annual net return, or cash flow, is \$100,000 at the end of the fifth year after startup, the contribution toward the overall project, based on the equations in Table 4.1 for a single payment present value factor, would be

$$\$100,000\frac{1}{(1+i)^n} = \$100,000\frac{1}{(1+i)^5}$$
$$= \mathcal{PS}_{i-5}(\$100,000)$$

For $i = 6\%$, this becomes

$$\mathcal{PS}_{6-5}(\$100,000) = 0.7473(\$100,000)$$
$$= \$74,730$$

This is illustrated in Fig. 5.11, where the diagram is replaced by a sum. To evaluate the present value of the complete project we sum all the present values of all annual net return, subtract the present values of investment (I_w, I_l, I_F), account for any scrap value and adjustments at the end of the project, and include retirement and replacement costs if these have not

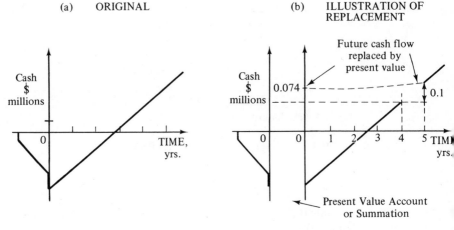

Figure 5.11. An illustration of how the cash position diagram is replaced by a sum of present values.

already been included in the annual return. All cash flows into the project are positive; all outward flows are negative.

A simple example illustrates the principles.

Problem: From Example 5.2 and the cash position curve in Fig. 5.12, calculate the present value if $i = 6\%$ compounded annually. Assume that $g = 8$ years and that the cash flows are discrete.

Sample solution: For this example, the average annual net profit is constant and equals $\$0.674 \times 10^6$. The book depreciation, assuming that $e = 0.10$, is $\$0.29 \times 10^6$. Hence, the annual cash flow $= (0.674 + 0.29) = \$0.964 \times 10^6$. If the cash flows are discrete, then discrete compounding is used. If, on the other

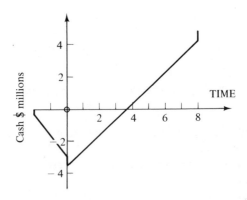

Figure 5.12. Cash position diagram assuming continuous flow.

hand, the cash flows were continuous, then continuous compounding would have been appropriate. Assume that all the fixed capital investment of 1.45×10^6 had to be available 2 years before the startup and that the remaining 1.45×10^6 had to be available 1 year before startup. Thus, the cash position of Fig. 5.12 is modified in the construction period and is shown in Fig. 5.13. Assume that the scrap value is zero and neglect the depreciation adjustment at the end of year 8 that arises because $d \neq e$.

The contribution to the present value, W, arising from the annual net returns is the sum of the present value of each annual net return. Thus,

$$
\begin{aligned}
W_{nr} = {}& \mathcal{PS}_{6-1}(\$0.964 \times 10^6) + \mathcal{PS}_{6-2}(\$0.964 \times 10^6) \\
& + \mathcal{PS}_{6-3}(\$0.964 \times 10^6) + \mathcal{PS}_{6-4}(\$0.964 \times 10^6) \\
& + \mathcal{PS}_{6-5}(\$0.964 \times 10^6) + \mathcal{PS}_{6-6}(\$0.964 \times 10^6) \\
& + \mathcal{PS}_{6-7}(\$0.964 \times 10^6) + \mathcal{PS}_{6-8}(\$0.964 \times 10^6) \\
= {}& 6.210(\$0.964 \times 10^6) \\
= {}& \$5.986 \times 10^6
\end{aligned}
$$

The negative contribution to the present value, W, from the capital expenditure is the present value of all capital expenditures:

$$
\begin{aligned}
W_I = {}& -\mathcal{SP}_{6-2}(\$100{,}000) - \mathcal{SP}_{6-2}(\$1.45 \times 10^6) \\
& -\mathcal{SP}_{6-1}(\$1.45 \times 10^6) - \$500{,}000 \\
= {}& -\$4.781 \times 10^6
\end{aligned}
$$

The positive contribution from the recovery of the working

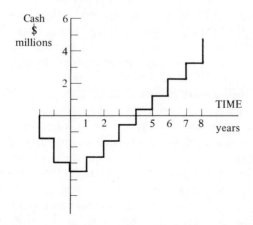

Figure 5.13. Cash position diagram for annual cash flows, Problem 5.2.

capital at the end of the project is

$$W_t = +\$\mathcal{P}_{6-8}(\$500,000)$$
$$= \$0.314 \times 10^6$$

We do not normally include the recovery of the land investment in the calculations. Hence, the total present value of this project is

$$W = W_{nr} + W_I + W_t \qquad (5.12)$$
$$= \$(5.986 - 4.781 + 0.314) \times 10^6$$
$$= +\$1.52 \times 10^6$$

There are two different methods that can be used based on this principle:

1. Assume an interest rate i and calculate the sum W; this is called the present value criterion.
2. Assume that the sum W is zero and calculate the interest rate i; this is called the internal-rate-of-return criterion.

Consider each in turn.

---

a. *Present Value Method* (synonyms: venture worth, present worth, incremental present worth, premium worth)

In this method, a value of the interest rate is selected and the alternative with the largest present value is the best alternative. The method can be illustrated by a tabular calculation of the present values of the cash flows each year.

Example 5.3:   The average unit cost per barrel of alkylate is given in Table 5.4. Assume that the fixed capital cost is $\$2.9 \times 10^6$, the land cost is $100,000, and the required working capital is $500,000. The tax life of the equipment is 15 years. Because of the rapidly changing technology, assume that our process will be obsolete in 8 years. The details are summarized in Table 5.5(a).

From Table 5.5(a) we note that 2 years are required between the start of construction and startup. During the first year (note that because we arbitrarily decided upon time = 0 at startup, this first year is -2), i.e., during the -2 year, there is a continuous expenditure into fixed investment. For simplicity we assume that at the start of year -2, we needed the complete amount, $2,400,000. The remaining $500,000 of capital investment occurs in year -1. At the beginning of year $+1$, i.e., at startup, we have an instantaneous working capital expenditure of $500,000. In the fifth year, we spend

TABLE 5.5(a)
INVESTMENTS AND SALES

Time (years)*		Land, I_l (10^6)	Fixed, I_F (10^6)	Working, I_w (10^6)	Annual sales, $\breve{q}$ (bbl 10^6)	Selling price, $\breve{S}$ ($/bbl)
		Capital costs				
−2:	S	0.10				
	D		2.4			
−1:	S					
	D		0.5			
1:	S			0.50		
End of						
1					0.20	8.50
2					0.38	8.40
3					0.52	8.20
4					0.64	8.00
5			0.10		0.64	8.00
6					0.64	8.00
7					0.64	8.00
8		0.10	0.40	0.50	0.64	8.00

*S means at the start of the year; D means during the year; all other times are at the end of the year.

$100,000 in fixed capital investment for plant improvement to reduce the cost from $4.75 to $4.70/bbl. At the end of the eighth year we recover the land and working capital, and the fixed investment has a scrap recovery value of $400,000.

For the operations, the annual sales increase to a maximum of 200 bbl of alkylate per day for 320 stream days/year or 0.64 million bbl/calendar year.

We assume that the selling price per barrel starts at $8.50 and gradually reduces to $8.00 as competition increases. For each year of operation we elect to pay the general expenses and the book depreciation regardless of production.

Problem: Assume that $i = 6\%$. Assume uniform depreciation for both tax and book value calculations. Calculate the present value of this proposal.

Sample solution: The tax depreciation is $0.0667. A summary of the annual revenues and disbursements is given in Table 5.5(b). Consider the table entries in detail. The total revenue is the product of the selling price and the number of units sold. For example, in year 3, 0.52 million barrels are sold at $8.20/bbl for a total revenue of 4.264×10^6.

TABLE 5.5(b)
ANNUAL REVENUES AND DISPERSEMENTS

Time (years)*	Revenue, $S\check{q}$ (10^6)	Total cost including $G = 0.35 \times 10^6$ before depreciation (10^6)	Gross profit excluding depreciation (10^6)	Depreciation for tax, dI_F (10^6)	Tax, 50% (10^6)	Net return (10^6)	$\$\mathcal{P}_{i-k}$ and $\mathcal{P}\$_{i-k}$ (6%)	Cash or project flows + (10^6)	− (10^6)
−2: S									0.112
D							1.124		2.698
−1: S							1.060		0.530
1: S							1.00		0.500
End of									
1	1.700	01.302	0.398	0.193	0.103	0.295	0.9434	0.278	
2	3.192	2.157	1.035	0.193	0.421	0.614	0.8900	0.546	
3	4.264	2.822	1.442	0.193	0.625	0.817	0.8396	0.686	
4	5.120	3.392	1.728	0.193	0.768	0.960	0.7921	0.760	
5	5.120	3.392	1.728	0.193	0.768	0.960	0.7473	0.717	0.075
6	5.120	3.360	1.760	0.200	0.780	0.980	0.7050	0.691	
7	5.120	3.360	1.760	0.200	0.780	0.980	0.6651	0.652	
8	5.120	3.360	1.760	0.200	0.780	0.980	0.6274	0.615	
								0.063	
								0.251	
								0.314	
Total								5.573	3.915
Present value								$1.658 million	

*S means at the start of the year; D means during the year; all other times are at the end of the year.

The total cost of the product is the sum of both the directly attributable costs and the fixed costs. For simplicity we exclude any form of depreciation. From Table 5.4, the unit cost for idealized production is the total cost $5.75 less general expenses less book depreciation = $4.75/bbl. Hence, the directly attributable cost is

$$0.52 \times 10^6 \text{ bbl sold} \times \$4.75 = \$2.470 \times 10^6$$

In this example, the general expense is recovered regardless of the sales. For 2000-bbl/day normal production this expense is $0.55/bbl. Hence, the annual expense to be recovered is

$$\$0.55/\text{bbl} \times 2000 \text{ bbl/yr} \times 320 \text{ days/yr} = \$0.352 \times 10^6$$

Hence, for year 3 the total cost excluding book depreciation is ($2.470 + 0.352) million or 2.822×10^6.

Note that in this example it was assumed that during the fifth year $100,000 was spent for process improvement such that in the seventh year the cost was reduced from $4.75 to $4.70/bbl.

The gross return before tax excluding book depreciation as an expense, $\check{R}^*$, is the difference between revenue and cost or for the third year: $4.264 - 2.822 = \$1.442 \times 10^6$.

A straight line depreciation is used for tax purposes. Since the tax depreciation is uniform and $y = 15$ years, $d = 0.0667$. Hence, the annual depreciation for tax purposes is independent of sales, equals dI_F, and hence in year 3 is $0.0667(\$2.9 \times 10^6) = \$0.1934 \times 10^6$.

The net return is the difference between the gross return and the tax. Note that this calculational procedure is independent of the book depreciation. Hence, the net return in year 3 is $0.817 million.

Finally, all contributions are brought to the present, or base year, by the $\mathcal{SP}$ factors for all years preceding the base year and by the $\mathcal{PS}$ factors for all years following the base year. Thus, for year 3, the $\mathcal{PS}_{6-3}$ factor is 0.8396, and hence the contribution is $0.686 million.

All the positive and negative contributions to the present value are added to yield the net present value. For this example the value is $1.658 million. For illustrative purposes, if at the end of the project the scrap value is less than the undepreciated balance, then the scrap value is not taxed. In this example the scrap value is less than the undepreciated balance for tax purposes, i.e., $V_S = \$0.4$ million $\leq \$1.4$ million $= I_F$

(of \$3.0 million) $- dI_F$ (of \$1.565 million). Hence, it is not taxed. Indeed, a portion of this net undepreciated balance of \$1.0 million may be considered as an expense during the eighth year of operation. If at the end of the project, the scrap value is greater than the undepreciated balance, then the difference $[V_s - (I_f - \sum d\check{I}_F)]$ would be taxed. However, such complications have not been included since the purpose of the example is to illustrate the calculational method and overall principles. This does emphasize, however, the need for the young professional to seek advice on the method of depreciation used for tax and book purposes, the taxation laws, etc.

More details and examples are given by Kempster (1967).

Consider now some mathematical relationships to represent the technique. For a base year at startup, the present value can be represented by

$$W = W_{nr} + W_I + W_t$$

$$= \underbrace{\sum_{k=1}^{k=g} \frac{1}{(1 + i)^k} \check{R}_k}_{\text{net return}} - \underbrace{\sum_{k=\text{construction start}}^{k=0} I_k(1 - i)^k}_{\text{capital expenditure}} + \underbrace{\begin{array}{c}\text{scrap value and tax re-} \\ \text{coveries at year } k = g\end{array}}_{\text{terminal recovery}}$$

(5.13)

where $g = $ design life in years,

$\check{R}_k = $ annual net return in year k.

The base year can be selected as any convenient year, and the summations and calculations adjusted accordingly. Care needs to be taken to be sure that all the terms have been included. Consider an expansion of Eq. (5.13) in terms of the return before tax, $\check{R}^*$. The result, when the investment or capital expenditure is assumed to be an instantaneous payment, is

$$W = \underbrace{\sum_{k=1}^{k=g} \frac{1}{(1 + i)^k} \check{R}^*(1 - t)\Big|_k + \sum_{k=1}^{k=y} \frac{1}{(1 + i)^k} t d_k I_F}_{\text{present worth of net return}} - \underbrace{(I_F + I_w)}_{\text{investment}}$$

$$+ \underbrace{[\wp S_{i-g}](1 - t)V_S}_{\substack{\text{scrap value recovery if} \\ g > y}} + \underbrace{\wp S_{i-g}(I_w)}_{\substack{\text{recovery of} \\ \text{working capital}}}$$

(5.14)

This result applies when the economic life is greater than the tax life. For this situation, at the end of the project an unexpected cash flow V_S occurs. This money would be considered as profit by the government, and therefore, subject to tax. If $g < y$, an accountant should be consulted to determine how to handle the scrap recovery.

Some interest formula relationships, from Table 4.2, that aid in the simplifications are

$$e = \frac{i}{(1 + i)^g - 1} = \Re\mathcal{S}_{i-g}$$

$$\sum_{k=1}^{k=g} \frac{1}{(1 + i)^k} = \frac{(1 + i)^g - 1}{i(1 + i)^g}$$

$$\frac{i(1 + i)^n}{(1 + i)^n - 1} = \frac{i}{(1 + i)^n - 1} + i$$

Hence, Eq. (5.14) becomes

$$W = \sum_{k=1}^{k=g} \frac{\check{R}^*(1 - t)}{(1 + i)^k} + \sum_{k=1}^{k=y} \frac{d_k I_F t}{(1 + i)^k} - I_F - i(\mathcal{P}\Re_{i-g})I_w + (\mathcal{P}\mathcal{S}_{i-g})(1 - t)V_S$$

$$(5.15)$$

So far we have seen that the present value method is based on the cash position diagram, can be calculated in a tabular format, and can be represented by equations expressed either in terms of the net return [Eq. (5.13)] or in terms of the gross return [Eq. (5.15)].

A rather surprising development, suggested by Happel (1958), is that exactly the same result is obtained from the project position diagram provided a cost of capital is included as an expense as $i(I_F + I_W)$. Thus, Happel suggests that a more general expression for the present value is given by

$$W = \sum \frac{1}{(1 + i)^k} \check{Q}_k \qquad (5.16)$$

This is more general because risk can be included in the cost of capital.

The reasoning for the preference for Eq. (5.16) over Eq. (5.13) is as follows: One accepts the philosophy that the money available as plowback to a company will be invested some way; it makes little difference really where the money is invested as long as the returns justify the risk. That is, one's emphasis is on the attractiveness of the return rather than on the total cash flow of invested capital. That is, if a company has 10×10^6 as plowback, the 10×10^6 will be invested somewhere. The question is, Will the project under consideration provide an annual return greater than an interest rate commensurate with the risk involved? Toward this end, Happel suggests that the present value is the sum of the present values of the annual venture profits including the appropriate corrections for cash flows at the end of the project. In this way, the investment does not appear per se as a cash outflow at the beginning of the project. Rather, the investment appears indirectly as an annual cost of capital of $i_m I_F + i I_w$ and as a portion of the investment that is considered as an expense each year. This portion is the book depreciation, which continues as an annual expense until the asset has been depreciated fully. The result of this method of considering the capital is the venture profit already discussed in Section 5.4. An important feature of this approach is that an allowance can be made for the risk involved in the different investments. To illustrate the similarities and differences between Eq. (5.16) and Eq. (5.13), Eq. (5.16) can be expanded in terms of either the annual return $\check{R}^*$ or $(\check{S} - \check{C})\check{q}$ based on Eq. (5.7) for venture profit. The result, expressed in terms of $\check{R}^*$, is

$$
\begin{aligned}
W = &\sum_{k=1}^{k=g} \frac{\check{R}_k^*(1 - t)}{(1 + i)^k} + \sum_{k=1}^{k=y} \frac{d_k I_F t}{(1 + i)^k} \\
&- (\mathcal{P}\mathcal{R}_{i-g})(i_m - i)I_F - I_F - i(\mathcal{P}\mathcal{R}_{i-g})I_w \\
&+ (\mathcal{P}\mathcal{S}_{i-g})(1 - t)V_S
\end{aligned}
\tag{5.17}
$$

This applies for $g \geq y$.

A comparison of Eq. (5.17) with Eq. (5.15) suggests that the results are equal if $i = i_m$. Thus, Eq. (5.15) is a special simplification of the more general Eq. (5.16). This is true provided book depreciation is represented by the sinking fund method. Equation (5.16) can be expressed in terms of $(\check{S} - \check{C})\check{q}$. The results are, when $g \geq y$:

$$
W = \underbrace{\sum_{k=1}^{k=g} \frac{(\check{S} - \check{C})\check{q}(1 - t)}{(1 + i)^k}\Bigg|_k}_{\text{net profit after tax}} + \underbrace{\sum_{k=1}^{k=y} \frac{t I_F d_k}{(1 + i)^k}}_{\substack{\text{depreciation adjust-}\\\text{ment for taxation}}} - \left\{\underbrace{\left[\frac{i}{(1 + i)^g - 1}\right]t}_{\substack{\text{annual depreciation}\\\text{into a sinking fund}}} + \underbrace{i_m}_{\substack{\text{cost of fixed}\\\text{investment}\\\text{capital}}}\right\}
$$

$$
\times \sum_{k=1}^{k=g} \frac{I_F}{(1 + i)^k} - \underbrace{\sum_{k=1}^{k=g} \frac{i I_w}{(1 + i)^k}}_{\text{cost for working capital}} + \underbrace{\left[\frac{i}{(1 + i)^g - 1}\right](1 - t)\sum_{k=1}^{k=g} \frac{V_S}{(1 + i)^k}}_{\text{recovery of scrap value}}
\tag{5.18}
$$

where y is the tax life of project in years.

Alternatively,

$$
W = \sum_{k=1}^{k=g} \frac{(\check{S} - \check{C})\check{q}(1 - t)}{(1 + i)^k}\Bigg|_k + \underbrace{\sum_{k=1}^{k=y} \frac{t I_F d_k}{(1 + i)^k}}_{\substack{\text{discounted cash}\\\text{credit}}} - \underbrace{\frac{t}{(1 + i)^g}I_F}_{\substack{\text{present worth of}\\\text{book depreciation}}}
$$

$$
- \underbrace{i_m\left[\frac{(1 + i)^g - 1}{i(1 + i)^g}\right]I_F}_{\substack{\text{present worth of return on}\\\text{fixed capital investment}}} - \underbrace{i\left[\frac{(1 + i)^g - 1}{i(1 + i)^g}\right]I_w}_{\substack{\text{present worth of return}\\\text{on working capital}}} + \frac{1}{(1 + i)^g}(1 - t)V_S
\tag{5.19}
$$

If the net return and the depreciation rate are constant for each year, k, then Eq. (5.19) simplifies to

$$W = \frac{(1 + i)^g - 1}{i(1 + i)^g}\langle(\ddot{S} - \ddot{C})\ddot{q}(1 - t)\rangle + \left[\frac{(1 + i)^y - 1}{i(1 + i)^y}\right]tI_Fd - \frac{I_Ft}{(1 + i)^g}$$
$$- i_m\left[\frac{(1 + i)^g - 1}{i(1 + i)^g}\right]I_F - i\left[\frac{(1 + i)^g - 1}{i(1 + i)^g}\right]I_w + \frac{1}{(1 + i)^g}(1 - t)V_S$$

$$(5.20)$$

In terms of interest rate factors already enumerated in Table 4.1, this becomes, when $y = g$,

$$W = (\mathcal{PR}_{i-g})\langle(\ddot{S} - \ddot{C})\ddot{q}(1 - t)\rangle$$
$$- (\mathcal{PR}_{i-g})(i_mI_F + iI_w) \qquad (5.21a)$$
$$+ (\mathcal{PS}_{i-g})(1 - t)V_S$$
$$= \mathcal{PR}_{i-g}\langle\breve{Q}\rangle \qquad (5.21b)$$

Happel (1958) provides other examples.

It should be appreciated that the calculations are very sensitive to the values used for i and i_m; care is needed in selecting these magnitudes. More details are given by Happel (1958), Kapfer (1969), and Blewitt (1967).

Although the examples presented here are worked in terms of discrete interest payments, similar relationships can be derived in terms of continuous compounding interest.

Problem: Rework Example 5.3 for $i = 6\%$ and $i_m = 15\%$ based on the venture-profit approach of Happel. Assume that the book-depreciation is based on the sinking fund method so that the equations are comparable.

Sample solution: The calculations are summarized in Table 5.6 based on the information given in Table 5.5(a) and (b). In these calculations the cost of the land has been omitted from the calculation. During the years of construction, the venture profit is negative and equal to the opportunity cost of the capital invested. Note also that the venture profit excludes the recovery of scrap value at the end of the project. That is, the term in Eq. (5.11)

$$\frac{i}{(1 + i)^g - 1}(1 - t)V_S$$

is not distributed throughout the project. Rather it is given as a lump sum in Table 5.6 for ease in comparison with Table 5.5. The recovery of working capital at the end of the project is not included because the method considers the working capital not as flowing into or out of the project, but rather as generating interest each year through the opportunity cost. The overall result is $-\$0.444$ million.

TABLE 5.6

SAMPLE CALCULATION OF PRESENT VALUE BASED ON ANNUAL VENTURE PROFIT

Time (years)		Net return (10^6)	Book depreciation, eI_F (10^6)	Net profit, $\check{p}$ (10^6)	$i_mI_F + iI_w$ (10^6) (i_m, 15%; i, 6%)	Venture profit, $\check{Q}$ (10^6)	$\delta\rho$ and $\delta\delta$ (6%)	Contributions + (10^6)	Contributions − (10^6)
−2:	S								
	D				0.360	−0.360	1.124		0.405
−1:	S								
	D				0.435	−0.435	1.06		0.461
1:	S				—	—	1.00		—
End of									
1		0.295	0.294	0.001	0.465	−0.464	0.9434		0.438
2		0.614	0.294	0.320	0.465	−0.145	0.8900		0.129
3		0.817	0.294	0.523	0.465	+0.058	0.8396	0.049	
4		0.960	0.294	0.666	0.465	0.201	0.7921	0.159	
5		0.960	0.294	0.666	0.480	0.186	0.7473	0.139	
6		0.980	0.304	0.676	0.480	0.196	0.7050	0.138	
7		0.980	0.304	0.676	0.480	0.196	0.6651	0.130	
8		0.980	0.304	0.676	0.480	0.196	0.6274	0.123	
								0.251	
Total								0.989	1.433
Present value									−0.444 million

Comment: The results are different because the interest rate to account for risk, i_m, was used.

---

b. *Internal Rate of Return* (synonyms: discounted cash flow, DCF, i_{irr}
profitability index, interest rate of return,
investor's method)

In the present value method, values for interest rate i (and i_m) were specified and then the present value was calculated. In the internal rate of return method the present value is specified as zero and the interest rate, i_{irr}, is calculated. (When the venture profit method of Happel is used to calculate the present value, $W = 0$ and we let $i = i_m = i_{irr}$ or i_{DCF}.) This is a trial and error calculation but reasonable trial rates for i_{irr} are 10% as a low trial value and 20% as a high trial value. The present value can be calculated at these two extreme trial values. Values for the internal rate of return outside this range mean the proposal is obviously attractive or unattractive. If the rate lies between the extremes, trial values can be obtained by plotting W against $(\mathcal{P}\mathcal{R}_{i-g})/g$. This can be seen to be an approximation to Eq. (5.21) [Malloy (1969)].

Sample calculations and discussion are given by Reul (1957), Happel (1958), Kempster (1967), and Edge (1960).

To apply this criterion, we accept the alternative with the largest internal rate of return.

Problem: Calculate the internal rate of return for Example 5.3. Base the calculations on (1) a cash flow basis and (2) the venture-profit concept.

Sample solution: The present value is calculated at $i_{irr} = 10\%$ and 20%. The cash flow approach is given in Table 5.7(a). In Fig. 5.14(a), two methods of interpolation-extrapolation are used to determine the approximate value of i_{irr}. The plot of W versus $(\mathcal{P}\mathcal{R}_{i-g})/g$ indicates that the abscissa $= 0.63$. Since $g = 8$ years, the value of i_{irr} corresponds with a $\mathcal{P}\mathcal{R}$ factor for 8 years of 5.01. This occurs for i_{irr} slightly less than 12%. The approximate value from a plot of W versus i_{irr} suggests that $i_{irr} \simeq 12\%$.

An alternative approach might be to use the venture-profit method of estimating the results. Here the resulting i_{irr} is about 11% from both graphical interpolation methods [Fig. 5.14(b)].

Again, these calculations are used in judging alternatives, and because the calculational procedure varies from company to company, care is needed in interpreting the results absolutely. This example is included to illustrate the calculational technique.

TABLE 5.7(a)

SAMPLE CALCULATION OF THE INTERNAL RATE OF RETURN FROM A CASH FLOW BASIS

Time (years)	Net return ($10^6)	$S\partial$ and ∂S (10%)	Cash flows ($10^6)		$S\partial$ and ∂S (20%)	Cash flows ($10^6)	
			+	−		+	−
−2: S		1.210		0.121	1.440		0.144
D				2.904			3.456
−1: S		1.10		0.550	1.200		0.600
D							
1: S		1.00		0.500	1.00		0.500
End of							
1	0.295	0.9091	0.268		0.8333	0.246	
2	0.614	0.8265	0.507		0.6944	0.426	
3	0.817	0.7513	0.614		0.5787	0.473	
4	0.960	0.6830	0.656		0.4823	0.463	
5	0.960	0.6209	0.596	0.062	0.4019	0.386	0.040
6	0.980	0.5645	0.553		0.3349	0.328	
7	0.980	0.5132	0.503		0.2791	0.274	
8	0.980	0.4665	0.457		0.2326	0.228	
			0.047			0.023	
			0.187			0.093	
			0.233			0.116	
			4.621	4.137		3.056	4.740
Present value			$0.484 million			−$1.684 million	

TABLE 5.7(b)
SAMPLE CALCULATION OF THE INTERNAL RATE OF RETURN FROM ANNUAL VENTURE PROFITS

Time (years)	Net profit, $(I_F + I_w)\langle\bar{P}\rangle$ (10^6)	i_{irr} (i_{irr} 10%)	Venture profit (10^6)	$\mathcal{SP}$ and $\mathcal{PS}$ (10%)	Cash flows (10^6) +	Cash flows (10^6) −	i_{irr} $(I_F + I_w)$ (i_{irr}, 20%)	Venture profit (10^6)	$\mathcal{SP}$ and $\mathcal{PS}$ (20%)	Cash flows (10^6) +	Cash flows (10^6) −
−2: S		0.240	−0.240	1.210		0.290	0.480	−0.480	1.440		0.691
−1: S		0.290	−0.290	1.10		0.319	0.580	−0.580	1.200		0.696
1: S				1.00					1.00		
1: E	0.001	0.340	−0.339	0.9091		0.308	0.680	−0.679	0.8333		0.566
2	0.320	0.340	−0.020	0.8265		0.016	0.680	−0.360	0.6944		0.250
3	0.523	0.340	0.183	0.7513	0.137		0.680	−0.157	0.5787		0.091
4	0.666	0.340	0.326	0.6830	0.223		0.680	−0.014	0.4823		0.007
5	0.666	0.350	0.316	0.6209	0.196		0.700	−0.034	0.4019		0.014
6	0.676	0.350	0.326	0.5645	0.184		0.700	−0.024	0.3349		0.008
7	0.676	0.350	0.326	0.5132	0.167		0.700	−0.024	0.2791		0.007
8	0.676	0.350	0.326	0.4665	0.152		0.700	−0.024	0.2326		0.006
					0.187					0.093	
Present value					1.246	0.933				0.093	2.336
					+$0.313 million					−$2.243 million	

129

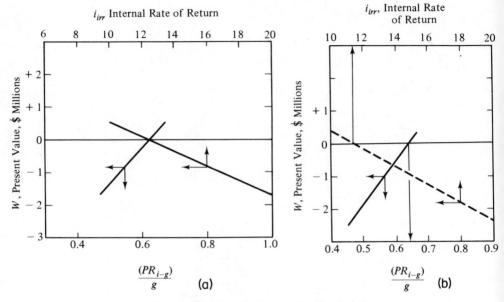

Figure 5.14. Graphical approximations of i_{irr}.

Leung (1970) developed a nomograph, given in Fig. 5.15, to assist in obtaining a reasonable trial value. It is based on a rearrangement of Eq. (5.17) with constant $\langle \check{R} \rangle$, $y = g$, $i = i_m = i_{irr}$, negligible V_S:

$$W = 0 = (\mathcal{P}\mathcal{R}_{i-g})[\langle \check{R} \rangle^*(1-t) + dI_F t - i_{irr}I_w] - I_F + \mathcal{P}\mathcal{S}_{i-g}(1-t)V_S \tag{5.22}$$

or

$$I_F = \mathcal{P}\mathcal{R}_{i-g}(\langle \check{R} \rangle - i_{irr}I_w) \tag{5.23}$$

If the working capital contribution is assumed to be small, then

$$\frac{I_F}{\langle \check{R} \rangle} \simeq \mathcal{P}\mathcal{R}_{i-g} \tag{5.24}$$

This is shown in Fig. 5.15.

This method has the advantage that it can be calculated without knowing "i". However, the method cannot be used to compare alternative solutions to the same problem or when the cash position curve crosses the abscissa more than once. In this latter case, there is no unique value for i_{irr}.

5.7 Special Methods for Selecting Among Alternatives Satisfying One Objective

In the preceding section, criteria were discussed for comparing alternative investments into completely different projects. Perhaps the choice is to invest in manufacturing pumps or spending money on research and development

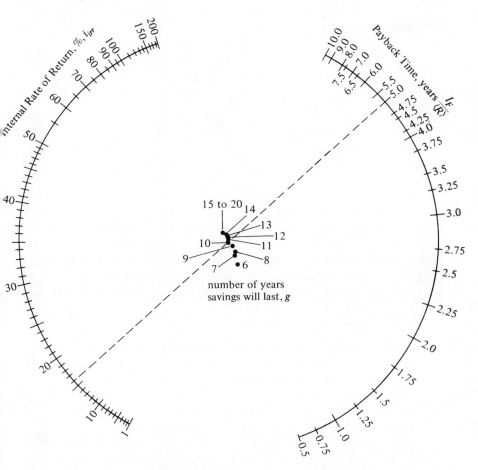

PROCEDURE: (1) Determine payback time, Eq 5-1, and (2) extend the
line joining payback time and number of years savings will last, to cut the rate-of-return arc.

Figure 5.15. Nomograph to yield trial values for the Internal-Rate-of-
Return. (*Courtesy of Leung*, "*Chemical Engineering*," *McGraw-Hill, Inc.,
1970.*)

to produce a new plastic. Consider now the special problem of choosing which
is the best way to satisfy one objective. For example, given the objective to
convert reactant A into product B, should the reactor be a fixed, fluidized, or
transported bed reactor? Any of the preceding methods could be used, but
two new methods that are especially applicable are capitalized cost and
marginal return on investment.

a. *Capitalized Cost* (synonym: sinking fund method) K

In this method we calculate the original cost plus the present value of
an infinite number of replacements, each g years. The capitalized cost is

therefore

$$K = I_F + (I_F - V_S)\underbrace{\left(\frac{1}{(1+i)^g - 1}\right)}_{\substack{\text{interest from a} \\ \text{sinking fund}}} \qquad (5.25)$$

$$\underbrace{}_{\substack{\text{first cost less} \\ \text{scrap value at} \\ \text{the end of the} \\ \text{gth year}}}$$

$$= I_F + (I_F - V_S)\left(\frac{\mathcal{RS}_{i-g}}{i}\right) \qquad (5.26)$$

$$= (I_F - V_S)\left[\frac{(1+i)^g}{(1+i)^g - 1}\right] + V_S$$

$$= (I_F - V_S)\left(\frac{\mathcal{RP}_{i-g}}{i}\right) + V_S \qquad (5.27)$$

Thus, the interest from the sinking fund generates enough money $(I_F - V_S)$ every g years to provide for an indefinite number of replacements. This method is applicable in selecting alternatives within a single project, for example, the type of reactor, boiler, or inert gas system for a process. To use this criterion, we select the alternative with the smallest K. See Jelen (1954).

Example 5.4: Two technically acceptable alternative reactor systems are available. All alternatives have the same economic life. The information is given in Table 5.8(a).

TABLE 5-8(a)
COST AND ECONOMIC LIFE INFORMATION

Reactor	I_F	V_S	g
A	6,000	1000	5
B	12,400	3000	5

Problem: Calculate the capitalized costs if $i = 6\%$.

Sample solution: From Eq. (5.25) the respective capitalized costs are

$$K_A = 6000 + (6000 - 1000)\frac{0.1774}{0.06} = \$20,800$$

$$K_B = 12,400 + (12,400 - 3000)\frac{0.1774}{0.06} = \$40,200$$

Based on this criterion, project A is more attractive because it has the smaller capitalized cost. Note that the value of the capitalized cost far exceeds the investment. This can be very misleading to the uninitiated.

b. *Marginal Return on Investment*

If we elect to attempt to maximize the profit over and above what money normally generates within the company, then we maximize the annual venture profit neglecting scrap value:

$$\max\{\langle \breve{Q} \rangle\} = \max\{\langle \breve{P} \rangle - i_m I_F - i I_w\} \qquad (5.28)$$

Taking the first derivative with respect to fixed capital investment and equating to zero yields

$$\frac{d\langle \breve{P} \rangle}{dI_F} = i_m \qquad (5.29)$$

That is, capital should be invested in the design until the last increment in investment above a base-acceptable, technically feasible alternative returns an incremental annual profit at a rate equal to the minimum acceptable rate of return, i_m. The method of calculation then is

Select the minimum investment that technically would satisfy the function; this is the initial base case.

Compare the next most expensive investment, $(I)_1$, with the base case, $(I)_b$, by comparing $(\Delta \text{ profit})/(\Delta \text{ investment})$ to i_m. If this is greater than i_m, then this investment $(I)_1$ is accepted and now becomes the base case.

Continue comparing each successive fixed investment to the base case until all alternatives have been considered.

The base case that survives this analysis is the recommended investment.

Example 5.5:   Two reactors A and B, from Example 5.4, have annual profits of $1200 and $2230. These profits correctly account for the scrap value, life, and depreciation. If $i_m = 15\%$, which reactor should we install?

Sample solution: The calculations are shown in Table 5.8(b). The $6000 reactor is the initial base case. The ratio of the marginal profits to marginal capital investment is greater than 0.15. Hence,

TABLE 5.8(b)
INFORMATION AND CALCULATIONS FOR ALTERNATIVES

Reactor	I_F	ΔI_F	Profit	$\Delta \breve{P}$	$\Delta \breve{P}/\Delta I$
A	$6000		1200		
		6400		1030	0.16
B	12400		2230		

reactor B becomes the base case. Since there are only the two alternatives, our calculations are complete and reactor B should be installed. A comparison of this answer with that in Example 5.4 shows that the conclusion is reversed when more information is considered.

Example 5.6: Four alternative systems are available to satisfy one function. Their installed and annual costs are summarized in Table 5.9. Which alternative should we select? Assume that $i_m = 15\%$.

Sample solution: The initial base case is alternative A. The $(\Delta \check{P}/\Delta I)_{B-A}$ for case B relative to A is 130/1600 or 8%. Therefore, case B does not become the base case. Now consider alternative C relative to A. The result for $(\Delta \check{P}/\Delta I)_{C-A}$ is $1158/6400 = 18\%$. Hence, since the incremental return is greater than i_m, case C becomes the base case. Now compare alternative D relative to C. The result, $(\Delta \check{P}/\Delta I)_{D-C}$, is $82/600 = 13.7\%$. Since this is below i_m, we do not accept D relative to C. Hence, the best alternative is the base case at the time calculations stopped, namely alternative C.

TABLE 5.9
ALTERNATIVE SYSTEMS

Alternative	Installed cost ($)	Total annual costs ($/year)
A	6,000	8720
B	7,600	8590
C	12,400	7562
D	13,000	7480

5.8 Interrelationships Among the Methods

Other methods of reporting the financial attractiveness of proposals are available (equivalent annual cost, MAPI) and the interested reader can learn about these from Szendrovits (1969), Taylor (1964), and Reisman (1968). The purpose of the previous section was to introduce the principles and concepts of calculating the commonly used criteria for the financial attractiveness of alternatives. The method used depends on the company and the preferences of the supervisor. While many apparently different methods of reporting the financial attractiveness of alternative proposals were described, some of them are merely simplifications of more versatile and general methods. A generalized interrelationship is shown in Fig. 5.16 with three basic

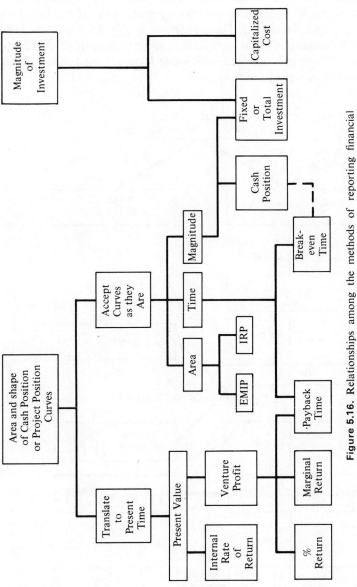

Figure 5.16. Relationships among the methods of reporting financial attractiveness.

branches: transcribing the cash position curve to the present time, accepting the cash position curve and identifying its characteristics, and the absolute magnitude of the investment.

Consider first the branch based on the present value representation of the cash flows. We start with the most general form of the present value method, Eq. (5.13) or (5.15). Then, as shown in Fig. 5.17, we can obtain the sequence of equations given in preceding sections. Eventually, after enough assumptions have been made we can relate W to $\langle \overset{\circ}{Q} \rangle$ and then to return on investment, r, and payback time, p.

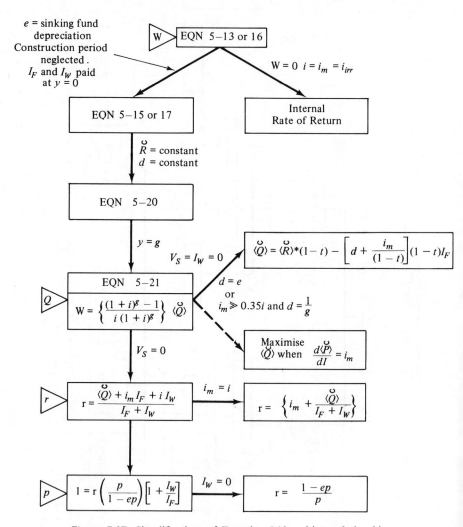

Figure 5.17. Simplifications of Equation 5.13 and interrelationships.

Furthermore, some very useful simplifications can be developed from these overall relationships. Happel (1958) has shown that the following approximation can be made for venture profit if $V_S = 0$:

$$\langle \breve{Q} \rangle = \langle \breve{R} \rangle^*(1 - t) + dtI_F - eI_F - i_mI_F - iI_w$$

$$= \left[\langle \breve{R} \rangle^* + \frac{dtI_F}{1 - t} - \frac{eI_F}{1 - t} - \left(\frac{i_mI_F + iI_w}{1 - t} \right) \right](1 - t) \tag{5.30}$$

An approximation for a sinking fund depreciation rate, e, can be used:

$$e = \frac{i}{(1 + i)^g - 1} \simeq \frac{1}{g} - 0.35i \tag{5.31}$$

If the governmental depreciation rate is straight line depreciation and if $g = y$, then

$$e \simeq d - 0.35i \tag{5.32}$$

Substitution of Eq. (5.32) into Eq. (5.30) yields

$$\frac{\langle \breve{Q} \rangle}{1 - t} = \left[\langle \breve{R} \rangle^* - dI_F + \frac{0.35iI_F}{1 - t} - \left(\frac{i_mI_F + iI_w}{1 - t} \right) \right] \tag{5.33}$$

If $I_w = 0$, then we obtain the simplification

$$\langle \breve{Q} \rangle = \langle \breve{R} \rangle^*(1 - t) - \left\{ d + \left[\frac{i_m - 0.35i}{1 - t} \right] \right\} I_F(1 - t) \tag{5.34}$$

If $d = e$ or if $0.35i$ is negligible relative to i_m, then

$$\langle \breve{Q} \rangle = \breve{R}^*(1 - t) - \left(d + \frac{i_m}{1 - t} \right) I_F(1 - t) \tag{5.35}$$

Alternatively, we could start with Eq. (5.30) and calculate the annual return for the special case when $\langle \breve{Q} \rangle = 0$ and $I_w = 0$. The result is

$$\breve{R}^* = \left[\frac{1}{g} - dt + i_m - 0.35i \right] \frac{I_F}{1 - t} \tag{5.36}$$

Rearrangement of the definition of the payback time, Eq. (5.2), yields the relationship for $\breve{R}^*$:

$$\breve{R}^* = \frac{I_F(1 - pdt)}{p(1 - t)}$$

Combining these relationships and solving for p yields

$$p = \frac{1}{(1/g) + i_m - 0.35i} \Big|_{\langle \breve{Q} \rangle = 0} \tag{5.37}$$

This relationship is independent of the method of depreciation used for tax purposes, d.

Happel (1958) prefers to use the before tax definition for payback time, p^*. The resulting relationship is [Happel (1958), pp. 12 and 57], for $\langle \breve{Q} \rangle$

$$= I_w = 0 \text{ and } d = 1/g,$$

$$p^* = \frac{1}{(1/g) + [(i_m - 0.35i)/(1 - t)]}\Big|_{\langle \check{Q} \rangle = 0} \qquad (5.38)$$

These relationships are important because

When simplifying assumptions can be made, we should recognize the equalities between the various criteria.

When different criteria are used by different individuals for the same overall risk and economic conditions, these relationships allow us to calculate values for each criterion that are consistent.

Example 5.7: Bill applies a preliminary screening for the projects he is submitting to his supervisor for approval. His supervisor uses payback time as a criterion and for the present economic conditions Bill can submit only those projects having a payback time of less than 2 years. What values for r, W, i_{irr}, and $\langle \check{Q} \rangle$ are consistent with $p = 2$ years if $i = 6\%$ and $g = 5$ years?

Sample solution: (1) *Relating to percentage return on investment:* If $I_w = 0$, then $r = (1 - ep)/p$. Reasonable values for book depreciation are 0.2 for straight line depreciation for $g = 5$ years or 0.18 for sinking fund depreciation. Hence,

$$r = \frac{1 - 0.2(2)}{2} \quad \text{or} \quad \frac{1 - 0.18(2)}{2}$$

$$= \frac{0.6}{2} \quad \text{to} \quad \frac{0.64}{2}$$

$$= 30\% \quad \text{to} \quad 32\%$$

As we shall see in Chapter 6, $I_w \simeq 0.2I_F$. For this condition

$$1 = r\left(\frac{p}{1 - ep}\right)\left(1 + \frac{I_w}{I_F}\right)$$

$$= r\left[\frac{2}{1 - 0.2(2)}\right]\left(1 + \frac{0.2I_F}{I_F}\right)$$

$$= r\left(\frac{2.4}{0.6}\right)$$

Hence,

$$r = \frac{0.6}{2.4} \quad \text{to} \quad \frac{0.64}{2.4}$$

$$= 25\% \quad \text{to} \quad 26\tfrac{1}{2}\%$$

(2) *Relating this to venture profit:* If we can assume that the scrap value $V_S = 0$, then

$$r = \frac{\langle \check{Q} \rangle + i_m I_F + i I_w}{I_F + I_w}$$

$$\langle \check{Q} \rangle = r(I_F + I_w) - i_m I_F - i I_w$$

If $I_w = 0$,
$$\langle \breve{Q} \rangle = [(0.30 \text{ to } 0.32) - i_m]I_F$$
If $I_w = 0.2I_F$, then
$$\langle \breve{Q} \rangle = (0.25 \text{ to } 0.265)(1.2I_F) - i_mI_F - 0.06(0.2I_F)$$
$$= [(0.29 \text{ to } 0.31) - i_m]I_F$$

(3) *Relating this to present worth:* From interest tables, $\mathcal{PR}_{6-5} = 4.212$. Hence, the corresponding value of the present worth when construction time is zero, Eq. (5.21) is applicable, and the scrap value is zero and we can neglect the recovery of working capital is

$$W = 4.212\langle \breve{Q} \rangle$$
$$= 4.212[(0.30 \text{ to } 0.32) - i_m]I_F \qquad \text{if } I_w = 0$$
$$= 4.212[(0.29 \text{ to } 0.31) - i_m]I_F \qquad \text{if } I_w = 0.2I_F$$

If the present value calculation is based on Eqs. (5.17) and (5.2), then for constant annual return and depreciation, zero construction time, and negligible scrap value, the results are

$$W = \mathcal{PR}_{i-g}[\breve{R}^*(1 - t) + dI_Ft] - I_F[1 + \mathcal{PR}_{i-g}(i_m - i)]$$
$$- I_w[i(\mathcal{PR}_{ig})]$$
$$= (\mathcal{PR}_{i-g})\frac{I_F}{p} - I_F[1 + (\mathcal{PR}_{i-g})(i_m - i)]$$
$$- I_w[i(\mathcal{PR}_{i-g})]$$

If the working capital is negligible, then

$$W = \frac{I_F}{p}[\mathcal{PR}_{i-g} - p - p(i_m - i)\mathcal{PR}_{i-g}]$$
$$= I_F\left[\frac{4.212 - 2 - 2(i_m - 0.06)4.212}{2}\right]$$
$$= 4.212(0.31 - i_m)I_F$$

If $I_w = 0.2I_F$, then the result is
$$W = 4.212(0.31 - i_m)I_F - 0.2i(4.212)I_F$$
$$= 4.212(0.30 - i_m)I_F$$

If the present value calculation is based on Eqs. (5.15) and (5.2), then for the same conditions the results are

$$W = \mathcal{PR}_{i-g}\left(\frac{I_F}{p}\right) - I_F(1 + \mathcal{PS}_{i-g}) - I_w[i(\mathcal{PR}_{i-g})]$$

If $I_w = 0$, $i = 0.06$, $g = 5$ years, and $p = 2$ years,

$$W = \mathcal{PR}_{6-5}\left(\frac{1}{p} - \frac{1}{\mathcal{PR}_{6-5}} - \frac{\mathcal{PS}}{\mathcal{PR}_{6-5}}\right)I_F$$
$$= 4.212\left(0.5 - \frac{1}{4.212} - \frac{0.7473}{4.212}\right)I_F$$
$$= 4.212(0.09)I_F$$

(4) *Relating this to internal rate of return:* We cannot use the results reported in section (3) because they assumed that $i = 0.06$. Hence, we need to rederive these results in terms of $i = i_m = i_{irr}$. For simplicity we shall assume that all the other conditions are valid.

From Eq. (5.17), the result, including book depreciation as an expense and assuming that $I_w = 0$, is

$$W = 0 = (\mathcal{PR}_{irr-5})\frac{I_F}{p} - I_F$$

For a payback time of 2 years, the result is

$$2 = \mathcal{PR}_{irr-5}$$

Hence, i_{irr} is between 40 and 50%.

From Eq. (5.15), again including book depreciation as an expense, and assuming $I_w = 0$, constant annual revenue, negligible construction period, and negligible scrap value, the result is

$$W = 0 = (\mathcal{PR}_{i_{irr}-5})\frac{I_F}{p} - I_F[1 + (\mathcal{PS}_{i_{irr}-5})]$$

$$\mathcal{PR}_{i_{irr}-5} = p[1 + (\mathcal{PS}_{i_{irr}-5})]$$

For a payback time of 2 years, the result is that i_{irr} is approximately 40%. This agrees reasonably well with the result obtained from Fig. 5.15.

Comment: Care needs to be taken to ensure that the assumptions involved are satisfied. In this example the book depreciation life was only 5 years. This value is commonly used because of the rapidly changing technology. However, some of these simplifications require that $d = e$ before they can be applied; normally the minimum tax life is 10 years (in Canada) and 11 years (in the United States) for chemical equipment. Hence, care is needed in applying these relationships.

A second branch of Fig. 5.16 accepts the cash position curve as it is. The EMIP and IRP study the areas between the curve and the abscissa, the cash position is the magnitude of the cash position-time relationship at a specified time, and break-even points and payback times are time locations related to special values of the cash position.

A third branch expresses the total amount of capital required in the project. This can be expressed either with or without some account being taken of the value of money.

5.9 Comparison and Evaluation of the Methods

The interrelationships among the various methods of reporting the financial attractiveness of alternatives have been discussed. Which method we use during our first professional years depends on the judgment of our supervisors. However, when we assume more responsibility it becomes our task to decide on the method. With this in mind, we shall outline some of the strengths and weaknesses of each method and compare the results for different examples.

Comparison

Table 5.10 lists the desirable features of an ideal criterion and indicates which of these features each method possesses. For a more detailed analysis, see Weaver et al. (1963), Kapfer (1967), and Happel (1958). Based on these characteristics, the two methods that are most strongly recommended by accountants, business administrators and engineers are the present value method and the internal-rate-of-return method, although Herron (1967) quite correctly points out that a variety of methods should be used because each method points out certain aspects of the attractiveness.

The relative merits of the present value and internal-rate-of-return methods have been argued and discussed in detail in the literature, and we leave this point to you to gain experience with both methods and decide on the method you prefer.

A suggested sample work sheet is given in Table 5.11 that presents the total financial commitment, the cash position, and the present-value calculations.

Example comparison

To illustrate the different answers that can be obtained by the use of the different evaluation methods, several alternatives are compared in Table 5.12. Only the answers have been reported to facilitate the comparison. In this table, the data for Table 5.5(a) and (b) were taken as case 1. From Table 5.5, the present value is about 1.6×10^6. All other cases were assigned values of I_F such that W was constant and equals 1.6×10^6 for $y = 15$ years, $g = 8$ years, $i_m = 15\%$, $i = 6\%$, $I_l = 3.5\%$ I_F; $I_w = 17.2\%$ I_F; and $\langle P \rangle$ = constant for all years. In the calculations, the startup expense, the construction period, and the tax rebate or undepreciated capital expense at the end of the eighth year were neglected.

In case 2, the annual net return was assumed to be 0.96×10^6. In case 3, it was 0.5 of this value, and in case 4, double this value.

The comparison between cases 1 and 2 is interesting. Case 1 describes varying cash flows and profits as given in Tables 5.5 and 5.6. For these varying

TABLE 5.10
SUMMARY OF CHARACTERISTICS OF DIFFERENT METHODS

	Present Value	Internal Rate of Return	Venture Profit	Return on Investment	Payback Time	EMIP IRP	Capitalized Cost	Cash Position Curve
Considers time value of money?	Yes ✓	Yes ✓	No, Average	No	No	No	In some way	✓ Yes
Consider time value of assets i.e. depreciation i.e. use diff. depreciation?	Yes ✓	Yes ✓	Average	Average	Average	Yes	In some way	Yes
Account for risk through interest rate. (Other than through g)?	Yes	No	Average	No	No	No	No	No
Consider income and variation with time?	Yes	Yes	No, Average	No, Average	No, Average	Yes	No	Yes
Account for construction period?	Yes	Yes	No	No	No	Yes	No	Yes
Flexible to allow for variation in sales volume, price?	Yes	Yes	No, Average	No	No	Yes	No	Yes
Variation in tax?	Yes	Yes	No	No	No	Yes	No	Yes
Illustrate the rate at which revenue is generated?	No	Yes	No	Yes	No	No	No	No
Reports magnitude of I_F?	No	No	No	No	No	No	Inflated impression	Yes
Considers reinvested profits?	Yes	Yes	Yes	No	No	No	No	No
Consider different service lives?	Yes	Yes	Partly	No	No	No	Care needed	Possible
Easy to use to compare alternatives (poor) 0 to 10 (excellent)	8	8	10	10	10	8	9	0
Ease in use in Optimization studies (poor) 0 to 10 (excellent)	8	6 Tend to minimize to maximize i_{rr}	9	4	4	?		0
Comments	If i too high, long term projects look poor	Average the interest into i...			Does not consider earning beyond year n.			

142

TABLE 5.11

SUGGESTED SAMPLE WORK SHEET

Total Capital Investment	Present Value	Return %											

		Cash Flows	$-$										
			$+$										
		Factor SP $-$ PS $-\%$											
		Net Return	$\circ$ R										
		Tax	$-\%$										
		Depr. for Tax	$d I_F$										
		Gross Profit excl. depr. and tax											
		Total Cost incl. G before deprec.											
		Revenue	S_q										
		Unit Selling Price	S										
		Annual Sales	$\circ$ q										
	Capital Costs		I_W										
		Land Field	I_F										
			I_l										
		Time											

conditions the arithmetic average net profit is \$0.545 million and the annual cash flow is \$0.823 million. Based on an assumed steady-state operation, at design capacity, case 2, these values are \$0.56 million and \$0.96 million, respectively.

For all these cases, the criteria described in preceding sections are calculated and summarized in Table 5.12. For case 1, the values of p, r, and Q are based on the arithmetic number averages of the pertinent components in Tables 5.5 and 5.6.

According to the present value criterion, all the projects are equally attractive. However, when the other criteria are applied, case 3 is most attractive. If case 3 were not available, then i_{irr} and EMIP suggest case 2 as most attractive; all the rest indicate case 1, as shown in Table 5.12 by the boxed figures. This example illustrates the variety of answers that can be obtained from the different criteria. Other comparisons have been reported by Reul (1968), Herron (1967), and Peters and Timmerhaus (1968), p. 259.

TABLE 5.12
COMPARISON OF ALTERNATIVES WITH THE DIFFERENT CRITERIA

	Cases			
	1	2	3	4
Background				
I_F (\$10⁶)	2.9	4.0	1.23	9.50
I_l (\$10⁶)	0.10	0.14	0.043	0.333
I_w (\$10⁶)	0.50	0.69	0.212	1.64
y (years)	15	15	15	15
dI_F (\$10⁶)	0.196	0.266	0.082	0.633
g (years)	8	8	8	8
eI_F (\$10⁶)	0.29	0.40	0.123	0.95
$\langle \breve{P} \rangle$ (\$10⁶)	0.545	0.56	0.357	0.97
$i_m I_F + i I_w$ (\$10⁶)	0.472	0.6414	0.1967	1.523
$\langle \breve{R} \rangle$ (\$10⁶)	0.823	0.960	0.480	1.92
Criteria				
I (\$10⁶)	3.4	4.69	1.44	11.14
p (years)	3.52	4.16	2.56	5.0
EMIP (years)	4.35	2.51	1.5	2.98
IRP (years)	—	5.0	3.0	6.0
r (%)	16.0	12.0	25	8.7
$\langle \breve{Q} \rangle$ (\$10⁶)	0.072	−0.0814	0.1603	−0.553
W (\$10⁶)	+1.65	+1.65	+1.65	+1.65
i_{irr} (%)	12	14	27	$7\frac{1}{2}$
K (\$10⁶)	7.8	10.7	3.3	25.5

Sensitivity

The accuracy of any comparison depends on the accuracy of the data used in the analysis. Because the accuracy is, in general, poor for many of the factors that contribute to the calculations, some appreciation of the sensitivity of the final result to the errors in the individual factors is useful.

A very qualitative summary of the factors, our ability to predict them and their effect on the result are shown in Table 5.13. Our ability to accurately predict the total product cost depends on the sensitivity of the cost to raw material costs. We cannot accurately predict the future governmental tax policies. For example, the government may instigate an R & D incentive scheme that will drastically affect one alternative and not another. This factor is not within the control of the estimator.

Since the uncertainty is great, a quantitative appreciation of the effect of variables on the results should be obtained. The simplest and least reliable approach is to recalculate the criteria for different values of one variable and keep all the other variables constant. Some results of such a study for the internal-rate-of-return method are reported, for example, in Figs. 26-11 and 26-12 by Weaver et al. (1963).

TABLE 5.13
QUALITATIVE SUMMARY OF THE EFFECT OF CONTRIBUTING
FACTORS ON THE FINAL ANSWER*

Factor	Ability to predict the factor accurately	Effect of error on calculated attractiveness	Usual values
Cost of land, I_l	Good	Minor	—
Fixed capital, I_F	Good	Major	—
Working capital, I_w	Fair	Major	—
Length of construction period	Good	Minor	0–2 years
Startup expense	Fair	Intermediate	—
Sales volume	Poor	Major	—
Selling price	Poor	Major	—
Total product costs	Good to fair	Major	—
Economic life	Poor	Intermediate	5–10 years
Tax life	Good	Intermediate	10–15 years
Salvage value	Poor	Minor	$0
Rate of taxation	Poor	Major	50%
Risk	Poor	Major	—
Internal interest rate, i	—	—	6%
Method of depreciation	—	Intermediate	—
Inflation	Poor	Major	$4\frac{1}{2}\%$
General business conditions	Poor	Reflected in other factors	—

*From *Chemical Business Handbook* J. H. Perry, ed., copyright 1963 by McGraw-Hill Book Company; used with permission.

TABLE 5.14

NORMAL DISTRIBUTIONS OF INPUT DATA FOR A PRESENT VALUE AND
INTERNAL-RATE-OF-RETURN ANALYSIS FOR A PLANT TO PRODUCE 10×10^6 LB/ANNUM*

Topic	Cumulative probability	Year									
		1965	1966	1967	1968	1969	1971	1973	1975	1977	1979
Research expense (10^6)	0.10	0.68	0.22	0.05	0.06						
	0.50	0.955	0.31	0.07	0.085						
	0.90	1.225	0.40	0.08	0.105						
Engineering and startup (10^6)	0.10				0.52						
	0.50			0.40	0.60						
	0.90				0.68						
Sales volume (10^6)	0.15					0	0.5	2.0	4.4	4.8	6.8
	0.50					1.7	3.2	5.7	8.2	9.7	13.4†
	0.90					4.1	6.1	8.8	11.6†	14.2†	18.4†
Selling price ($/lb)	0.001					0.80	0.80	0.80	0.80	0.80	0.80
	0.50					0.90	0.90	0.90	0.90	0.90	0.90
	0.999					1.00	1.00	1.00	1.00	1.00	1.00

Cumulative probability	I_F $million		I_w (no. of months)	Raw materials R_A ($/lb)	R_B ($/lb)	Variable costs ($/lb)	By-product credit ($/lb)	Lab. (10^6/year)	Maintenance (% I_F)	Taxes and insurance (% I_F)	Depreciation, g years		Sales, corp. and research expense (10^6/year)
	BL	Aux.									BL	Aux.	
0.10	3.19	1.13	1.8	0.087	0.068	0.044	0.0099	0.66	6.2	1.5	12	15	0.075
0.50	3.37	1.41	3.0	0.10	0.073	0.062	0.0113	0.75	7.0				0.100
0.90	3.57	1.55	3.6	0.117	0.080	0.079	0.0123	0.9	7.8				0.195

*Courtesy of DeFriece et al. (1967) and the American Association of Cost Engineers.
†The design capacity of plant, 10×10^6 lb/year, is exceeded.

146

With computers, however, more ambitious studies can be made, and usually it is worth the effort and expense. A sample set of input and output data of an analysis in which the input data are represented by normal distributions has been given by DeFriece et al. (1967). This is reproduced in Table 5.14 and Fig. 5.18. Doig (1969) introduces a method of using the first moments of the probability distribution about the mean as a measure of the risk.

In summary, the values of financial attractiveness are sensitive to errors in the input data, and this should be appreciated.

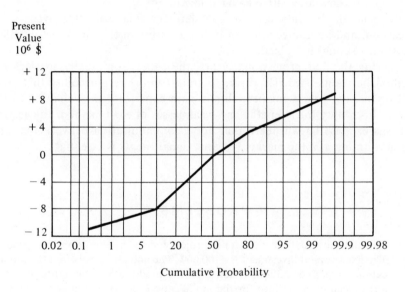

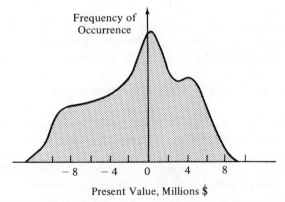

Figure 5.18. Cumulative distribution of the present value for $i = i_m = 15\%$ and inputs given in Table 5.14. (*Courtesy of DeFriece, Hamilton, and Larson and The American Association of Cost Engineers.*)

5.10 Summary

Many methods are available to indicate which alternative is the most financially attractive. These methods essentially are various representations of the cash position curves and simplifications thereof. Although no single method should be used in isolation, the present worth and the total investment correctly account for the time value of money and of assets and are flexible enough to allow for variations in sales, selling price, annual depreciation, etc., for any alternative being studied.

In general, the data used to calculate the financial attractiveness are uncertain, and an appreciation of how the errors in the input factors affect the results should be gained.

During the first professional years, the supervisor usually specifies the method he wants used. However, to train for the responsibility that soon will be his, the young engineer should gain experience in evaluating to the best of his ability the strengths and weaknesses of each method. In carrying out this exercise he will learn that good communication between him and the accounting and the market research departments is essential.

PROBLEMS

5.1. Calculate the payback time for a project for the modification to a process. The fixed capital investment is $100,000. The annual costs before the modification were $3.5 million. Because of the modification, the costs including a depreciation allowance for the modification are $3.395 million. The book depreciation rate is $e = 0.15$, and the government depreciation rate is $d = 1.10$.

5.2. Calculate the payback time for a plant costing $3 million. The annual return is expected to be $2 million/year, and the depreciation rate allowed by the government is uniform with $d = 0.10$. State the assumptions and limitations of your answer.

5.3. Calculate the simple rate of return for Problems 5.1 and 5.2. Assume that $I_w = 0.15 I_F$.

5.4. Your supervisor likes to receive the answers expressed in terms of payback time. You calculate the payback time for a project to be 1.2 years. However, the internal rate of return for this project is 2%. You therefore believe that the project would be economically disastrous to undertake. Write a letter to your supervisor giving him the results of your payback time calculations.

5.5. Table 5.12 summarizes conditions where different criteria indicate that different alternatives are attractive. Synthesize your own examples to illustrate this.

5.6. Draw a cash position curve for a project in which the annual returns are not constant. Use this information to calculate the internal rate of return and the present value of the proposal.

5.7. From Dr. E. M. Tory: The Christian Capitalist Party and the Free Enterprise Party are both against sin and for private enterprise but differ in the details of their programs. The C.C.P. offers a 2-year write-off (straight line) and a 50% tax. The F.E.P. allows a depreciation rate of 30% of the unrecovered (un-depreciated) value but offers a 40% tax. Which party offers the best program?

5.8. From Dr. E. M. Tory: For an investment of $1 million, the Makabuk Chemical Company can derive a gross profit of $400,000/year for 5 years, $300,000 for the sixth year, $200,000 for the seventh, and $100,000 for the eighth, after which the plant will be closed and the unrecovered value (if any) claimed as a loss. If $i = 0.10 = i_m$, what is the *difference* in the venture worths obtained under the above programs?

5.9. A project requires $2 million for fixed investment and $300,000 for working capital. The expected life of the project is 25 years. The annual profit after tax is given below:

Year	$\langle P \rangle$ ($)
1	400,000
2	500,000
3	555,000
4	555,000
5–25	560,000

Assume that the annual government depreciation rate is 0.10 and that the book depreciation is uniform. Calculate the internal rate of return. Neglect the construction period.

5.10. For Problem 5.9, assume that $i_m = 15\%$. Calculate the present value by two methods: Happel's venture profit method and the method based on the project position. The return on investment is 20%. If the working capital is 10% of the fixed capital investment and the depreciation is 5% of the net profit (after tax and after depreciation), what is the payback time?

5.11. The following four different types of molding presses are available for our extrusion plant, worth $3 million. Which one should we install if the company expects a 10% return on capital investment?

	1	2	3	4
Installed cost	6000	7600	12,400	13,000
Power ($/year)	680	680	1,200	1,260
Labor ($/year)	6600	5000	3,200	3,700
Maintenance per year	2%	3%	$3\frac{1}{2}\%$	2%
Taxes and insurance	2%	2%	2%	2%
Economic life per year	5	3	5	10

Estimation of the Capital Investment

6

In Chapter 5, we saw that all criteria for the financial attractiveness of proposals needed a value for the capital investment, I. The total investment includes the fixed capital investment for equipment and buildings, land, and working capital; interest for money borrowed during construction; and startup costs. We shall consider the fixed capital investment first. The fixed capital investment, I_F, can include such items as

An installed heat exchanger and associated piping.

The addition of a new distillation column and associated equipment to an existing process.

The construction of a complete process within an existing building.

The construction of a complete process on an existing piece of land available within an existing factory. This normally consists of capital requirements to install the actual process operations equipment and that required to add to the company's existing storage, utility, and service facilities to adequately serve the new process. We refer to process operation installations as battery limits installations and refer to those additions to storage, utility, and service facilities as the auxiliaries. This is shown in Fig. 6.1.

The construction of a complete process together with all the related required auxiliaries: storage and handling, utilities, and services (such

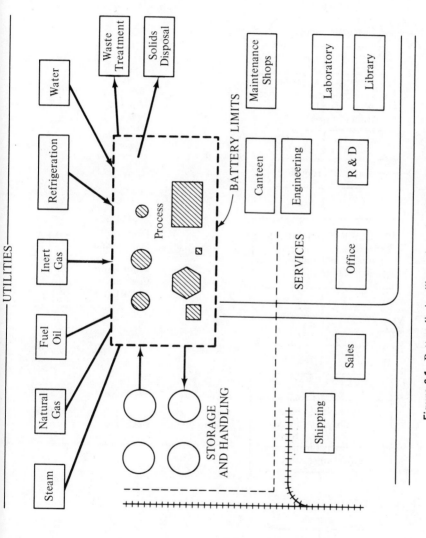

Figure 6.1. Battery limits, illustration of relationship with other sections of a site. (*Courtesy of C.A. Miller of Canadian Industries Ltd.*)

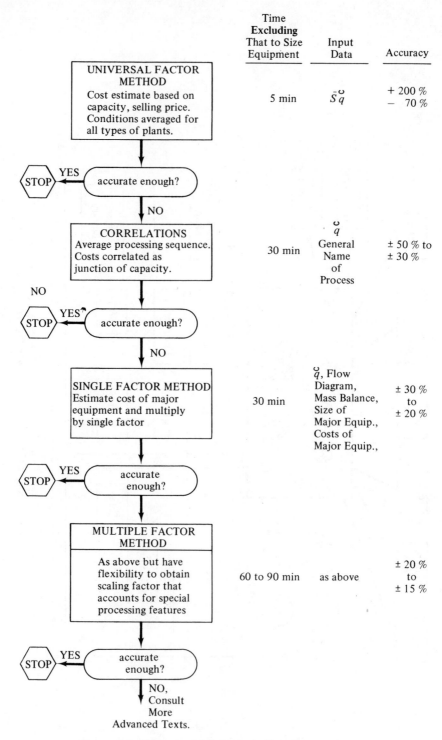

Figure 6.2. Methods of estimating fixed capital investment.

as laboratories, lunchrooms, offices, gatehouse, etc.). This is called a green-field or grass-roots plant.

Thus, we have a very wide variety of answers required.

The data available for cost estimates vary as well:

Cost correlations developed many years ago.
Costs available for equipment similar to that of our present needs yet for another capacity.
Quotations from suppliers.

The accuracy and the time required to obtain such data vary.

Finally, the time available for cost estimations varies from problem to problem. Our task, then, is to select the methods available to estimate the capital costs in the calculational time available, based on the data available, and for the problem at hand. In this book, the classification used is the calculational time available.

6.1 Time Available and the Principle of Successive Approximation

Recall from Chapter 1 that for any problem we should start simply and apply the principle of successive approximation. Such application to the capital cost estimation problems results in the scheme outlined in Figs. 6.2 and 6.3. The first method we could apply is the turnover ratio or universal factor method, which takes about 5 min of calculational time without having to resort to looking up much data. The method is relatively inaccurate. If the answer suggests that the project is worth continuing and we want a more accurate method of estimating the capital costs, we can search for cost correlation data.

If such a correlation is unavailable, inapplicable, or too inaccurate, we encounter a step change in time required because the more accurate methods require a material balance and the key sizes of the major pieces of equipment. The time required to do this depends on the computer-aided systems available, the amount of and order of the recycle, and the number of components over which a balance is made. Estimates of the time required vary between 8 and 50 hr. With this input information, the equipment cost can be estimated and thence, via multiplication by various factors, the total fixed capital investment. There is a range of such factor methods. These are shown in Fig. 6.2.

More accurate methods are available. However, the time required can extend to several man-years and demand the skill of professional estimators. The interested reader is referred to Bauman (1964) and Chilton (1960).

In summary, we should become acquainted with the variety of estimation techniques available, the time and data required, and the resulting accuracy. Such information is necessary so that we can develop the required professional judgment.

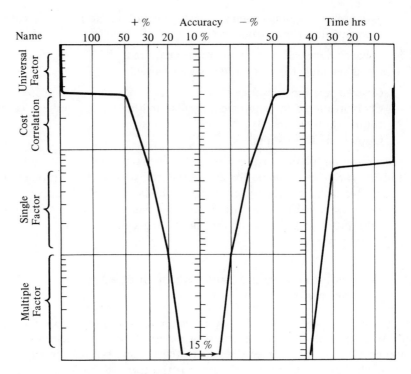

Figure 6.3. Qualitative relationship between time and accuracy for capital investment estimation techniques.

6.2 Universal Factor Method

The total fixed capital cost (of either green-field or battery limit installations) can be estimated from the present selling price of the product and the annual capacity of the plant. (Synonyms include turnover ratio or capital ratio method.)

The method

The fixed capital investment is given by

$$I_F = \frac{\ddot{S}\breve{q}}{w} \tag{6.1}$$

where $\ddot{S}$ = selling price per unit of production

$\breve{q}$ = annual capacity of the proposed plant expressed in the same units of production as $\ddot{S}$

$w =$ universal factor or turnover ratio or the reciprocal of the capital ratio

Values of w are given in Table 6.1. A distribution of the values of w is shown in Fig. 6.4. The data reported in Fig. 6.4 should be interpreted with caution since any type of distribution can be obtained depending on the number and

TABLE 6.1
VALUES OF THE UNIVERSAL FACTOR OR THE TURNOVER RATIO, w

	w
General applicability	1
Large-volume organic intermediates with dominant raw material or labor costs [Kiddoo (1951)]	1.4
Range	0.2–8.0

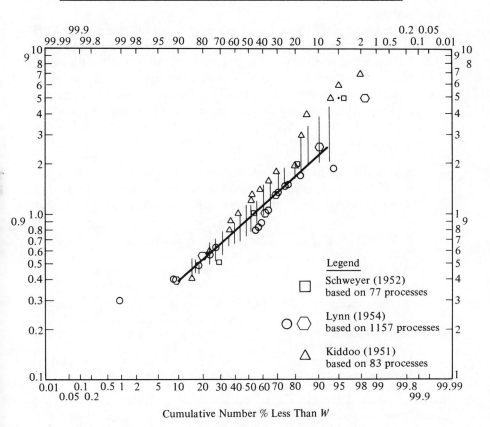

Figure 6.4. Illustrative distribution of values of turnover ratios, w.

type of processes included in the set of processes studied. For this plot, Lynn's work summarizes over 1000 processes, which are distributed as follows: carbon black, 21; petroleum, 75; heavy inorganics, 129; synthetic fibers, 51; pulp and paper, 69; general chemicals, 310; explosives, 20; sulfur, 20; glass, 40; resins and plastics, 61; rubber, 38; paints, pigments, and inks, 55; processed foods, 72; pharmaceuticals and fine chemicals, 138; soaps and detergents, 18; and distilled beverages, 40. Because of both the distribution and quantity of data, Lynn's work was accepted as representative of the distribution of w values. For comparison, the data of Schweyer and Kiddoo for primarily organic petrochemical and petroleum processes are included. The data suggest that w is log normally distributed and with a geometric standard deviation of about 2. This means that 95% of the time the estimates of the fixed capital investment are within the range $+200\%$ and -66% of the estimate. That is, if we estimate the fixed capital investment as $\$1 \times 10^6$, for 95% of the processes the fixed capital investment lies between 0.33 million (when the true turnover ratio is 3.0) and 3 million (when the true turnover ratio is 0.34).

For further reading about the details of this method, see Kiddoo (1951), Schweyer (1952), Lynn (1954), Wessell (1953), and Peters and Timmerhaus (1968). It should be realized that the great value of this method is its simplicity. This advantage is lost if we resort to searching through lists of turnover ratios for the particular process we have in mind. Hence, the term *universal factor* is used because the factor w is meant to be applicable to any process.

The input information

The capacity of the plant should be known from the definition of the problem. If not, then order-of-magnitude estimates are given in Table 6.2.

The selling price of the products are usually available through the resources

TABLE 6.2
ORDER-OF-MAGNITUDE CAPACITIES OF PLANTS*

Commodity	Average production from a single plant (lb/year)	
	Canada	United States
Heavy chemicals	10×10^6	100×10^6
Intermediate chemicals	5×10^6	50×10^6
Fine chemicals	0.5×10^6	5×10^6
Development, speciality pharmaceuticals	0.01 to 0.1×10^6	0.1 to 1×10^6

*From Street and Corrigan (1967).

TABLE 6.3
SOURCES OF COSTS OF CHEMICAL COMMODITIES

The Chemical Marketing Newspaper, New York (weekly newspaper), formerly called *Oil, Paint and Drug Reporter,* New York	Current prices of over 2500 chemicals; includes commentary, news, and some market data
Canadian Chemical Processing, *Southam Business Publication,* Don Mills, Ontario (monthly magazine)	Prices and market data for chemicals that are made in Canada
Fisher Chemical Index, Fisher Scientific Company, Toronto, Ontario (annual book)	Average annual price list for speciality and small-quantity sales; lists over 7000 inorganic and organic chemicals
Aldrich Chemical Catalog, The Aldrich Chemical Company, Milwaukee, Wis. (annual book)	Same as above; includes organic compounds
Alfa Inorganic Limited, Inorganic and organometallic research chemicals, Beverly, Mass. (annual book)	Same as above; includes costs for over 2200 inorganic, organometallic, and metallic compounds

listed in Table 6.3. Note that up-to-date selling prices should be used; data listed in tables given by Aries and Newton (1955), Happel (1958), and Peters (1958) are of historical interest only. We should realize that the selling prices quoted in the open literature are for general sales; prices for large- or small-volume sales can be quite different. In addition, special contract prices can be arranged for mutual benefit between some companies. Nevertheless, the sources listed in Table 6.3 are reasonable.

Figure 6.5 illustrates a general relationship between selling price and production capacity for a plant. This should not be used for capital cost calculations. The figure is included to illustrate the general trend.

Massey and Black (1969) suggest, provided selling price and market volume evolve rather than experience revolutionary technological break-throughs, that the selling price can be estimated from the relationship

$$\sum_i (\ddot{S}\breve{q})_i = k\theta^m \tag{6.2}$$

where θ = time, in years, when we wish to know the selling price $\ddot{S}_{\theta}$
k = constant
m = slope constant
$\breve{q}$ = total U.S. national annual production of commodity

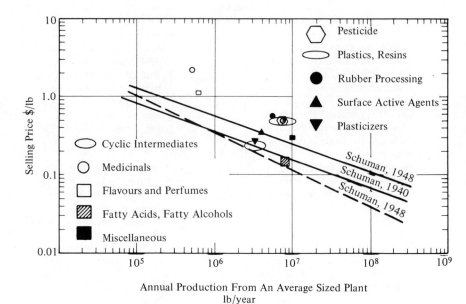

Figure 6.5. Generalized relationship between selling price and production capacity. (*Data from Zabel and Marchitto, 1958.*)

Sample values of the constants k and m are given in Table 6.4. Values for the total national production are given by the Stanford Research Institute or the *Minerals Yearbook*, U.S. Bureau of Mines.

Example

Problem: Estimate the fixed capital cost of a plant to produce 10^5 1b/year of tetraethylene pentamine. The present selling price is 60 cents/1b. Use the turnover ratio method.

Answer: The turnover ratio method is synonymous with the universal factor method. For general applicability a reasonable value for w is 1.0. Hence, the result is [from Eq. (6.1)]

$$I_F = \frac{\$0.60 \times 10^5}{1.0}$$

$$= \$60,000$$

A 5-min estimate of the capital cost is $60,000.

TABLE 6.4
SAMPLE VALUES OF CONSTANTS FOR SELLING PRICE RELATIONSHIPS*

	Average slope, $\langle m \rangle$	Deviation, σ for m	Average constant, $k/(S\bar{q})_1$	Deviation, $\sigma, k/(S\bar{q})_1$
Chemicals				
Organic acids	1.45	0.12	0.44	0.057
Alcohols	1.49	0.20	0.40	0.066
Aldehydes	1.60	0.20	0.33	0.047
Chlorinated hydrocarbons	1.64	0.23	0.34	0.083
Esters	1.46	0.34	0.51	0.15
Hydrocarbons	1.99	0.30	0.24	0.01
Inorganic acetates	1.55	0.22	0.35	0.09
Mixed organics	1.68	0.16	0.40	0.07
Organic acetates	1.47	0.50	0.48	0.14
Mean	1.76		0.31	
Minerals				
Asbestos	1.62		0.42	
Bauxite	1.51		0.36	
Feldspar	1.33		0.47	
Graphite	1.55		0.42	
Gypsum	1.46		0.40	
Phosphate rock	1.50		0.38	
Potash	1.62		0.35	
Mean	1.58		0.40	
Metals				
Aluminum	2.05		0.22	
Copper	1.66		0.44	
Pig iron	1.66		0.43	
Lead	1.31		0.83	
Magnesium	2.46		0.20	
Nickel	1.65		0.31	
Titanium	1.28		0.60	
Zinc	1.28		0.65	
Mean	1.62		0.43	

*From Massey and Black (1969) and Black (1971).

6.3 Cost Correlations for Fixed Capital Investments

Often the costs of plants and equipment have been correlated satisfactorily in terms of one variable.

Estimating costs of battery limit or green-field installations from cost correlations

For these correlations the details of the flow diagram are not necessary. We do, however, need to know the raw material or some identifying feature of the process when more than one process is available to produce the product.

The costs are usually correlated in terms of a production capacity, kilograms per year, metric tons per year, etc. That is, the correlating equation is of the form

$$(I_F)_1 = (I_F)_0 \left\{ \frac{\text{capacity factor}_1}{\text{capacity factor}_0} \right\}^n \tag{6.3}$$

The correlations are often reported as nomographs or graphs [see, for example, Dryden and Furlow (1966), Chilton (1960) and articles that appear periodically in *British Chemical Engineering* and *Chemical Engineering*]. However, tables of the correlating parameters are often more useful when mathematical calculations are required, as, for example, in economic balances. Hence, in this book tables of exponents are given. For each correlation we should know the range of applicability; the intercept; the exponent, n; the standard deviation, σ, and the time or date when the data apply.

Usually included in the battery limits or grass-roots costs are the additional costs required to modify or install the necessary auxiliary services; they represent the costs up to plant startup. Appendix B summarizes some of these cost correlation data.

Estimating costs of equipment from cost correlations

Sometimes an estimate is needed of the cost of a single piece of equipment rather than for a complete process. Cost correlations have been developed for individual pieces of equipment. Care needs to be taken, however, in interpreting the data because the cost of the equipment can be reported as FOB the manufacturer or fabricator, delivered or installed, and often the cost used is not clearly identified. A second point to note is that the cost is correlated in terms of a parameter that is not always capacity (as was the case for the fixed capital investment described in the preceding subsection). Thus, the cost of heat exchangers is often correlated in terms of surface area; refrigeration units, in tons; continuous thickeners, in feet; etc. The correlating parameter is chosen to give the most significant correlation. Appendix C provides some results of the correlations.

The common form of the correlating equation is

$$(I_F)_1 \text{ or } (E_{\text{FOB}})_1 \text{ or } (E_D)_1 \text{ or } (E_I)_1 = \{\text{cost of reference } 0\} \left\{ \frac{\text{capacity}_1}{\text{capacity}_0} \right\}^n \tag{6.4}$$

Thus, comparison of Eq. (6.3) with (6.4) suggests that the same general correlation techniques are used.

Extrapolation of data

Cost data from any of the correlations for processes or for individual equipment pieces may not apply to our particular problem because

The only data available are for plants or equipment of a different size or capacity; for example, we know the cost of a 500-ton/day plant but seek the cost of a 600-ton/day plant.

The costs are available for a different time than what we want; for example, we know the price of a heat exchanger in 1967, but we want to know the price now.

To account for changes in capacity and time, we have developed a set of averaging procedures that can be used as a last resort to estimate the pertinent costs when no other data are available.

Extrapolating the Size or Capacity. A study of Appendices B and C indicates, provided we can identify the correlating parameter, that we may account for the changes in capacity through

$$\frac{(I_F)_0}{(I_F)_1} = \left(\frac{\text{capacity}_0}{\text{capacity}_1}\right)^n \tag{6.5}$$

where n is the the scale-up exponent. Average values for n range from 0.6 to 0.7. This equation should not be applied if the capacity ratio exceeds 50 or if the capacities are outside the minimum-maximum size limits.

Adjusting for Variations with Time. Inflation indices have been developed to adjust costs for variations in time. The generalized equation is

$$\frac{(I_F)_1}{(I_F)_2} = \frac{(CI_1)}{(CI_2)} \tag{6.6}$$

where $(I_F)_\theta$ is the capital investment cost of a complete plant or of a piece of equipment at time θ. (In Eq. 6.6 the two specific times are $\theta = 1$ and $\theta = 2$.) Note that this equation does not apply to selling prices of chemicals. CI_θ is the value of the inflation index at time θ.

Each index is an average of some set of economic or cost factors believed to represent wages, fringe benefits, productivity, costs of materials, and general economic conditions. Each type of index uses different combinations of the ingredients. An index is a number that relates the average cost of these factors at some time θ relative to a base reference year when the costs are assigned a value of 100. Usually the indices available are 6–12 months behind times because of the time delay in gathering and correlating the information.

Many companies and countries develop their own indices. About 40 of the inflation indices published in the United States for building, general construction, plant construction, price of materials, wages and labor, transportation, equipment rental, and maintenance are listed and qualitatively evaluated in the *AACE Bulletin* (1967) or Waller (1969). For the engineer working in a company that does not develop its own inflation index, Table 6.5 lists the most pertinent indices. Annual average values of five of these indices are shown in Fig. 6.6 and Table 6.6. In Fig. 6.6 all indices are referred to a base year 1948–1949 = 100 to illustrate the differences and similarities

TABLE 6.5
SOME INFLATION INDICES

Title	Purpose and description	Availability	Rating
Marshall and Stevens Index [see Stevens (1947)]	Index for equipment cost compiled quarterly for industries. Developed primarily for insurance companies interested in changing values of plant assets. Index given as overall average for all industries and as averages for each of 8 process industries and 4 related industries. For each there is a generalized component breakdown: for example, process machinery, 25%; tankage, 24%; pipe and fittings, 12%; maintenance equipment, 2%; installation labor, 19%; power, 12%; administrative, 6% (excludes buildings and engineering manpower).	Published in each edition of *Chemical Engineering*; 1926 = 100.	The most applicable for equipment costs for Canada [Miller (1966)]. Seems highly rated in the U.S. [*AACE Bulletin* (1965)]
Chemical Engineering Magazine Index [see Arnold and Chilton (1963) and Chilton (1966)]	Developed primarily as a plant construction index. Provides separate indices for equipment, construction labor, buildings, engineering, and supervision, plus further breakdown of equipment costs. The overall index is a weighted average of these components. Sufficient details are supplied so that engineer can synthesize his own index.	Published in each edition of *Chemical Engineering*; 1957 – 59 = 100.	Rated highly by users primarily in the U.S. in *AACE Bulletin* (1965). Miller (1966) believes it has a downward bias over intermediate periods when applied in Canada.
Nelson Refinery Construction and Equipment Inflation Indices [see Nelson (1967a and b)]	Cost of duplicating a refinery installation at another date without reference to technological changes. Combination of 20% iron and steel, 8% nonmetallic building materials, 12% miscellaneous equipment, 39% skilled labor, and 21% unskilled labor. Also provides indices, through the components, for pumps, electrical machinery, internal combustion engines, instruments, and heat exchangers.	1946 = 100; published in *The Oil and Gas Journal*, first issue of each month with summaries in first issues of Jan., April, July, and Oct.	

TABLE 6.5 CONTINUED

Title	Purpose and description	Availability	Rating
Nelson True-Cost Index [see Nelson (1968a)]	Measures the relative cost of constructing a barrel of refining or process capacity at various dates. Attempts to account for the average technological improvements in processing. Data for refineries that are actually built.	Same as above	Of historical interest only for most chemical engineering purposes. Often data reported early in the literature use ENR index.
Engineering News Record Construction Index see [*Engineering News-Record* (1949)]	An average of 20 U.S. and 2 Canadian cities ( ) of the cost of 2500 (1500) lb of structural steel 1800 (1580 for Montreal and 1190 for Toronto), board feet of lumber, 6 (10) bbl of cement, and 200 hr of common labor. The bracketed terms refer to the quantity priced for the two Canadian cities.	*Engineering News-Record magazine*; base 1913 = 100	Seems to have general acceptance in the industry although in Canada Ontario has produced another index based on activated sludge as the secondary treatment unit.
EPA-STP Treatment Plant Index (PHS-STP or WPC-STP index) [see Federal Water Pollution Control Administration (1968)]	Index for complete primary and secondary domestic waste treatment plants. Monthly summaries prepared by the Division of Construction Grants, U.S. Environmental Protection Agency Index— excl land, engineering, legal and fiscal services, contingencies. Plant to treat a daily average flow of 1 million U.S. gal/day (maximum 2.5 million) with a BOD of 200 mg/l, recirculation ratio of 1.5/l and an overall BOD reduction of 92%. The plant incl. comminutor, bar screen, Parshall flume, grit chamber, primary and secondary clarifiers, high rate trickling filter, chlorine contact tank, primary and secondary digestors, sludge filter building incl. office and laboratory. Costs reported monthly for 20 U.S. cities and arithemetically averaged.	Reproduced in the WPCF Journal 1957 − 59 = 100	

163

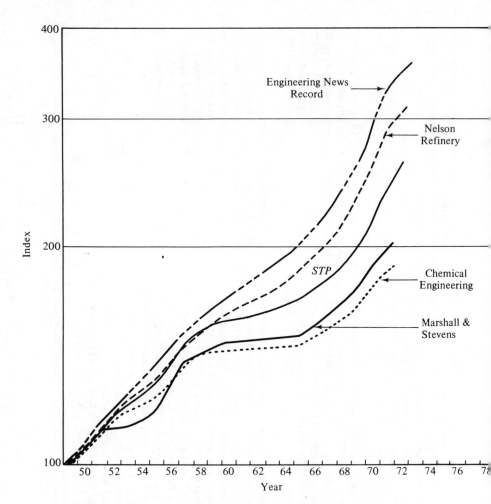

Figure 6.6. Comparison of inflation indices, base 1940 = 100.

among the inflation indices. Although any base year could be selected, base years of 1949 = 100 or 1959 = 100 are attractive because the inflation indices were relatively constant for these two periods. For a comparison, the displacement of one curve relative to the others does depend on the base year chosen so care is needed in assessing the relative trends. For example, for the base 1949 = 100, both the E.N.R. Construction Index and the Nelson Refinery Index seem to predict values higher than the Marshall and Stevens Equipment Cost Index and the Chemical Engineering Cost Index. However, for a base year 1959 = 100, the Nelson Refinery index follows the Chemical Engineering and Marshall and Stevens Indices closely after 1959 but falls below these two for times earlier than 1952. For a comparison with a base year of 1957–1959 = 100 see Norden (1968) or Chilton (1966).

Table 6.6
Annual Average Values for Inflation Indices

Year	Marshall and Stevens installed equipment index, 1926 = 100		Chemical Engineering plant construction cost index, 1957 = 100		Nelson refinery construction index, 1946 = 100		Engineering News-Record construction index, 1913 = 100	Environmental Protection Agency STP 1957 – 59 = 100, United States national average
	All industry	Process industry	Total plant	Equipment	Inflation	True cost		
1947	151	149	65	60	117	106	413	56
1948	163	162	70	66	133	108	460	65
1949	161	162	71	67	140	109	477	66
1950	168	167	74	70	146	110	510	69
1951	180	178	80	78	157	109	543	74
1952	181	179	81	78	164	109	569	77
1953	183	181	85	81	174	108	600	81
1954	185	184	86	82	180	105	628	83
1955	191	189	88	85	184	103	660	87
1956	209	206	94	93	195	102	690	92
1957	225	224	99	99	206	103	724	98
1958	229	228	100	100	214	104	759	102
1959	235	232	102	102	222	104	797	104
1960	238	237	102	102	228	103	824	105
1961	237	236	102	100	233	102	847	106
1962	239	237	102	101	238	100	872	107
1963	239	238	102	101	244	99	901	109
1964	242	241	103	101	252	100	936	110
1965	245	244	104	102	261	101	971	112

TABLE 6.6 CONTINUED

Year	Marshall and Stevens* installed equipment index, 1926 = 100		Chemical Engineering plant construction cost index, 1957 = 100		Nelson refinery construction index, 1946 = 100		Engineering News-Record construction index, 1913 = 100	Environmental Protection Agency STP 1957 – 59 = 100 United States national average
	All industry	Process industry	Total plant	Equipment	Inflation	True cost		
1966	252	252	107	105	273	103	1021	116
1967	263	260	110	108	288	104	1070	119
1968	273	268	114	112	304	108	1165	124
1969	285	283	119	116	329	106	1272	133
1970	303	301	126	123	365	118	1418	144
1971	321	321	132	130	406	118	1620	160
1972	332	332	137	135	429	122	1670	172
1973	344	344	144	142	468	127	1896	
1974								
1975								
1976								
1977								
1978								
1979								

*Sometimes referred to as the Marshall and Swift index.

Consider briefly some of the errors inherent in using the indices. First, the index used should be relative to the problem at hand; that is, the E.N.R. construction index should not be applied to the cost of heat exchangers or to the cost of a chemical plant to produce nylon because the ingredients in the index do not represent what is needed to construct heat exchangers or chemical plants. The second error is that the indices reflect past flow diagrams and design techniques. They do not reflect radical technological changes in process technology nor do they account for improvements in processing because of process refinements and learning about the process. That is, because of process improvements through learning the 1969 cost of catalytic cracking plants has decreased to less than 43% of the cost for a plant of the same capacity in 1946. Ethylene plants cost less than 40% of what they cost in 1958. Yet the Marshall and Stevens inflation indices for chemical plant construction have increased by 130% over that in 1946 and increased by 20% over that in 1958. For more discussion consult Norden (1968) and Nelson (1968a).

Hence, the indiscriminate use of inflation indices should be avoided, and some knowledge of the technological improvements in processing is essential. Some suggestions on preparing your own inflation index are given by Patterson (1969).

Discussion and implications

Consider now a brief discussion of the error in these methods, the use of scale factors, extensions to other problems, and the interrelationships between equipment and plant costs.

Errors and Simplifications. In general, we should be aware of four errors in this correlation method: the error of attempting to correlate cost in terms of a single independent variable (this could be called a correlation error), the error of representing the data by a simple exponential relationship (a linearization error), the error of not being able to account for technological or learning behavior in the correlations, and an error of special circumstances. Consider each in turn.

What we seek is a compromise between simplicity and accuracy. In general, we select the single independent variable to minimize the error. However, this often introduces error. For example, Figs. 6.7, 6.8, and 6.9 summarize data for Dowtherm furnaces, for storage tanks, and for crystallizers. The data are plotted against "the most significant independent variable" and were collected over a relatively short period of time. The spread of data indicates how difficult it is to represent some costs by simple correlations and hence the error involved in such simplicity.

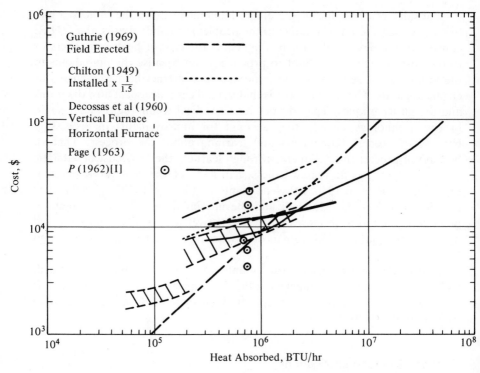

Figure 6.7. Cost correlation for Dowtherm furnaces (M and S Equipment = 300) to illustrate discrepancies among data.

Although this is a weakness of most of the cost correlations reported in Appendix C, few authors indicate the significance of their correlation or the error. Hence, in using cost correlations we should appreciate that there is a correlation error. [Other examples of the scatter in the data are shown by Bauman (1964), Fig. 4.1, p. 42; Denzler (1952); Guthrie (1969a) and Woods (1974).]

A second error arises because we attempt to correlate the data in the simple exponential form of Eq. (6.3). Often the data are as shown in Fig. 6.10, where the costs are not a simple exponential function, or as in Fig. 6.11, where there exists a central exponential portion bounded by two tails. Data such as that given in Fig. 6.10 are usually approximated by a series of straight lines or by an equation of the form

$$I_F = a\{\text{capacity} + b\}^{n^1} \tag{6.7}$$

where a and b are constants and n^1 is a scale-up exponent which should not be equated to n because different correlating equations are used.

On the other hand, the tail portions shown in Fig. 6.11 are usually not correlated. They represent the maximum and minimum size of equipment

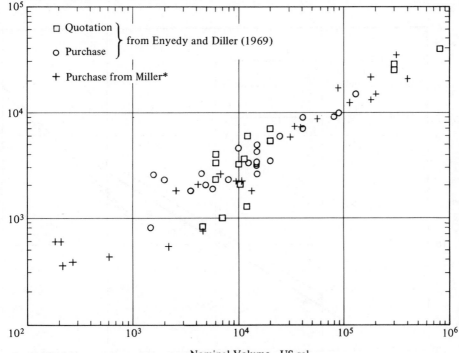

Figure 6.8. Cost data for vertical, cylindrical storage vessels. Conical roof (fixed) atmospheric pressure, carbon steel, M and S = 280 chemical industry. (*Data courtesy of C.A. Miller of Canadian Industries Ltd.*)

for usual production techniques. Thus, these tails of the cost correlations should be replaced by size constraints. Increasing capacity above the maximum size is obtained by duplicating the equipment. For sizes less than the minimum size, probably the minimum size should be purchased subject to the appropriate modifications. For example, in Fig. 6.11 the minimum commercial diameter bubble cap distillation column is about 3 ft and the maximum, for simple construction, is about 12 ft. These ranges vary as new fabrication techniques are developed. It is our responsibility to determine the appropriate ranges that apply today.

The third error concerns technological advances; when new methods of fabricating or constructing equipment are developed, the "old" cost correlations usually no longer apply. Since many cost correlations are updated by inflation indices, care is needed to ensure that the correlation refers to the fabrication techniques used today.

The error of special circumstances occurs because correlations can be based on the straight list price of the supplier, on the actual purchase price within a company, or a mixture of these. The price of actual sale depends on

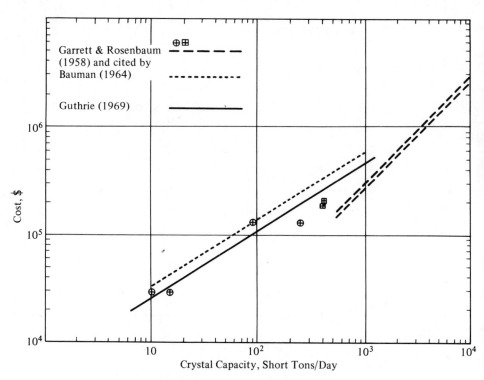

Figure 6.9. Cost correlation-data for crystallizers: mild steel, MS = 300. Delivered classification, growth type vacuum.

such factors as how anxious the supplier is for business, and on the past business relationships between the buyer and seller. Bulk buying is also a factor. This is discussed next.

Correction Factors. The data given in Appendix C reflect the accepted materials of construction (standard design with no special requirements) and do not allow for special contract prices. For the most part, the data are list prices. For example, the costs of distillation trays can be expressed as the purchase of a standard unit together with a correction chart to account for the bulk buying. Such a correction chart is shown in Fig. 6.12. Figure 6.13 shows a correction to the cost of heat exchangers for nonstandard length of exchanger tubes.

Extension to Other Problems and Interrelationship Between Equipment and Plant Costs. The costs of single pieces of equipment can be extended to the cost of convenient collections of equipment. Blair (1963), for example, illustrates how a combination of a typical reaction-separation train can be

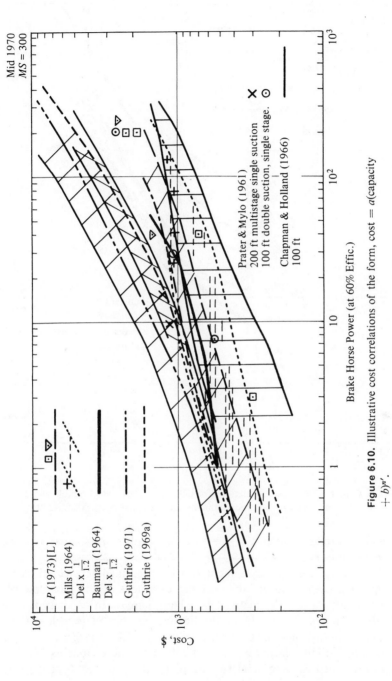

Figure 6.10. Illustrative cost correlations of the form, cost $= a$(capacity $+ b)^{n'}$.

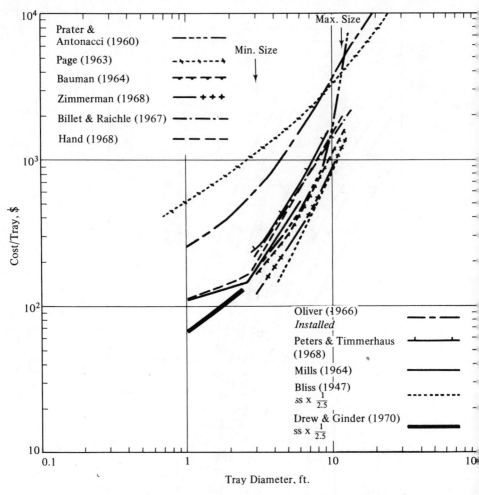

Figure 6.11. Cost correlations for delivered carbon steel bubble cap distillation trays with common commercial size constraints, MS = 280.

generalized to give the cost of the system as a function of capacity. An example is given in Fig. 6.14.

Indeed the costs of equipment can be combined to yield the cost of a complete process. Indeed, the scale-up exponent of the complete plant, n in Eq. (6.3), reflects the method by which increase in capacity is achieved. If larger capacity is gained by duplicating equipment, which is the major cost contributor, then the exponent approaches 1.0. If larger capacity can be gained by building larger equipment following the exponents listed in Appendix C, then the exponent for the plant approaches 0.6 or may be even smaller.

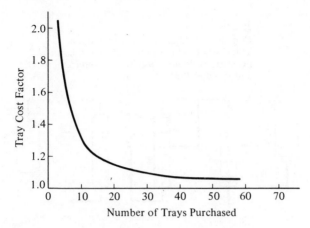

Figure 6.12. Sample of correction for unit costs because of bulk buying. (*Courtesy of A.G. Blair.*)

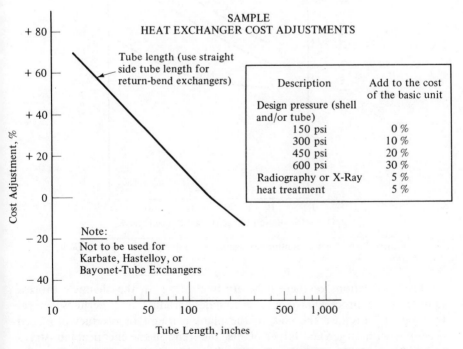

Figure 6.13. Correction factors for "Non-Standard Heat Exchangers." (*Courtesy A.G. Blair, 1963.*)

BASIS:

Complete Distillation System Including
Three Still Columns in Series, Calandrias,
Condensers, Pumps, and Feed, Product,
and Residue Tanks

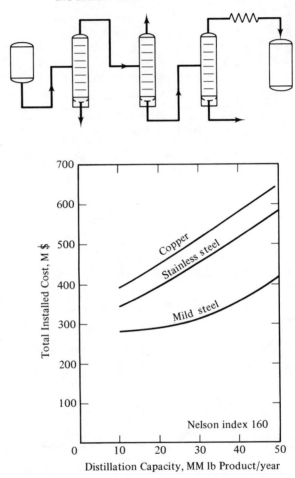

Figure 6.14. Cost of continuous distillation system. (*Courtesy A.G. Blair, 1963.*)

The implications of these data are interesting. In the chemical process industry, one process produces one major product and perhaps several by-products. Because the cost of the plant per unit of product produced *decreases* with larger and larger plants, the trend in the chemical industry is to build larger plants. On the other hand, in the metallurgy process industry, the variety of the finishing sections and the demand for different types of steel and steel products mean that flexibility is more important than the savings in fixed capital investment that could be gained by building a large-scale single-train unit.

In summary, correlations are available to provide estimates of the "average" costs of building a process (Appendix B) or buying equipment (Appendix C). These costs can be adjusted, with care, to specific problems at different times or sizes.

6.4 Factor Methods of Cost Estimation

The costs of plant installations as estimated from cost correlations (Section 6.3) are based on average, acceptable, past processing sequences. These do not allow the flexibility of changing process sequences. What is wanted might be the cost of a processing sequence radically different from the average. Hence, to permit this flexibility, estimation methods are developed to allow a process to be modularly connected together from whatever equipment the designer wishes. The sources of expenditure for a capital investment are summarized in Table 6.10. These cost contributions are often grouped as cost contributions to:

> the cost of the major pieces of equipment,
> cost of the *complete* installation of the equipment,
> auxiliary equipment necessary to make the process work,
> engineering and field expenses,
> contractor's fees and contingencies.

In the factor method, the cost of the major pieces of equipment is multiplied by an appropriate factor to yield the desired cost. Thus, the total fixed capital investment might equal the delivered equipment cost times a factor 5 (to account for the complete installation, the auxiliaries, the engineering and field expenses and the contractor's fees and contingencies).

There is a great variety of factors; their choice and use depends on the time and accuracy expected:

(a)   one factor for the average of all the cost contributions (about 5).
(b)   one factor for each of the cost contributions averaged over all equipment in the process (assume the piping cost factor is 0.40).
(c)   one factor for each of the cost contributions for each type of equipment (assume the piping cost factor for a pump with drive is 0.30).

Complicating the discussion of these methods is the fact that the value of the factor depends on the materials of construction of the equipment (or the alloy), and whether the equipment cost is expressed as f.o.b., delivered or installed equipment.

The input information required for the factor methods to work is the base cost. This, in turn, usually requires a knowledge of the equipment size, and this requires mass and energy balances for the proposed process sequence. Hence these methods cannot be used unless the equipment has been sized to allow for cost estimation of the equipment. First, the method of obtaining the cost of the major or main plant items of equipment is discussed. Then the various factor methods are described and compared.

Obtaining the equipment or base cost

Most factor methods use the cost of the main plant equipment as the base cost. The equipment cost can be expressed as installed, delivered, or FOB. The last means "free on board" the delivery vehicle where the equipment is manufactured or at a specified location.

The main decision is, What equipment should be included in the base cost? In general, the base equipment includes all equipment within the battery limits whose cost is as significant as the cost of a pump. That is, the cost of storage tanks, knockout drums, accumulators, pumps, and heat exchangers should contribute to the base equipment cost or the cost of the main plant items (MPI's).

A literal application of this criterion is, however, dangerous. The equipment included in the base case must also be that which requires piping, instrumentation, foundations, etc. We can see this constraint when we appreciate that the total base cost is multiplied by piping factors, for example, to obtain the investment cost.

The inclusion of some items in the base equipment or MPI's depends on the stage in the development of the flow diagram. Early in the development, the flow diagram shows major processing units; later, heat exchangers are indicated; then the details of pumps, steam ejectors, accumulators, and knockout drums are given. Eventually, details for intermediate storage, startup, shutdown, and disposal are provided. Through these different stages of development of the flow diagram the base equipment increases. This should be kept in mind in establishing the cost of the base equipment or MPI's.

Consider, for example, the selection of the base equipment for the alkylation plant shown in Fig. 6.15. From this diagram the equipment summarized in Table 6.7 would be selected. The additional pumps, storage, and intermediate equipment installed on the plant are given in Tables 6.8 and 6.9.

To attempt to obviate this difficulty, Miller (1964) gives a correction factor to be applied to the main equipment items to give the base equipment. The factor depends on the stage in flow diagram development when the estimate is made.

Early in the development of the process flow diagram the main plant item costs should be increased by 10–20% to account for additional equip-

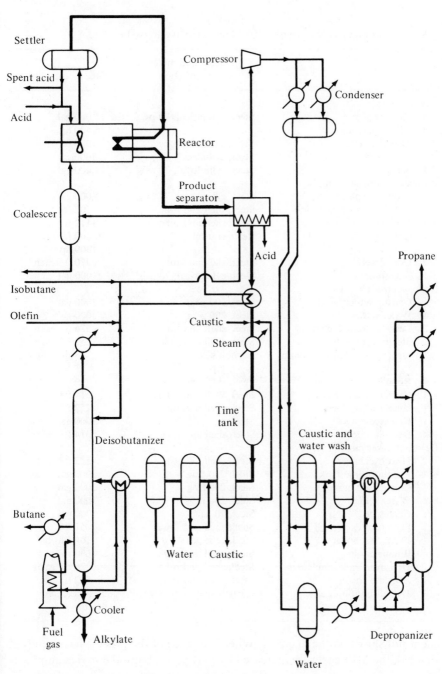

Figure 6.15. Flow diagram of alkylation plant. (*Courtesy of Crowe et al., "Chemical Plant Simulation," Prentice-Hall, Inc., 1971.*)

TABLE 6.7
EQUIPMENT SELECTED AS BASE EQUIPMENT BASED ON FIG. 6.15

		Comments and material of construction	Size or capacity
Reactor			
1	Reactor vessel	Steel, cylindrical, 70 psig	11,000 gal
1	Mixer in reactor		400 hp
1	H/E in reactor	Steel, shell and tube	7300 ft^2
1	Coalescer	Steel, cylindrical, 70 psig	1000 gal
1	Settler	Steel, cylindrical, 70 psig	13,000 gal
Product separation (initial)			
1	Product separator	Steel, cylindrical, 70 psig	15,000 gal
1	H/E in product separator	Steel, shell and tube	302 ft^2
1	Feed H/E	Steel, shell and tube	1112 ft^2
1	Compressor	Refrigeration	20,000 ft^3/min
			1000 hp
2	Condensers	Steel, shell and tube	2410 ft^2 each
1	Accumulator	Steel, cylindrical, 70 psig	1000 gal
Depropanizer circuit			
1	Caustic settler	Steel, 200 psig	3000 gal
1	Water settler	Steel, 200 psig	3000 gal
2	Feed-bottoms exchanger	Steel, shell and tube	526 ft^2 each
2	Steam feed heater	Steel, shell and tube	252 ft^2 each
1	Deprop distillation column	Carbon steel	48-in. diameter, 37 Koch
1	Reboiler	Steel, shell and tube	460 ft^2
1	Overhead condenser	Steel, shell and tube	1314 ft^2
1	Overhead cooler	Steel, shell and tube	252 ft^2
1	Coalescer	Steel	1000 gal
4	Bottoms cooler	Steel, shell and tube	1314 ft^2 each
Deisobutanizer circuit			
2	Heat exchanger	Steel, shell, 50 psig	522 ft^2 each
1	Reaction time tank	Steel, 200 psig	3000 gal
1	Caustic settler	Steel, 200 psig	3000 gal
1	Water settler	Steel, 200 psig	1000 gal
1	Coalescer	Steel, 70 psig	1000 gal
1	Feed heat exchanger	Steel, shell and tube	1051 ft^2
1	Furnace reboiler	Steel, tube gas fired	10^6 Btu/hr
1	Butane cooler	Steel, shell and tube	630 ft^2
2	DIB overheads condenser	Steel, shell and tube	6220 ft^2 each
2	Alkylate cooler	Steel, shell and tube	522 ft^2 each
1	DIB distillation column	Carbon steel, 150 psig	48 in., 80 Koch flexitrays

ment not shown in the diagram. When the scope of the process has been well defined, the MPI costs are increased by 1–10% to obtain the basic equipment costs.

A final warning concerning equipment costs is that some equipment will be purchased installed; some quotations will be for FOB prices and some for

TABLE 6.8

ADDITIONAL BASE EQUIPMENT INCLUDING PUMPS AND INTERMEDIATE
STORAGE THAT WOULD BE REASONABLE FOR THE DEVELOPMENT OF FIG. 6.15

	Comments and material of construction	Size or capacity
Reactor		
1 Acid feed pump		75 hp
1 Fresh acid storage	Steel, vertical cylinder, atm.	20,000 gal
Product separator		
1 Pump bottoms product separator		75 hp
1 Pump bottoms accumulator		100 hp
Depropanizer circuit		
1 Caustic settler circulating pump		3 hp
1 Water wash circulating pump		3 hp
1 Deprop reflux pump		20 hp
Debutanizer circuit		
1 Caustic settler Circulating pump		3 hp
1 Water wash circulating pump		3 hp
1 Bottoms pump		125 hp
1 Overhead pump		125 hp

TABLE 6.9

MISCELLANEOUS EQUIPMENT NEEDED FOR STARTUP AND OPERATIONS
FOR EXTENSIONS OF TABLE 6.8 AND FIG. 6.15

	Comments and material of construction	Size or capacity
Reactor		
1 Spent acid storage	Steel, vertical, cylindrical, atm.	20,000 gal
1 Spent acid pump		3 hp
1 Acid decanter	Steel, cylindrical, 70 psi	940 gal
1 Pump acid to neutralize caustic		10 hp
Product separator section		
1 Caustic storage	Steel	1000 gal
2 Caustic pumps		3 hp each
2 Utility water pumps		3 hp each
Depropanizer		
1 Caustic neutralizer tank	Steel, 4 psig	1000 gal
Deisobutanizer circuit		
1 Isobutane surge tank	Steel, cylindrical, 100 psig	20,000 gal

delivered equipment. Each should be kept separate because different sets of factors apply. For an order-of-magnitude appreciation of the differences,

Freight, taxes, and duties can amount to 5% on tax for domestic purchases and 10–12% on freight and 10–15% for duties for imports. These percentages are all based on material costs. Thus,

$$E_D = 1.1 \quad \text{to} \quad 1.25 E_{FOB}$$

where $\qquad E_D = $ cost of equipment delivered

Installation costs include uncrating, mounting, and hooking up to existing auxiliaries or utilities. These costs depend greatly on the type and size of the equipment. Overall averages are in the range 40–120%. Thus,

$$E_I = 1.4 \quad \text{to} \quad 2.2 E_D$$

where $\qquad E_I = $ cost of equipment installed

These are meant only to provide an early appreciation for the need to keep the different costs separate. We shall see later that the term "installed" has many meanings, and care is needed to prevent confusion.

Single-factor methods for scaling equipment costs to grass roots or battery limits costs

The complete installed cost is a single factor, f, times the base cost. The base cost can be FOB, delivered, or installed cost for the major equipment within the battery limits. Care needs to be taken to clarify which is the base cost referred to in the tabulated factors.

The single-factor method allows flexibility in the process equipment costing but averages the sources of expenditure, given in Table 6.10, into one

TABLE 6.10
SOURCES OF EXPENDITURE FOR A CAPITAL INVESTMENT

FOB cost of equipment and materials
Sales tax and import duties
Shipping and freight
Uncrating, construction of supports
Installation of manways, skirt supports, installation of supports,
    drains, pipes, supports for piping structural steel, foundations,
    piling, underground piping, electrical wiring and lighting,
    instruments, supports and instrument lines, insulation, painting,
    safety installations, control rooms, buildings to house equipment,
    maintenance stores and shops, warehouses and loading/unloading
    facilities, safety and security facilities, service facilities
    (utilities, offices, distribution, and sales), land, site preparation,
    costs to engineers and contractors, overheads during the construction
    period

---

single factor. This method is easy to remember and apply and takes little time but does not offer the most flexibility or the greatest accuracy. The accuracy is $\pm 30\%$.

The factors are listed in Table 6.11 and are applied according to the following equations:

$$I_F = fE$$

$$(I_F)_{BL} = [^{BL}f^{FOB}]E_{FOB} \quad \text{or} \quad (I_F)_{GR} = [^{GR}f^{FOB}]E_{FOB}$$
$$= [^{BL}f^D]E_D \qquad\qquad = [^{GR}f^D]E_D \qquad (6.8)$$
$$= [^{BL}f^I]E_I \qquad\qquad = [^{GR}f^I]E_I$$

The equation and factors used depend on whether the equipment cost is expressed as FOB, delivered, or installed. The total cost includes expenses for site preparation and the necessary auxiliaries but does not include the cost of land. These factors depend on whether the process is dominated by solids-handling equipment (identified by the symbol S in Tables 6.11 and 6.12); by piping, as would occur in fluids handling processes (symbol F); or by a mixture of the two processes (symbol S-F). For example, a fertilizer, lime, or cement kiln process would typify an S process; an acetic acid, butanol, or alkylation process would typify an F process; and a sulfuric acid, acetylene from carbide, alumina, or soy bean processing would represent an S-F process. The boundaries of these classifications are not clear, and judgment is required in the selection of the factor for the process under consideration.

Values for all three classifications are given in the tables so that the factor can be selected that is most applicable to the process being studied.

The original analysis of cost factors was done by Lang (1947a and b, 1948). He analyzed the costs of 14 plants; it is not clear whether this was for

TABLE 6.11
SINGLE FACTORS TO SCALE EQUIPMENT COSTS TO GRASS-ROOTS
AND BATTERY LIMIT PLANT COSTS INCLUDING AUXILIARIES BUT
EXCLUDING LAND FOR CARBON STEEL CONSTRUCTION

Type of plant	$^{GR}f^{FOB}$	$^{GR}f^D$	$^{GR}f^I$
Solid processing (S) Solid-fluid processing (S-F) Fluid processing (F)		4.3 (1968)	

Type of plant	$^{BL}f^{FOB}$	$^{BL}f^D$	$^{BL}f^I$
Solid processing (S)		3.8 (1963) 3.1 (1947)	2.2 (1967)
Solid-fluid processing (S-F)		4.1 (1963) 3.6 (1947)	2.5 (1967)
Fluid processing (F)		4.8 (1963) 4.7 (1947)	3.3 (1967)

grass-roots or battery limits installations. His three factors were 3.1 for solid processing, 3.6 for solid-fluid processing, and 4.7 for fluid processing. These Lang factors are still quoted by many authors [see Street and Corrigan (1967) for battery limits analysis].

The values reported in Table 6.11 are based on the extensive study made by Arnold and Chilton (1963) that forms the basis for the Chemical Engineering Inflation Index described in Section 6.3. The latter work considered grass roots, battery limits, and plant additions within an existing structual work.

Multiple-factor methods based on activity

In the preceding subsection we discussed the use of a single, average factor to represent the costs listed in Table 6.10. Consider now a more flexible system that permits us to select a weighting for each cost contribution.

First, the costs can be divided into four groups: the cost of the physical plant within the battery limits, the cost of the auxiliaries, the cost of engineering and field expenses, and the cost of the contractor's fees and an allowance for contingency. The major emphasis of this subsection and the next two subsections and Section 6.5 is on estimating the physical plant cost within the battery limit. Details of some methods of estimating the three other costs are given near the end of Section 6.4. However, some indication of these costs as functions of the base equipment costs is given in the present subsections so that the relationship between the single factor and the multiple factors will be clear.

The overall relationship among these costs is given in Fig. 6.16. Consider, then, the estimation of the factors to yield the total physical plant cost.

The cost contributions toward the physical plant cost, listed in Table 6.10, can be classified according to the total cost for a given activity (piping, painting, insulation, etc.) or divided further according to whether the cost contributions come from material or labor. In this subsection, we shall relate the factor to an activity and do not separate material from labor costs. Typical factors are listed in Table 6.12.

The cost factors have been correlated in terms of the delivered, installed, or FOB costs of the main plant items. Included in the main plant items are all equipment shown on the flow diagram that are as significant a cost item as pumps. That is, the cost of storage tanks, knockout pots, pumps, heat exchangers—any equipment that costs as much as the smallest pump—should contribute to the cost of the equipment or base cost.

In Table 6.12 the auxiliaries and site preparation are factors of the equipment cost except for Miller's analysis, which expresses the auxiliary costs as factors of the BL cost.

The relationship between Tables 6.11 and 6.12 should be noted. The sum of all factors in Table 6.12 equals the single factor given in Table 6.11.

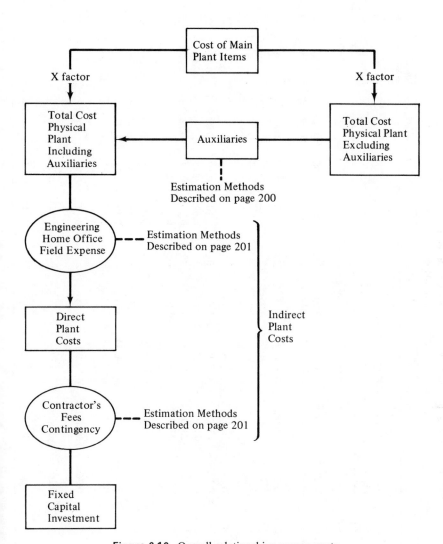

Figure 6.16. Overall relationships among costs.

Thus, for a battery limits installation of an S-F process the sum of the factors based on delivered equipment cost is 4.07, as reported in Table 6.12; in Table 6.11 a single factor of 4.1 is given.

Because of the variation of some of the factors, it is worthwhile discussing some of the features of Table 6.12. For a grass-roots, fluid installation, the factors for installation, foundations, and the battery limit buildings seem larger than we would expect. However, the cost of the auxiliaries has been

TABLE 6.12

FACTORS TO CONVERT EQUIPMENT COSTS INTO THE FIXED CAPITAL INVESTMENT FOR CARBON STEEL INSTALLATIONS

	Grass-roots plants						Battery limits installations				
	Crushing* plant	Conc.* plant	Typical† mineral processing	S-F	Domestic◊ waste treatment	F	S	S-F	F	General††	Metal-lurgy**
Equipment FOB											
Freight											
Delivered	1.00	1.00	1.00	1.00	1.00	1.00	1.00	1.00	1.00	1.00	1.00
Install	0.15	0.15	0.19–0.23	0.39–0.43	0.12	0.76	0.45	0.39	0.27–0.47	0.15	0.7–1.
Installed					0.77						
Piping	0.037	0.23	0.07–0.23	0.30–0.39	0.25	0.33	0.16	0.31	0.66–1.20	0.20	
Structural steel	0.17	0.23			0.08	0.28	—	—	0–0.13	—	
Foundations and reinforced concrete	0.01	0.03									
Insulation and painting										0.13	
Electrical	0.09	0.175	0.13–25	0.08–0.17	0.42	0.09	0.10	0.10	0.09–0.11	0.12	
Instruments	0.014	0.08	0.03–0.12	0.13	0.12‡	0.13	0.09	0.13		0.15	
BL building and service	0.11	0.23	0.33–0.50	0.26–0.35	0.10	0.45	0.25	0.39	0.18–0.34	0.60	1.1–1.4
Excavation and fill site preparation			0.03–0.18	0.08–0.22	0.16	—	0.13	0.10	0.10–		
Auxiliaries			0.14–0.30	0.48–0.55		incl above	0.40	0.55	0.70–	excluded	0.3–0.5
Total Physical plant				2.97		3.04	2.58	2.87	3.40–3.46	2.35	
Field expense		0.28	0.10–0.12	0.35–0.43	0.24		0.39	0.34	0.41		
Engineering		0.12		0.35–0.43	excluded	0.41	0.33	0.32	0.33		
Direct plant costs				3.71–3.75			3.30	3.53	4.14		
Contractor fees, overhead, profit	0.26	0.26	0.30–0.33	0.09–0.17	0.54		0.17	0.18	0.21		
Contingency	0.26	0.26	excluded	0.39			0.34	0.36	0.42		
I_F: **Total fixed capital investment**			2.3–3.28	4.27			3.81	4.07	4.87		3.1–3.9

*Katell (1973) †Balfour and Papucciyan (1972) ◊FWPCA (1968) ††Miller (1964) **Luth & Konig (1967) for OH. Auxil = casting bay ‡Filter media.

absorbed into these factors so that the factor for the total physical plant seems too small. We would expect the factor to be about 3.50 based on the corresponding data for the battery limits installations. The cost of the auxiliaries also seems to have been absorbed into the factors reported by Nelson (1960) for fluid processing. Hence, the young professional is cautioned to study all the data available so that he can select values that seem consistent for his problem. One feature of the table is that most analyses provide reasonably consistent factors for engineering (0.35), field expense (0.43), contractors fees (0.15), and contingency (0.36). Hence, the major problem is in determining the factor for the total physical plant. A more detailed breakdown of these factors for the total physical plant is given in Tables 6.13 and 6.14. In Table 6.13 the classification S, S-F, and F is not used specifically; rather a range is given for each classification. It should be noted that the analysis excludes sales tax and that the base cost includes an allowance for miscellaneous equipment. Thus, the delivered equipment cost (excluding sales tax) is increased by 1–20% (depending on the stage of development of the flow diagram and on the complexity of the process) to obtain the base cost. The factors are expressed as percentages rather than as fractions. The result obtained is the total physical plant cost within battery limits excluding the auxiliaries. A reasonable, average analysis of these factors, 2.35, is given, for comparison, in Table 6.12. We note that if an auxiliary factor of 0.50 is included, then the overall factor of 2.85 is certainly consistent with the factors suggested by other authors. Estimation procedures for the auxiliary costs will be given later in Section 6.4. Estimation procedures for the sales tax are given in Table 6.15. The factors in Table 6.14 apply to fluids processing only. Judgment is required in selecting the magnitude of the factors. Sokullu (1969) has suggested that the piping factor based on the delivered equipment cost can be calculated from the flow diagram from the correlation:

$$\text{factor} = 11 \text{ (pipe to equipment ratio)}^{1.6}$$

where the pipe to equipment ratio is the number of actual pipes carrying material (solids, liquids, gases, excluding elevators, conveyors, etc.) shown on the flow diagram divided by the number of major process equipment units. Drives are included with the pumps, compressors, etc. as *one* equipment unit. In general, most processes are built essentially of carbon steel. Indeed, these factors, presented in Tables 6.12, 6.13, 6.15, 6.16 and 6.17 are based on the assumption that the material of construction is primarily carbon steel. While experienced estimators can appropriately account for the presence of a significant amount of non-carbon-steel equipment by the judicious choice of factors in Tables 6.13 and 6.14, those learning to develop judgment should use the following method of Hirsch and Glazier (1960) if there is a significant portion of alloy materials used. To illustrate the effect alloy material has on the total factor, Clerk (1963) and Gallagher (1967) have suggested trends in

TABLE 6.13
FACTOR METHOD OF MILLER BASED ON DELIVERED EQUIPMENT COSTS = 100*

		Battery limit costs (range of factors in % of basic equipment), Average Unit Cost of M.P.I. (1958 $)†						
		Under $3000	$3000 to $5000	$5000 to $7000	7000 to $10,000	$10,000 to $13,000	$13,000 to $17,000	Over $17,000
Field erection of basic equipment	High percentage of equipment involving high field labor	23/18	21/17	19.5/16	18.5/15	17.5/14.2	16.5/13.5	15.5/13
	Average (mild steel equipment)	18/12.5	17/11.5	16/10.8	15/10	14.2/9.2	13.5/8.5	13/8
	High percentage of corrosion materials and other high-unit-cost equipment involving little field erection	12.5/7.5	11.5/6.7	10.8/6	10/5.5	9.2/5.2	8.5/5	8/4.8
Equipment foundations and structural supports	High: Predominance of compressors or mild steel equipment requiring heavy foundations			17/12	15/10	14/9	12/8	10.5/6
	Average: For mild steel fabricated equipment solids			12.5/7	11/6	9.5/5	8/4	7/3
	Average: For predominance of alloy and other high-unit-price fabricated equipment	7/3	8/3	8.5/3	7.5/3	6.5/2.5	5.5/2	4.5/1.5
	Low: Equipment more or less sitting on floor	5/0	4/0	3/0	2.5/0	2/0	1.5/0	1/0
	Piling or rock excavation				Increase above values by 25–100%			
Piping, includes ductwork, excludes insulation	High: Gases and liquids, petrochemicals, plants with substantial ductwork	105/65	90/58	80/48	70/40	58/34	50/30	42/25
	Average for chemical plants: Liquids, electrolytic plants	65/33	58/27	48/22	40/16	34/12	30/10	25/9
	Liquids and solids	33/13	27/10	22/8	16/6	12/5	10/4	9/3
	Low: Solids	13/5	10/4	8/3	6/2	5/1	4/0	3/0

*Courtesy C. A. Miller of Canadian Industries Ltd. and the American Association of Cost Engineers.

†The average unit cost of the main plant items is the total cost of the M.P.I. divided by the total number of items.

186

TABLE 6.13 CONTINUED

		Battery limit costs (range of factors in % of basic equipment), Average Unit Cost of M.P.I. (1958 $)						
		Under $3000	$3000 to $5000	$5000 to $7000	$7000 to $10,000	$10,000 to $13,000	$13,000 to $17,000	Over $17,000
Insulation of equipment only	Very high: Substantial mild steel equipment requiring lagging and very low temperatures	13/10	11.5/8.5	10/7.4	9/6.2	7.8/5.3	6.8/4.5	5.8/3.5
	High: Substantial equipment requiring lagging and high temperatures (petrochemicals)	10.3/7.5	9/6.3	7.8/5.2	6.7/4.2	5.7/3.4	4.7/3.8	4.8/2.5
	Average for chemical plants	7.8/3.4	6.5/2.6	5.5/2.1	4.5/1.7	3.6/1.4	2.9/1.1	2.2/.8
	Low	3.5/0	2.7/0	2.2/0	1.8/0	1.5/0	1.2/0	1/0
Insulation of piping only	Very high: Substantial mild steel piping requiring lagging and very low temperatures	22/16	19/13	16/11	14/9	12/7	9/5	6/3.5
	High: Substantial piping requiring lagging and high temperatures (petrochemicals)	18/14	15/12	13/10	11/8	9/6	7/4	4.5/2.5
	Average for chemical plants	16/12	14/10	12/8	10/6	8/4	6/2	4/2
	Low	14/8	12/6	10/5	8/4	6/3	4/2	2/1
All electrical‡ except building, lighting, and instrumentation	Electrolytic plants, includes rectification equipment		55/42	50/38	45/33	40/30	35/26	
	Plants with mild steel equipment, heavy drives, solids	26/17	22.5/15	19.5/12.5	17/10	14/8.5	12/7	10/6
	Plants with alloy or high-unit-cost equipment, chemical and petrochemical plants	18/9.5	15.5/8.5	13/6.5	11/5.5	9/4.5	7.3/3.5	6/2.5

‡Note: Above figures include to 3 % for BL outside lighting, which is not covered in building services.

187

TABLE 6.13 CONTINUED

		Battery limit costs (range of factors in % of basic equipment), Average Unit Cost of M.P.I. (1958 $)						
		Under $3000	$3000 to $5000	$5000 to $7000	$7000 to $10,000	$10,000 to $13,000	$13,000 to $17,000	Over $17,000
Instrumentation§	Substantial instrumentation, central control panels, petrochemicals		58/31	46/24	37/18	29/13	23/10	18/7
	Miscellaneous chemical plants		32/13	26/10	20/7	15/5	11/3	8/2
	Little instrumentation, solids		21/9	17/7	13/5	10/3	7/2	5/1
Miscellaneous, includes site preparation, painting, and other items not accounted for above	Top of range—large complicated processes; bottom of range—smaller, simple processes	Range for all values of basic equipment is 6 to 1%						

Building evaluation when most of process units are located inside buildings

	High, brick and steel	Medium	Low, economical	Evaluation
Quality of construction	+4	+2	0	
	Very high unit cost equipment	Mostly alloy steel	Mixed materials	Mostly carbon steel
Type of equipment	−3	−2	−1	0
	Very high	Intermediate	Atmosphere	
Operations pressures	−2	−1	0	

Building class = algebraic sum =

Buildings—architectural and structural, excludes building services¶

§*Note:* Total instrumentation cost does not vary a great deal with size and hence is not readily calculated as a percentage of basic equipment. This is particularly true for distillation systems. If in doubt, detailed estimates should be made.

¶*Note:* When building specifications and dimensions are known, a high-grade building cost projects is recommended. ...

TABLE 6.13 CONTINUED

Building class		Average unit cost of M.P.I. (1958 $)						
		Under $3000	$3000 to $5000	$5000 to $7000	$7000 to $10,000	$10,000 to $13,000	$13,000 to $17,000	Over $17,000
Most of process Units inside buildings	+2	92/68	82/61	74/56	67/49	59/44	52/39	46/33
	+1 to −1	72/49	62/43	56/38	51/33	45/29	41/26	36/21
	−2	50/37	44/33	40/29	35/25	30/21	27/18	23/15
Open-air plants with minor buildings		37/16	32/13	28/11	24/8	20/6	17/4	14/2

Building services**	High	Normal	Low
Compressed air for general service only	4	1½	0.5
Electric lighting	18	9	5
Sprinklers	10	6	5
Plumbing	20	12	3
Heating	25	16	8
Ventilation:			
Without air conditioning	18	8	0
With air conditioning	45	35	25
Total overall average***	85	55	20

The above factors apply to those items normally classified as building services. They do not include

1. Services located outside the building such as substations, outside sewers, and outside water lines, all of which are considered to be outside the battery limit, as well as outside the building.

2. Process services.

**Note: The following factors are for battery limit (process) buildings only and are expressed in percentage of the building—architectural and structural cost. They are not related to the basic equipment cost.

***The totals provide the ranges for the type of building involved and are useful when the individual service requirements are not known. Note that the overall averages are not the sum of the individual columns.

189

Table 6.14
Bach's Factors for Cost Components for Fluid Processes*

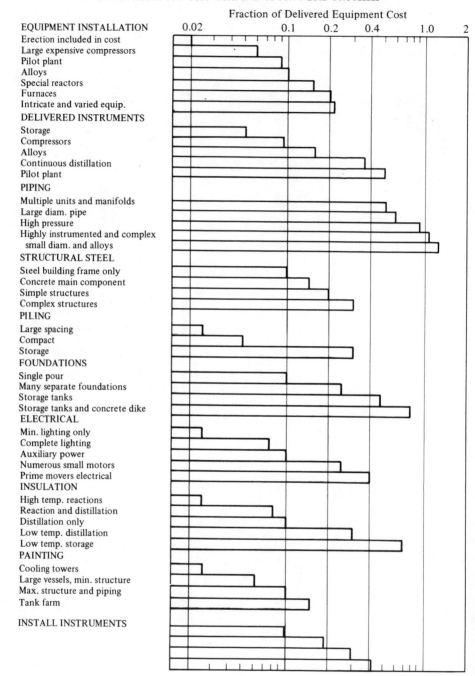

Fraction of Delivered Equipment Cost

EQUIPMENT INSTALLATION
Erection included in cost
Large expensive compressors
Pilot plant
Alloys
Special reactors
Furnaces
Intricate and varied equip.

DELIVERED INSTRUMENTS
Storage
Compressors
Alloys
Continuous distillation
Pilot plant

PIPING
Multiple units and manifolds
Large diam. pipe
High pressure
Highly instrumented and complex
  small diam. and alloys

STRUCTURAL STEEL
Steel building frame only
Concrete main component
Simple structures
Complex structures

PILING
Large spacing
Compact
Storage

FOUNDATIONS
Single pour
Many separate foundations
Storage tanks
Storage tanks and concrete dike

ELECTRICAL
Min. lighting only
Complete lighting
Auxiliary power
Numerous small motors
Prime movers electrical

INSULATION
High temp. reactions
Reaction and distillation
Distillation only
Low temp. distillation
Low temp. storage

PAINTING
Cooling towers
Large vessels, min. structure
Max. structure and piping
Tank farm

INSTALL INSTRUMENTS

*From Bach (1958).

TABLE 6.15
ESTIMATING SALES TAX ON MATERIAL COSTS

Country	Suggestion
United States	Guthrie (1969a) suggests 3% of direct material dollars as overall average
Canada	1969 sales tax conditions were Federal: 12% on materials (usually included in quoted prices but the engineer should be clear about this) Provincial: Varies from province to province with 5% of material costs for buildings and services as reasonable average

Estimations of material content [Miller (1966)]

	Within BL	Auxiliaries
Total material	70–80% of total physical plant cost, X	65–75% of auxiliary cost
Material in buildings and services	60–70% of building costs	65–75% of auxiliary cost

TABLE 6.16
TYPICAL ANALYSIS OF THE FACTORS WITH A SEPARATION OF MATERIALS AND LABOR*

	Total factor	f_m, materials	f_l, labor
Equipment delivered	1.00		
Installation	0.09		0.09
Instruments (installed)	0.13	0.09	0.04
Piping	0.29	0.155	0.13
Foundations and steel	0.18	0.08	0.10
Insulation painting	0.11	0.025	0.085
Electrical	0.18	0.06	0.12
BL building	0.21	0.13	0.08
Site preparation	0.08		
Auxiliaries	0.55		
Physical plant cost	2.82		
Engineering and home office	0.31	0.01	0.30
Field expense	0.43	0.30	0.12
	3.56		
Contractor's fees	0.17		
Contingency	0.39		
Fixed capital investment	4.12		

*Based on Bauman (1964) for essentially carbon steel equipment.

TABLE 6.17
RELATIVE LABOR RATIOS IN DIFFERENT COUNTRIES

	Construction labor cost in 1961 (U.S.$)			Content index			Labor ratio: product of cost and content and accounting for work week		
U.S. average	1.00*	1.0†	1.0‡	1.0*	1.0†	1.0‡	1.00*	1.0†	1‡
Canada	0.62	—	0.78	1.5	—	1.11	1.08	—	0.86
England	0.32	0.58	0.24	1.7	2.0	1.54	0.69	1.16	0.37
Germany	0.36	0.59	0.24	2.4	1.82	1.33	1.08	1.08	0.32
Brazil	0.09	—	—	11.4	—	—	1.23	—	—
France	0.23	0.58	0.41	2.8	2.0	1.54	0.81	1.16	0.63
Italy	0.23	0.58	0.25	4.7	2.5	1.33	1.35	1.45	0.34
Australia	0.31	—	—	1.7	—	—	0.66	—	—
Mexico	0.12	—	—	10.6	—	—	1.54	—	—
Spain	0.07	—	—	—	—	—	—	—	—
Japan	0.13	0.69	0.09	5.3	3.33	1.54	1.00	2.30	0.14
India	0.043	—	—	—	—	—	—	—	—

*Bauman (1962).
†Kastens (1962).
‡Grosselfinger (1962a).
For other discussion, see Nelson (1963).

the factor as shown in Fig. 6.17. The ordinate is the total Lang or single factor by which the delivered equipment cost of the alloy equipment should be multiplied to give the total investment. The abscissa is the ratio of the FOB cost of the equipment of alloy material to that for carbon steel. Some values are given in the table with Fig. 6.17, and details are provided for the different types of equipment by Woods (1974). This figure is illustrative only.

Hirsch and Glazier (1960) correlate their battery limit physical plant costs for fluid and for fluid-solid systems by the following correlations, which require little judgment in selecting the magnitude of the factors:

$$^{BL}[\text{physical plant cost}]_F = E^1_{FOB}(1 + f_{piping} + f_{labor} + f_{misc.}) + E^1_{install.} + C_{alloy} \tag{6.9}$$

$$^{BL}[\text{physical plant cost}]_{F-S} = E^1_{FOB}(1 + f_{misc.}) + (E^1_{FOB})_f(f_{piping} + f_{labor})_{fluid} + (E^1_{FOB})_s(0.65 f_{labor})_{solid} + E^1_{install.} + C_{alloy} \tag{6.10}$$

In their correlations all the equipment costs are for carbon steel equipment unless the material of construction was chosen for some reason other than corrosion. Then a correction factor is applied, C_{alloy}. In these expressions, the installed equipment $E^1_{install}$, is separated from the equipment that is

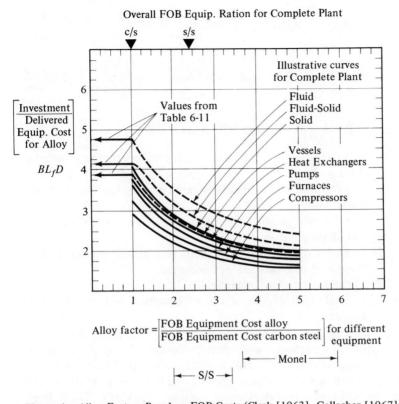

Figure 6.17. Effect of materials of construction on single factor to scale delivered equipment cost to the complete investment value. Illustrative only.

Illustrative Alloy Factors Based on FOB Costs (Clerk [1963], Gallagher [1967] and P)

Alloy	Vessels	Heat Exchangers	Pumps	Furnaces	Mixers
Carbon steel	1	1	1	1	1
Stainless steel 304	2.50 to 2.75	3.2	1.8	1.5	1.12
					1.17
Stainless steel 316	3.0	3	2		1.4
Monel	4 to 6.5	3.6	2.5		

priced FOB, E^1_{FOB}. For the fluid-solid system the engineer uses judgment to identify the equipment that essentially handles solids.

With reference to Table 6.12, they found that all the factors contributing to the physical plant cost could be reduced to three: a piping factor, a labor factor, and a miscellaneous factor. These factors could, in turn, be represented by

$$\log_{10} f_{\text{labor}} = 0.635 - 0.154 \log_{10} 0.001 E^1_{\text{FOB}} - 0.992 \frac{e}{E^1_{\text{FOB}}} + 0.506 \frac{f}{E^1_{\text{FOB}}}$$
(6.11)

$$\log_{10} f_{\text{piping}} = -0.266 - 0.014 \log_{10} 0.001 E^1_{\text{FOB}} - 0.156 \frac{e}{E^1_{\text{FOB}}} + 0.556 \frac{p}{E^1_{\text{FOB}}}$$
(6.12)

$$f_{\text{misc.}} = 0.344 + 0.033 \log_{10} 0.001 E^1_{\text{FOB}} + 1.194 \frac{t}{E^1_{\text{FOB}}} \qquad (6.13)$$

where e = FOB cost of all the heat exchangers less the incremental cost
of alloy
f = FOB cost of all field fabricated vessels less the incremental
cost of alloy
p = FOB cost of all pumps including drives less the incremental
cost of alloy
t = FOB cost of all tower shells less incremental cost of alloy
(trays and internals are not included)
E^1 = carbon steel equipment cost
C_{alloy} = total dollar value of the incremental cost of alloy for all
equipment.
In their correlations, they base all costs on carbon steel except where an
alloy is required for purposes *other* than corrosion. Hence, if the FOB cost
of a stainless steel tower is \$173,000 but the alloy was chosen for corrosive
reasons, then the cost contribution to both t and to the total FOB cost, E^1_{FOB},
should be based on a carbon steel tower, costing say \$32,000. The difference,
\$141,000, is a component of C_{alloy}. Detailed examples are given by Hirsch
and Glazier (1960). A nomograph has been developed by Walas (1961).
Off-site auxiliaries and the indirect expenses need to be added to the physical
plant cost.

Multiple-factor methods that separate materials and labor

The methods described here are similar to those in the preceding subsection except that labor and materials are considered separately. Hence,
we can allow for the efficiency and costs of labor in different parts of the
country and in different countries.
Many authors give examples of methods that separate the cost contributions of material and labor: Arnold and Chilton (1963), Happel (1958),
Bauman (1964), and Guthrie (1969a). To illustrate the approaches taken,
the method of Bauman will be described.

Bauman subclassifies most components of Table 6.12 into material and labor components. His data are quoted as ranges and medians of the percentage of the total fixed capital investment in his Tables 11.3 and 11.4. In Table 6.16, for illustrative purposes, his data are normalized and expressed as factors of the equipment cost. Where the breakdown is not apparent the total factor is left intact, for example, for the site preparation and the auxiliaries. Since the installation and building components could be further divided into foundations, steel, insulation, painting, etc., this was included. The data apply to a grass-roots installation.

Once we know the relative factors for materials and labor, then we can account for both inflation of material prices and changes in labor costs and efficiency. To illustrate why the separation is useful, consider the simplified problem of estimating the capital cost for a new set of construction conditions.

The equation we could use to estimate the cost of the physical plant could be

$$\text{[physical plant cost]} = \frac{(CI)}{(CI)_0} E_D(\Sigma f_m) + E_D(\Sigma f_l)\left(\frac{DI_1}{DI_0}\right)\left(\frac{LI_1}{LI_0}\right)$$

(6.14)

where CI = inflation index for materials or construction as described in Table 6.6.

Σf_m = sum of all the material factors
Σf_l = sum of all the labor factors
DI = content index for labor
LI = cost index for labor

Subscripts 0 and 1 refer to reference conditions and conditions under study, respectively. The content index refers to the relative number of hours it takes to complete a job. The higher the index, the longer it takes. The index could be high because of adverse working conditions (intense heat or cold, humidity, high altitude, etc.) and because tools and labor-saving devices are not available.

Table 6.17 summarizes some values for the content and cost indices for labor. The product of the content and cost indices and the total number of hours paid for but not worked is the labor ratio.

Example 6.1:   The cost of a 50t/day plant built in Toronto, Canada in 1964 is $300,000.

Problem: Estimate the cost of a 100t/day plant to be built in 1969 in Mexico. Assume that the cost distribution is represented by the data in Table 6.16.

Sample Solution: The breakdown of the cost contributions, based on the factors in Table 6.16, is

$$\text{physical plant cost} = \$300,000 \frac{2.82}{4.12} = \$205,000$$

$$\text{delivered equipment} = \$300,000 \frac{1.00}{4.12} = \$72,800$$

$$\begin{array}{l}\text{materials costs (assuming}\\ \text{50\% for site preparation}\\ \text{and auxiliaries)}\end{array} = \$300,000 \frac{0.855}{4.12} = \$62,200$$

$$\begin{array}{l}\text{labor costs (assuming 50\%}\\ \text{for site preparation and}\\ \text{auxiliaries)}\end{array} = \$300,000 \frac{0.960}{4.12} = \$70,000$$

$$\begin{array}{l}\text{percentage cost of indirect}\\ \text{expenses}\end{array} = \frac{\text{total} - \text{physical plant cost}}{\text{total cost}}$$

$$= \frac{4.12 - 2.82}{4.12} \times 100$$

$$= 31.5\%$$

From Table 6.17, values for the labor ratio for Canada and Mexico are, respectively, 1.08 and 1.54. For illustrative purposes only, assume that the material costs are the same in the two countries. Hence an estimate of the physical plant cost is

$$X = 72,800 + 62,200 + 70,000 \times \frac{1.54}{1.08}$$

$$= \$235,000$$

If the indirect costs are still 31.5% of the fixed investment, then the fixed investment is

$$\text{fixed investment} = \frac{\$235,000}{1 - 0.315}$$

$$= \$343,000$$

Comments: The purpose of this problem was solely to demonstrate why it is beneficial to separate material and labor contributions. Details of the actual calculational procedures are given in more advanced texts, such as Bauman (1964).

More sophisticated factor methods or the bare module approach

In the previous two subsections we introduced factors that converted the total cost of the equipment into the cost of the complete plant. These factors are average factors; for example, the average cost of the piping is the total equipment cost times an average factor. In this section we shall introduce factors that give the cost of piping, installation, etc., for individual types of equipment. Now, instead of multiplying the sum of the equipment costs by factors averaged over the whole plant, we shall sum the products of the costs of individual equipment units by factors representative of that unit.

This can be expressed in terms of equations. In the previous two subsections the physical plant cost was given as

$$X = \sum_i f_i \sum_i E_{Di} \qquad (6.15)$$

In this section, the physical plant cost is given as

$$X = \sum_i f_i E_{Di} + \text{site development} + \text{buildings} + \text{auxiliaries} \qquad (6.16)$$

Table 6.18(a) summarizes average factors for the major equipment units. Details for other equipment units are given in Guthrie (1969a), and Woods (1974). His field installation factors yield the physical unit cost excluding site preparation and auxiliaries. Note that Guthrie separates the contributions from labor and materials. Earlier data by Hand (1958) are given, for comparison, in Table 6.18(b). Other data are given by Wroth (1960).

The major developer of the module costing approach has been Guthrie. He bases all his calculations on the FOB equipment cost, E_{FOB}. To this, via factors, is added the total material needed to complete the module. The total he calls $(E_{\text{FOB}} + m)$ or M.

To install the module directly requires labor and hence, from a knowledge of labor to material cost ratio (L/M), or a direct calculation of the labor (L), the total $(L + M)$ factor can be determined. The "indirects" cost of freight, taxes, insurance, engineering and field expense are added to $(L + M)$ to yield the bare module cost (BM). This excludes contingency, contractor fees, and auxiliaries, site development, land and industrial buildings. The total module factor would include an allowance for these.

Summary of the factors used to estimate the physical plant cost

In this section factors methods are described for estimating the capital costs of a plant given as a base cost the FOB, delivered, or installed cost of the main plant equipment. The overall outline of the factor methods is given in Figs. 6.16 and 6.18.

The simplest and sloppiest method is to use a single factor that scales up the base cost to the complete capital investment, I_F. Next in order of sloppiness is a set of component factors that are averages over all types of processes. Such average component factors can be used to determine either the physical plant cost, X, or the complete fixed capital investment, I_F. In this method part of the difficulty is in developing judgment as to which value of a range of values should be selected for each factor.

TABLE 6.18(a)

FACTORS FOR INDIVIDUAL PIECES OF EQUIPMENT BASED ON FOB COST OF EQUIPMENT = 1.00
(BASED ON CARBON STEEL)*

	Furnaces	Exchangers		Vessels		Pump and driver	Compressors and driver	Tanks
		Shell-tube	Air-cooled	Vertical	Horizontal			
FOB Equipment	1.00	1.00	1.00	1.00	1.00	1.00	1.00	1.00
Piping	0.18	0.46	0.18	0.61	0.42	0.30	0.21	
Concrete	0.10	0.05	0.02	0.10	0.06	0.04	0.12	
Steel	—	0.03	—	0.08	—	—	—	
Instruments	0.04	0.10	0.05	0.12	0.06	0.03	0.08	
Electrical	0.02	0.02	0.12	0.05	0.05	0.31	0.16	
Insulation	—	0.05	—	0.08	0.05	0.03	0.03	
Paint	—	—	0.01	0.01	0.01	0.01	0.01	
Total materials $(E + m) = M =$	1.34	1.71	1.38	2.05	1.65	1.72	1.61	1.20
Erection and setting (L)	0.30	0.63	0.38	0.95	0.59	0.70	0.58	0.13
X, excluding site preparation and auxiliaries ($M + L$)	1.64	2.34	1.76	3.00	2.22	2.42	2.19	1.33
Freight, insurance, and taxes	—	0.08	—	0.08	0.08	0.08	0.08	0.08
Engineering and home office, construction overhead, or field expense	0.60	0.95	0.70	0.22	0.92	0.97	0.89	
Total or Bare Module Factor (BM)	2.24	3.37	2.46	4.30	3.22	3.47	3.16	

*From Guthrie (1969a).

TABLE 6.18(b)

FACTORS FOR INDIVIDUAL PIECES OF EQUIPMENT BASED ON FOB COST OF EQUIPMENT $= 1.00$
TO OBTAIN TOTAL BATTERY LIMIT COST (BASED ON CARBON STEEL)*

	Furnaces†	Exchangers	Vessels		Pump and driver	Compressors and driver	Instruments	Miscellaneous equipment
			Columns	Pressure				
FOB Equipment	1.00	1.00	1.00	1.00	1.00	1.00	1.00	1.00
Piping	0.10	0.50	0.60	0.65	0.30	0.15	0.50	0.15
Concrete	0.10	0.05	0.10	0.05	0.05	0.05	0.05	0.05
Steel	—	0.25	0.15	0.20	—	—	0.20	0.10
Instruments	—	—	—	—	—	—	—	—
Electrical	0.05	0.03	0.05	0.05	0.75	0.15	0.40	0.10
Insulation	0.07	0.14	0.25	0.12	0.07	0.07	0.07	0.07
Paint	0.03	0.03	0.03	0.03	0.03	0.03	0.03	0.03
Building	—	—	—	—	0.10	0.15	0.15	0.10
Total materials (M)	1.35	2.00	2.18	2.10	2.30	1.60	2.40	1.60
Erection and setting labor (L)	0.15	0.65	0.82	0.90	0.70	0.30	0.60	0.30
X, total physical cost ($M + L$)	1.50	2.65	3.00	3.00	3.00	1.90	3.00	1.90
Indirects	0.50	0.85	1.00	1.00	1.00	0.60	1.00	0.60
Total factor for BL or BM factor	2.00	3.50	4.00	4.00	4.00	2.50	4.00	2.50

*From Hand (1958).
†Based on erected cost.

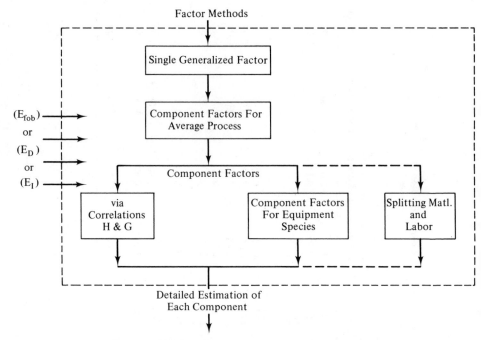

Factor Methods

Figure 6.18. Overall relationships among factor methods.

It is partly for this purpose that more complicated methods of assessing the factors for each components were developed. On the one hand, Hirsch and Glazier develop correlations that relate the component factors to the types of equipment that make up the major pieces of equipment. Alternatively, Hand (1958) and Guthrie (1969a) provide component factors for each type of equipment. By these methods, more mathematical methods are applied to the selection of the values for the component factors.

In the long run, better estimates of the component factors can be made if we know the relative contributions of materials and labor to each component factor. Although this may appear to be rather specialized now, improved estimation will be based on accounting for these two separate contributions. We should note that what we are trying to estimate is the cost I_F. What many of these methods yield is physical plant cost, X. Hence, some factor methods or correlations are needed for the auxiliaries and the indirect expenses to yield I_F. These will be discussed next.

Estimating the costs of auxiliaries

Estimates of the total capital cost for either a grass-roots or battery limits installation normally should include the additional costs of modifying or installing the necessary auxiliary services.

The cost of auxiliaries can be expressed as a fraction of the equipment cost (as was done in Table 6.12), or expressed as fractions of the investment or correlated as packaged units.

Table 6.19 summarizes the cost correlations of generalized auxiliaries as functions of the total physical plant cost within the battery limit. Table 6.20 summarizes cost correlations of specific auxiliary items as a function of the total fixed capital investment, I_F.

Appendix D is a summary of cost correlations of specific auxiliary items. These correlations assume that this auxiliary is not a modification to existing equipment.

Estimating other costs for fixed capital investment or the indirects

Other costs that contribute to the fixed capital investment are engineering, field expense, contractor's fees, and contingencies. Sometimes they are referred to as the indirect expenses.

TABLE 6.19
COST CORRELATIONS FOR AUXILIARIES AS FUNCTIONS OF TOTAL PHYSICAL
PLANT COST WITHIN BATTERY LIMITS, X*

| | Factors of battery limit plant cost X | | |
| | | Battery limits installation on existing site | |
Auxiliary	Grass-roots installation	Chemical plant	Refineries
Storage and handling (S & H)			
Low	2	0	
Average	15–25	2–6	
High	70	20	
	20–36†	16–25†	6–13†
Utilities (U)			
Low	15	3	
Average	20–30	6–14	
High	50	30	
	38–53†	7–25†	13–19†
Services expressed as % of BL + S & H + U			
Low	5	0	
Average	10–16	2–6	
High	20	15	
	14–29†	3–21†	0–6†

*Data from Miller (1964).
†Dickens and Douglas (1960).

TABLE 6.20

COST CORRELATIONS FOR AUXILIARIES AS A PERCENTAGE OF THE TOTAL
FIXED CAPITAL INVESTMENT, I_F. (These data apply for grass-roots installations)*

Auxiliary	Range	Median (%)
Auxiliary buildings	3.0–9.0	5.0
Steam generation	2.6–6.0	3.0
Refrigeration, including distribution	1.0–3.0	2.0
Water supply cooling and pumping	0.4–3.7	1.8
Finished product storage	0.7–2.4	1.8
Electric main substation	0.9–2.6	1.5
Process waste systems	0.4–1.8	1.1
Raw material storage	0.3–3.2	1.1
Steam distribution	0.2–2.0	1.0
Electric distribution	0.4–2.1	1.0
Air compression and distribution	0.2–3.0	1.0
Water distribution	0.1–2.0	0.9
Fire protection system	0.3–1.0	0.7
Water treatment	0.2–1.1	0.6
Railroads	0.3–0.9	0.6
Roads and walks	0.2–1.2	0.6
Gas supply and distribution	0.2–0.4	0.3
Sanitary waste disposal	0.1–0.4	0.3
Communications	0.1–0.3	0.2
Yard and fence lighting	0.1–0.3	0.2

*Courtesy of H. C. Bauman and *Chemical Engineering Progress.*

The total of all these indirect costs is given by Bauman (1964) as 15–30%
of the total fixed investment, I_F. O'Donnell (1953) proposes a relationship
expressing the indirects as a percentage of the total fixed investment, I_F.
Thus,

$$\text{total indirects} = 35\% \left[\frac{I_F}{10^6} \right]^{-0.10} \tag{6.17}$$

Guthrie (1969a) suggests that the total indirects are about 55% of the total
physical plant cost, X, or about 37% of the total fixed capital investment.
Bauman's values seem low and Guthrie's seem high. However, with these
three sources a reasonable appreciation of the overall magnitude can be
gained.

Of course, in Table 6.12, the components of the indirect costs were expressed as functions of the base equipment cost. More accurate methods of
estimation of these components are available. They will be discussed in turn.

Engineering Expenses. This expense refers to the cost of the engineering
man-hours and associated home office costs for designing the process. This
includes the process and project engineering, drafting, purchasing, accounting
and cost engineering, travel and living expenses for the engineers, reproduction and communications, and general office expenses. Many correlate this

expense as a function of either the physical plant cost, X, or the total fixed capital investment I_F.

Bauman (1964) gives the relationships for the engineering expense as a percentage of the fixed capital investment, I_F, for battery limits chemical processes:

$$\text{engineering expense as } \% \text{ of } I_F = 17\% \left[\frac{I_F}{10^5}\right]^{-0.22} \pm 40\% \qquad (6.18)$$

For complex chemical, grass-roots chemical, or pilot plants,

$$\text{engineering expense as } \% \text{ of } I_F = 30\% \left[\frac{I_F}{10^5}\right]^{-0.24} \pm 40\% \qquad (6.19)$$

These relationships agree with the single correlation suggested by O'Donnell (1953).

Guthrie (1969a) estimates the engineering costs to be 10% of the physical plant cost including both auxiliaries and battery limits equipment and provides corrections to this value depending on the magnitude of the investment, the ratio of labor to materials, and the type of process. Guthrie's values are lower than those of Bauman. However, as we shall see shortly, Guthrie's estimates of the other components are higher, so that the net result seems to be the same, provided a consistent method of estimation is used.

Field Expenses. This includes the construction and operations of temporary field offices, roads, fences, etc; construction equipment (including rental), small tools; and construction supervision, purchasing, fringe benefits for employment, field tests, miscellaneous expenses for job cleanup, public liability insurance, etc.

Guthrie (1969a) suggests that this is 17.8% of the physical plant cost, X; this corresponds with 11.3% of I_F. He provides correction charts to account for variations in the total magnitude of the investment and the labor to materials ratio. Bauman (1964), on the other hand, gives a breakdown of the contributions to the field expenses and expresses these as ranges of percentages of the total fixed investment, I_F, in his Table 11.4, p. 176. The overall range is 6–14%, with a suggested median of 10% I_F.

Contractor's Fees. Normally, the contractor's fees are 3–5% of the total of the physical plant cost plus engineering expenses plus the field expenses.

Contingencies. This allowance for the unforeseen events that affect the cost is usually 10% of everything but the contractor's fees. That is, the contingencies $= 10\%(X + \text{engineering and field expenses})$. The magnitude of this percentage depends on the details available when the cost estimate is done.

If the scope and details are well defined, a reasonable contingency is about 8–10%. If the cost analysis is done when the flow diagram is just developed and many fine details have not been considered, then the contingency should be closer to 20%.

6.5 Detailed Estimation for Each Component

If greater accuracy is needed, more accurate estimates of the components are needed. Indeed, no longer are the components calculated as fractions of the base equipment cost. Since this topic is beyond the scope of this text, only a summary of sources of information is given in Table 6.21.

TABLE 6.21
SOURCES OF MORE DETAILED COST ESTIMATION TECHNIQUES

Cost component	Source
Equipment	From your own experience files, obtain quotations from suppliers
Piping, valves	Guthrie (1969b), Dickson (1950), Dinning (1967), Lamberton (1963), Bauman (1959), Keating (1962), Bauman (1964), Zimmerman (1970a)
Equipment installation	Peters and Timmerhaus (1968), Table 7; Bauman (1964); Page (1963); Mills (1964).
Instruments	Liptak (1962); Bauman (1964), Chap. 8; Liptak (1970a)
Electrical	Auld (1963); Bauman (1964), Chap. 8
Buildings	Bauman (1964), Chap. 5
Insulation	Bauman (1964)

6.6 Estimating Additional Capital Expenditures

The total financial commitment to a project requires more than just the capital for the fixed investment, I_F. Additional expenditures are required for working capital, I_w, land, I_l; starting up the plant; and interest charged on the capital during the construction period.

The working capital can be expressed as a fraction of the fixed capital investment or the annual revenue from sales, $\breve{S}$, or can be based on estimated inventory needs. The equations are

$$I_w = 0.1 \text{ to } 0.15 I_F \qquad (6.20)$$

$$= 0.25 \text{ to } 0.30 \breve{S} \qquad (6.21)$$

The inventory and capital needs can be approximated as

One-month capacity of raw material at $\ddot{N}$, the unit cost of the raw material.

Two-month capacity of finished product at price $\ddot{C}$ to represent the cash on hand and the finished product stored in the warehouse.

One month of accounts receivable at $\ddot{S}$.

For more details, see, for example, Bechtel (1960).

The cost of land can be estimated as a first approximation as

$$I_l = 0.01 \text{ to } 0.02 I_F \qquad (6.22)$$

A wide variety of suggestions have been made to estimate the cost of starting up the plant. Bauman (1964) suggests that the cost is rarely more than 10% of I_F. Indeed, although the range is from 0.4 to 25% of I_F, the average is 1.1% I_F [Bauman (1960) or Bauman (1964), Table 9.3, p. 150]. Barr (1960) suggests that the costs represent 50 days of total operating costs.

Guthrie (1969b) provides a correlation for testing installed equipment. This is only a component of the startup cost. Nelson (1960) suggests that acceptance tests are about 17% of the delivered equipment costs.

Barr (1960) suggests that the interest on the capital required during the construction period is 6% for half the total construction period.

6.7 Overall Summary and Recommendations

Many methods are available to estimate the capital investment required for a project. The emphasis has been on methods for estimating the fixed capital cost for complete processes. However, the principles can be applied to individual pieces of equipment.

Application of the principle of optimum sloppiness suggests that the estimates should be attempted first by the turnover or universal factor method, from a cost correlation method and then from a factor method.

The universal factor method is simple and inaccurate, yet it quickly gives the young professional an order of magnitude of the cost.

Cost correlations have many pitfalls: They apply only over a limited range, have inherent errors because of the simplifications made to obtain the correlation, and are a continuous correlation for discrete choices of size.

The factor methods are based on the cost of the major pieces of equipment. These methods are probably the most important for the young professional to master. A wide range of different factor methods was described. To gain experience in selecting the factors, the factors can be estimated from the variety of methods mentioned.

A recommended work sheet for the factor method is given in Table 6.22.

Methods are given to estimate the capital requirements other than that needed for the fixed capital investment. In Tables 6.13 and 6.22, low, probable, and high factors are selected. Because the low, probable, and high values have been used consistently throughout the analysis, and because the probability of either all lows or all highs occurring simultaneously is remote, Miller recommends that 10% be added to the low values and be subtracted from the high values.

TABLE 6.22
RECOMMENDED WORK SHEET FOR THE FACTOR METHOD*

TITLE _Chlorine Plant_					DATE _June '65_

CAPACITY					

Number of Main Plant Items	Inflation Indices		FACTOR OR ACCURACY	LOW	PROBABLE	HIGH
	1958	Current				
100	100	112				

		FACTOR/ACCURACY	LOW	PROBABLE	HIGH
Average Unit Cost of MPI's in 1958 $ _9000_					
Main Plant Items (MPI)	Estimated			1,000,000	
Misc. Unlisted Equip. (MUE)	_7%_			70,000	
Basic Equipment MPI + MUE _Excluding sales taxes and catalyst_	+10 −10		963,000	1,070,000	1,177,000

Installation of Basic Equipment	Remarks _Slightly under ave._	8	10	12
Foundations	_Average_	5	7	9
Instruments	_Lower range of ave. for chem._	6	10	14
Piping	_Ave. for chem. pl._	20	28	35
Insulation: Equip.	_Rel. low_	0.5	1	2
Pipe	_Rel. low_	4	5	6
Electrical	_Electrolytic Plant_	35	39	43
Misc.		3	4	5
Building: Arch and Str	_Eval −1 to −2_	30	35	40

Services

Compressed Air	1.5				
Elect. and Lighting	9				
Sprinklers	—	45% =	14	16	18
Plumbing	10				
Heating	8				
Vent and Air Cond	15				
Total Services	45				

		FACTOR	LOW	PROBABLE	HIGH
Sub-total of Factors		125	155	184	
Adjustments Lows _+10_ High _−10_		138	155	166	
Total Adjusted Factors		138	155	166	1,330,000 1,660,000 1,955,000
Physical Plant Cost X excluding taxes and catalyst	−16	+15	2,293,000	2,730,000	3,132,000

*Courtesy C. A. Miller of Canadian Industries Ltd.

TABLE 6.22 CONTINUED

	FACTORS			LOW	PROBABLE	HIGH
Direct Cost of Battery Limit (B/L)				2,293,000	2,730,000	3,132,000
Storage and Handling *Only warehouse + related handling*	6	8	10	164,000	218,000	273,000
Utilities *Rectifiers incl. in B/L Water supply avail. Little steam " "*	7	10	15	191,000	273,000	410,000
Services *Somewhat less than average* (*as % of* B/L + S & H + U)	7	10	13	226,000	322,000	418,000
Total B/L + Auxiliaries		+19%		2,274,000	3,540,000	4,233,000
Taxes B/L { *Fed.* 11% *on* 75%				189,000	225,000	258,000
Prov. 3% *on* 65%				9,000	11,000	12,000
Aux { *Fed.* 11% *on* 70%				45,000	63,000	85,000
Prov. 3% *on* 70%				12,000	17,000	23,000
Total Direct Cost				3,129,000	3,859,000	4,611,000
Indirect Costs.						
Construction Field		15%		470,000	580,000	691,000
Catalyst (*incl. installation*)				500,000	600,000	700,000
Royalties				NIL	NIL	NIL
Engineering		5%		180,000	222,000	265,000
Total Indirect Costs				1,150,000	1,402,000	1,656,000
Total Direct + Indirect		±19%		4,279,000	5,261,000	6,267,000
Contingencies		10%		427,000	526,000	—
Total Fixed Investment		+8% −19%		4,706,000	5,707,000	6,267,000

PROBLEMS

6.1. Based on an announcement of new construction (the cost and capacity) and the present selling price, estimate the turnover ratio for at least 10 chemicals. Construction information can be obtained from newspapers, *Financial Post*, *Hydrocarbon Processing*, and *Chemical Engineering*.

6.2. From annual reports, calculate the turnover ratios for three companies.

6.3. In describing the universal factor method, no care was taken to differentiate between grass-roots and battery limits plants. Why?

6.4. Prepare a plot of the variation of selling price with time for a number of chemicals. Some historical information can be obtained from Aries and Newton (1955) and Happel (1958).

6.5. The costs of chemicals vary greatly with the amount purchased. Compare the prices of seven common chemicals as quoted in *The Chemical Marketing Newspaper* and by laboratory supply companies such as Fisher Scientific, E. H. Sargent and Co., and Aldrich Chemical. Does this suggest a method of estimating the large-scale costs of some rather exotic chemicals that are not normally reported in *The Chemical Marketing Newspaper*.

6.6. Compare the selling price of the same chemicals in at least three different countries. (Costs of chemicals in Canada are reported in *Canadian Chemical Processing*. *European Chemical News* has other data.)

6.7. Many writers suggest that the investment cost per unit of capacity is a useful method of estimating the capital investment, for example, Peters (1958), p. 103; Peters and Timmerhaus (1968); Chilton (1949); Wilcoxon in Chilton (1960); Kiston et al. in Chilton (1960); and Aries and Newton (1955). This method is not included in this text. Why? In answering this question, carefully identify its advantages and disadvantages.

6.8. A reasonable range of values for factors to represent installed piping as a fraction of delivered equipment cost is (Circle a reasonable answer.)

$$0.0–0.2$$
$$0.2–0.6$$
$$0.2–2.0$$
$$0.4–1.0$$
$$0.8–2.0$$
$$2.0–4.0$$
$$1.6–5.0$$

6.9. Estimate the capital cost of a plant that is to produce 3000 bbl of alkylate per day. This battery limit installation is to be estimated
  a. By the universal factor method.
  b. From a cost correlation.
  c. By a single Lang's factor method.
  d. By Miller's method.

   e. By Guthrie's method.

   f. By Hirsch and Glazier's method.

6.10. Determine the capital cost of a green-field plant that is to produce 600 tons of sulfuric acid per day via the contact process

   a. By the universal factor method.

   b. From a cost correlation.

   c. By Lang's factor method.

   d. By Miller's factor method.

   e. By Guthrie's method.

   f. By Hirsch and Glazier's method.

6.11. Determine the capital cost of a plant that is to produce 370 tons of sulfuric acid per day from metallurgical off-gas by the different methods cited in Problem 6.9.

6.12. Your design section head is going to a meeting in 5 min. He wants a rough ($\pm80\%$) capital cost estimate for a 50-ton/day heavy chemical plant producing product X, 1.4 cents/lb. The green-field plant consists of

     6 shell and tube exchangers, total area 12,000 ft²

     1 anion exchanger, 350 ft³

     6 bronze centrifugal pumps, 80 gal/min each

     1 glass-lined reactor, 600 gal (U.S.)

     2 glass-lined tanks, atmospheric pressure of 5000 gal (U.S.) each

Your boss also wants a better ($\pm40\%$) estimate by the time the meeting is over.

6.13. Estimate the fixed capital investment of a plant that is to produce 6×10^5 lb of barium carbonate per year. The present selling price of barium carbonate is \$117/long ton.

6.14. The FOB equipment cost for the major equipment for a typical solids process to produce ultramarine blue powder is \$500,000. What is the fixed capital investment for a battery limit plant?

6.15. If the manufacturing cost of ultramarine blue is 15 cents/lb, what would be a 1-min estimate of a reasonable selling price (cents per pound).

6.16. Based on your answers to Problems 6.14 and 6.15, how many pounds of ultramarine blue per year is this plant designed to produce? Is this reasonable?

Estimation of the Cost and Selling Price of a Product

7

The costs of a large number of components contribute to the cost of a product. Indeed, probably the most challenging problem in product cost estimation is to ensure that all components are correctly included in the cost. To aid in keeping track of the cost contributions, the component costs are usually classified as to how the costs originate or, in other words, how the costs can be attributed to the product in question. Usually, we refer to the costs as being directly attributable, indirectly attributable, and general. The directly attributable components are those that we can readily visualize as contributing to the product cost. For example, all the raw material costs can be visualized as affecting the cost of the product. Indirectly attributable costs are those that somehow are related to the product but where the relationship is not precise. For example, the cost of running the chemical laboratory is related to the number of analyses done on the complete factory site. The samples from the process under consideration are part of this demand. Hence, we can indirectly allocate a portion of the cost of the laboratory to the cost of the product perhaps based on a percentage of the time spent analyzing the samples. Finally, there are general expenses (administrative, legal, clerical, etc.). No clear-cut way of apportioning these total costs to the product is available. We see this when we ask, How much of the sales manager's time is spent thinking about product X? Yet these costs need to be equitably distributed among all products. This classification, together with other groupings of the cost components, is summarized in Table 7.1. This classification is the basis for most methods of estimating the product cost. First, we estimate the product cost at a fixed rate of production, usually the design capacity. Then, we consider methods of interpreting the costs as a function of the rate of production.

7.1 Estimation of the Product Cost at a Fixed Production Rate

We can apply the principle of optimum sloppiness to the estimation of the product cost. The overall algorithm is shown in Fig. 7.1. This approach does not have as many possibilities as did the estimation of the capital cost.

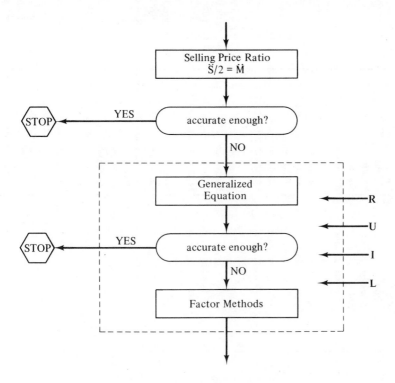

Figure 7.1. Algorithm for product cost estimation.

TABLE 7.1
COMPONENTS OF THE PRODUCT COST

Classified according to variation with the rate of production	Components	Classified according to ability to attribute the cost to a product	Classified according to source
C_L Costs vary about linearly with production rate	Raw materials Utilities Packing, containers Shipping Royalties	M_D Directly attributable	$C_m = f$(materials)
C_R Costs vary with production rate but are not zero at zero production rate	Operating labor Direct supervision Maintenance Plant supplies Laboratory analyses		$C_l = f$(labor)
C_F Costs independent of production rate	Rent Insurance Taxes Depreciation	M_F Directly attributable and independent of production rate	$C_L = f$(investment)
	Medical Safety and protection General plant overheads Payroll Restaurant Recreation Storage facilities	M_I Indirectly attributable to a product	
	Administration Sales, market research, and advertising Research and development Financing	G General expenses not easily attributable to a given product	$C_{OBL} = f$(costs outside BL)

C (overall) M (spans M_D, M_F, M_I)

Time and the estimation of product cost

The first possible method to estimate the cost assumes that we know the selling price. Then as a first approximation the manufacturing cost, M, is about one-half of the selling price. Alternatively, the cost is about 0.6 selling price. This procedure is analogous to the universal factor method for capital cost estimation. The result is so sloppy that the major value is being able to estimate a cost in a minute.

The next method of calculating the cost is to substitute values of the raw material cost, R, the utility costs, U, the fixed capital investment, I, and the labor costs, L, into a generalized equation. We should appreciate that different levels of accuracy are available for values of $RUIL$. This range is shown in Fig. 7.2.

A more accurate method of calculating the product cost is to select appropriate values of the factors for each component. Normally, all the contributions are correlated in terms of the $RUIL$ terms. Consider first selecting a basis and then each method in turn.

Selecting a basis

Before we can do any calculations we need to select a basis for our product costing. That is, we can determine the annual cost, the cycle cost, or the cost per unit of production. The most commonly selected basis is *per unit of production*, i.e., per pound, per ton, or per gallon or per cubic meter of final

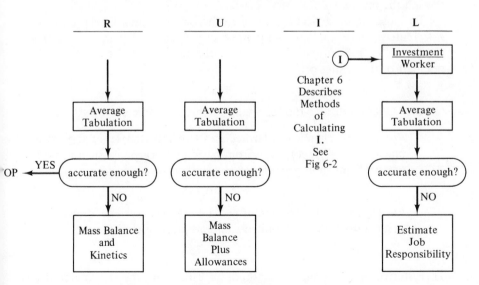

Figure 7.2. Algorithm for determining *RUIL*.

product of a given specification. Note that the size of the unit, the name, and the specification should be identified. Confusion can result, for example, when one author reports the costs per ton of acid when he means per ton of 98 % w/w sulfuric acid because this is how the product is sold, whereas another writer interprets this as per ton of 100% equivalent sulfuric acid. Clarity is essential.

Another problem concerns the relationship between annual costs and unit costs. Depreciation and maintenance are known on an annual basis; raw material usage is most often known per unit of final product. However, there are not 365 operating days/year. Hence, the daily production rate cannot be multiplied by 365 days to obtain the annual production rate. The number of operating or stream days is usually 300–340 days/year depending on the process. Hence, the annual number of stream days should be specified.

Selling price ratio method

Often, the selling price can be estimated, or it is known. If it is to be estimated, very crude estimates might be made from Fig. 6.5 or from a knowledge of the universal factors, w, and the fixed capital investment. Then the costs can be estimated as

$$\ddot{M} = 0.5\ddot{S} \tag{7.1}$$

$$\ddot{C} = 0.6\ddot{S} \tag{7.2}$$

These are gross generalizations but may serve to give some appreciation, even though the results are not very accurate.

To illustrate the inaccuracy, some other rules-of-thumb relating just the raw material cost to the selling price are given by Schuman (1955) and Grumer (1967). Schuman suggests that the raw material cost, $\ddot{R}$, is about one-half of the selling price, or

$$\ddot{R} = 0.5\ddot{S}$$

Grumer (1967) indicates the following for bulk organic chemicals:

> For organic chemical intermediates (such as acetylene, acrylonitrile, phenol, and styrene) made from basic hydrocarbons (such as natural gas, ethylene, and propylene),
>
> $$\ddot{R} = 0.35\ddot{S}$$
>
> For organics made from intermediate organics (such as for acetic acid, acetic anhydride, acrylonitrile, and adipic acid),
>
> $$\ddot{R} = 0.75\ddot{S}$$

This illustrates that even the methods of estimating the raw material cost vary greatly.

Determining the *RUIL*

The next set of methods requires some knowledge of the raw material cost, R, the utility cost, U, the investment cost, I, and the labor cost L. Consider each in turn.

The raw material cost, R, is the product of yield or amount of raw material needed per unit of production of the product and the delivered cost of the raw material. The quantity of raw material needed is often tabulated in the references describing processes (such as in Table 7.2). A summary of some of these is given in Appendix E. If a more accurate answer is needed, we need to do a detailed study of the reaction, the conversions, and the side reactions including coke formation and summarize the requirements with a material balance. The cost of the raw material can be determined from the sources listed in Table 6.3.

Problem: Estimate the yield of ketene from acetic acid.

Sample solution: The acetic acid goes to ketene plus water as the major reaction. For every mole of acetic acid, about 0.765 mole follows this major reaction to form 0.765 mole of ketene and 0.765 mole of water. About 0.018 mole of acetic acid decomposes to light components. The remaining 0.217 mole does not react or decompose to carbon. About 0.018 mole of ketene decomposes to light components and about 0.005 mole polymerizes to diketene and heavier components. Hence, the net amount of ketene is $0.765 - 0.018 - 0.005 = 0.742$ mole. Thus, the yield is 0.742 mole of ketene per 1 mole of acetic acid fed to the reactor.

The utility cost, U, is the product of the usage and the unit cost of the utilities. The average, tabulated values of the usages are given in Appendix E. Some simple observations may be useful in checking the consistency of steam and water usages around distillation columns. For an organic separation, the number of pounds of steam is the total boilup divided by 5. The factor 5 results because the latent heat for most organics is about 200 BTU/lb, while for water it is about 1000 BTU/lb. The cooling water requirement for the condenser for a 10°C rise is 5–6 imperial gal/lb of steam.

A more accurate calculation of the utility usage can be determined from a mass balance. Certain utilities, such as steam, water, and electricity, should be increased by 25–50% to compensate for building and service needs and losses.

Average costs of most utilities are summarized in Table 7.3. The young professional should plot the trends in utility costs within the company so that he can anticipate changes in policy (i.e., steam turbines versus electricity). A

TABLE 7.2

REFERENCES USEFUL FOR LOCATING INFORMATION ABOUT PROCESSES
CLASSIFIED ACCORDING TO ORDER OF SEARCHING

Reference	Comment
1. Kirk, H. F., McKetta, J. J., Jr., Othmer, D. F. (1972) *Kirk-Othmer Encyclopedia of Chemical Technology*, 2nd ed., John Wiley & Sons, New York.	
2. Faith et al. (1965)	Excellent general coverage
3. Shreve, R. H., *Chemical Process Industries*, 2nd ed., McGraw-Hill, New York, 1956; 3rd ed., 1967	Descriptive but often lacks the quantitative numbers

Next we should consider specific textbooks. Consult the card catalog of the library. Articles and smaller reports may be found in the following collections.

4. *Modern Chemical Processes*, multivolume series describing chemical manufacturing plants, Van Nostrand Reinhold, New York, 1950ff.	Collections of detailed articles on specific industries; excellent source for details if the process is included
5. Company publications Unilever's Educational Series, Unilever, Blackfriars, London, E.C.4.	Booklets describing processes within their company
Lurgi Contractors' Manual, Lurgi Gesellschaften, Frankfurt am Main, Germany	Photographs and limited technical detail of processes they construct
Imperial Oil Ltd.'s *Petrochemical Flow Charts*	List intermediate and raw materials for various products; no data given
6. Flow diagrams Chemical and metallurgical engineering, "Chemical Engineering Flowsheets," *Chemical Engineering*	Flow diagrams plus utility usage for many processes
Chemical Engineering "Flow Diagrams"	Each issue presents a flow diagram and some details
Hydrocarbon Processing and *Petroleum Refiner* "Petroleum Handbook Issue"	Reviews flow diagrams and gives process descriptions of about 200 processes annually in the November issue
7. Noyes, R., or Sittig, M., *Chemical Process Monographs*, Noyes Development Corporation, Pearl River, N.Y., 14 vols	Recent single volumes for different chemicals, e.g., sodium hydroxide and acrylonitrile; draws primarily from the patent literature
8. Groggins, P. H., *Unit Processes in Organic Synthesis*, 5th ed., McGraw-Hill, New York, 1958	
9. Kobe, A. K., *Inorganic Process Industries*, Macmillan, New York, 1948	

TABLE 7.2   CONTINUED

Reference	Comment
10. Riegel, E. R., *Industrial Chemistry*, 4th ed., Van Nostrand Reinhold, New York, 1942	
11. BIOS and CIOS reports: British Intelligence Objectives Sub-Committee and Combined Intelligence Objectives Sub-Committee reports (1946–1947)	Gives details of production and processes in Germany in the early 1940s; although much is out of date, the data are often more complete than from other sources; the related FIAT reports concentrate on science and engineering fundamentals and do not give process descriptions
12. *European Chemical News*	
13. *Advances in Petroleum Chemistry and Refining* (K. A. Kobe, and J. J. McKetta, Jr., eds.), Wiley-Interscience, New York	Multivolume series with at least one chapter per volume on chemical processes
14. LePrince, P. et al (1971) "Procédés de Pétrochimie caractéristiques, techniques et économiques" Éditions Technip, Paris	Excellent review of important processes in the late 1960's. Flow diagrams, comparisons, costs, unit usages
15. Hahn, A. V. (1970) "The Petrochemical Industry: Market, and Economics" McGraw-Hill, New York	Good review of many processes. Flow diagrams, capital investment, product costs
16. United Nations, ECE, UNIDO, ECAFE publications.	A wide variety of data available in this often-overlooked resource.
17. OECD documents.	Process data not that frequent but some available
18. Wayman, M (1973) "Guide for Planning Pulp and Paper Enterprises", FAO, Rome	
19. Austin, G. T. (1974ff) Series of articles in *Chemical Engineering* starting *81*, 2, p. 132	Series of articles briefly reviews reactions, market and use of about 100 organics
20. Luth, F.A.K. and Konig, H. (1967) "The Planning of Iron and Steel Works" 3rd ed. Springer-Verlag, Berlin.	

sample is shown in Fig. 7.3. He should be aware of the differences in costs from one country to another. The latter knowledge is important in assessing patented processes and developments in other countries.

Methods of estimating the capital costs, I, have already been described in detail in Chapter 6.

The labor cost, L, is the product of the man-hours required per unit of production and the cost of labor. A very simple estimate of the number of

TABLE 7.3
AVERAGE COSTS OF UTILITIES (1967–1970, U.S. $)*

	Canada ($)	United States ($)	U.K. ($)	Japan ($)	Europe ($)
Sources of heat					
Steam per 1000 lb or per 10^6 Btu					
600 psig		0.90–1.20			
500 psig	0.60–1.20	0.60–1.20	1.50–1.80		
300 psig		0.60			
150 psig		0.55			
100 psig	0.50–1.00	0.50–1.00	1.1–1.70		
50 psig		0.50			
Exhaust	0.25–0.40	0.25–0.40			
Electricity per kWh					
Purchased	0.006–0.010	0.008–0.028	0.015–0.020	0.010	0.010
Self-generated		0.006–0.015			
Per 10^6 Btu		2.70			
Fuel oil per U.S. gal	0.05–0.15	0.05–0.15			
Heavy per U.S. gal			0.09		
Gas oil per U.S. gal			0.135		
Bunker C per 10^6 Btu		0.32			
Fuel gas (1000 Btu/ft³)					
Natural per 1000 scf or per 10^6 Btu	0.05	0.20–0.60		0.49–0.95	
Manufactured per 1000 scf (~ 1000 Btu/ft³)		0.50–1.50			
LPG per 1000 scf	0.18	0.25			
Propane per U.S. gal (550 Btu/ft³) per 10^6 Btu		0.17–0.50	0.8–1.00		0.12–0.20
Hydrogen per 1000 scf		0.16			
Coal					
Coal per ton		7.00–14.00			
Coal per 10^6 Btu		0.30–0.40	0.52–0.54	0.57	
Sources of cooling					
Water per 1000, U.S. gal			0.11–0.20		
Cooling					
Well	0.01–0.02	0.02–0.06			
River		0.02–0.0			
Tower					

Table 7.3 Continued

	Canada ($)	United States ($)	U.K. ($)	Japan ($)	Europe ($)
Refrigeration per 10^6 Btu					
0°C		1.80			
−15°C		2.10			
−35°C		3.00			
(ton-day = 0.288×10^6 Btu or ton = 200 Btu/min)					
Processing needs					
Inert gas per 1000 scf					
Nitrogen					
Trailers	6.00				
Large-scale	0.20–6.00				
N_2-H_2 mixtures (6–75% H_2)	0.25–0.50		4.50		
Compressed air per 1000 scf					
Process	0.10	0.02–0.06			
Filtered and dried for instruments		0.04–0.12			
Process water per 1000 U.S. gal					
City	0.17	0.10–0.35	0.40		
Filtered and softened		0.15–0.40	1.10		
Boiler water feed		0.95			
Distilled		0.70–1.20			
Waste treatment					
Water per 1000 U.S. gal treated					
Contaminated water, sewage		0.30–0.40			
Nonchemically contaminated, sewage		0.02			
Chemical treatment	0.20				
Biological treatment	0.08–0.10				
Filtering, coagulating, chlorinating lake or well water for drinking purposes	0.02–0.03				

*Based on data from Rudd et al. (1973); Peters and Timmerhaus (1968); Liebson and Trischman (1971); West (1965); process description articles in *Chemical Engineering, British Chemical Engineering,* and *Hydrocarbon Processing;* and private discussions with colleagues in industry.

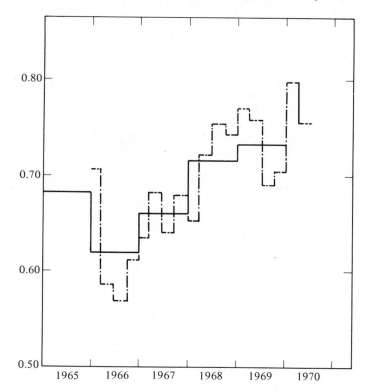

Figure 7.3. Sample quarterly and annual variation in utility costs. (*Sample data for high pressure steam includes maintenance and losses for Company A.*)

workers is to use the capital investment, I, and the information that the investment per worker is about $60,000, or whatever might seem reasonable for the process under study. For example, the capital investment in the chemical industry per worker is greater than $10,000/worker. For example, Aries and Newton (1955) suggest that in the 1950s for existing plants it was $25,000/worker; in the 1950s for new plants it was $40,000/worker. In 1964 in the Shell Canada Plant at Bronte, Ontario the investment was $120,000/worker. Noranda Mines Ltd. installed an aluminum reduction plant at New Madrid, Mo., in 1967 for $100,000/worker. In 1967, International Pulp and Paper Co. built a pulp and paper mill near Lake Champlain for $76,000/worker.

This method is useful only when little other information is available. The usual sources of information are tabulated values such as are summarized in Appendix E. Some authors have suggested labor requirements for different processing steps or units, for example, Wessel (1953) and Aries and Newton (1955). However, it takes a lot of experience before such methods can be used to yield realistic answers. A more accurate estimate of the labor requirement can be gained by studying the job responsibilities. In obtaining a man-hour per ton estimate from this method we should realize that the labor is hired on an annual basis and that four shifts are required to maintain three shifts for 7 days/week. In the steel industry, data on the man-hours per ton are not very useful because of the wide variation in their value. Sometimes the data are expressed as the number of men per shift. To convert this to man-hours per ton, the number of men per shift is multiplied by 8760 and divided by the annual tonnage production.

The cost of labor varies from country to country and even within different sections of a country. Furthermore, the cost should include the fringe benefits as well as the actual hourly rate. A value of about \$10,000/man-year was a reasonable average wage in 1970. Now we have values for $RUIL$.

Generalized equation method

Given values for $RUIL$, the total unit cost, $\ddot{C}$, can be estimated from the relationship

$$\ddot{C} = 1.2(\ddot{R} + \ddot{U} + \ddot{F}) + 2.5\ddot{L} + 0.36\frac{I_F}{\breve{q}} \tag{7.3}$$

where F is the container or packaging cost per unit of product. This equation is derived from the following relationships:

$$\ddot{C} = \dot{M}_D + \dot{M}_F + \dot{M}_I + \ddot{G} \tag{7.4}$$
$$= \dot{M} + \ddot{G} \tag{7.5}$$
$$= \ddot{R} + \ddot{U} + \ddot{F} + 2.1\ddot{L} + 0.3\frac{I_F}{\breve{q}} + \ddot{G} \tag{7.6}$$

$$\ddot{G} = 1.2\dot{M} \tag{7.7}$$

The components in all these relationships represent overall averages.

Detailed $RUIL$—factor method

Given values for $RUIL$, the product cost, $\ddot{C}$, can be estimated by summing the cost components for each component listed in Table 7.1. Each component can be expressed as a factor or fraction of the basic components I or $\ddot{L}$. Such factors are summarized in Table 7.4. For example, unit maintenance cost has been correlated in terms of the fixed investment per unit of production and in terms of the labor cost. The correlating percentages are given as double entries in Table 7.4; that is, one or the other but not both should be used. Since the process industry is becoming less dependent on labor, it is preferred to correlate in terms of the fixed investment. Either the fixed costs can be averaged at 10% of $I_F/\breve{q}$ or the individual components can be specified. The indirectly attributable costs are correlated in terms of the labor, maintenance,

TABLE 7.4

METHODS OF ESTIMATING THE COST OF PRODUCTS: VALUES OF FACTORS*

Cost component	Symbol	Correlating parameter							Generalized breakdown not to be used for cost estimation	
		$\ddot{R}$	$\ddot{U}$	$I_F/\ddot{q}$	$I/\ddot{q}$	$I/\ddot{q}$	$\ddot{L}$	$\ddot{M}$	$\ddot{C}$	$\ddot{S}$
Raw materials	$\ddot{R}$	1.00							0.20	0.35–0.55
Utilities	$\ddot{U}$		1.00				0.035		0.10–0.20	0.05
Containers	$\ddot{F}$							0.5 cent/lb bulk chemicals 1 cent/lb specialty chemicals		
Operating labor	$\ddot{L}$						1.00		0.05–0.20	0.01–0.11
Operating superv.	$\ddot{A}$						0.10–0.40			
Operating supplies	$0.15\ddot{J}$			0.005–0.01†			0.10†			
Maintenance	$\ddot{J}$			0.02–0.15†			0.06†			
Royalties									0–0.06	
Total	$\ddot{M}_D$								0.60	0.06–0.07
Depreciation	$e\,I_F/\ddot{q}$			0.08–0.20						
Rent										
Insurance				0.004–0.01						
Property tax				0.01–0.04						
Total	$\ddot{M}_F$			0.10					0.10–0.20	0.06
Indirectly attributable costs	$\ddot{M}_I$						$0.75(\ddot{L}+\ddot{J}+\ddot{A})$		0.05–0.15	0.01–0.06
Total manufacturing cost $= \ddot{M}_D + \ddot{M}_F + \ddot{M}_I$	$\ddot{M}$									

TABLE 7.4 CONTINUED

Cost component	Symbol	Correlating parameter						Generalized breakdown not to be used for cost estimation	
		$\breve{R}$	U	$I_F/\ddot{q}$	$I/\ddot{q}$	L	$\ddot{M}$	$\ddot{C}$	$\breve{S}$
General expense	$\ddot{G}$								
Administrative cost							0.20 / 0.03–0.06		0.10 / 0.02– / 0.035
Selling cost							0.05–0.22 / 0.5 cent/lb bulk / 1 cent/lb specialty	0.02–0.20	0.05
Research cost							0.035–0.08	0.05	0.02– / 0.05
Financing cost					0.02–0.04				
Total cost	$\ddot{C}$								0.84
Income tax									0.08
Net earnings									0.08
Selling price	$\breve{S}$					2.0			

$$\ddot{C} = \ddot{M}_D + \ddot{M}_F + \ddot{M}_I + \ddot{G}$$
$$\breve{S} = \ddot{C} + \text{tax} + \text{net earnings}$$

*Based on personal files plus data from DeCicco (1968), Chilton (1951a, b, and c), Wessel (1953), and Aries and Newton (1955).
†Double entry: Use only one.

and supervision costs. The general expense, $\ddot{G}$, is usually averaged at 20% of $\dot{M}$. However, the components and their averages are given as fractions of $\dot{M}$ or of $I/\breve{q}$ for the financing cost. Also included in this table for information and not for estimation purposes is a generalized breakdown of the contributions of each component as a percentage of $\breve{C}$ and $\breve{S}$.

Complications

Two major complications are how to handle by-products and such downstream services as environmental control equipment. Many chemical processes produce more than one product. Indeed, often there are many by-products from one raw material from one set of *RUIL*. If a plant product A is priced too low and by-product B is too high, then A is sold and B builds up in inventory. One method suggested by Dershowitz et al. (1960) is to cost a hypothetical alternative method of making products in ratios different from that used for the process. From an algebraic analysis, the cost of each can be determined. For example, we want to make acetaldehyde by the dehydrogenation of ethanol. Hydrogen is a by-product. If we do not have an accepted price for the hydrogen, then we could cost the production of acetaldehyde from the oxidation of ethanol. Here the by-product is water. Thus, a cost for producing acetaldehyde can be determined directly, and thence a price for hydrogen can be estimated. This discussion has mainly served to make the young professional aware of the complications of by-products to cost analysis. Further analysis is beyond the scope of this text.

Normally it is easy for us to account for all storage, processing, and handling costs upstream of the process. However, we should be aware that auxiliary waste treatment and disposal flare systems and air pollution control expenses must be accounted for somewhere in the overall costing.

Cost estimation of nonprocess products

In the preceding sections the emphasis has been on cost estimation in the sanitary, mining, mineral, chemical or metallurgical industry. Methods and data for estimating the cost of machining, fabrication, mechanical processing of materials, and bonding are given by McNeill and Clark (1966).

7.2 Estimation of the Product Cost at Reduced Rates of Production

In Section 7.1, methods were given for estimating the product cost at a fixed rate of production. This is usually the design production rate. However, often the plant operates at capacities other than the design capacity. Hence, it is very useful to be able to estimate the product cost as a function of production.

Not all the cost contributions vary the same way with production rate. In the short run, the costs can be independent, directly dependent, and partly dependent on the production rate, $\breve{q}$. Some examples are shown in Fig. 7.4. The costs that are independent of production rate, C_F, include depreciation, land, tax, rent, insurance, medical expenses, safety and protection, payroll, restaurant, recreation, storage facilities, engineering, administration, sales, and research.

Regulated expenses, C_R, are proportional but not linear and do not go through the origin. These include labor, supervision, maintenance, plant supplies, and laboratory expenses.

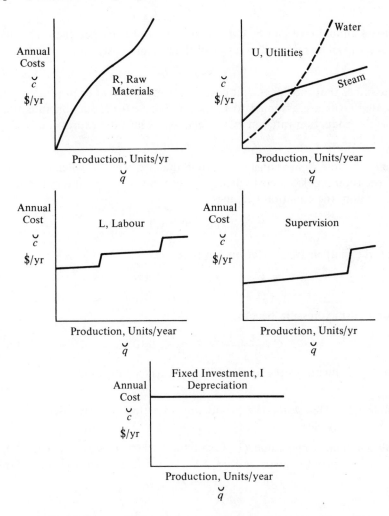

Figure 7.4. The variation of directly attributable expenses with production rate.

Those expenses that vary linearly with production rate, C_L, include raw materials, packing containers, utilities, shipping, royalties, and credit for by-products.

The two major advantages of this method are that we obtain mathematical expressions for the cost that are easy to use in optimization work and that the results are easy to visualize graphically on a so-called break-even curve. Although some of these costs often undergo step changes, average or smoothed variations are assumed.

A convenient basis is "a calendar year of operation." The total cost equation for the annual cost is

$$C = C_F + C_L + C_R \tag{7.8}$$

The fixed annual cost can be expressed as total dollars per year. The linear annual cost can be reported in terms of the per unit cost; thus,

$$\check{C}_L = \ddot{C}_L \check{q} = a_0 \check{q} \tag{7.9}$$

This assumes that the linear unit cost, C_L, is independent of production rate. Regulated costs are assumed to be positive at zero production rate and to vary with production rate but not directly so. Thus, the expression could be

$$\check{C}_R = a_1 + b_1(\check{q})^{c_1+1} \tag{7.10}$$

where a_1, b_1, and c_1 are constants. Often, the intercept, a_1, when $\check{q} = 0$ is 0.3 times the total regulated cost when $\check{q}$ corresponds with maximum profit. For this situation, the equation becomes

$$\check{C}_R = \frac{0.3}{0.7} b_1(\check{q}\,\text{max})^{c_1+1} + b_1(\check{q})^{c_1+1}$$

Hence, the mathematical relationship becomes

$$\check{C} = \check{C}_F + a_0\check{q} + a_1 + b_1(\check{q})^{c_1+1}$$
$$= (\check{C}_F + a_1) + a_0\check{q} + b_1(\check{q})^{c_1+1} \tag{7.11}$$

The unit cost expression becomes

$$\check{C} = \frac{\check{C}_F + a_1}{\check{q}} + a_0 + b_1(\check{q})^{c_1} \tag{7.12}$$

Example 7.1 illustrates the applicability of this classification.

Example 7.1: Determine the production rate that will give the maximum profit.

Sample solution: The value $\check{Q}$ = maximum when $d\check{P}/d\check{q} = 0$. The annual profit is given as $\check{P} = \check{q}(\ddot{S} - \check{C})$. Substitution yields

$$\frac{d\check{P}}{d\check{q}} = \frac{d}{d\check{q}}\check{q}\left(\ddot{S} - \frac{\check{C}_F + a_1}{\check{q}} - a_0 - b_1(\check{q})^{c_1}\right)$$
$$= \ddot{S} - a_0 - b_1(c + 1)q^c$$

Hence, the maximum profit occurs when the production rate is

$$\check{q}_{op} = \left[\frac{\ddot{S} - a_0}{b(c + 1)}\right]^{1/c}$$

This form of cost expression is easy to use in mathematical calculations. Consider now a graphical representation of costs as a function of production rate, $\check{q}$.

Normally the annual dollars from sales and all costs including depreciation are plotted as a function of $\check{q}$ as in Fig. 7.5. The cost contributions are the fixed costs, the regulated costs, and the linear costs. These yield the total cost. To this could be added an opportunity cost. Note that Eqs. (7.9) and (7.10) apply only for a rate of production less than that where unit costs are a minimum. This can be seen from Fig. 7.6(a) and (b).

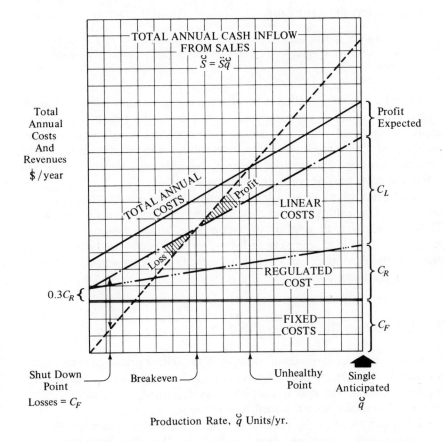

Figure 7.5. Variation in costs as a function of production rate: break-even curve.

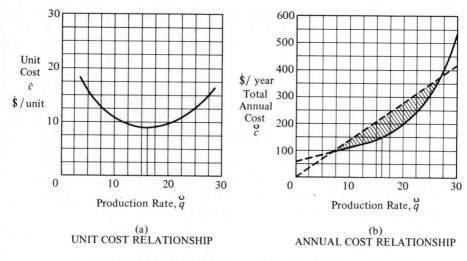

(a)
UNIT COST RELATIONSHIP

(b)
ANNUAL COST RELATIONSHIP

Figure 7.6. Relationship between unit and annual costs ($\ddot{c}$ and $\check{c}$) to illustrate production rate in break-even curves. (a) Unit costs. (b) Annual costs.

Figure 7.5 is often called a break-even curve because from such a plot where the revenue is superimposed on the costs the production rate can easily be identified where the revenue and costs are equal or the company breaks even. Other production rates referred to are the shutdown point when the fixed costs are balanced by the cost less sales, and the unhealthy point where the costs plus opportunity costs balance sales.

Some precautions about using such relationships are that they apply only for the economic short run and only for $\check{q}$ less than where cost is a minimum. These models can be applied to a complete company [see, for example, Anderson (1963)], a complete industry, or a process producing a single product. Break-even curves do not have much meaning when valuable by-products are produced.

7.3 Estimating the Selling Price

Some discussion of methods of estimating the selling price has been given in Section 5.6. In general, the most commonly used method is the cost-plus method. That is, the cost is estimated, as described in Section 7.2, and a profit and tax allowance is added to give the selling price.

The main question is, How does one select the minimum profit or an acceptable profit? Rudd and Watson (1968) use the following criterion: The minimum selling price is such that the average annual venture profit, $\langle \check{Q} \rangle$, is zero. Thus, the minimum selling price is given by

$$\ddot{S} = \ddot{C} + \frac{tI_F(e - d) + i_m I_F + iI_w}{\ddot{q}(1 - t)} \tag{7.13}$$

Based on this criterion, the minimum selling price can be estimated easily.

7.4 Summary

The product cost must account for a host of cost contributions. In general, the major contribution for a chemical is the cost of the raw materials, which accounts for as much as half the selling price. Other significant cost contributions come from labor, utilities, and the financing of the capital investment (or depreciation). Methods were reviewed for estimating these contributions; the method and the accuracy depend on the time available.

Not all production is at a fixed rate. A break-even curve was developed to provide a convenient representation of how the cost and different cost contributions vary with production rate. Finally, a method of estimating the selling price was given.

PROBLEMS

7.1. Estimate the selling price for low-purity 95% oxygen. We want to produce 500 tons/day. The operating usages are

> 0.2 man-hour/ton
> 0.22 kWh/lb
> 2.2 lb of steam/lb
> 13.0 U.S. gal of cooling water/lb

Assume reasonable costs for all the pertinent resources required and reasonable values for any other information required. Justify these assumptions where appropriate.

7.2. Estimate the product cost and the percentage return on investment of producing chlorine from the electrolysis of brine. The per tonnage usages are (per ton of chlorine)

> salt: 1.75 tons
> graphite: 3 kg
> mercury: 0.2 kg
> water: 2400 U.S. gal
> steam: 23,000 lb
> electricity: 3300 kWh for cell
> 75 kWh for miscellaneous
> operating labor: 4.8 mh/ton

These usages are based on a plant that produces 1.15 tons of 75% caustic soda, 1 ton of chlorine, and 10,000 scf of hydrogen. In 1952, an installation of 10 tons/day of chlorine cost $620,000 and required 26 tons of mercury for initial installation. The cost prices are

> salt: $10.00/ton
> graphite: $1/kg
> mercury: $515/76-lb flask

Assume reasonable values for other items. The present selling prices are

> chlorine: $5/100 lb
> hydrogen: $0.30/1000 scf
> sodium hydroxide: $3/100 lb

7.3. From Dr. Emil Nenniger: The capital cost estimate for a 250-MW nuclear power generating station is as follows:

> total physical plant cost (including heavy water
> and excluding fuel): $66 million
> engineering, inspection, construction, contractors'
> fees, staff training, and contingency: $24 million

Interest during construction is to be considered as part of the total capital cost. The interest rate will be $5\frac{1}{2}\%$ per annum and the expenditure is expected to proceed as follows:

6 months	18 months	30 months	42 months	54 months	66 months	78 months
0.5%	4%	31%	50%	75%	97%	100%

Estimate the total capital cost, excluding fuel, based on funding simultaneously with expenditures. Calculate the unit energy cost in mills per kilowatt hour for an 80% capacity factor.

Direct operating cost—fuel (only) at $25/lb of UO_2:

> burn up = 8000 MWatt-days/metric ton U.
> station efficiency = 29.85%

The remainder—for all practical purposes—is considered as fixed annual charges as follows:

operation and maintenance, including staff, services, materials, heavy water, upkeep, interest on fuel inventory, and grant in lieu of local taxes: $1.5 million/year

> capital charges: plant, equipment, and fuel
> interest: 5.5%
> sinking fund (depreciation):   ?   (to be invested at 5% for 30 years)
> administration, etc.:   2.0%
> cost of initial fuel charge: $3 million

7.4. Determine the product cost for alkylate based on the mass balance information and usage information given in Table 5.4. The accuracy expected is $\pm20\%$. Unit costs include acid, \$8.68/bbl; butylene, \$3.55/bbl; propylene, \$1.20/bbl; i-C_4, \$3/bbl; n-butane, \$3.60/bbl; and propane, \$3.60/bbl.

7.5. Calculate the selling price for alkylate as dollars per barrel such that the venture worth is positive when $y = 10$ years, $g = 5$ years, $i_m = 15\%$, and $i = 7\%$. Neglect the construction and startup periods. Enumerate the assumptions made.

7.6. A flow diagram for the production of acetaldehyde from ethylene is given in *Hydrocarbon Processing 46*, No. 11, p. 135. Two alternative processes are proposed. Assume that the oxygen plant facilities are already available, but that the air compression unit is not and that the contributions to the costs have the following unit values:

$$
\begin{array}{rl}
\text{ethylene:} & \$0.05/\text{lb} \\
\text{air:} & \text{free} \\
\text{hydrochloric acid:} & \$0.18/\text{lb} \\
\text{cooling water:} & \$0.01/1000 \text{ gal} \\
\text{cold water:} & \$0.005/1000 \text{ gal} \\
\text{demineralized water:} & \$0.05/1000 \text{ gal} \\
\text{steam:} & \$0.75/1000 \text{ lb} \\
\text{electricity:} & \$0.008/\text{kWh} \\
\text{supervisors:} & \$4/\text{man-hour} \\
\text{operators:} & \$3.50/\text{man-hour}
\end{array}
$$

Assume that we want to produce 150,000 long tons/year with 8000 hr in an operating year.
a. What would the price of oxygen have to be if the two alternatives are to have the same unit costs?
b. What are the total unit cost and a proposed selling price?

7.7. What would it cost per ton of final product to make 2000 I gph of ethyl alcohol from molasses given the following extra information:
a. Molasses, 2.5 gal/gal of 190 proof alcohol.
b. Specific gravity of 190 proof $= 0.84$.
c. Plant operates 300 days of the year.
d. Unit costs of molasses: \$0.15/gal
$$
\begin{array}{rl}
\text{steam:} & \$1/1000 \text{ lb} \\
\text{electricity:} & \$0.6/100 \text{ kWh} \\
\text{water:} & \$0.15/1000 \text{ gal} \\
\text{labor:} & \$4/\text{hr.}
\end{array}
$$
e. Annual depreciation: 10%.

7.8. Estimate the present-day total cost per ton of sulfuric acid via the contact process for a plant producing 1000 tons of acid per day.

$$
\begin{array}{rl}
\text{sulfur:} & 668 \text{ lb/ton} \\
\text{electricity:} & 5 \text{ kWh/ton for turbine-driven system} \\
\text{electricity:} & 30 \text{ kWh/ton if the blower is electrically driven}
\end{array}
$$

water for boiler :   350 U.S. gal of city water/ton
for acid :   34 U.S. gal of city water/ton
for cooling :   3600 U.S. gal of bay water/ton
Steam used at 120 psig
on plant excluding
turbine blower :   0.1 lb/lb
Steam at 120 psig for
sale :   1700 lb/ton from turbine plant
Steam at 300 psig for
sale :   2000 lb/ton if turbine is electrically driven
Labor :   0.64 mh/ton
Costs :   sulfur : $10/ton
electricity : $0.54/100 kWh
city water : $0.20/1000 Imp. gal
bay water : $0.02/1000 Imp. gal
steam, 120 psig : $0.50/1000 lb
steam, 300 psig : $1.00/1000 lb
labor : $3.50/hr

There are no royalties. The plant operates 300 days of the year. Depreciation is based on 10% of the fixed capital investment. Corrosive liquids are involved. The plant we are considering is

a. A steam turbine-driven plant that has 120 psig steam to sell as a credit.
b. An electrically driven blower system so that the steam is available to sell at 300 psig.

7.9. Courtesy of Dr. Emil Nenniger: For a plant of 200,000-lb/year capacity, a fixed capital cost estimate was prepared in 1955 when the C. E. Equipment Cost Index was 88.6. This cost was analyzed to ascertain the cost of those components which would be increased in number and those which would be increased in size in a plant of greater capacity.

units varying by number	$150,000
units varying by size	200,000
fixed capital	$350,000

A breakdown of the manufacturing cost estimate for the above capacity for present conditions is

raw materials, utilities, packaging :	$0.250/lb
fixed expenses (depreciation, property taxes, insurance) and maintenance on units varying in number :	0.090/lb
fixed expenses and maintenance on units varying by size :	0.085/lb
labor and proportional expenses on units varying by number :	0.200/lb
labor and proportional expenses on units varying by size :	0.080/lb
manufacturing cost :	0.705/lb
general expenses (administration, sales, research, and finance), 10% manufacturing cost :	0.071/lb
total production cost :	0.776/lb

Market research has shown that a market of 500,000 lb/year will exist at a sale price of $1/lb.

a. What will be the present total fixed capital required for a 500,000-lb/year plant?

b. What will be the total production cost per pound for the 500,000-lb/year plant?

c. What will be the return on fixed capital before income taxes?

d. What will be the return on investment after income taxes?

e. What will be the present value if $i = 6\%$ and $i_m = 20\%$?

Using Costs to Generate Ideas for Screening Studies and Process Improvement

8

We have introduced methods of considering the financial attractiveness of alternative proposals and of estimating the cost of fixed assets and of products. However, the overall objective of a young professional is to decide what policy or alternative to select that will give an attractive financial return for the risk involved. Part of the responsibility is to identify alternatives that might be attractive. From another viewpoint, the alternatives we are called upon to study are often complicated. Hence, it is useful to realize that other cost criteria besides the present value or internal rate of return may be useful guidelines. The word *guidelines* is emphasized because present value or internal rate of return is the method that should be used to ultimately establish the most attractive alternative. However, in screening alternatives and in the identification of areas where improvements can be made, such criteria as the cost increments through each processing stage, the cost per mole, the cost per similar processing function, the cost of alternatives with similar attributes, and the cost per property are useful additional criteria to the usual annual and unit product costs. These criteria are summarized in Table 8.1.

For example, the unit cost of alkylate is summarized in Table 5.4. However, it would be useful to know where the major cost increments occurred in the flow diagram shown in Fig. 6.15; the breakdown of costs into the contribution from material, labor, utilities, and overheads at each stage; the cost of alkylate per octane number or per unit of energy as opposed to that

TABLE 8.1
USEFUL FINANCIAL CRITERIA FOR PROCESS SCREENING OR IDENTIFICATION

Financial criteria	Elaboration
1. Return or outlay Internal rate of return } Present value	To be used in final selection. Details given in Chapter 5.
2. Cost per unit of production of product or	Useful as overall preamble to an analysis of structure. Can be used for overall economic balances.
Cost per year or	Serves as most useful basis for criteria 1 and for overall economic balances.
Cost per cycle	Useful basis for time efficiency studies.
3. Cost increments	Useful for identifying cost-sensitive operations and gaining an appreciation of costs if the product specifications are changed. From this study will come the cost of each functional stage in the process flow diagram.
4. Cost components of materials, utilities, labor, overheads at each cost increment	
5. Cost components and unit costs for reduced and overcapacity conditions	Too often we forget that the process is not working at design capacity all the time. This type of analysis can be very revealing.
6. Cost increments when all effluents and by-products are assigned representative values	Normally unwanted waste streams are assigned zero worth at the condition of discharge. However, some streams have a negative worth because they must be treated before they can be discharged into the environment and some, such as condensate, are valuable.
7. Cost per property for raw materials, utilities, and product	The properties included density, alkalinity or acidity, moles, heat capacity, resistivity, thermal conductivity, boiling point degrees, melting point, compressibility, yield, tensile or shear strengths, hardness, reflectivity, etc.
8. Cost per comparison for similar attributes for all raw materials, utilities, and products	The attributes that could be similar are toxicity, power, energy, weight, shape of molecule, serviceability, reactivity, selectivity, acidity, etching power, etc.

obtained from the competing products; the cost per mole of the raw materials and the product; and the cost of each functional stage. Let us elaborate on the cost ratios or relationships that can be useful in screening or in process improvements.

8.1 The Cost Per Function of Equipment in the Process Flow Diagram

Establishing the cost per function

From the analysis of function or of structure [Woods (1969) and Crowe et al. (1971), Chap. 4], the mass and energy balances, the installed equipment costs for depreciation and maintenance, the operating labor costs, the utilities, and overheads costs, the cost per function can be estimated easily. For example, a heat exchanger is shown in Fig. 8.1. All costs are given on an hourly basis. The net cost of the steam is $4/hr, and the depreciation and maintenance is about $2/hr. If the costs of labor and overheads are neglected, the cost/heat exchange function is $6/hr. The calculations can be based on a year or an hour, but the calculations are hard to do per unit flow through each unit.

A similar analysis can be done for each piece of equipment and for design, overdesign, and underdesign capacities.

Using the cost per function

The cost per function for the processing scheme used can be compared with the cost per function from alternative devices. Note that this is not a comparison of the *capital* costs of equipment that performs the same function.

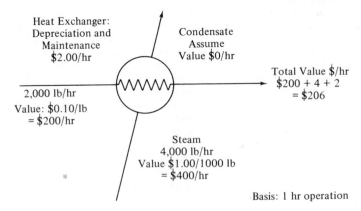

Figure 8.1. Establishing the cost/function and the dollar flow for a heat exchanger.

Such a plot of capital costs is given by Corrigan et al. (1967). While such a comparison is useful, the comparison that is valid for the present purposes would be an hourly cost to perform the same function. Such an analysis can be used to identify possible alternative methods of satisfying the same function.

Second, the cost per function can be listed for each functional set of equipment in the process. A sample is given in Table 8.2. We can thus identify the most expensive cost increment. Often each cost per function can be divided into components of utilities, materials, labor, and overheads.

Thus, the cost per function can be used to help identify possible alternative equipment that may be attractive financially and to identify the sources of major cost contributions in the process flow diagram.

TABLE 8.2
COST PER FUNCTION FOR PROCESS FLOW DIAGRAM

Equipment or unit number	Function	Basis: $/24-hr day					Overall rank
		Utilities	Maintenance and depreciation	Materials	Labor	Total	
1	Separate	0.51	0.50	—	0.02	1.03	3
2	React	0.10	0.18	—	0.02	0.30	6
3	Separate	0.62	1.00	0.15	0.02	1.79	1
4	Mix	0.01	1.09	—	0.02	1.12	2
5	Size Increase	0.01	0.15	—	0.18	0.34	4
6	Separate	0.01	0.20	—	0.02	0.23	7
7	Package	0.01	0.30	—	0.02	0.33	5
Total		1.27	3.42	0.15	0.30	5.14	

8.2 Cost Per Function of Utilities and Effluents

Just as the cost per function of equipment can be assessed, the cost per function or property of the utilities and the effluents can be evaluated. For example, the cost per Btu removed can be evaluated for condensers or coolers. The uses of the effluents and by-products can be established and the cost of the stream evaluated accordingly. For example, the cost of condensate per Btu available from the condensate and the cost of condensate per gallon of treated water available are useful calculations. These data help identify areas where different utilities can be utilized or where major processing or recovery systems should be investigated.

8.3 Raw Material Costs : Cost Per Mole
or Cost Per Property

A study can be made of all materials used in the process: raw materials, adsorbents, catalysts, fillers, promoters, support materials, etc. The property that is the most important for each material can be identified. Then the costs can be calculated relative to this property. This helps to identify areas for future improvement.

For raw materials, a key property is the molecular or equivalent weight. Normally costs are reported per unit weight or volume. However, a classification per mole, as in Table 8.3, is useful in screening processes.

TABLE 8.3
COST PER MOLE FOR SOME CHEMICALS

Chemical	Cost (U.S. cents/g mole)	Cost ($) (April 1970)
Water	0.0001	0.20/1000 gal
Ammonia	0.10	55.00/ton
Salt (rock)	0.11	0.87/100 lb
Ethylene	0.20	0.33/lb
Methanol	0.29	0.27/gal
Sulfuric acid	0.37	33.95/ton
Benzene	0.64	0.25/gal
Butylene	0.78	0.0625/lb
Acetaldehyde	0.87	0.09/lb
Isopropanol	1.0	0.49/gal
Acetic acid	1.2	9.00/100 lb
Butadiene	1.2	0.10/lb
Ethylbenzene	1.4	0.06/lb
Magnesium hydroxide	2.7	0.21/lb
Acetic anhydride	3.2	0.14/lb
Adipic acid	5.8	0.18/lb
Pyridine	9.1	0.52/lb

8.4 Product Specifications and Costs Per
Property or Comparisons Per Attribute

One area where cost improvements can often be made is through changes in the specifications of the product. To appreciate the actual value of the changes in product specifications we can study the dollar flow through the process flow diagram, the cost of the product per property used by the customers, and the cost per attribute of the product.

Dollar flow through the process

The cost per function can be combined with an analysis of the dollar flows in the streams to study the cost of the stream at any location in the process. In this dollar flow analysis, the costs per function are added to the value of each input stream to each unit. If, for example, in Fig. 8.1 the 2000-lb/hr input to the heat exchanger had a value of \$200/hr, then the dollar flow is \$206/hr for the process effluent. This assumes that the condensate has zero value. For this simple example the calculations are simple. However, when material recycles and when material streams branch, realistic values are needed to attribute the costs among the streams. For example, for the flow diagram in Fig. 8.2, the value of stream 11 requires that the cost accumulated in stream 6 and for unit 5 needs to be equitably divided between streams 7 and 8. However, the value of stream 6 is itself dependent on the cost of stream 8 because these costs recycle. A sample calculation, with the allocation factors α_4, α_5, α_9, β_8, β_7, γ_{11}, and γ_{10} indicated, is given in Fig. 8.2. Based on the dollar flows the cost can easily be estimated for any stream in the process.

Cost per property

If the product is sold to supply octane rating, then the cost of alkylate per octane rating can be compared with the cost of alternative competing products.

8.5 Summary

Sometimes young professionals are so overwhelmed by the complexity of the processes that they cannot see easily where they should start to try to improve a process. Too often they start trying to apply their mathematical and engineering science skills where negligible benefit will result. One fruitful approach would be to prepare a cash position diagram, as outlined in Chapter 3, and to scrutinize each flow. One could try to minimize the working capital, keep the inventory small and level and try to maintain an even flow of money without violent fluctuations.

Alternatively, one could look at the more technical aspects of the process and try to identify areas where different technical equipment should be used or where alternative processing sequences would be beneficial. This short chapter highlights some of the cost guidelines that can be used to uncover potential savings.

System :

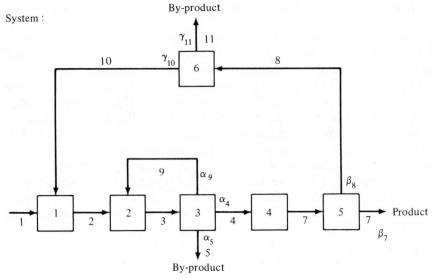

Costs associated with equipment		
Equipment unit	Cost, $/hr	
1	$ 1,000	
2	2,000	
3	3,000	
4	4,000	
5	5,000	
6	6,000	
Total operating cost	$21,000/hr	
Raw material cost	$10,000/hr	
Total	$31,000/hr	

Allocation factors among products 5,7,
and 11: $\delta_5 = 0.306$; $\delta_{11} = 0.097$.

Stream   5 = 0.306($31,000)   = $ 9,500
         11 = 0.097($31,000) = $ 3,000
         7 = $31,000 − 12,500 = $18,500

Costs associated with the streams

Assume $\alpha_9 = 0$; $\alpha_4 = \alpha_5 = 0.50$;
$\beta_8 = 0$; $\gamma_{11} = \gamma_{10} = 0.50$.

Stream	Cost, $/hr	
	Intermediate	Product
1	$10,000	
2	14,000	
3	16,000	
4	9,500	
5	—	9,500
6	13,500	
7	—	18,500
8	0	
9	0	
10	3,000	
11	—	3,000
Total		$31,000

Figure 8.2. Dollar flows for a recycle problem. (*Courtesy of the authors Crowe et al, Chemical Plant Simulation, Prentice-Hall, Inc., 1971.*)

PROBLEMS

8.1. You have just been assigned to work on a hydrodesulfurization process described in *Hydrocarbon Processing 47*, No. 9, p. 202 (1968) and by Blume et al. (1968). Where would you concentrate your efforts to improve this process?

8.2. Repeat Problem 8.1 for any process. Some processing details can be found through the use of the references listed in Table 7.2.

8.3. Develop tables of cost per mole data for raw materials pertinent to your industry if reactions are important. Study the development of new processes and generate rules-of-thumb for how to use the cost per mole information for screening studies of reaction routes for new processes.

Financial Decision Making: Summary 9

Engineers make key decisions in the process industry that affect all society. Good decisions account for a host of sometimes conflicting criteria: technical, safety, environmental, originality, benefits to society, market, political, economic, ethical, resources, time, financial, and financial attractiveness. Engineers must generate ideas that will benefit society, consider these many criteria, and make decisions—this is what this book is about.

In an esoteric sense, money is one of the most convenient measures of good or bad decisions. Indeed, in this general sense, many of the criteria— environmental, resources, time, etc.—can be expressed in terms of money. In this sense, good decisions based on multicriteria can be based on financial attractiveness provided a satisfactory method is used to quantify the unit of measurement. Hence, an important and major theme of this book was the calculation of the financial attractiveness criterion as being the backbone of good decision making.

In a very practical sense, money is the fabric of the process industry. Young professionals need a good understanding of not only the material flows that keep an industry healthy but the money flows without which it dies. A brief survey of economic modeling and theory led to a look at different facets of the process industry and the cash flows associated with each.

In general, goods or commodities are manufactured to bring benefit to man in society. A reasonable price is paid in return for the use of these commodities. The price yields a fair profit to the manufacturers. Supply by the manufacturers and the demand by society interact in the market. If the supply is excessive, money is tied up unnecessarily in the commodity as it sits on the shelf or in the warehouse. If the supply is insufficient, customers are disappointed.

The overall concepts of economics help to provide insight into what happens for different marketing and production policies. Two important ideas are the law of diminishing returns and the idea that profit is a maximum where marginal revenue and marginal cost are equal.

For a real company producing a product, the overall decisions include where to obtain the money or capital needed to run the business, how much product to make, and how to distribute the available money among the many activities of the company. The problem of obtaining the capital necessary for the projects was discussed.

The three major areas for the distribution of the money resources are in operations (or efficiency), design (or expansion), and R & D (or invention–innovation). The young professional is employed mainly in these areas. His responsibility is to identify directions and actions that the company should take and to prove technically, economically, financially, sociologically, and environmentally that they are feasible. His arguments need to be expressed in financial terms that are understood by supervisors, vice-presidents, etc.

Methods of identifying the financial attractiveness of proposals were described and compared. The present value and the internal-rate-of-return methods were recommended because of their flexibility and reliability.

The engineer will be required to estimate the capital and product costs of his proposals. Since many proposals can be dismissed without much detailed calculation, it is extremely important to start simply and calculate only the necessary information. Toward this goal, this book has presented algorithms of different sequential calculational procedures.

To help identify areas for potential savings, some simple concepts of value and cost per function were introduced in Chapter 8.

Bibliography

AACE Bulletin (1967), "AACE Cost Index Committee Information Survey," American Association of Cost Engineers Bulletin 7, No. 4, p. 145 (Dec.).

ALGER, P. L., CHRISTENSEN, N. A., and OLMSTED, S. P. (1965). "Ethical Problems in Engineering," sponsored by the American Society of Engineering Education.

ALI, A. M. (1970). "Inventory Problems" in *Cost and Optimization Engineering* (F. C. Jelen, ed.), McGraw-Hill, New York, Chap. 10.

ALLEN, D. H. (1967). "Two New Tools for Project Evaluation," *Chem. Eng. 74*, No. 15, p. 75.

ANDERSON, R. E. (1963). "Financial Management in the Chemical Industry" in *Administration of the Chemical Enterprise* (C. Berenson, ed.), Wiley-Interscience, New York, Chap. 9.

ARIES, R. S. (1966). "Trade Secrets: Robert Aries Airs His Views," *Chem. Eng. 73*, No. 8, p. 175.

ARIES, R. S., and NEWTON, R. D. (1955). *Chemical Engineering Cost Estimation*, McGraw-Hill, New York.

ARNOLD, T. H., and CHILTON, C. H. (1963). "New Index Shows Plant Cost Trends," *Chem. Eng. 70*, No. 4, p. 143.

AULD, J. R. (1963). "Capital Cost Estimates for Chemical Plants Electrical Systems," paper presented at the CIC conference in Montreal, Oct. 23.

AUSTIN, G. T. (1974). "The Industrially Significant Organic Chemicals," *Chem. Eng. 81*, No. 2, p. 132, No. 4, p. 125 ff.

BACH, N. G. (1958). "More Accurate Plant Cost Estimates," *Chem. Eng. 65*, No. 19, p. 155 and reprinted in Chilton (1960).

BACKMAN, J. (1970). *The Economics of the Chemical Industry*, Manufacturing Chemists Assoc., 1825 Connecticut Ave. N. W., Washington, D.C.

BALFOUR, F. J. and PAPUCCIYAN, T. L. (1972). "Capital Cost Estimating for Mineral Processing Plants," *Canadian Mining Journal 93*, No. 6, pp. 88–96. (June).

BARISH, N. H. (1962). "Economic Analysis for Engineering and Managerial Decision Making," McGraw-Hill, New York.

BARR, F. T. (1960). "Techniques for Evaluating Petroleum Processes," *Chem. Eng. Prog. 56*, No. 12, p. 53.

BAUMAN, H. C. (1959). "Costing Piping, The Bugaboo of Chemical Plant Estimating," *Ind. Eng. Chem. 51*, No. 1, p. 81A.

BAUMAN, H. C. (1960). "Cost of Starting Up the Chemical Process Plant." *Ind. Eng. Chem. 52*, No. 3, p. 51A.

BAUMAN, H. C. (1962). "What Is the Real Cost of Labor Abroad?," *Ind. Eng. Chem. 54*, No. 7, p. 34.

BAUMAN, H. C. (1964). *Fundamentals of Cost Engineering in the Chemical Industry*, Van Nostrand Reinhold, New York.

BEAM, K. A. (1970). "The Availability of Risk Capital in Canada," report submitted to Dept. of Chemical Engineering, McMaster University, Hamilton, Ontario, Canada.

BECHTEL, L. R. (1960). "Estimate Working Capital Needs," *Chem. Eng. 67*, No. 4, p. 127.

BERENSON, C. (1963a). *Administration of the Chemical Enterprise*, Wiley-Interscience, New York.

BERENSON, C. (1963b). "Marketing in the Chemical Industry" in *Administration of the Chemical Enterprise* (C. Berenson, ed.) Wiley-Interscience, New York, Chap. 1.

BILLET, R., and RAICHLE, L. (1967). Optimizing Method for Vacuum Rectification, Part II, *Chem. Eng. 74*, No. 4, p. 149.

BIRD, R. B., STEWART, W. E., and LIGHTFOOT, E. N. (1960). *Transport Phenomena*, Wiley, New York.

BLACK, J. H. (1971). "Correlating Marketing Variables for Chemicals, Minerals and Metals," *Trans. Am. Assoc. Cost Engineers*, Montreal Annual Meeting, published by the AACE.

BLAIR, A. G. (1963). "Estimating Equipment Costs," paper presented at the CIC conference in Montreal, Oct 23.

BLEWITT, B. J. (1967). "Development and Application of the Criteria for Economic Comparison and Profitability Studies," *AIChE Today Ser.*, Nov.

BLISS, H. (1947). "Data for Equipment Cost Estimates," *Chem. Eng. 54*, No. 5, p. 126 and reprinted in Chilton (1960).

BLISS, H. (1947). "Process Equipment Cost Data II. *Chem. Eng. 54*, No. 6, p. 100.

BLUME, J. H., MILLER, D. R., and NICOLAI, L. A. (1968). "Refining Process Developments—Remove Sulfur From Fuel Oil at Lowest Cost," *Hydrocarbon Processing 47*, No. 9, p. 131.

BOFFEY, P. M. (1971). "Nader and the Scientists: A Call for Responsibility," *Science 171*, p. 549, Feb.

BRANSCOM, L. M. (1971). "Taming Technology," *Science 171*, p. 972.

BROWN, R. G. (1967). *Decision Rules for Inventory Management*, Holt, Rinehart and Winston, Inc., New York.

CANADIAN RESEARCH AND DEVELOPMENT (1969). *Where Canada Spends Her R & D Dollars*, p. 7, Dec.

CARSON, R. (1962). *The Silent Spring*, Houghton-Mifflin Co., Boston.

CHAPMAN, F. S. and HOLLAND, F. A. (1966). "New Cost Data for Centrifugal Pumps," *Chem. Eng. 73*, No. 15, p. 200.

Chemical Engineering EDITORIAL STAFF (1963). "Engineers Speak Out on Ethics," *Chem. Eng. 70*, No. 25, p. 177.

Chemical Engineering News' annual September review of comparative financial data for selected companies.

Chemical Equipment Catalog, Van Nostrand Reinhold, New York.

CHILTON, C. H. (1949). "Cost Data Correlated," *Chem. Eng. 56*, No. 6, p. 97.

CHILTON, C. H. (1960). *Cost Engineering in the Process Industry*, McGraw-Hill, New York.

CHILTON, C. H. (1966). "Plant Cost Index Points Up Inflation," *Chem. Eng., 73*, No. 9, p. 184.

CLERK, J. (1963). "Multiplying Factors Give Installed Costs of Process Equipment," *Chem. Eng., 70*, No. 4, p. 182.

COMMONER, B. (1971). *The Closing Circle: Nature, Man and Technology*, Knopf, New York.

CORRIGAN, T. E., LEWIS, W. E., and McKELVEY, K. N. (1967). "What Do Chemical Reactors Cost in Terms of Volume?" *Chem. Eng. 74*, No. 11, p. 214.

CRANE, B. (1964). *The Sophisticated Investor*, newly revised and expanded by S. C. Eisenlohr, Simon and Schuster, New York.

CRANE CANADA LTD. (1957). "Flow of Fluids Through Valves, Fittings and Pipe," *Technical Paper 410-C*, Engineering Division, Chicago. Available from Crane Canada Ltd., Box 70, Montreal, P. Q.

CROWE, C. M., HAMIELEC, A. E., HOFFMAN, T. W., JOHNSON, A. I., SHANNON, P. T., and WOODS, D. R. (1971). *Chemical Plant Simulation*, Prentice-Hall, Englewood Cliffs, N. J.

DASGUPTA, A. K. and PEARCE, D. W. (1972). *Cost Benefit Analysis: Theory and Practice*, MacMillan, London.

DeCicco, R. W. (1968). "Economic Evaluation of Research Projects—By Computer," *Chem. Eng. 75*, No. 12, p. 84.

DeCossas, K. M., Koltun, S. P., and Patton, E. L. (1960). "Equipment Costs," *Chem. Eng. Prog. 56*, No. 12, p. 60.

DeFriece, A. N., Hamilton, G. E., and Larson, C. E. (1967). "Monte Carlo Simulation Applications in Research Project Evaluation," *Trans. Am. Assoc. Cost Engineers*, Cleveland, Annual Meeting, pub. by AACE, University, Alabama.

de Garmo, E. P. (1967). *Engineering Economy*, 4th ed., Macmillan, New York.

Denzler, R. E. (1952). "Blower and Fan Costs," *Chem. Eng. 59*, No. 10, p. 130. and reprinted in Chilton (1960).

Dershowitz, A. F. and McEntree, H. R. (1958). "Joint Products and Byproducts," *Chem. Eng. 65*, No. 26, p. 61, and reprinted in Chilton, (1960).

Dickens, S. P., and Douglas, F. R. (1960). "Off-site Investment and Working Capital," *Chem. Eng. Prog. 56*, No. 12, p. 44.

Dickson, R. A. (1950). "Pipe Cost Estimation," *Chem Eng. 57*, No. 1, p. 123.

Dinning, T. N. (1967). "Factored System for Pricing Piping Installations," *Trans. Am. Assoc. Cost Engineers*, Cleveland, Annual Meeting, published by the AACE, University, Alabama, p. 159.

Doig, I. D. (1969). *A Measurement of Venture Risk Using Expected Values*, Dept. of Chemical Engineering, The University of New South Wales, Kensington, N.S.W. 2033, Australia, Oct.

Doody, F. S. (1965). *Introduction to the Use of Economic Indicators*, Random House, Inc., New York.

Drew, J. W., and Ginder, A. F. (1970). How to Estimate the Cost of Pilot Plant Equipment. *Chem. Eng. 77*, No. 3, p. 100.

Dryden, C. E., and Furlow, R. H. (1966). *Chemical Engineering Costs*, Ohio State University, Columbus.

Edge, C. G. (1960). *A Practical Manual on the Appraisal of Capital Expenditure*, The Society of Industrial and Cost Accountants of Canada, Hamilton, Ontario, Canada.

Engineering News Record (1949). "ENR Construction and Building Cost Indexes," *Engineering News Record 142*, No. 11, p. 161.

Enyedy, G., Jr., and Diller, R. M. (1969). "COME Project Progress," *AACE Bull. 11*, No. 3, p. 106.

Erskine, M. G. (1969). *Chemical Conversion Factors and Yields*. Chemical Information Services, Menlo Park, California.

Faith, W. L., Keyes, D. B., and Clark, R. L. (1965). *Industrial Chemicals*, 3rd ed., Wiley, New York.

Federal Water Pollution Control Administration (1968). "*Treatment Plant Construction Cost Index*." Division of Construction Grants, Washington, D.C.

FIEGEL, L. J. (1972). "Marketing-Research and Development," *Trans. Am. Assoc. Cost Engineers*, Grossingers, Annual Meeting, published by the AACE, p. 129.

FISHBURN, PETER C. (1968). "Utility Theory," *Management Science Theory 14*, p. 335.

FORRESTER, J. (1970). *World Dynamics*, Wright-Allen Press Inc., Cambridge, Mass.

GABOURY, J. A. M. (1949). *Tables of Conversion Factors: Weights and Measures*, distributed with the compliments of Canadian Industries Ltd., Chemical Dept., Montreal.

GALLAGHER, J. T. (1967). "Rapid Estimation of Plant Costs," *Chem. Eng. 74*, No. 26, p. 88.

GANIS, B., and JORDON, W. A. (1963). "Advertising and Publicity in the Chemical Industry" in *Administration of the Chemical Enterprise* (C. Berenson, ed.), Wiley-Interscience, New York, Chap. 4.

GERSHEFSKI, G. W. (1972). "The Design and Use of Computer Assisted Financial Planning Systems," paper presented at the Annual Meeting of the American Institute of Chemical Engineers, Nov. 26–30, New York.

GLOBE AND MAIL, THE, Sept. 1, 1969, p. 25, Toronto, Canada.

GORDON COMMISSION (1958). Royal Commission *Canada's Economic Prospects*, Queen's Printer, Ottawa.

GRANT, E. L., and IRESON, W. G. (1970). *Principles of Engineering Economy*, 5th ed., Ronald, New York.

GREGORY, J. C. (1946). *Interest Tables for Determining Rate of Return*, Atlantic Richfield Co., Philadelphia.

GROSSELFINGER, F. B. (1962). "Capital Cost vs. Sales Price," *Chem. Eng. Prog. 58*, No. 2, p. 23.

GROSSELFINGER, F. B. (1962). "Capital Cost Effects on the US Chemical Industry's Foreign Competition," *Chem. Eng. Prog. 58*, No. 3, p. 60.

GRUMER, E. L. (1967). "Selling Price vs. Raw-material Cost," *Chem. Eng.*, *74*, No. 9, p. 190.

GUSHEE, D. E. (1965). "Keeping Sophistication in Perspective," *Ind. Eng. Chem. 57*, No. 10, p. 5.

GUTHRIE, K. M. (1969a). "Data and Techniques for Preliminary Capital Cost Estimating," *Chem. Eng. 76*, No. 6, p. 114.

GUTHRIE, K. M. (1969b). "Costs" in *A Complete Guide to Liquid Handling*, *Chem. Eng. 76*, No. 8, p. 201.

GUTHRIE, K. M. (1971). "Pump and Valve Costs" *Chem. Eng. 78*, No. 23, p. 151, and reproduced in Popper (1970) p. 161.

HAHN, A. V. (1970). *The Petrochemical Industry: Market and Economics*. McGraw-Hill, New York.

HAND, W. E. (1958). "From Flowsheet to Cost Estimate." *Pet. Ref. 37*, No. 9, p. 331.

HAPPEL, J. (1958). *Chemical Process Economics*, Wiley, New York.

HARBERGER, A. C. (1973). *Project Evaluation: Collected Papers*. Markham Publishing Co., Chicago. LD. 74-165981, BIN-8410-2021-3. Chapter 2. Survey of Literature.

HARRIS, J. S. (1961). "Selecting Potentially Profitable Products," *Chem. Eng. News. 39*, No. 16, p. 110, April 17.

HERRON, D. P. (1967). "Comparing Investment Evaluation Methods," *Chem. Eng., 74*, No. 2, p. 125.

HIRSCH, J. H., and GLAZIER, E. M. (1960). "Estimating Plant Investment Costs," *Chem. Eng. Prog. 56*, No. 12, p. 37.

HIRSCHMANN, W. B., and BRAUWEILER, J. R. (1970). "Continuous Interest and Discounting" in *Cost and Optimization Engineering* (F. C. Jelen, ed.), McGraw-Hill, New York, Chap. 4.

HODGINS, J. W. (1970). "Macro-ethics," *Professional Engineer Eng. Digest*, June.

HOUGEN, O. A., WATSON, K. M., and RAGATZ, R. A. (1959). *Chemical Process Principles*, Vol. II, 2nd ed., Wiley, New York.

HULL, A. P. (1971). "Radiation in Perspective—Some Comparisons of Environmental Risks from Nuclear-Fueled and Fossil-Fueled Power Plants." *Nuclear Safety 12*, p. 185.

Hydrocarbon Processing annual refining and petrochemical handbook issues, Gulf Publishing Co., Houston.

IMPERIAL OIL LTD. *Petrochemical Flow Charts*. Available from Imperial Oil Ltd., Chemical Products Dept., 111 St. Clair Ave. W., Toronto, Canada.

INDUSTRIAL AND ENGINEERING CHEMISTRY (1950 ff.). *Modern Chemical Processes*, Van Nostrand Reinhold, New York.

JELEN, F. C. (1954). "Next Time Use Capitalized Costs," *Chem. Eng. 61*, No. 2, p. 199.

JELEN, F. C. (1970). "Depreciation and Taxes—Equivalence After Taxes" in *Cost and Optimization Engineering* (F. C. Jelen, ed.), McGraw-Hill, New York.

JORDAN, D. G. (1968). *Chemical Process Development*, Part 1, Wiley-Interscience, New York.

KAPFER, W. H. (1967). "Development of Object Functions for Engineering Economic Analysis," *AIChE Today Ser.*, Nov.

KAPFER, W. H. (1969). "Appraising Rate of Return Methods," *Chem. Eng. Prog. 65*, No. 11, p. 55.

KARDOS, G. (1969). *Heron Road Bridge*, Case ECL 133A in Engineering Case Library Stanford Engineering Case Program, Stanford University, Stanford, Calif.

KASTENS, M. L. (1962). "Productivity Factor Critical," *Chem. Eng. Prog. 58*, No. 2, p. 22.

KATELL, S. (1973). "Cost Engineering in the Minerals Industry." Video tapes and study guide available from the Process Evaluation Group, United States Dept. of the Interior, Bureau of Mines, Morgantown, W. Va.

KAZANOWSKI, A. D. (1968a). "A Standardized Approach to Cost-Effectiveness Evaluations" in *Cost-Effectiveness: The Economic Evaluation of Engineered Systems* (J. M. English, ed.), Wiley, New York.

KAZANOWSKI, A. D. (1968b). "Cost-Effectiveness Fallacies and Misconceptions Revisited" in *Cost Effectiveness: the Economic Evaluation of Engineered Systems* (J. M. English, ed.), Wiley, New York.

KEATING, C. J. (1962). "Accurate Way To Estimate Pipe Installation Costs," *Chem. Eng. 69*, No. 13, p. 125.

KEENEY, R. L., "A Decision Analysis with Multiple Objectives: The Mexico City Airport." *The Bell Journal of Economics and Management Science 4*, No. 1, p. 101.

KEMPSTER, J. H. (1967). "Financial Analysis to Guide Capital Expenditure Decisions," *Research Report 43*, National Association of Accountants, New York.

KHARBANDA, O. P. (1958). *Nomograms for Chemical Engineers*, Academic Press, New York.

KIDDOO, G. (1951). "Turnover Ratios Analyzed," *Chem. Eng. 58*, No. 10, p. 145 and reprinted in Chilton (1960).

KIEFER, D. M. (1964). "Winds of Change in Industrial Chemical Research," *Chem. Eng. News, 42*, No. 12, p. 88, March 23.

KIRK, H. F. McKETTA, J. J., JR. and OTHMER, D. F. (1972). *Kirk-Othmer Encyclopedia of Chemical Technology*, 2nd ed., Wiley, New York.

KOBE, K. A. and McKETTA, J. J., *Advances in Petroleum Chemistry and Refining* Wiley-Interscience, New York.

KRATHWOHL, D., et al. (1964). *Taxonomy of Educational Objectives: Affective Domain*, McKay, New York.

LAMBERTON, C. H. (1963). "Estimating Piping Costs," paper presented at the CIC conference in Montreal, Oct. 23.

LANG, H. J. (1947a). "Engineering Approach to Preliminary Cost Estimates," *Chem. Eng., 54*, No. 9, p. 130.

LANG, H. J. (1947b). "Cost Relationships in Preliminary Cost Estimation," *Chem. Eng., 54*, No. 10, p. 117.

LANG, H. J. (1948). "Simplified Approach to Preliminary Cost Estimation," *Chem. Eng., 55*, No. 6, p. 112.

LEAR, J. (1970). "Predicting the Consequences of Technology," *Saturday Review*, p. 44, March 28.

LePrince, P., Chauvel, A., Catry, J. P., and Castex, L. (1971). Procédes de Pétrochimie charactéristiques, techniques et économiques. Editions Technip. 27 Rue Ginoux, Paris 15ᵉ.

Leung, T. K. Y. (1970). "New Nomograph: Quick Route to Discounted Cash Flow," *Chem. Eng. 77*, No. 12, p. 208.

Liebson, I., and Trischman, C. A. (1971). "Spotlight on Operating Cost: Economic Analysis, Part 1," *Chem. Eng. 78*, No. 12, p. 69.

Liptak, B. G. (1962). "Flow Instruments: Cost vs. Size," *Chem. Eng. 69*, No. 6, p. 196.

Liptak, B. G. (1970a). "Process Instruments, Part 1," *Chem. Eng. 77*, No. 20, p. 60.

Liptak, B. G. (1970b). "Process Instruments, Part 2," *Chem. Eng. 77*, No. 21, p. 175.

Liptak, B. G. (1970c). "Process Instruments, Part 3," *Chem. Eng. 77*, No. 22, p. 83.

Liptak, B. G. (1970d). "Process Instruments, Part 4, *Chem. Eng. 77*, No. 24, p. 94.

Lurgi Manual (1961). Lurgi Gesellschaften, Frankfurt am Main, Germany.

Luth, F. A. D., and Konig, H. (1967). *The Planning of Iron and Steelworks*, 3rd ed., translated by Gordon Cockburn, Springer-Verlag, New York.

Lynn, L. (1954). "Making the Most of Capital Ratios," *Chem. Eng., 61*, No. 4, p. 175.

Magee, J. F., and Boodman, D. M. (1967). *Production Planning and Inventory Control*, 2nd ed., McGraw-Hill, New York.

Malloy, J. B. (1969). "Instant Economic Evaluation," *Chem. Eng. Prog. 65*, No. 11, p. 47.

Man-Made World (1971). Three-volume Engineering Concepts Curriculum Project, McGraw-Hill, New York.

Marglin, S. A. (1967). *Public Investment Criteria: Benefit-Cost Analysis for Planned Economic Growth.* George Allen and Unwin, Ltd. Ruskin House, Museum Street, London.

Massey, D. J., and Black, J. H., (1969). "Predicting Chemical Prices," *Chem. Eng., 76*, No. 23, p. 150.

McGraw-Hill Department of Economics (1967). Index published with each issue of *Chemical Engineering, Chem. Eng., 74*, No. 8, p. 197.

McNeill, T. F., and Clark, D. S. (1966). *Cost Estimating and Contract Pricing*, American Elsevier, New York.

Merrill Lynch, Pierce, Fenner & Smith, Inc. (1971). *How To Read a Financial Report*, rev. ed., New York.

Miles, L. D. (1961). *Techniques of Value Analysis and Engineering*, McGraw-Hill, New York.

MILLER, C. A. (1964). "Estimating the Costs of Chemical Plants," *Chem. in Canada*, p. 34, Jan.

MILLER, C. A. (1965). "Factor Estimating Refined for Appropriation of Funds." *AACE Bull.* 7, No. 3, p. 92, Sept.

MILLER, C. A. (1966). Notes distributed to the senior class, McMaster University, Hamilton, Ontario, Canada.

MILLS, H. E. (1964). "Costs of Process Equipment," *Chem. Eng.*, *71*, No. 6, p. 133.

Minerals Yearbook, U.S. Bureau of Mines, U.S. Department of the Interior, Washington, D.C.

MUELLER, J. W. (1963). "Accounting and the Chemical Business" in *Administration of the Chemical Enterprise* (C. Berenson, ed.), Wiley-Interscience, New York, Chap. 8.

MYER, J. N. (1968). *Understanding Financial Statements*, Mentor Executive Library Books, MQ 794, New York.

MYERS, A. L., and SIEDER, W. D. (1973). *Chemical Process Logic*, to be published by Prentice-Hall, Inc., Englewood Cliffs, N.J.

NADER, R. (1971). *Conference on Professional Responsibility*, Washington, D.C., Jan. 30.

NADER, R., PETKAS, P. and BLACKWELL, K. (1972). *Whistle Blowing*, Bantam Books, Inc., New York.

NATIONAL BUREAU OF ECONOMIC RESEARCH (1954). *Long Range Economic Projection: Studies in Income and Wealth*, Princeton University Press, Princeton, N.J.

NATIONAL SCIENCE FOUNDATION (1966). *Review of Data on Science Resources*, No. 7, Jan.

NELSON, W. L. (1960). Reported in Hirsch and Glazier (1960).

NELSON, W. L. (1963). "Foreign Costs and Industrial Productivity," *Chem. Eng. Prog. 59*, No. 3, p. 22.

NELSON, W. L. (1967a). "Tabulated Values of Construction Cost Index," *Oil Gas J.*, *65*, p. 110, March 6.

NELSON, W. L. (1967b). "How Nelson Index Is Computed," *Oil Gas J., 65,* p 97, May 15.

NELSON, W. L. (1968a). "Cost Indexes Without Productivity Mean Little," *Trans. Am. Assoc. Cost Engineers,* Houston, Annual Meeting, published by the AACE, University, Alabama, p. 45–1.

NORDEN, R. B. (1968). "Development of a Cost Index," *Trans. AACE 12th National Meeting*, Houston, June 17–19. Published by the AACE, University, Alabama, p. 46–1.

O'DONNELL, J. P. (1953). "New Correlation of Engineering and Other Indirect Project Costs," *Chem. Eng. 60*, No. 1, p. 188.

OLIVER, E. D. (1966). *Diffusional Separation Processes: theory, design and evaluation*. Wiley, New York.

OLSEN, R. A. (1968). *Manufacturing Management: A Quantitative Approach*, International Textbook Co., Scranton, Pa.

O'MEARA, J. T., JR. (1961). "Selecting Profitable Products," *Harvard Business Rev.*, p. 83, Jan.–Feb.

OSBURN, J. P., and KAMMERMEYER, K. (1958). *Money and Chemical Engineer*, Prentice-Hall, Inc., Englewood Cliffs, N.J.

OTTO, E. A. (1963). "The Primary Securities Market-Venture Capital Pools," *Essays on Business Finance*, 4th ed., Masterco Press, Ann Arbor, Mich.

PACKARD, V. (1957). *The Hidden Persuaders*, Penguin Books, Baltimore, Chap. 3.

PAGE, J. S. (1963). *Estimator's Manual of Equipment and Installation Costs*, Gulf Publishing Co., Houston.

PATTERSON, W. H. (1969). "Preparing and Maintaining a Construction Cost Index," *Trans. Am. Assoc. Cost Engineers,* Pittsburgh, Meeting, published by the AACE, University, Alabama, p. 272.

PERRY, J. H. (1950). *Chemical Engineer's Handbook*, 3rd ed., McGraw-Hill, New York.

PERRY, J. H. (1954). *Chemical Business Handbook*, McGraw-Hill, New York.

PETERS, M. (1958). *Plant Design and Economics for Chemical Engineers*, McGraw-Hill, New York.

PETERS, M., and TIMMERHAUS, K. (1968). *Plant Design and Economics for Chemical Engineers*, 2nd ed., McGraw-Hill, New York.

POPPER, H., and the staff of *Chemical Engineering* (1970). *Modern Cost Engineering Techniques*, McGraw-Hill, New York.

POPPER, H., and HUGHSON, R. V. (1970). "How Would *You* Apply Engineering Ethics to Environmental Problems," *Chem. Eng. 77*, No. 24, p. 88.

Popular Mechanics (1970). "Current U.S. Used Car Prices," p. 89, June.

PRATER, N. H. and ANTONACCI, D. W. (1960). "How to Estimate Fractionating Column Costs." *Pet. Refiner. 39*, No. 7, p. 119.

PRATER, N. H. and MYLO, J. (1961). "Equipment Cost Data File: Centrifugal Pumps (Multi-Stage, Vertically Split) (Double Suction, Single Stage, Horizontally Split)." *H.P. and Pet. Ref. 40*, No. 12, p. 159.

REILLY, P. M., and JOHRI, H. P. (1969). "Decision Making Through Opinion Analysis," *Chem. Eng. 76*, No. 7 p. 122; or in H. Popper, New York, 1970. p. 342.

REISMAN, A. (1968). "Methods for Choosing Among Competing Investment Opportunities." *Heating, Piping and Air Conditioning 40*, No. 9, p. 130, Sept.

REUL, R. I. (1957). "Profitability Index for Investments." *Harvard Business Rev. 35*, No. 4, p. 116.

REUL, R. I. (1968). "Which Investment Appraisal Technique Should You Use," *Chem. Eng.*, *75*, No. 9, p. 212.

RIGGS, J. L. (1968). *Economic Decision Models for Engineers and Managers*, McGraw-Hill, New York.

ROYAL COMMISSION ON BANKING AND FINANCE (1964). Submission by the Canadian Small and Independent Business Federation, Queen's Printer, Ottawa.

RUDD, D. F., and WATSON, C. C. (1968). *The Strategy of Process Engineering*, Wiley, New York.

RUDD, D. F., POWERS, G. J. and SIRROLA, J. J. (1973). *Process Synthesis*. Prentice-Hall, Inc., Englewood Cliffs, N.J.

SCHUMAN, S. C. (1940). Cited in Schuman (1955b).

SCHUMAN, S. C. (1948). Cited in Schuman (1955a).

SCHUMAN, S. C. (1955a). "New Look at Economics of Pricing." *Chem. Eng. 62*, No. 3, p. 180.

SCHUMAN, S. C. (1955b). "How Plant Size Affects Unit Costs," *Chem. Eng. 62*, No. 5, p. 173.

SCHWEYER, H. C. (1952). "Capital Ratios Analyzed," *Chem. Eng. 59*, No. 1, p. 164.

SCIENCE COUNCIL OF CANADA (1968). "Towards a National Science Policy for Canada," *Report 4*, Oct., Queen's Printer, Ottawa.

SHELDRICK, M. G. (1969). "Deep Well Disposal: Are Safeguards Being Ignored?," *Chem. Eng. 76*, No. 7, p. 74.

SHREVE, R. N. (1967). *Chemical Process Industries*, 3rd ed., McGraw-Hill, New York.

SIMMONDS, W. H. C. (1969). "Stepwise Expansion and Profitability," *Chem. in Canada*, p. 16, Sept.

SITTIG, M. (1967). *Organic Chemical Process Encyclopedia*. Noyes Development Corp., Mill Rd. at Grand Ave., Park Ridge, New Jersey.

SOKULLU, E. S. (1969). "Estimating Piping Costs from Process Flowsheets, *Chem. Eng. 76*, No. 3, p. 148.

STANFORD RESEARCH INSTITUTE. *Chemical Economics Handbook*, updated periodically, Menlo Park, Calif.

STARR, C. (1969). "Social Benefit Versus Technological Risk." *Science 165*, p. 1232.

STEVENS, R. W. (1947). "Equipment Cost Indexes for Process Industries." *Chem. Eng. 54*, No. 11, p. 124. Reprinted in Chilton (1960) p. 20.

STREET, G. L., and CORRIGAN, T. E. (1967). Make Quick Evaluation Estimates," *Hydrocarbon Processing 46*, No. 12, p. 147.

SZENDROVITS, A. Z. (1969). *An Introduction to Production Management*, McMaster University Bookstore, Hamilton, Canada.

SZENDROVITS, A. Z. (1971). *Business Simulation Participants' Manual*, McMaster University Bookstore, Hamilton, Canada.

TAYLOR, G. A. (1964). *Managerial and Engineering Economy*, Van Nostrand Reinhold, New York.

TELLER, A. J. (1966). "Thoughts on Professionalism," *Chem. Eng.*, *73*, No. 20. p. 138.

THATCHER, C. M. (1962). *Fundamentals of Chemical Engineering*, C. E. Merrill Books, Columbus, Ohio.

THUESEN, H. G., and FABRYCKY, W. J. (1964). *Engineering Economy*, 3rd ed. Prentice-Hall, Inc., Englewood Cliffs, N.J.

TOFFLER, A. (1970). *Future Shock*, Bantam, Random House, New York.

TWADDLE, W. W., and MALLOY, J. B. (1966) "Evaluating and Sizing New Chemical Plants." *Chem. Eng. Prog. 62*, No. 7, p. 90; or *AACE Bull. 8*, No. 3, p. 135.

UHL, V. W., and HAWKINS, A. W. (1971). *Technical Economics for Engineers*, AIChE Continuing Education Series 5. American Institute of Chemical Engineers, New York.

U. S. DEPARTMENT OF COMMERCE (1967). *Technological Innovation: Its Environment and Management*, report by the panel on Invention and Innovation. Washington, D.C.

WALAS, S. M. (1961). "Plant Investment Costs by the Factor Method," *Chem. Eng. Prog. 57*, No. 6, p. 68.

WALLER, T. C. (1969). "Cost Index Committee—Report to Membership," *1969 Trans. Am. Assoc. Cost Engineers,* Annual Meeting, Pittsburgh, published by the AACE, University, Alabama, p. 281.

WAYMAN, M. (1973). "Guide for Planning Pulp and Paper Enterprises." *FAO Forestry and Forest Product Studies.* No. 18. Food and Agriculture Organization of the United Nations, Rome.

WEAVER, J. B., BAUMAN, H. C., and HENEGHAN, W. F. (1963). "Cost and Profitability Estimation" in *Chemical Engineer's Handbook*, 4th ed. (R. H. Perry et al., eds.), McGraw-Hill, New York.

WESSEL, H. E. (1953). "How To Estimate Costs in a Hurry," *Chem. Eng. 60*, No. 1, p. 168.

WEST, A. S. (1965) of Rohm and Haas, submission to the design project at the University of Pennsylvania.

WHITE, T. H. (1970). *The Making of the President—1969*, Simon and Schuster, New York.

WOODS, D. R. (1969). *An Analysis of Structure with Example Application to the Alkylation and Sulfuric Acid Processes*, Dept. of Chemical Engineering, McMaster University, Hamilton, Ontario, Canada.

WOODS, D. R. (1974) *Cost Data for the Process Industries.* McMaster University Bookstore, McMaster University, Hamilton, Ontario, Canada.

WROTH, W. F. (1960). "Factors in Cost Estimation," *Chem. Eng. 67*, No. 21, p. 204.

ZABEL, H. W. and MARCHITTO, M. (1959). "What Price Can I Get for My Chemical?" *Chem. Eng. 66*, No. 21, p. 112. Reprinted in Chilton (1960).

ZIMMERMAN, O. T. (1968a). "Elements of Capital Cost Estimation." *Cost Eng. 13*, No. 4, p. 4.

ZIMMERMAN, O. T. (1970b). "Capital Investment Cost Estimation" in *Cost and Optimization Engineering* (F. C. Jelen, ed.), McGraw-Hill, New York, Chap. 15.

Nomenclature

The terms used in this text are defined in the Glossary. The system of nomenclature for these terms embodies two principles that impart consistency and simplicity:

1. Capital letters represent monetary values. Lowercase letters refer to nonmonetary values.
2. Linguistic-accent superscripts are used to differentiate between annual rates and per unit production rates. Bird et al. (1960) used $\wedge$ and $\sim$ to differentiate between per unit mass and per unit mole. Of the remaining linguistic-accent superscripts, the Russian $\smile$ was chosen to represent *annual rates* or *per year* basis. The German umlaut ($\cdot\cdot$) refers to *per unit of production*.

Once these principles were established, it remained only to match symbols with concepts. Wherever possible the symbols common to five major engineering economics texts were chosen. Where this was not possible (i.e., two concepts using the same symbol) the unallocated symbol that most closely sounded like the concept was chosen. For example, two texts used the symbols h and p for container and shipping cost. Neither symbol is acceptable. Symbols C for container or S for shipping are already allocated. Hence, F for freight was chosen.

An asterisk (*) refers to items reported before tax, whereas the absence of a superscript indicates items reported after tax. Thus, $\breve{R}^*$ is annual return before tax, and $\breve{R}$ is annual return after tax.

257

Symbol	Concept
A	Operating supervision cost
B	Amount of outstanding borrowed capital
C	Total cost including book depreciation
C_F	Cost that does not vary with the rate of production: fixed costs
C_L	Linear costs that vary with production rate and are zero at zero production rate
C_R	Regulated costs that vary with the production rate but are not zero at the zero production rate
ΔC	Marginal cost
D	Depreciation cost
E	Equipment cost
E_D	Delivered equipment cost
E_{FOB}	FOB equipment cost
E_I	Installed equipment cost
F	Container and shipping cost of product excluding directly attributable labor
G	General expenses
H	Cash position at time b years
I	Total capital investment
I_F	Fixed capital investment
I_W	Working capital investment
J	Maintenance cost
K	Capitalized cost
L	Operating labor cost
M	Total manufacturing cost
M_D	Directly attributable manufacturing cost that varies with production rate
M_F	Directly attributable manufacturing cost that is independent of production rate
M_I	Indirectly attributable manufacturing cost
N	Raw material expense, dollars per pound of raw material
P	Profit after taxes including book depreciation.
P^*	Profit before taxes including book depreciation
Q	Venture profit
R	Return, raw material cost contribution to the product cost; profit excluding book depreciation
S	Selling price: revenue less any allowances for bulk volume, discounts, etc.
ΔS	Marginal revenue, incremental revenue
U	Utility cost
V	Original value of some (completely installed) asset.
V_b	Book value of some asset of asset value
V_S	Scrap value of some asset, salvage value

Symbol	Concept
W	Present value
X	Physical plant cost
Z	Replacement cost of asset, $= V - V_s$
$\mathcal{I}$	Total amount of interest during n interest periods
$\mathcal{P}$	Principal/total amount borrowed/present sum of capital on which interest is paid: present worth
$\mathcal{R}$	End of period payment to give in uniform series ordinary annuity
$\mathcal{S}$	Single payment at the end of nth period; sum at future date; amount of principal plus interest due
b	Number of years at which cash position is measured from initial operation
c	Fixed percentage for depreciation purposes
d	Depreciation rate for tax purpose
e	Depreciation rate for internal accounting purposes
f	Number of days in an interest period
f	Factor to scale costs
g	Project life as estimated for design, years
h	Insurance premium $i_m - i$
i	Current earning rate in company; interest rate based on length of one interest period with no risk
i_m	Minimum acceptable with risk
j	Nominal interest rate; approximate interest rate based on a 1-year interest period
k	Maintenance: fraction of investment year
l	Man-hours of labor excluding maintenance
m	Number of times interest is compounded per year
n	Number of interest periods
p	Payout time after taxes
p^*	Payout time before taxes
q	Quantity produced, demanded, sold
r	Percentage return on total investment after taxes
r^*	Percentage return on total investment before taxes
t	Income tax rate
w	Turnover ratio or 1/capital ratio
y	Number of time units (service life in years) specified for tax purposes by government; taxable period of plant life

Glossary of Accounting, Engineering, and Business Terms

Accounts payable An amount owing to creditors, representing a liability for purchases of goods or services.

Accounts receivable An amount claimed against a debtor, usually money rights arising from the sale of goods or services.

Administrative expense The classification for financial statement purposes of those expenses of an organization relating to the overall direction of its affairs; as opposed to those expenses incurred for other specialized functions; e.g., costs of manufacturing, selling, financing, or research and development are *not* included in the administrative expense.

Allocation of costs Distribution of expenses to processing units or to products.

Annual cost Dollars per calendar year (approximately 365 days).

Appurtenances Equipment added to process or nonprocess equipment to make it function, e.g., piping, insulation, instrumentation, electrical.

Asset An economic resource of an entity (including money resources, physical resources, and intangible resources).

Auxiliary facilities (*Synonyms:* off-site or off-battery limits.) Facilities that serve battery limits processing but do not produce a chemical product that is sold. For example, *utilities* (substations, boiler house, compressed air, refrigeration, water supply, inert gas, drains and sewers including normal sewage treatment); *storage* *and handling* (warehouses, storage tanks, loading and unloading facilities for raw materials and finished products—but does not include storage facilities for in-process material within battery limits or for materials required for utilities); *services* (all remaining investment items on the plant site; includes offices, laboratories, shops, lunchrooms, fences, roads, etc.).

Balance sheet   A formal statement of financial position, showing the assets, liabilities, and owner's equity of the accounting entity at a particular moment of time.

Bare module   (*See* Module, cost of bare.)

Base case   A single set of consistent data describing normal operation of a process, or the technically acceptable alternative that requires the smallest capital investment.

Battery limits   The geographic boundary, real or imaginary, around all the process equipment including that for the pollution abatement inside process area needed to provide effluents satisfactory to the rest of the plant operation. However, it excludes the auxiliary facilities.

Bid design   Stage in engineering activity when detailed plans, specifications, and layout are such that construction can be performed without further information. (Fixed capital investment cost estimates are accurate to $\pm 5\%$.) Sometimes called detailed design.

Book value, internal   The amount at which an item appears in the books of account and financial statements for the purpose of internal company accounting. In accordance with generally accepted accounting principles, most assets are recorded at their original cost, less such amounts as have been written off as expense since acquisition, such as depreciation or depletion. The original cost is not adjusted for changes in the "real" (market value) value of the asset itself or for changes in the value of the monetary unit (inflation/deflation). If the asset is scrapped, the book value drops immediately to zero.

Book value, tax   Net asset value for purposes of governmental taxation. Same as internal book value except that the depreciation deducted is that which is allowed for by the federal government taxation department.

Building costs   Costs within the battery limits including buildings, structural steel for the building, heating, ventilating, lighting, wiring but excluding foundations and supports for process equipment and process plumbing such as drains and vents.

Burden   Usually a synonym for *overhead*.

Capital, cost of   The cost of obtaining the total capital employed by a company, expressed as an interest rate. (Includes both the cost of equity capital and the cost of borrowed funds.) The weighted average of (1) the after tax cost of long term debt, (2) the yield on any outstanding preferred stock, and (3) the cost of common equity capital.

Capital, fixed investment   The total original cost of installed physical facilities that cannot be deducted for tax purposes as a current expense in the year of acquisition but for which depreciation is allowed by the taxation authorities. Land is not considered as fixed capital. Costs incurred in site preparation are not included as fixed capital investment.

Capital, sources of Suppliers of capital to a business enterprise (stockholders, banks, creditors).

Capital, working The funds over and above the fixed capital and land investment needed to start and maintain a project (excluding startup costs). Includes cash, inventory, accounts receivable, extracting solvents, goods in process less accounts payable. Characteristically, these funds can be converted readily into cash. Working capital is normally assumed recovered at the end of the project without loss. By definition, current assets minus current liabilities.

Capital recovery The process by which the original fixed capital investment is recovered over its life.

Capitalized cost In accounting, charging of an expenditure to a capital asset account rather than to an expense account. In profitability studies, the sum of money which, at a given interest rate, provides an infinite series of uniform payments without diminishing the original sum.

Cash Includes currency, coins, readily transferable money orders and checks, and demand deposits in bank accounts. Refers only to those items which are unrestricted as to use and are available readily for the payment of any obligations.

Cash basis Accounting procedure whereby revenue and expense are recognized when cash is received and paid, as opposed to the accrual basis or production basis.

Cash flow The net passage of dollars into or out of a firm or project as a result of operations. The usual convention is to consider cash outflows negative (investments, expenses, increased tax, etc.) and cash inflows positive (savings in reduced expenses, increased profit before or after tax depending on which is desired, reduced tax, etc.). Depreciation is *not* a cash flow but merely a book transaction.

Cash position The net financial result at time of all cash flows since the start of the project is the cash position at time *t*.

Compound interest (*See* Interest, compound.)

Compounding Use of compound interest to determine sums later in time which are equivalent to an earlier, smaller sum.

Construction expense (*See* Field expense.)

Container expense Cost of the physical device used to package the product. Does not include labor, material, and overhead costs. This is a subset of packaging expense.

Contingencies An allowance for unforeseeable elements of cost (particularly in fixed investment estimates) which previous experience has shown to be statistically likely to occur. Includes items overlooked in construction costs, slight changes in process design, unforeseen engineering fees, and added costs due to strikes or delays and may allow for the escalation of equipment prices.

Continuous interest (*See* Interest, continuous.)

Contract Legal agreement between two parties. In the construction of a process plant, the contract can be bonus-penalty, cost-plus, guaranteed maximum, lump sum, etc.

Contract, bonus-penalty Contractor is guaranteed a bonus for each day the project is completed ahead of schedule and agrees to pay a similar penalty for each day after the scheduled completion date that is required to complete the project.

Contract, cost-plus Contractor furnishes all material, equipment, and labor at actual cost plus an agreed upon percentage fee for his services.

Contract, guaranteed maximum Same as cost-plus together with a guarantee that the total cost to owner will not exceed a stipulated maximum amount.

Contract, lump sum Contractor agrees to furnish a completely erected facility at a single price.

Contract, turnkey A lump sum agreement plus startup with guarantees of quality, quantity, and yield.

Contractor's fees The fee for services of the contractor on the installation of fixed capital.

Control lab costs Cost of chemical and physical testing for routine production purposes and minor trouble shooting but does not include research.

Cost, product All manufacturing costs associated with the product and thus included in determining costs of goods sold and inventory valuations. Includes directly and indirectly attributable expenses, general expenses, and depreciation that can be equitably attributed to a product.

Cost of goods sold (*See* Cost, product.)

Cost indices (*See* Inflation index.)

Current With respect to income determination, means that item is applicable to the period now under consideration.

Current asset An asset that in the normal course of operations is expected to be converted into cash or consumed in the production of revenue within 1 year (or within normal operating cycle where that is longer than 1 year).

Current expense Amounts (usually cost) chargeable against the revenue of this period.

Current income Income for the current year or current period.

Depletion A reduction in quantity of wasting assets, as a result of consumption or removal of natural resources, e.g., standing timber, mines. *Also:* A noncash allowance made in the accounts to reflect the cost of portion of wasting assets consumed or removed. This is allowed as a tax deduction.

Depreciation Gradual exhaustion of the service potential of fixed assets which is not restored by maintenance practices. *Also:* A proportionate charge as expense to an accounting period based on cost or other recorded value of fixed assets.

Depreciation, for company purposes Depreciation provisions as reflected in company's financial statements as opposed to these in tax return statement. Yields the book value.

Depreciation, for tax purposes Depreciation provisions as reflected in tax return statement (also called capital cost allowance—usually allowing for accelerated writing off of assets).

Detailed design (*See* Bid design.)

Direct expenses Confusing term because *direct* may mean "directly attributable to a given product" or "varies with product rate."

Direct production cost (*See* Directly attributable expense.)

Directly attributable expense With reference to fixed capital investment, the cost of all material and labor directly attributable to the actual installation of facilities. With reference to product costs, costs of materials and labor and other expenses that can be easily identified and attributed to the manufacture of a specific product.

Discounted cash flow   (*See* Internal rate of return.) (*Synonyms:* investor's method, profitability index, internal rate of return, interest rate of return.)

Discounting   The use of compound interest to determine sums earlier in time which are equivalent to a later, larger sum (opposite of *compounding*).

Economic life   (*See* Life, economic.)

Employee benefits   (*See* Fringe benefits.)

Engineering bid design   (*See* Bid design.)

Engineering cost   All costs (including profit) incurred in making surveys, tests, drawings, and specifications complete enough for a contractor (includes salaries and overheads for administration, engineering, drafting, purchasing, cost estimation, expediting, communications, reproduction, and supervision of construction). (Sometimes called engineering and supervision.) See O'Donnell (1953).

Equipment cost, delivered   Cost of equipment delivered to the construction site but not uncrated. (FOB cost plus transportation, taxes, and duties.)

Equipment cost, FOB   Cost of equipment crated and on board the delivery vehicle at the equipment manufacturer's location. Does not include tax, import duties, freight, or shipping expense.

Equipment cost, installed   (This term needs to be carefully defined in the context in which it is used.) Delivered equipment cost plus all costs incurred in getting it uncrated, laid on foundations, supported, and electrically wired. Includes materials and labor. Normally does not include piping, utility hookup, insulation, instrumentation applied to the system, painting, or buildings. However, different authors include a variety of costs.

Equity   Source of financing the assets of the firm.

Equity capital   The ownership claim by the shareholders in the assets of the firm.

Equivalent annual cost method   The cost stream for each project is converted into the equivalent perpetual annuity at an appropriate rate of interest.

Escalation   (*See* Inflation index.)

Excess capacity   Productive capacity not in use because potential volume cannot be sold economically. (*See* Utilization factor.)

Expansion   Any increase in capacity of a plant or process unit, usually through capital expenditure.

Extra work   Work added to contract drawings and specifications, at an extra charge, after original contract was let, due to errors and design modifications.

Fabrication   The assembly of previously designed portions of the plant.

Feasibility study   Investigation of all phases of a project (financial, technical, environmental, market) in as much detail as is necessary to justify dropping it or continuing the project through the next stage.

Field expense   Indirectly attributable costs incurred by the contractor during the construction of the plant.

Financing   (*See* Capital, sources of.)

Financing expense   (*See* Capital, cost of.)

Firm estimate   (*See* Bid design.)

Fixed capital   (*See* Capital, fixed investment.)

Fixed cost   A cost which, for a given time period and range of activity (called the relevant range), does not change in total but becomes progressively smaller on a per unit basis as volume increases.

Force majeure   A clause in all construction contracts that frees the contractor from any obligations imposed on him due to strikes, floods, catastrophes, national emergencies, etc.

Freight   The delivery charge to bring products, materials, or equipment from *supply* location to *use* location.

Fringe benefits   Payroll costs other than wages not paid directly to the employee. These include holidays, pensions, insurance, savings plans, etc.

General expense   An expense not otherwise classified. For product costs this is an indirectly attributable expense of administration, sales, research, and financing activities.

Grass roots plant   A complete plant erected on a virgin site. The investment includes all costs of site preparation, battery limits facilities, and auxiliary facilities.

Gross   Whole or entire.

Gross margin   Excess of sales over cost of goods sold.

Gross profit   (*See* Gross margin.)

Income   *Income* of an enterprise measures its effectiveness as an operating unit and is the change in net assets arising out of (1) the excess or deficiency of revenues over reported expired costs and (2) other gains or losses to the enterprise from sales, exchanges, or other conversion of assets.

Income statement   (Statement of profit and loss, statement of revenue and expense.) A statement of a business, summarizing the revenues and expenses for a stated period and change in net assets.

Incremental approach   (Also called out-of-pocket approach or marginal cost method.) A cost estimation technique based on changes in cash flows which can actually be foreseen as occurring rather than through using accounting conventions.

Incremental cost   (*See* Marginal cost.)

Indirectly attributable expense   *As applied to fixed capital investment:* construction overhead, engineering expenses, taxes and insurance, contingencies, and contractor's fee. *As applied to product costs:* all factory costs other than directly attributable material and labor. Book depreciation may be included. Also called factory overhead, burden, etc.

Inflation index   Historical time series of numbers relative to a base index of 100, established at a reference time, to approximate the relative change in value of the dollar with elapsed time in a particular segment of the economy.

Ingredients   (*See* Raw materials.)

Instantaneous compounding   (*See* Interest, continuous.)

Instrumentation   Cost of control valves, data logging equipment, instruments. May or may not be the installed cost.

Insurance   The cost of obtaining financial protection to replace the value of an element (such as equipment, time, money) in case of loss.

Intangibles   Nonphysical elements that have an effect on a project.

Interest   Compensation paid for the use of borrowed capital called the principal.

Interest, compound   Interest for the period (usually 1 year) based on principal and interest up to the beginning of the period.

Interest, continuous   The use of interest factors assuming an instantaneous base period for compounding (rather than quarterly or annually).

Interest, simple   The calculation of the money generated from interest is made at discrete, recurring time intervals. The usual time period is 1 year. Ordinary interest rates are based on a 360-day year. Exact interest rates are based on a 365-day year.

Internal rate of return   The discounting rate that equates the present value of expected cash outflows with the present value of expected cash inflows. Generally calculated after tax. May or may not include opportunity costs and book depreciation as expenses. (Interest rate of return, discounted cash flow, profitability index, investor's method.)

Inventory   The supply of raw materials, products in process, finished products, and supplies for maintenance, catalysts, and chemicals presently held.

Investor's method   (*See* Internal rate of return.)

Labor, operating (directly attributable)   That portion of the labor force in the battery limits that can be directly attributed to the product. Usually excludes transportation and maintenance but includes packaging.

Land cost   Cost of unimproved real estate.

Life, book life   The life of an asset according to a company's internal depreciation schedule.

Life, design   Same as economic life except that it is estimated *before* the plant is designed.

Life, economic (production)   The longevity of a proposed process or product due to obsolescence, changing economic conditions, or the physical life of the plant. This is an engineering decision determined for an existing plant.

Life, physical   The period which an asset could operate before shutting down due to physical deterioration.

Life, tax (service)   The physical life of the asset as specified for depreciation purposes by the taxation agencies.

Linear costs   Those variable costs which have a linear relationship to volume of production.

Load factor   Use utilization factor.

Lump-sum contract   (*See* Contract, lump sum.)

Maintenance   Labor, material, and overhead expense required to keep equipment or other installations in suitably operable conditions. Those items that cannot be expended within the year purchased are not included and are considered as fixed capital.

Manufacturing costs   The sum of directly attributable labor, materials, and factory overhead costs chargeable to manufacture a given product excluding administrative and selling financing. Usually includes directly attributable book depreciation.

Marginal cost   The amount by which the total costs are increased by the last unit of output at any given volume of production (differential cost).

Material in process   The value of materials that have left raw material storage but have not been consigned to product inventory.

Minimum acceptable rate of return (MAR)   The return on investment chosen as acceptable for discounting purposes. This includes an allowance for risk.

Minimum unit cost   The unit cost at that operating level of an existing facility which produces the lowest average manufacturing cost per unit of output.

Module   A completely operating and functional process is divided into a system of modules for each type of major processing equipment by constructing imaginary boundaries around each equipment. This boundary, approximately 3 meters from the equipment, encloses all appurtenances to create the working unit of equipment. Thus, there are heat exchanger modules, pressure vessel modules, pump modules, etc. Included in the module will be the appropriate piping, instrumentation, insulation, and piping and equipment supports. This excludes cost of building structures, land and site development.

Module, cost of bare   Cost of equipment and appurtenances to create a working module or unit of equipment. Includes labor and material cost to uncrate and install, the freight, taxes, insurance, engineering and field expense.

Module, cost of total   Cost of bare module plus contingency and contractor fees. Sometimes it also includes an allowance for auxiliaries, site development, land and industrial buildings.

Net   Free from all deductions.

Net sales   Dollar volume of sales less allowances made for discounts, bulk shipments, etc.

Noncash expense   An expense for accounting purposes which does not require an outlay of funds of the same amount in the same year (e.g., depreciation).

Nonprocess equipment   The equipment part of auxiliary facilities.

Obsolescence   Decrease in value of physical equipment due to technological or economical changes rather than physical deterioration.

Off-site facilities   (*See* Auxiliary facilities.)

Operating costs   Use manufacturing costs.

Operating supplies   Directly attributable materials that are required in the production but that do not appear as part of the final product.

Opportunity costs   The estimate of values which are foregone by undertaking one alternative instead of another.

Out-of-pocket costs   (*See* Marginal cost.)

Overhead   Those manufacturing costs of a manufacturing company which are not directly attributable to any one product and therefore are attributed on an arbitrary yet equitable basis. (Includes indirectly attributable costs plus general expenses for a product.) For plant construction, overhead equals indirectly attributable expense .

Packaging expense   Total cost of putting a product in a package. Includes labor, materials, and overheads.

Payables   (*See* Accounts payable.)

Payout time   The measure of the time needed to recoup in the form of cash inflow from operations the initial amount invested as fixed capital (payback time or period).

Physical life   (*See* Life, physical.)

Piping   The cost of the labor, materials, and overhead for the installed piping, valves, and fittings associated directly with the process equipment.

Plant overhead   (*See* Overhead.)

Present value method   Current value of cash flows as obtained by discounting. Specifically it is the discounted after tax revenues less the discounted costs. An investment evaluation procedure based on discounting revenues and costs at an interest rate representing the cost of capital or a minimum acceptable rate of return. (*Synonyms:* present worth, venture worth.) May or may not include book depreciation and opportunity costs as expenses.

Present worth   (*See* Present value method.)

Price   Rate at which a commodity or service is exchanged for money. The revenue received for a unit of product.

Principal   The amount of capital upon which interest is paid.

Process equipment   All equipment and appurtenances included in the actual manufacturing process. Usually it all lies within the battery limits.

Profit   (*See* Income.) The accounting approximation of the amount of return of the project or enterprise after taxes and product costs. (Depreciation is included in the product cost.)

Profit, gross   (*See* Gross profit.)

Profitability   A general term for the amount of profit achieved or to be achieved from a given project.

Profitability index   (*See* Internal rate of return.)

Project position   The net financial result at time *t* of all money flow since the start of the project. Book depreciation is considered an expense.

Purchase cost   Define specifically: FOB, delivered, installed, turnkey.

Rate of return   Abbreviation for rate of return on investment. (*See* Internal rate of return.)

Rate of return on investment   General criterion for evaluating projects.

Raw materials   Materials that end up in the final product. Materials, such as catalysts, that do not appear in the final product are operating supplies.

Receivables   (*See* Accounts receivable.)

Regulated costs   Those variable costs that are not zero at zero production rate (includes operating labor).

Reinvestment   A problem facing those using the profitability method involving compound interest; related to the disposal of those funds potentially earned by the funds generated by the investment being considered.

Replacement   Facility proposed to take the place of an existing facility without increasing its capacity.

Replacement, retirements and repairs expense   Money used to maintain capacity of a unit over and above the anticipated maintenance expenses.

Research and development expense   An overhead expense incurred in searching for new and improved products and processes.

Return   Net sales less manufacturing costs excluding book depreciation as an expense.

Return on average investment   Ratio of average annual profits over the economic life to the average book value of the investment including working capital.

Return on investment   Abbreviation for rate of return on investment.

Return on original investment   The ratio of the average annual profits over the economic life to the total capital investment.

Return on sales   Ratio of annual profits to annual revenue.

Revenue   Gross dollar flow from sales before deduction of costs. Revenue results from sale of goods and services and is measured by charge made to customers for goods and services rendered to them. It also includes gains from sale or exchange of assets, interest and dividends earned, and investments and other increases in equity.

Risk   Condition where there is a known probability of alternative events occurring in the future.

Royalties   Payments for the use of patented methods and processes.

Sales   Total volume of goods sold; sales revenue is the total value of such sales.

Sales, net   Revenue from the sale of goods less allowance made for discounts, bulk shipments, etc.

Sales expense   The classification for financial statement purposes of those expenses of an organization relating to the selling or marketing of an organization's goods or services, as opposed to those expenses incurred for other specialized functions, e.g., administration, financial, and manufacturing.

Salvage value   Value that can be recovered from equipment or other facilities when taken out of processing use and sold to an outside party. Usually assumed to be net of the removal expenses.

Scale-up exponent   The exponent, usually 0.6, that relates fixed investment costs to capacity or size; thus, $\text{cost}_1/\text{cost}_2 = (\text{size}_1/\text{size}_2)^n$.

Scrap value   (*See* Salvage value.)

Service facilities   (*See* Auxiliary facilities.)

Service life   (*See* Life, tax.)

Shared facilities   Facilities are shared by the production requirements for various products. The facility expense must then be equitably attributed to the different products.

Site preparation costs   The cost of preparing the plant site for the installation of process facilities. Includes demolition, cleanup, grading, landscaping, and road and railway siding installation.

Six-tenths factor   (*See* Scale-up exponent.)

Sizing factor   (*See* Scale-up exponent.)

Startup expense   Those nonrecurring costs between the completion of plant construction and the time when the plant is capable of operating at an acceptable capacity.

Stream days   Time utilization expressed as operating days per year.

Sunk costs   A historical cost which has already been incurred and cannot be recovered and which, therefore, is irrelevant to the decision-making process.

Supervision   Plant operating costs of shift supervisors and foremen who are assigned to process facilities producing more than one product.

Surplus material   Uninstalled materials purchased for a fixed investment project but left unused after construction is complete. (Includes pipe fittings, valves, etc.)

Taxes   Includes property—federal, provincial, or state—and sales taxes. Each can usually be identified from the context.

Terminal cash flow   Cash flows at the end of economic life.

Time utilization   The fraction of the total time when a facility is on stream producing.

Turnkey contract　(*See* Contract, turnkey.)

Turnover ratio　The ratio of annual revenue to the total assets (can be different depending on whether total assets available or total assets employed is considered). (Universal factor ratio, or capital ratio.)

Uncertainty　Condition where alternative events may occur in the future but the probability of each alternative is not known.

Unit cost　*As applied to fixed investment:* cost of any activity divided by a convenient capacity or size. For example, $50 fixed investment per ton of capacity. *As applied to manufacturing cost:* total manufacturing costs divided by the number of units of production completed.

Utilization factor　Ratio of actual to ideal or design value. Applied to utilization of time, capacity, supply.

Variable costs　A cost which is uniform per unit but which fluctuates in total in direct proportion to the changes in related total activity or volume.

Venture profit　Annual net profit after tax including book depreciation as an expense less opportunity costs.

Venture worth　(*See* Present value method.)

Work in process, cost　The total costs of directly attributable labor, material, and factory overhead applied to the production of units at any given stage in the process.

Working capital　(*See* Capital, working.)

Yard preparation　(*See* Site preparation costs.)

Discrete Rate-of-Return Factors[*]

A

*From *Engineering Economy*, *4th Edition*, Thuesen, H. Fabrycky, W., and Thuesen, G., Prentice-Hall, Inc., Englewood Cliffs, N.J., 1971.

TABLE A.1
1% INTEREST FACTORS FOR ANNUAL COMPOUNDING INTEREST

	Single payment		Equal payment series			
n	Compound-amount factor SP	Present-worth factor PS	Compound-amount factor SR	Sinking-fund factor RS	Present-worth factor PR	Capital-recovery factor RP
1	1.010	0.9901	1.000	1.0000	0.9901	1.0100
2	1.020	0.9803	2.010	0.4975	1.9704	0.5075
3	1.030	0.9706	3.030	0.3300	2.9410	0.3400
4	1.041	0.9610	4.060	0.2463	3.9020	0.2563
5	1.051	0.9515	5.101	0.1960	4.8534	0.2060
6	1.062	0.9421	6.152	0.1626	5.7955	0.1726
7	1.072	0.9327	7.214	0.1386	6.7282	0.1486
8	1.083	0.9235	8.286	0.1207	7.6517	0.1307
9	1.094	0.9143	9.369	0.1068	8.5660	0.1168
10	1.105	0.9053	10.462	0.0956	9.4713	0.1056
11	1.116	0.8963	11.567	0.0865	10.3676	0.0965
12	1.127	0.8875	12.683	0.0789	11.2551	0.0889
13	1.138	0.8787	13.809	0.0724	12.1338	0.0824
14	1.149	0.8700	14.947	0.0669	13.0037	0.0769
15	1.161	0.8614	16.097	0.0621	13.8651	0.0721
16	1.173	0.8528	17.258	0.0580	14.7179	0.0680
17	1.184	0.8444	18.430	0.0543	15.5623	0.0643
18	1.196	0.8360	19.615	0.0510	16.3983	0.0610
19	1.208	0.8277	20.811	0.0481	17.2260	0.0581
20	1.220	0.8196	22.019	0.0454	18.0456	0.0554
21	1.232	0.8114	23.239	0.0430	18.8570	0.0530
22	1.245	0.8034	24.472	0.0409	19.6604	0.0509
23	1.257	0.7955	25.716	0.0389	20.4558	0.0489
24	1.270	0.7876	26.973	0.0371	21.2434	0.0471
25	1.282	0.7798	28.243	0.0354	22.0232	0.0454
26	1.295	0.7721	29.526	0.0339	22.7952	0.0439
27	1.308	0.7644	30.821	0.0325	23.5596	0.0425
28	1.321	0.7568	32.129	0.0311	24.3165	0.0411
29	1.335	0.7494	33.450	0.0299	25.0658	0.0399
30	1.348	0.7419	34.785	0.0288	25.8077	0.0388
31	1.361	0.7346	36.133	0.0277	26.5423	0.0377
32	1.375	0.7273	37.494	0.0267	27.2696	0.0367
33	1.389	0.7201	38.869	0.0257	27.9897	0.0357
34	1.403	0.7130	40.258	0.0248	28.7027	0.0348
35	1.417	0.7059	41.660	0.0240	29.4086	0.0340
40	1.489	0.6717	48.886	0.0205	32.8347	0.0305
45	1.565	0.6391	56.481	0.0177	36.0945	0.0277
50	1.645	0.6080	64.463	0.0155	39.1961	0.0255
55	1.729	0.5785	72.852	0.0137	42.1472	0.0237
60	1.817	0.5505	81.670	0.0123	44.9550	0.0223
65	1.909	0.5237	90.937	0.0110	47.6266	0.0210
70	2.007	0.4983	100.676	0.0099	50.1685	0.0199
75	2.109	0.4741	110.913	0.0090	52.5871	0.0190
80	2.217	0.4511	121.672	0.0082	54.8882	0.0182
85	2.330	0.4292	132.979	0.0075	57.0777	0.0175
90	2.449	0.4084	144.863	0.0069	59.1609	0.0169
95	2.574	0.3886	157.354	0.0064	61.1430	0.0164
100	2.705	0.3697	170.481	0.0059	63.0289	0.0159

TABLE A.2

$1\frac{1}{2}\%$ INTEREST FACTORS FOR ANNUAL COMPOUNDING INTEREST

	Single payment		Equal payment series			
n	Compound-amount factor $S\!P$	Present-worth factor $P\!S$	Compound-amount factor $S\!R$	Sinking-fund factor $R\!S$	Present-worth factor $P\!R$	Capital-recovery factor $R\!P$
1	1.015	0.9852	1.000	1.0000	0.9852	1.0150
2	1.030	0.9707	2.015	0.4963	1.9559	0.5113
3	1.046	0.9563	3.045	0.3284	2.9122	0.3434
4	1.061	0.9422	4.091	0.2445	3.8544	0.2595
5	1.077	0.9283	5.152	0.1941	4.7827	0.2091
6	1.093	0.9146	6.230	0.1605	5.6972	0.1755
7	1.110	0.9010	7.323	0.1366	6.5982	0.1516
8	1.127	0.8877	8.433	0.1186	7.4859	0.1336
9	1.143	0.8746	9.559	0.1046	8.3605	0.1196
10	1.161	0.8617	10.703	0.0934	9.2222	0.1084
11	1.178	0.8489	11.863	0.0843	10.0711	0.0993
12	1.196	0.8364	13.041	0.0767	10.9075	0.0917
13	1.214	0.8240	14.237	0.0703	11.7315	0.0853
14	1.232	0.8119	15.450	0.0647	12.5434	0.0797
15	1.250	0.7999	16.682	0.0600	13.3432	0.0750
16	1.269	0.7880	17.932	0.0558	14.1313	0.0708
17	1.288	0.7764	19.201	0.0521	14.9077	0.0671
18	1.307	0.7649	20.489	0.0488	15.6726	0.0638
19	1.327	0.7536	21.797	0.0459	16.4262	0.0609
20	1.347	0.7425	23.124	0.0433	17.1686	0.0583
21	1.367	0.7315	24.471	0.0409	17.9001	0.0559
22	1.388	0.7207	25.838	0.0387	18.6208	0.0537
23	1.408	0.7100	27.225	0.0367	19.3309	0.0517
24	1.430	0.6996	28.634	0.0349	20.0304	0.0499
25	1.451	0.6892	30.063	0.0333	20.7196	0.0483
26	1.473	0.6790	31.514	0.0317	21.3986	0.0467
27	1.495	0.6690	32.987	0.0303	22.0676	0.0453
28	1.517	0.6591	34.481	0.0290	22.7267	0.0440
29	1.540	0.6494	35.999	0.0278	23.3761	0.0428
30	1.563	0.6398	37.539	0.0266	24.0158	0.0416
31	1.587	0.6303	39.102	0.0256	24.6462	0.0406
32	1.610	0.6210	40.688	0.0246	25.2671	0.0396
33	1.634	0.6118	42.299	0.0237	25.8790	0.0387
34	1.659	0.6028	43.933	0.0228	26.4817	0.0378
35	1.684	0.5939	45.592	0.0219	27.0756	0.0369
40	1.814	0.5513	54.268	0.0184	29.9159	0.0334
45	1.954	0.5117	63.614	0.0157	32.5523	0.0307
50	2.105	0.4750	73.683	0.0136	34.9997	0.0286
55	2.268	0.4409	84.530	0.0118	37.2715	0.0268
60	2.443	0.4093	96.215	0.0104	39.3803	0.0254
65	2.632	0.3799	108.803	0.0092	41.3378	0.0242
70	2.835	0.3527	122.364	0.0082	43.1549	0.0232
75	3.055	0.3274	136.973	0.0073	44.8416	0.0223
80	3.291	0.3039	152.711	0.0066	46.4073	0.0216
85	3.545	0.2821	169.665	0.0059	47.8607	0.0209
90	3.819	0.2619	187.930	0.0053	49.2099	0.0203
95	4.114	0.2431	207.606	0.0048	50.4622	0.0198
100	4.432	0.2256	228.803	0.0044	51.6247	0.0194

TABLE A.3
2% INTEREST FACTORS FOR ANNUAL COMPOUNDING INTEREST

	Single payment		Equal payment series			
n	Compound-amount factor SP	Present-worth factor PS	Compound-amount factor SR	Sinking-fund factor RS	Present-worth factor PR	Capital-recovery factor RP
1	1.020	0.9804	1.000	1.0000	0.9804	1.0200
2	1.040	0.9612	2.020	0.4951	1.9416	0.5151
3	1.061	0.9423	3.060	0.3268	2.8839	0.3468
4	1.082	0.9239	4.122	0.2426	3.8077	0.2626
5	1.104	0.9057	5.204	0.1922	4.7135	0.2122
6	1.126	0.8880	6.308	0.1585	5.6014	0.1785
7	1.149	0.8706	7.434	0.1345	6.4720	0.1545
8	1.172	0.8535	8.583	0.1165	7.3255	0.1365
9	1.195	0.8368	9.755	0.1025	8.1622	0.1225
10	1.219	0.8204	10.950	0.0913	8.9826	0.1113
11	1.243	0.8043	12.169	0.0822	9.7869	0.1022
12	1.268	0.7885	13.412	0.0746	10.5754	0.0946
13	1.294	0.7730	14.680	0.0681	11.3484	0.0881
14	1.319	0.7579	15.974	0.0626	12.1063	0.0826
15	1.346	0.7430	17.293	0.0578	12.8493	0.0778
16	1.373	0.7285	18.639	0.0537	13.5777	0.0737
17	1.400	0.7142	20.012	0.0500	14.2919	0.0700
18	1.428	0.7002	21.412	0.0467	14.9920	0.0667
19	1.457	0.6864	22.841	0.0438	15.6785	0.0638
20	1.486	0.6730	24.297	0.0412	16.3514	0.0612
21	1.516	0.6598	25.783	0.0388	17.0112	0.0588
22	1.546	0.6468	27.299	0.0366	17.6581	0.0566
23	1.577	0.6342	28.845	0.0347	18.2922	0.0547
24	1.608	0.6217	30.422	0.0329	18.9139	0.0529
25	1.641	0.6095	32.030	0.0312	19.5235	0.0512
26	1.673	0.5976	33.671	0.0297	20.1210	0.0497
27	1.707	0.5859	35.344	0.0283	20.7069	0.0483
28	1.741	0.5744	37.051	0.0270	21.2813	0.0470
29	1.776	0.5631	38.792	0.0258	21.8444	0.0458
30	1.811	0.5521	40.568	0.0247	22.3965	0.0447
31	1.848	0.5413	42.379	0.0236	22.9377	0.0436
32	1.885	0.5306	44.227	0.0226	23.4683	0.0426
33	1.922	0.5202	46.112	0.0217	23.9886	0.0417
34	1.961	0.5100	48.034	0.0208	24.4986	0.0408
35	2.000	0.5000	49.994	0.0200	24.9986	0.0400
40	2.208	0.4529	60.402	0.0166	27.3555	0.0366
45	2.438	0.4102	71.893	0.0139	29.4902	0.0339
50	2.692	0.3715	84.579	0.0118	31.4236	0.0318
55	2.972	0.3365	98.587	0.0102	33.1748	0.0302
60	3.281	0.3048	114.052	0.0088	34.7609	0.0288
65	3.623	0.2761	131.126	0.0076	36.1975	0.0276
70	4.000	0.2500	149.978	0.0067	37.4986	0.0267
75	4.416	0.2265	170.792	0.0059	38.6771	0.0259
80	4.875	0.2051	193.772	0.0052	39.7445	0.0252
85	5.383	0.1858	219.144	0.0046	40.7113	0.0246
90	5.943	0.1683	247.157	0.0041	41.5869	0.0241
95	6.562	0.1524	278.085	0.0036	42.3800	0.0236
100	7.245	0.1380	312.232	0.0032	43.0984	0.0232

TABLE A.4
3% INTEREST FACTORS FOR ANNUAL COMPOUNDING INTEREST

	Single payment		Equal payment series			
n	Compound-amount factor $\mathcal{SP}$	Present-worth factor $\mathcal{PS}$	Compound-amount factor $\mathcal{SR}$	Sinking-fund factor $\mathcal{RS}$	Present-worth factor $\mathcal{PR}$	Capital-recovery factor $\mathcal{RP}$
1	1.030	0.9709	1.000	1.0000	0.9709	1.0300
2	1.061	0.9426	2.030	0.4926	1.9135	0.5226
3	1.093	0.9152	3.091	0.3235	2.8286	0.3535
4	1.126	0.8885	4.184	0.2390	3.7171	0.2690
5	1.159	0.8626	5.309	0.1884	4.5797	0.2184
6	1.194	0.8375	6.468	0.1546	5.4172	0.1846
7	1.230	0.8131	7.662	0.1305	6.2303	0.1605
8	1.267	0.7894	8.892	0.1125	7.0197	0.1425
9	1.305	0.7664	10.159	0.0984	7.7861	0.1284
10	1.344	0.7441	11.464	0.0872	8.5302	0.1172
11	1.384	0.7224	12.808	0.0781	9.2526	0.1081
12	1.426	0.7014	14.192	0.0705	9.9540	0.1005
13	1.469	0.6810	15.618	0.0640	10.6350	0.0940
14	1.513	0.6611	17.086	0.0585	11.2961	0.0885
15	1.558	0.6419	18.599	0.0538	11.9379	0.0838
16	1.605	0.6232	20.157	0.0496	12.5611	0.0796
17	1.653	0.6050	21.762	0.0460	13.1661	0.0760
18	1.702	0.5874	23.414	0.0427	13.7535	0.0727
19	1.754	0.5703	25.117	0.0398	14.3238	0.0698
20	1.806	0.5537	26.870	0.0372	14.8775	0.0672
21	1.860	0.5376	28.676	0.0349	15.4150	0.0649
22	1.916	0.5219	30.537	0.0328	15.9369	0.0628
23	1.974	0.5067	32.453	0.0308	16.4436	0.0608
24	2.033	0.4919	34.426	0.0291	16.9356	0.0591
25	2.094	0.4776	36.459	0.0274	17.4132	0.0574
26	2.157	0.4637	38.553	0.0259	17.8769	0.0559
27	2.221	0.4502	40.710	0.0246	18.3270	0.0546
28	2.288	0.4371	42.931	0.0233	18.7641	0.0533
29	2.357	0.4244	45.219	0.0221	19.1885	0.0521
30	2.427	0.4120	47.575	0.0210	19.6005	0.0510
31	2.500	0.4000	50.003	0.0200	20.0004	0.0500
32	2.575	0.3883	52.503	0.0191	20.3888	0.0491
33	2.652	0.3770	55.078	0.0182	20.7658	0.0482
34	2.732	0.3661	57.730	0.0173	21.1318	0.0473
35	2.814	0.3554	60.462	0.0165	21.4872	0.0465
40	3.262	0.3066	75.401	0.0133	23.1148	0.0433
►45	3.782	0.2644	92.720	0.0108	24.5187	0.0408
50	4.384	0.2281	112.797	0.0089	25.7298	0.0389
55	5.082	0.1968	136.072	0.0074	26.7744	0.0374
60	5.892	0.1697	163.053	0.0061	27.6756	0.0361
65	6.830	0.1464	194.333	0.0052	28.4529	0.0352
70	7.918	0.1263	230.594	0.0043	29.1234	0.0343
75	9.179	0.1090	272.631	0.0037	29.7018	0.0337
80	10.641	0.0940	321.363	0.0031	30.2008	0.0331
85	12.336	0.0811	377.857	0.0027	30.6312	0.0327
90	14.300	0.0699	443.349	0.0023	31.0024	0.0323
95	16.578	0.0603	519.272	0.0019	31.3227	0.0319
100	19.219	0.0520	607.288	0.0017	31.5989	0.0317

TABLE A.5
4% INTEREST FACTORS FOR ANNUAL COMPOUNDING INTEREST

	Single payment		Equal payment series			
n	Compound-amount factor $S P$	Present-worth factor $P S$	Compound-amount factor $S R$	Sinking-fund factor $R S$	Present-worth factor $P R$	Capital-recovery factor $R P$
1	1.040	0.9615	1.000	1.0000	0.9615	1.0400
2	1.082	0.9246	2.040	0.4902	1.8861	0.5302
3	1.125	0.8890	3.122	0.3204	2.7751	0.3604
4	1.170	0.8548	4.246	0.2355	3.6299	0.2755
5	1.217	0.8219	5.416	0.1846	4.4518	0.2246
6	1.265	0.7903	6.633	0.1508	5.2421	0.1908
7	1.316	0.7599	7.898	0.1266	6.0021	0.1666
8	1.369	0.7307	9.214	0.1085	6.7328	0.1485
9	1.423	0.7026	10.583	0.0945	7.4353	0.1345
10	1.480	0.6756	12.006	0.0833	8.1109	0.1233
11	1.539	0.6496	13.486	0.0742	8.7605	0.1142
12	1.601	0.6246	15.026	0.0666	9.3851	0.1066
13	1.665	0.6006	16.627	0.0602	9.9857	0.1002
14	1.732	0.5775	18.292	0.0547	10.5631	0.0947
15	1.801	0.5553	20.024	0.0500	11.1184	0.0900
16	1.873	0.5339	21.825	0.0458	11.6523	0.0858
17	1.948	0.5134	23.698	0.0422	12.1657	0.0822
18	2.026	0.4936	25.645	0.0390	12.6593	0.0790
19	2.107	0.4747	27.671	0.0361	13.1339	0.0761
20	2.191	0.4564	29.778	0.0336	13.5903	0.0736
21	2.279	0.4388	31.969	0.0313	14.0292	0.0713
22	2.370	0.4220	34.248	0.0292	14.4511	0.0692
23	2.465	0.4057	36.618	0.0273	14.8569	0.0673
24	2.563	0.3901	39.083	0.0256	15.2470	0.0656
25	2.666	0.3751	41.646	0.0240	15.6221	0.0640
26	2.772	0.3607	44.312	0.0226	15.9828	0.0626
27	2.883	0.3468	47.084	0.0212	16.3296	0.0612
28	2.999	0.3335	49.968	0.0200	16.6631	0.0600
29	3.119	0.3207	52.966	0.0189	16.9837	0.0589
30	3.243	0.3083	56.085	0.0178	17.2920	0.0578
31	3.373	0.2965	59.328	0.0169	17.5885	0.0569
32	3.508	0.2851	62.701	0.0160	17.8736	0.0560
33	3.648	0.2741	66.210	0.0151	18.1477	0.0551
34	3.794	0.2636	69.858	0.0143	18.4112	0.0543
35	3.946	0.2534	73.652	0.0136	18.6646	0.0536
40	4.801	0.2083	95.026	0.0105	19.7928	0.0505
45	5.841	0.1712	121.029	0.0083	20.7200	0.0483
50	7.107	0.1407	152.667	0.0066	21.4822	0.0466
55	8.646	0.1157	191.159	0.0052	22.1086	0.0452
60	10.520	0.0951	237.991	0.0042	22.6235	0.0442
65	°12.799	0.0781	294.968	0.0034	23.0467	0.0434
70	15.572	0.0642	364.290	0.0028	23.3945	0.0428
75	18.945	0.0528	448.631	0.0022	23.6804	0.0422
80	23.050	0.0434	551.245	0.0018	23.9154	0.0418
85	28.044	0.0357	676.090	0.0015	24.1085	0.0415
90	34.119	0.0293	817.983	0.0012	24.2673	0.0412
95	41.511	0.0241	1012.785	0.0010	24.3978	0.0410
100	50.505	0.0198	1237.624	0.0008	24.5050	0.0408

TABLE A.6
5% INTEREST FACTORS FOR ANNUAL COMPOUNDING INTEREST

	Single payment		Equal payment series			
n	Compound-amount factor S^P	Present-worth factor P^S	Compound-amount factor S^R	Sinking-fund factor R^S	Present-worth factor P^R	Capital-recovery factor R^P
1	1.050	0.9524	1.000	1.0000	0.9524	1.0500
2	1.103	0.9070	2.050	0.4878	1.8594	0.5378
3	1.158	0.8638	3.153	0.3172	2.7233	0.3672
4	1.216	0.8227	4.310	0.2320	3.5460	0.2820
5	1.276	0.7835	5.526	0.1810	4.3295	0.2310
6	1.340	0.7462	6.802	0.1470	5.0757	0.1970
7	1.407	0.7107	8.142	0.1228	5.7864	0.1728
8	1.477	0.6768	9.549	0.1047	6.4632	0.1547
9	1.551	0.6446	11.027	0.0907	7.1078	0.1407
10	1.629	0.6139	12.587	0.0795	7.7217	0.1295
11	1.710	0.5847	14.207	0.0704	8.3064	0.1204
12	1.796	0.5568	15.917	0.0628	8.8633	0.1128
13	1.886	0.5303	17.713	0.0565	9.3936	0.1065
14	1.980	0.5051	19.599	0.0510	9.8987	0.1010
15	2.079	0.4810	21.579	0.0464	10.3797	0.0964
16	2.183	0.4581	23.658	0.0423	10.8378	0.0923
17	2.292	0.4363	25.840	0.0387	11.2741	0.0887
18	2.407	0.4155	28.132	0.0356	11.6896	0.0856
19	2.527	0.3957	30.539	0.0328	12.0853	0.0828
20	2.653	0.3769	33.066	0.0303	12.4622	0.0803
21	2.786	0.3590	35.719	0.0280	12.8212	0.0780
22	2.925	0.3419	38.505	0.0260	13.1630	0.0760
23	3.072	0.3256	41.430	0.0241	13.4886	0.0741
24	3.225	0.3101	44.502	0.0225	13.7987	0.0725
25	3.386	0.2953	47.727	0.0210	14.0940	0.0710
26	3.556	0.2813	51.113	0.0196	14.3752	0.0696
27	3.733	0.2679	54.669	0.0183	14.6430	0.0683
28	3.920	0.2551	58.403	0.0171	14.8981	0.0671
29	4.116	0.2430	62.323	0.0161	15.1411	0.0661
30	4.322	0.2314	66.439	0.0151	15.3725	0.0651
31	4.538	0.2204	70.761	0.0141	15.5928	0.0641
32	4.765	0.2099	75.299	0.0133	15.8027	0.0633
33	5.003	0.1999	80.064	0.0125	16.0026	0.0625
34	5.253	0.1904	85.067	0.0118	16.1929	0.0618
35	5.516	0.1813	90.320	0.0111	16.3742	0.0611
40	7.040	0.1421	120.800	0.0083	17.1591	0.0583
45	8.985	0.1113	159.700	0.0063	17.7741	0.0563
50	11.467	0.0872	209.348	0.0048	18.2559	0.0548
55	14.636	0.0683	272.713	0.0037	18.6335	0.0537
60	18.679	0.0535	353.584	0.0028	18.9293	0.0528
65	23.840	0.0420	456.798	0.0022	19.1611	0.0522
70	30.426	0.0329	588.529	0.0017	19.3427	0.0517
75	38.833	0.0258	756.654	0.0013	19.4850	0.0513
80	49.561	0.0202	971.229	0.0010	19.5965	0.0510
85	63.254	0.0158	1245.087	0.0008	19.6838	0.0508
90	80.730	0.0124	1594.607	0.0006	19.7523	0.0506
95	103.035	0.0097	2040.694	0.0005	19.8059	0.0505
100	131.501	0.0076	2610.025	0.0004	19.8479	0.0504

TABLE A.7
6% INTEREST FACTORS FOR ANNUAL COMPOUNDING INTEREST

	Single payment		Equal payment series			
n	Compound-amount factor $S\!P$	Present-worth factor $P\!S$	Compound-amount factor $S\!R$	Sinking-fund factor $R\!S$	Present-worth factor $P\!R$	Capital-recovery factor $R\!P$
1	1.060	0.9434	1.000	1.0000	0.9434	1.0600
2	1.124	0.8900	2.060	0.4854	1.8334	0.5454
3	1.191	0.8396	3.184	0.3141	2.6730	0.3741
4	1.262	0.7921	4.375	0.2286	3.4651	0.2886
5	1.338	0.7473	5.637	0.1774	4.2124	0.2374
6	1.419	0.7050	6.975	0.1434	4.9173	0.2034
7	1.504	0.6651	8.394	0.1191	5.5824	0.1791
8	1.594	0.6274	9.897	0.1010	6.2098	0.1610
9	1.689	0.5919	11.491	0.0870	6.8017	0.1470
10	1.791	0.5584	13.181	0.0759	7.3601	0.1359
11	1.898	0.5268	14.972	0.0668	7.8869	0.1268
12	2.012	0.4970	16.870	0.0593	8.3839	0.1193
13	2.133	0.4688	18.882	0.0530	8.8527	0.1130
14	2.261	0.4423	21.015	0.0476	9.2950	0.1076
15	2.397	0.4173	23.276	0.0430	9.7123	0.1030
16	2.540	0.3937	25.673	0.0390	10.1059	0.0990
17	2.693	0.3714	28.213	0.0355	10.4773	0.0955
18	2.854	0.3504	30.906	0.0324	10.8276	0.0924
19	3.026	0.3305	33.760	0.0296	11.1581	0.0896
20	3.207	0.3118	36.786	0.0272	11.4699	0.0872
21	3.400	0.2942	39.993	0.0250	11.7641	0.0850
22	3.604	0.2775	43.392	0.0231	12.0416	0.0831
23	3.820	0.2618	46.996	0.0213	12.3034	0.0813
24	4.049	0.2470	50.816	0.0197	12.5504	0.0797
25	4.292	0.2330	54.865	0.0182	12.7834	0.0782
26	4.549	0.2198	59.156	0.0169	13.0032	0.0769
27	4.822	0.2074	63.706	0.0157	13.2105	0.0757
28	5.112	0.1956	68.528	0.0146	13.4062	0.0746
29	5.418	0.1846	73.640	0.0136	13.5907	0.0736
30	5.744	0.1741	79.058	0.0127	13.7648	0.0727
31	6.088	0.1643	84.802	0.0118	13.9291	0.0718
32	6.453	0.1550	90.890	0.0110	14.0841	0.0710
33	6.841	0.1462	97.343	0.0103	14.2302	0.0703
34	7.251	0.1379	104.184	0.0096	14.3682	0.0696
35	7.686	0.1301	111.435	0.0090	14.4983	0.0690
40	10.286	0.0972	154.762	0.0065	15.0463	0.0665
45	13.765	0.0727	212.744	0.0047	15.4558	0.0647
50	18.420	0.0543	290.336	0.0035	15.7619	0.0635
55	24.650	0.0406	394.172	0.0025	15.9906	0.0625
60	32.988	0.0303	533.128	0.0019	16.1614	0.0619
65	44.145	0.0227	719.083	0.0014	16.2891	0.0614
70	59.076	0.0169	967.932	0.0010	16.3846	0.0610
75	79.057	0.0127	1300.949	0.0008	16.4559	0.0608
80	105.796	0.0095	1746.600	0.0006	16.5091	0.0606
85	141.579	0.0071	2342.982	0.0004	16.5490	0.0604
90	189.465	0.0053	3141.075	0.0003	16.5787	0.0603
95	253.546	0.0040	4209.104	0.0002	16.6009	0.0602
100	339.302	0.0030	5638.368	0.0002	16.6176	0.0602

TABLE A.8
7% INTEREST FACTORS FOR ANNUAL COMPOUNDING INTEREST

	Single payment		Equal payment series			
n	Compound-amount factor SP	Present-worth factor PS	Compound-amount factor SR	Sinking-fund factor RS	Present-worth factor PR	Capital-recovery factor RP
1	1.070	0.9346	1.000	1.0000	0.9346	1.0700
2	1.145	0.8734	2.070	0.4831	1.8080	0.5531
3	1.225	0.8163	3.215	0.3111	2.6243	0.3811
4	1.311	0.7629	4.440	0.2252	3.3872	0.2952
5	1.403	0.7130	5.751	0.1739	4.1002	0.2439
6	1.501	0.6664	7.163	0.1398	4.7665	0.2098
7	1.606	0.6228	8.654	0.1156	5.3893	0.1856
8	1.718	0.5820	10.260	0.0975	5.9713	0.1675
9	1.838	0.5439	11.978	0.0835	6.5152	0.1535
10	1.967	0.5084	13.816	0.0724	7.0236	0.1424
11	2.105	0.4751	15.784	0.0634	7.4987	0.1334
12	2.252	0.4440	17.888	0.0559	7.9427	0.1259
13	2.410	0.4150	20.141	0.0497	8.3577	0.1197
14	2.579	0.3878	22.550	0.0444	8.7455	0.1144
15	2.759	0.3625	25.129	0.0398	9.1079	0.1098
16	2.952	0.3387	27.888	0.0359	9.4467	0.1059
17	3.159	0.3166	30.840	0.0324	9.7632	0.1024
18	3.380	0.2959	33.999	0.0294	10.0591	0.0994
19	3.617	0.2765	37.379	0.0268	10.3356	0.0968
20	3.870	0.2584	40.996	0.0244	10.5940	0.0944
21	4.141	0.2415	44.865	0.0223	10.8355	0.0923
22	4.430	0.2257	49.006	0.0204	11.0613	0.0904
23	4.741	0.2110	53.436	0.0187	11.2722	0.0887
24	5.072	0.1972	58.177	0.0172	11.4693	o.0872
25	5.427	0.1843	63.249	0.0158	11.6536	0.0858
26	5.807	0.1722	68.676	0.0146	11.8258	0.0846
27	6.214	0.1609	74.484	0.0134	11.9867	0.0834
28	6.649	0.1504	80.698	0.0124	12.1371	0.0824
29	7.114	0.1406	87.347	0.0115	12.2777	0.0815
30	7.612	0.1314	94.461	0.0106	12.4091	0.0806
31	8.145	0.1228	102.073	0.0098	12.5318	0.0798
32	8.715	0.1148	110.218	0.0091	12.6466	0.0791
33	9.325	0.1072	118.933	0.0084	12.7538	0.0784
34	9.978	0.1002	128.259	0.0078	12.8540	0.0778
35	10.677	0.0937	138.237	0.0072	12.9477	0.0772
40	14.974	0.0668	199.635	0.0050	13.3317	0.0750
45	21.002	0.0476	285.749	0.0035	13.6055	0.0735
50	29.457	0.0340	406.529	0.0025	13.8008	0 0725
55	41.315	0.0242	575.929	0.0017	13.9399	0.0717
60	57.946	0.0173	813.520	0.0012	14.0392	0.0712
65	81.273	0.0123	1146.755	0.0009	14.1099	0.0709
70	113.989	0.0088	1614.134	0.0006	14.1604	0.0706
75	159.876	0.0063	2269.657	0.0005	14.1964	0.0705
80	224.234	0.0045	3189.063	0.0003	14.2220	0.0703
85	314.500	0.0032	4478.576	0.0002	14.2403	0.0702
90	441.103	0.0023	6287.185	0.0002	14.2533	0.0702
95	618.670	0.0016	8823.854	0.0001	14.2626	0.0701
100	867.716	0.0012	12381.662	0.0001	14.2693	0.0701

TABLE A.9
8% INTEREST FACTORS FOR ANNUAL COMPOUNDING INTEREST

	Single payment		Equal payment series			
n	Compound-amount factor SP	Present-worth factor PS	Compound-amount factor SR	Sinking-fund factor RS	Present-worth factor PR	Capital-recovery factor RP
1	1.080	0.9259	1.000	1.0000	0.9259	1.0800
2	1.166	0.8573	2.080	0.4808	1.7833	0.5608
3	1.260	0.7938	3.246	0.3080	2.5771	0.3880
4	1.360	0.7350	4.506	0.2219	3.3121	0.3019
5	1.469	0.6806	5.867	0.1705	3.9927	0.2505
6	1.587	0.6302	7.336	0.1363	4.6229	0.2163
7	1.714	0.5835	8.923	0.1121	5.2064	0.1921
8	1.851	0.5403	10.637	0.0940	5.7466	0.1740
9	1.999	0.5003	12.488	0.0801	6.2469	0.1601
10	2.159	0.4632	14.487	0.0690	6.7101	0.1490
11	2.332	0.4289	16.645	0.0601	7.1390	0.1401
12	2.518	0.3971	18.977	0.0527	7.5361	0.1327
13	2.720	0.3677	21.495	0.0465	7.9038	0.1265
14	2.937	0.3405	24.215	0.0413	8.2442	0.1213
15	3.172	0.3153	27.152	0.0368	8.5595	0.1168
16	3.426	0.2919	30.324	0.0330	8.8514	0.1130
17	3.700	0.2703	33.750	0.0296	9.1216	0.1096
18	3.996	0.2503	37.450	0.0267	9.3719	0.1067
19	4.316	0.2317	41.446	0.0241	9.6036	0.1041
20	4.661	0.2146	45.762	0.0219	9.8182	0.1019
21	5.034	0.1987	50.423	0.0198	10.0168	0.0998
22	5.437	0.1840	55.457	0.0180	10.2008	0.0980
23	5.871	0.1703	60.893	0.0164	10.3711	0.0964
24	6.341	0.1577	66.765	0.0150	10.5288	0.0950
25	6.848	0.1460	73.106	0.0137	10.6748	0.0937
26	7.396	0.1352	79.954	0.0125	10.8100	0.0925
27	7.988	0.1252	87.351	0.0115	10.9352	0.0915
28	8.627	0.1159	95.339	0.0105	11.0511	0.0905
29	9.317	0.1073	103.966	0.0096	11.1584	0.0896
30	10.063	0.0994	113.283	0.0088	11.2578	0.0888
31	10.868	0.0920	123.346	0.0081	11.3498	0.0881
32	11.737	0.0852	134.214	0.0075	11.4350	0.0875
33	12.676	0.0789	145.951	0.0069	11.5139	0.0869
34	13.690	0.0731	158.627	0.0063	11.5869	0.0863
35	14.785	0.0676	172.317	0.0058	11.6546	0.0858
40	21.725	0.0460	259.057	0.0039	11.9246	0.0839
45	31.920	0.0313	386.506	0.0026	12.1084	0.0826
50	46.902	0.0213	573.770	0.0018	12.2335	0.0818
55	68.914	0.0145	848.923	0.0012	12.3186	0.0812
60	101.257	0.0099	1253.213	0.0008	12.3766	0.0808
65	148.780	0.0067	1847.248	0.0006	12.4160	0.0806
70	218.606	0.0046	2720.080	0.0004	12.4428	0.0804
75	321.205	0.0031	4002.557	0.0003	12.4611	0.0803
80	471.955	0.0021	5886.935	0.0002	12.4735	0.0802
85	693.456	0.0015	8655.706	0.0001	12.4820	0.0801
90	1018.915	0.0010	12723.939	0.0001	12.4877	0.0801
95	1497.121	0.0007	18701.507	0.0001	12.4917	0.0801
100	2199.761	0.0005	27484.516	0.0001	12.4943	0.0800

TABLE A.10
9% INTEREST FACTORS FOR ANNUAL COMPOUNDING INTEREST

	Single payment		Equal payment series			
n	Compound-amount factor S^p	Present-worth factor P^S	Compound-amount factor S^R	Sinking-fund factor R^S	Present-worth factor P^R	Capital-recovery factor R^P
1	1.090	0.9174	1.000	1.0000	0.9174	1.0900
2	1.188	0.8417	2.090	0.4785	1.7591	0.5685
3	1.295	0.7722	3.278	0.3051	2.5313	0.3951
4	1.412	0.7084	4.573	0.2187	3.2397	0.3087
5	1.539	0.6499	5.985	0.1671	3.8897	0.2571
6	1.677	0.5963	7.523	0.1329	4.4859	0.2229
7	1.828	0.5470	9.200	0.1087	5.0330	0.1987
8	1.993	0.5019	11.028	0.0907	5.5348	0.1807
9	2.172	0.4604	13.021	0.0768	5.9953	0.1668
10	2.367	0.4224	15.193	0.0658	6.4177	0.1558
11	2.580	0.3875	17.560	0.0570	6.8052	0.1470
12	2.813	0.3555	20.141	0.0497	7.1607	0.1397
13	3.066	0.3262	22.953	0.0436	7.4869	0.1336
14	3.342	0.2993	26.019	0.0384	7.7862	0.1284
15	3.642	0.2745	29.361	0.0341	8.0607	0.1241
16	3.970	0.2519	33.003	0.0303	8.3126	0.1203
17	4.328	0.2311	36.974	0.0271	8.5436	0.1171
18	4.717	0.2120	41.301	0.0242	8.7556	0.1142
19	5.142	0.1945	46.018	0.0217	8.9501	0.1117
20	5.604	0.1784	51.160	0.0196	9.1286	0.1096
21	6.109	0.1637	56.765	0.0176	9.2923	0.1076
22	6.659	0.1502	62.873	0.0159	9.4424	0.1059
23	7.258	0.1378	69.532	0.0144	9.5802	0.1044
24	7.911	0.1264	76.790	0.0130	9.7066	0.1030
25	8.623	0.1160	84.701	0.0118	9.8226	0.1018
26	9.399	0.1064	93.324	0.0107	9.9290	0.1007
27	10.245	0.0976	102.723	0.0097	10.0266	0.0997
28	11.167	0.0896	112.968	0.0089	10.1161	0.0989
29	12.172	0.0822	124.135	0.0081	10.1983	0.0981
30	13.268	0.0754	136.308	0.0073	10.2737	0.0973
31	14.462	0.0692	149.575	0.0067	10.3428	0.0967
32	15.763	0.0634	164.037	0.0061	10.4063	0.0961
33	17.182	0.0582	179.800	0.0056	10.4645	0.0956
34	18.728	0.0534	196.982	0.0051	10.5178	0.0951
35	20.414	0.0490	215.711	0.0046	10.5668	0.0946
40	31.409	0.0318	337.882	0.0030	10.7574	0.0930
45	48.327	0.0207	525.859	0.0019	10.8812	0.0919
50	74.358	0.0135	815.084	0.0012	10.9617	0.0912
55	114.408	0.0088	1260.092	0.0008	11.0140	0.0908
60	176.031	0.0057	1944.792	0.0005	11.0480	0.0905
65	270.846	0.0037	2998.288	0.0003	11.0701	0.0903
70	416.730	0.0024	4619.223	0.0002	11.0845	0.0902
75	641.191	0.0016	7113.232	0.0002	11.0938	0.0902
80	986.552	0.0010	10950.574	0.0001	11.0999	0.0901
85	1517.932	0.0007	16854.800	0.0001	11.1038	0.0901
90	2335.527	0.0004	25939.184	0.0001	11.1064	0.0900
95	3593.497	0.0003	39916.635	0.0000	11.1080	0.0900
100	5529.041	0.0002	61422.675	0.0000	11.1091	0.0900

TABLE A.11
10% INTEREST FACTORS FOR ANNUAL COMPOUNDING INTEREST

	Single payment		Equal payment series			
n	Compound-amount factor SP	Present-worth factor PS	Compound-amount factor SR	Sinking-fund factor RS	Present-worth factor PR	Capital-recovery factor RP
1	1.100	0.9091	1.000	1.0000	0.9091	1.1000
2	1.210	0.8265	2.100	0.4762	1.7355	0.5762
3	1.331	0.7513	3.310	0.3021	2.4869	0.4021
4	1.464	0.6830	4.641	0.2155	3.1699	0.3155
5	1.611	0.6209	6.105	0.1638	3.7908	0.2638
6	1.772	0.5645	7.716	0.1296	4.3553	0.2296
7	1.949	0.5132	9.487	0.1054	4.8684	0.2054
8	2.144	0.4665	11.436	0.0875	5.3349	0.1875
9	2.358	0.4241	13.579	0.0737	5.7590	0.1737
10	2.594	0.3856	15.937	0.0628	6.1446	0.1628
11	2.853	0.3505	18.531	0.0540	6.4951	0.1540
12	3.138	0.3186	21.384	0.0468	6.8137	0.1468
13	3.452	0.2897	24.523	0.0408	7.1034	0.1408
14	3.798	0.2633	27.975	0.0358	7.3667	0.1358
15	4.177	0.2394	31.772	0.0315	7.6061	0.1315
16	4.595	0.2176	35.950	0.0278	7.8237	0.1278
17	5.054	0.1979	40.545	0.0247	8.0216	0.1247
18	5.560	0.1799	45.599	0.0219	8.2014	0.1219
19	6.116	0.1635	51.159	0.0196	8.3649	0.1196
20	6.728	0.1487	57.275	0.0175	8.5136	0.1175
21	7.400	0.1351	64.003	0.0156	8.6487	0.1156
22	8.140	0.1229	71.403	0.0140	8.7716	0.1140
23	8.954	0.1117	79.543	0.0126	8.8832	0.1126
24	9.850	0.1015	88.497	0.0113	8.9848	0.1113
25	10.835	0.0923	98.347	0.0102	9.0771	0.1102
26	11.918	0.0839	109.182	0.0092	9.1610	0.1092
27	13.110	0.0763	121.100	0.0083	9.2372	0.1083
28	14.421	0.0694	134.210	0.0075	9.3066	0.1075
29	15.863	0.0630	148.631	0.0067	9.3696	0.1067
30	17.449	0.0573	164.494	0.0061	9.4269	0.1061
31	19.194	0.0521	181.943	0.0055	9.4790	0.1055
32	21.114	0.0474	201.138	0.0050	9.5264	0.1050
33	23.225	0.0431	222.252	0.0045	9.5694	0.1045
34	25.548	0.0392	245.477	0.0041	9.6086	0.1041
35	28.102	0.0356	271.024	0.0037	9.6442	0.1037
40	45.259	0.0221	442.593	0.0023	9.7791	0:1023
45	72.890	0.0137	718.905	0.0014	9.8628	0.1014
50	117.391	0.0085	1163.909	0.0009	9.9148	0.1009
55	189.059	0.0053	1880.591	0.0005	9.9471	0.1005
60	304.482	0.0033	3034.816	0.0003	9.9672	0.1003
65	490.371	0.0020	4893.707	0.0002	9.9796	0.1002
70	789.747	0.0013	7887.470	0.0001	9.9873	0.1001
75	1271.895	0.0008	12708.954	0.0001	9.9921	0.1001
80	2048.400	0.0005	20474.002	0.0001	9.9951	0.1001
85	3298.969	0.0003	32979.690	0.0000	9.9970	0.1000
90	5313.023	0.0002	53120.226	0.0000	9.9981	0.1000
95	8556.676	0.0001	85556.760	0.0000	9.9988	0.1000
100	13780.612	0.0001	137796.123	0.0000	9.9993	0.1000

TABLE A.12

12% INTEREST FACTORS FOR ANNUAL COMPOUNDING INTEREST

	Single payment		Equal payment series			
n	Compound-amount factor SP	Present-worth factor PS	Compound-amount factor SR	Sinking-fund factor RS	Present-worth factor PR	Capital-recovery factor RP
1	1.120	0.8929	1.000	1.0000	0.8929	1.1200
2	1.254	0.7972	2.120	0.4717	1.6901	0.5917
3	1.405	0.7118	3.374	0.2964	2.4018	0.4164
4	1.574	0.6355	4.779	0.2092	3.0374	0.3292
5	1.762	0.5674	6.353	0.1574	3.6048	0.2774
6	1.974	0.5066	8.115	0.1232	4.1114	0.2432
7	2.211	0.4524	10.089	0.0991	4.5638	0.2191
8	2.476	0.4039	12.300	0.0813	4.9676	0.2013
9	2.773	0.3606	14.776	0.0677	5.3283	0.1877
10	3.106	0.3220	17.549	0.0570	5.6502	0.1770
11	3.479	0.2875	20.655	0.0484	5.9377	0.1684
12	3.896	0.2567	24.133	0.0414	6.1944	0.1614
13	4.364	0.2292	28.029	0.0357	6.4236	0.1557
14	4.887	0.2046	32.393	0.0309	6.6282	0.1509
15	5.474	0.1827	37.280	0.0268	6.8109	0.1468
16	6.130	0.1631	42.753	0.0234	6.9740	0.1434
17	6.866	0.1457	48.884	0.0205	7.1196	0.1405
18	7.690	0.1300	55.750	0.0179	7.2497	0.1379
19	8.613	0.1161	63.440	0.0158	7.3658	0.1358
20	9.646	0.1037	72.052	0.0139	7.4695	0.1339
21	10.804	0.0926	81.699	0.0123	7.5620	0.1323
22	12.100	0.0827	92.503	0.0108	7.6447	0.1308
23	13.552	0.0738	104.603	0.0096	7.7184	0.1296
24	15.179	0.0659	118.155	0.0085	7.7843	0.1285
25	17.000	0.0588	133.334	0.0075	7.8431	0.1275
26	19.040	0.0525	150.334	0.0067	7.8957	0.1267
27	21.325	0.0469	169.374	0.0059	7.9426	0.1259
28	23.884	0.0419	190.699	0.0053	7.9844	0.1253
29	26.750	0.0374	214.583	0.0047	8.0218	0.1247
30	29.960	0.0334	241.333	0.0042	8.0552	0.1242
31	33.555	0.0298	271.293	0.0037	8.0850	0.1237
32	37.582	0.0266	304.848	0.0033	8.1116	0.1233
33	42.092	0.0238	342.429	0.0029	8.1354	0.1229
34	47.143	0.0212	384.521	0.0026	8.1566	0.1226
35	52.800	0.0189	431.664	0.0023	8.1755	0.1223
40	93.051	0.0108	767.091	0.0013	8.2438	0.1213
45	163.988	0.0061	1358.230	0.0007	8.2825	0.1207
50	289.002	0.0035	2400.018	0.0004	8.3045	0.1204

TABLE A.13
15% INTEREST FACTORS FOR ANNUAL COMPOUNDING INTEREST

	Single payment		Equal payment series			
n	Compound-amount factor $\mathcal{SP}$	Present-worth factor $\mathcal{PS}$	Compound-amount factor $\mathcal{SR}$	Sinking-fund factor $\mathcal{RS}$	Present-worth factor $\mathcal{PR}$	Capital-recovery factor $\mathcal{RP}$
1	1.150	0.8696	1.000	1.0000	0.8696	1.1500
2	1.323	0.7562	2.150	0.4651	1.6257	0.6151
3	1.521	0.6575	3.473	0.2880	2.2832	0.4380
4	1.749	0.5718	4.993	0.2003	2.8550	0.3503
5	2.011	0.4972	6.742	0.1483	3.3522	0.2983
6	2.313	0.4323	8.754	0.1142	3.7845	0.2642
7	2.660	0.3759	11.067	0.0904	4.1604	0.2404
8	3.059	0.3269	13.727	0.0729	4.4873	0.2229
9	3.518	0.2843	16.786	0.0596	4.7716	0.2096
10	4.046	0.2472	20.304	0.0493	5.0188	0.1993
11	4.652	0.2150	24.349	0.0411	5.2337	0.1911
12	5.350	0.1869	29.002	0.0345	5.4206	0.1845
13	6.153	0.1625	34.352	0.0291	5.5832	0.1791
14	7.076	0.1413	40.505	0.0247	5.7245	0.1747
15	8.137	0.1229	47.580	0.0210	5.8474	0.1710
16	9.358	0.1069	55.717	0.0180	5.9542	0.1680
17	10.761	0.0929	65.075	0.0154	6.0472	0.1654
18	12.375	0.0808	75.836	0.0132	6.1280	0.1632
19	14.232	0.0703	88.212	0.0113	6.1982	0.1613
20	16.367	0.0611	102.444	0.0098	6.2593	0.1598
21	18.822	0.0531	118.810	0.0084	6.3125	0.1584
22	21.645	0.0462	137.632	0.0073	6.3587	0.1573
23	24.891	0.0402	159.276	0.0063	6.3988	0.1563
24	28.625	0.0349	184.168	0.0054	6.4338	0.1554
25	32.919	0.0304	212.793	0.0047	6.4642	0.1547
26	37.857	0.0264	245.712	0.0041	6.4906	0.1541
27	43.535	0.0230	283.569	0.0035	6.5135	0.1535
28	50.066	0.0200	327.104	0.0031	6.5335	0.1531
29	57.575	0.0174	377.170	0.0027	6.5509	0.1527
30	66.212	0.0151	434.745	0.0023	6.5660	0.1523
31	76.144	0.0131	500.957	0.0020	6.5791	0.1520
32	87.565	0.0114	577.100	0.0017	6.5905	0.1517
33	100.700	0.0099	664.666	0.0015	6.6005	0.1515
34	115.805	0.0086	765.365	0.0013	6.6091	0.1513
35	133.176	0.0075	881.170	0.0011	6.6166	0.1511
40	267.864	0.0037	1779.090	0.0006	6.6418	0.1506
45	538.769	0.0019	3585.128	0.0003	6.6543	0.1503
50	1083.657	0.0009	7217.716	0.0002	6.6605	0.1501

TABLE A.14

20% INTEREST FACTORS FOR ANNUAL COMPOUNDING INTEREST

	Single payment		Equal payment series			
n	Compound-amount factor $S\mathcal{P}$	Present-worth factor $\mathcal{P}S$	Compound-amount factor $S\mathcal{R}$	Sinking-fund factor $\mathcal{R}S$	Present-worth factor $\mathcal{P}\mathcal{R}$	Capital-recovery factor $\mathcal{R}\mathcal{P}$
1	1.200	0.8333	1.000	1.0000	0.8333	1.2000
2	1.440	0.6945	2.200	0.4546	1.5278	0.6546
3	1.728	0.5787	3.640	0.2747	2.1065	0.4747
4	2.074	0.4823	5.368	0.1863	2.5887	0.3863
5	2.488	0.4019	7.442	0.1344	2.9906	0.3344
6	2.986	0.3349	9.930	0.1007	3.3255	0.3007
7	3.583	0.2791	12.916	0.0774	3.6046	0.2774
8	4.300	0.2326	16.499	0.0606	3.8372	0.2606
9	5.160	0.1938	20.799	0.0481	4.0310	0.2481
10	6.192	0.1615	25.959	0.0385	4.1925	0.2385
11	7.430	0.1346	32.150	0.0311	4.3271	0.2311
12	8.916	0.1122	39.581	0.0253	4.4392	0.2253
13	10.699	0.0935	48.497	0.0206	4.5327	0.2206
14	12.839	0.0779	59.196	0.0169	4.6106	0.2169
15	15.407	0.0649	72.035	0.0139	4.6755	0.2139
16	18.488	0.0541	87.442	0.0114	4.7296	0.2114
17	22.186	0.0451	105.931	0.0095	4.7746	0.2095
18	26.623	0.0376	128.117	0.0078	4.8122	0.2078
19	31.948	0.0313	154.740	0.0065	4.8435	0.2065
20	38.338	0.0261	186.688	0.0054	4.8696	0.2054
21	46.005	0.0217	225.026	0.0045	4.8913	0.2045
22	55.206	0.0181	271.031	0.0037	4.9094	0.2037
23	66.247	0.0151	326.237	0.0031	4.9245	0.2031
24	79.497	0.0126	392.484	0.0026	4.9371	0.2026
25	95.396	0.0105	471.981	0.0021	4.9476	0.2021
26	114.475	0.0087	567.377	0.0018	4.9563	0.2018
27	137.371	0.0073	681.853	0.0015	4.9636	0.2015
28	164.845	0.0061	819.223	0.0012	4.9697	0.2012
29	197.814	0.0051	984.068	0.0010	4.9747	0.2010
30	237.376	0.0042	1181.882	0.0009	4.9789	0.2009
31	284.852	0.0035	1419.258	0.0007	4.9825	0.2007
32	341.822	0.0029	1704.109	0.0006	4.9854	0.2006
33	410.186	0.0024	2045.931	0.0005	4.9878	0.2005
34	492.224	0.0020	2456.118	0.0004	4.9899	0.2004
35	590.668	0.0017	2948.341	0.0003	4.9915	0.2003
40	1469.772	0.0007	7343.858	0.0002	4.9966	0.2001
45	3657.262	0.0003	18281.310	0.0001	4.9986	0.2001
50	9100.438	0.0001	45497.191	0.0000	4.9995	0.2000

TABLE A.15
25% INTEREST FACTORS FOR ANNUAL COMPOUNDING INTEREST

	Single payment		Equal payment series			
n	Compound-amount factor SP	Present-worth factor PS	Compound-amount factor SR	Sinking-fund factor RS	Present-worth factor PR	Capital-recovery factor RP
1	1.250	0.8000	1.000	1.0000	0.8000	1.2500
2	1.563	0.6400	2.250	0.4445	1.4400	0.6945
3	1.953	0.5120	3.813	0.2623	1.9520	0.5123
4	2.441	0.4096	5.766	0.1735	2.3616	0.4235
5	3.052	0.3277	8.207	0.1219	2.6893	0.3719
6	3.815	0.2622	11.259	0.0888	2.9514	0.3388
7	4.768	0.2097	15.073	0.0664	3.1611	0.3164
8	5.960	0.1678	19.842	0.0504	3.3289	0.3004
9	7.451	0.1342	25.802	0.0388	3.4631	0.2888
10	9.313	0.1074	33.253	0.0301	3.5705	0.2801
11	11.642	0.0859	42.566	0.0235	3.6564	0.2735
12	14.552	0.0687	54.208	0.0185	3.7251	0.2685
13	18.190	0.0550	68.760	0.0146	3.7801	0.2646
14	22.737	0.0440	86.949	0.0115	3.8241	0.2615
15	28.422	0.0352	109.687	0.0091	3.8593	0.2591
16	35.527	0.0282	138.109	0.0073	3.8874	0.2573
17	44.409	0.0225	173.636	0.0058	3.9099	0.2558
18	55.511	0.0180	218.045	0.0046	3.9280	0.2546
19	69.389	0.0144	273.556	0.0037	3.9424	0.2537
20	86.736	0.0115	342.945	0.0029	3.9539	0.2529
21	108.420	0.0092	429.681	0.0023	3.9631	0.2523
22	135.525	0.0074	538.101	0.0019	3.9705	0.2519
23	169.407	0.0059	673.626	0.0015	3.9764	0.2515
24	211.758	0.0047	843.033	0.0012	3.9811	0.2512
25	264.698	0.0038	1054.791	0.0010	3.9849	0.2510
26	330.872	0.0030	1319.489	0.0008	3.9879	0.2508
27	413.590	0.0024	1650.361	0.0006	3.9903	0.2506
28	516.988	0.0019	2063.952	0.0005	3.9923	0.2505
29	646.235	0.0016	2580.939	0.0004	3.9938	0.2504
30	807.794	0.0012	3227.174	0.0003	3.9951	0.2503
31	1009.742	0.0010	4034.968	0.0003	3.9960	0.2503
32	1262.177	0.0008	5044.710	0.0002	3.9968	0.2502
33	1577.722	0.0006	6306.887	0.0002	3.9975	0.2502
34	1972.152	0.0005	7884.609	0.0001	3.9980	0.2501
35	2465.190	0.0004	9856.761	0.0001	3.9984	0.2501

TABLE A.16

30% INTEREST FACTORS FOR ANNUAL COMPOUNDING INTEREST

	Single payment		Equal payment series			
n	Compound-amount factor SP	Present-worth factor PS	Compound-amount factor SR	Sinking-fund factor RS	Present-worth factor PR	Capital-recovery factor RP
1	1.300	0.7692	1.000	1.0000	0.7692	1.3000
2	1.690	0.5917	2.300	0.4348	1.3610	0.7348
3	2.197	0.4552	3.990	0.2506	1.8161	0.5506
4	2.856	0.3501	6.187	0.1616	2.1663	0.4616
5	3.713	0.2693	9.043	0.1106	2.4356	0.4106
6	4.827	0.2072	12.756	0.0784	2.6428	0.3784
7	6.275	0.1594	17.583	0.0569	2.8021	0.3569
8	8.157	0.1226	23.858	0.0419	2.9247	0.3419
9	10.605	0.0943	32.015	0.0312	3.0190	0.3312
10	13.786	0.0725	42.620	0.0235	3.0915	0.3235
11	17.922	0.0558	56.405	0.0177	3.1473	0.3177
12	23.298	0.0429	74.327	0.0135	3.1903	0.3135
13	30.288	0.0330	97.625	0.0103	3.2233	0.3103
14	39.374	0.0254	127.913	0.0078	3.2487	0.3078
15	51.186	0.0195	167.286	0.0060	3.2682	0.3060
16	66.542	0.0150	218.472	0.0046	3.2832	0.3046
17	86.504	0.0116	285.014	0.0035	3.2948	0.3035
18	112.455	0.0089	371.518	0.0027	3.3037	0.3027
19	146.192	0.0069	483.973	0.0021	3.3105	0.3021
20	190.050	0.0053	630.165	0.0016	3.3158	0.3016
21	247.065	0.0041	820.215	0.0012	3.3199	0.3012
22	321.184	0.0031	1067.280	0.0009	3.3230	0.3009
23	417.539	0.0024	1388.464	0.0007	3 3254	0.3007
24	542.801	0.0019	1806.003	0.0006	3.3272	0.3006
25	705.641	0.0014	2348.803	0.0004	3.3286	0.3004
26	917.333	0.0011	3054.444	0.0003	3.3297	0.3003
27	1192.533	0.0008	3971.778	0.0003	3.3305	0.3003
28	1550.293	0.0007	5164.311	0.0002	3.3312	0.3002
29	2015.381	0.0005	6714.604	0.0002	3.3317	0.3002
30	2619.996	0.0004	8729.985	0.0001	3.3321	0.3001
31	3405.994	0.0003	11349.981	0.0001	3.3324	0.3001
32	4427.793	0.0002	14755.975	0.0001	3.3326	0.3001
33	5756.130	0.0002	19183.768	0.0001	3.3328	0.3001
34	7482.970	0.0001	24939.899	0.0001	3.3329	0.3001
35	9727.860	0.0001	32422.868	0.0000	3.3330	0.3000

Cost Correlations
for Processes

B

The total fixed capital investments for Battery Limits installations are given in terms of the total annual production capacity in metric tons or Mg./year. These data can be converted to daily capacities by dividing by the appropriate number of operating days per year: usually 330 days/year. More data and details are given by Woods (1974). All costs refer to North American values for mid 1970 corresponding to a MS = 300.

Product	Process	Size 10^3 Mg/yr.	Cost 10^6 $	Range	n	Error (%)
Acetaldehyde	Ex ethanol	23	1.2			
	Ex ethylene	50	4.1	25–100	0.70	10
Acetic acid	Ex methanol	10	23	2–50	0.68	15
Acetone	Ex propylene	10	7.5	2–50	0.45	20
	Ex isopropanol	25	7			
Acetylene	Ex natural gas or petrochemical source	15	7	2–150	0.70	10
Acrylic acid	Ex propylene with methyl acrylate as by-product	1.1	3.2			
Acrylic fiber		10	8.2	4–20	0.69	

Product	Process	Size 10^3 Mg/yr.	Cost 10^6 \$	Range	n	Error (%)
Acrylonitrile	Ex acetylene and HCN	100	32	10–500	0.60	30
Adipic acid		10	6.5	5–50	0.53	
Alkyl benzene (linear)		40	2.8	10–120	0.70	
Alum (liquid)		10	0.9	7–350	0.71	
Alumina	Ex bauxite	200	37	100–400	0.66	
Aluminum	Ex alumina	50	53	25–200	0.80	
Aluminum sulfate		50	1.8	10–500	0.71	25
Ammonia (anhydrous, liquefied)	Ex steam reforming of naphtha	150	11	30–330	0.70	40
	Ex steam reforming of natural gas ($\times$ 0.8)					
	Ex partial oxidation of natural gas ($\times$ 1.0), naphtha ($\times$ 1.15), fuel oil ($\times$ 1.3), coal ($\times$ 1.70)					
Ammonium nitrate	Ex ammonia, nitric acid	100	2.8	15–300	0.65	
Propylene oxide	via chlorohydrin	40	4.3	25–60	0.90	
	proplyene plus isobutane	60	12.8			
	electrochemical	60	11.7			
Protein	Ex paraffinic concentrates	60	10			
Pseudocumene	distillation separation	32	1.8			
Pulp: alkaline chemical (sulfite, sulfate, Kraft)	Ex softwood, bleached incl. recovery, as air dry pulp. slush pulp is $\times$ 0.9 these costs. Ex hard wood = $\times$ 1.05	100	33	8–200	0.87	
	unbleached nonintegrated	30	9	8–300	0.62	
	bleached nonintegrated	30	12.5	8–60	0.62	
Pulp: acid sulfite	bleached with recovery	50	20	8–200	0.78	100
	without recovery	50	18	8–200	0.86	100
Pulp: semi-chemical	bleached with recovery	30	13	8–65	0.72	100
	unbleached = $\times$ 0.67	65	23	65–160	1.00	
Pulp: chemm-mechanical	cold caustic soda	30	8	8–65	0.70	100
	bleached	65	13.5	65–160	1.00	
Pulp: ground wood	unbleached slush = $\times$ 0.58	30	6.8	8–200	0.71	100

Product	Process	Size 10^3 Mg/yr.	Cost 10^6 \$	Range	n	Error (%)
Resorcinal	sulfonation	1.8	1.1			
Soap		3	0.26	1.5–7	0.23	
Sodium		18	7.9			
Sodium Carbonate	Solvay Process	120	0.38	60–200	0.55	
(Soda Ash)	Ex natural brine	360	39			
Sodium Chlorate		30	5	15–60	0.66	
Sodium Hydroxide	Electrolysis of brine	30	10	3–300	0.38	
Sorbitol	Ex corn sugar	4.5	0.8			
Steel	Integrated	500	230	150–4000	0.65	
Styrene	Ex benzene, ethylene	100	10.5	20–400	0.67	
	Ex ethyl benzene	40	3.5			
	Ex reformate aromatics	32	6.5			
Sugar	Ex sugar cane: operates 120 days/yr	10	3.2	6–30	0.41	

Cost Correlations
for Equipment

C

All prices refer to North American prices for mid 1970 corresponding to a Marshall–Stevens index of 300. Most prices are for carbon steel (c/s) equipment although some are quoted for stainless steel (s/s) construction.

More details are given by Woods (1974).

	Size	Unit	Cost 10^3 \$	Range	n	Error %
Activated sludge unit excl. disposal: Installed	1	capacity, 10^6 US gal/d	54	$0.01 - 10^2$	0.78	
Adsorber, L, carbon for waste water: Installed	1	capacity, 10^6 US gpd	420	$0.025 - 10^2$	0.62	
G, air drying: Delivered	$\{^{40}_{400}$	capacity, cfm 100°F	$\{^{1.9}_{5.8}$	$10 - 150$ / $150 - 1500$	0.32 / 0.67	
Aeration Tank (only): Installed	100	volume, 10^3 ft³	120	$3 - 10^3$	0.77	
Bag Filters, GS, shaker type: FOB incl motors	10	capacity, 10^3 scfm	5	$1 - 50$	0.79	50
reverse jet: FOB excl compressor	10	capacity, 10^3 scfm	6.4	$5 - 60$	0.71	
Barometric condensers, c/s multijet: Del	500	water flow rate, US gpm	2.6	$50 - 10^4$	0.60	40
Basins:						
Aeration: earthwork: Installed	10^3	volume, 10^3 US gal	90	$100 - 2 \times 10^5$	0.67	40
Chlorination contact, concrete: Installed	10^2	volume, 10^3 US gal	32	$1 - 10^3$	0.63	
Equalization, earthwork: Installed	10^2	volume, 10^3 US gal	19	$70 - 7 \times 10^7$	0.51	
Evaporation, plastic lined: Installed	1	volume, 10^7 US gal	115	$0.3 - 5$	0.64	30
Sludge storage and drying: Installed	1	volume, 10^7 US gal	56	$0.03 - 50$	0.60	
Waste stabilization: Installed	1	volume, 10^7 US gal	10	$0.5 - 100$	0.91	60
Blenders:						
Rotary double cone, c/s: FOB incl motor	30	capacity, ft³	5.1	$7 - 150$	0.41	20
Twin shell c/s: FOB incl motor	30	capacity, ft³	2.8	$25 - 150$	0.54	
Vertical spiral: FOB excl motor	300	capacity, ft³	1.8	$100 - 400$	0.82	
Horizontal spiral ribbon: FOB incl motor	$\{^{3}_{50}$	capacity, ft³	$\{^{2.5}_{5.2}$	$1 - 18$ / $18 - 400$	0.19 / 0.46	
Pan: FOB incl motor	10	capacity, ft³	9	$1 - 40$	0.74	
Blowers:						
Centrifugal, 4 psi: Del excl motor	10	capacity, 10^3 scfm	20	$0.5 - 150$	0.60	60
Rotary lobe, 10 psi: FOB incl motor	50	drive, hp.	3.3	$5 - 300$	0.55	
Rotary sliding vane: Del excl motor	3	capacity, 10^2 scfm	4	$0.3 - 15$	0.48	
Centrifuges:						
Sedimentation type:						
Tube c/s: FOB excl motor	4	tube diam., in	6.8	$1.5 - 6$	1.54	

	Size	Unit	Cost 10³ $	Range	n	Error %
Disc bowl c/s: FOB excl motor	10	drive, hp	7.4	0.5 – 200	0.67	
Horizontal scroll discharge c/s: FOB excl motor	40	drive, hp	22	8 – 200	0.60	
Filtering type:						
Vertical basket top drive c/s: FOB excl motor	30	basket diam., in	8.2	10 – 80	1.00	
bottom drive c/s: FOB excl motor	20	filter area, ft²	12	10 – 40	0.44	
Automatic batch horizontal basket c/s: FOB	20	filter area, ft²	30	7 – 80	0.65	
Pusher conveyor c/s: FOB excl motor	30	basket diam., in	37	10 – 60	1.00	
Classifiers:						
Air cyclone: Del complete	3	capacity, ston/hr	13	1 – 10	0.42	
Cyclone, wet: Del	3	capacity, ston/hr	1.7	1 – 4	0.45	
Rake: tank size: Del incl motor	7	(width, ft)(length, ft)$^{0.2}$	13.5	4.5 – 12	1.80	
Spiral: Del incl motor	50	spiral diam., in.	12.5	25 – 75	1.53	
Coagulation unit: municipal waste: Installed	1	capacity, 10⁶ US gal/d	62	0.1 – 100	0.62	60
Compressors:						
centrifugal <1000 psi: Del incl motor	{1, 20}	}drive, 10² hp	18, 145	0.3 – 7, 7 – 70	0.82, 0.40	30, 50
Station: installed incl land	30	drive, 10² hp	720	3 – 200	0.65	60
Compressor:						
Axial 5 stage: Delivered incl turbine	{25, 100, 200}	capacity, 10³ scfm	{220, 370, 650	10 – 50, 50 – 120, 120 – 300	0.25, 0.61, 0.84	
Helical screw: FOB incl motor	1	drive, 10² hp	15	0.4 – 2.5	0.95	
Reciprocating <1000 psi: FOB incl motor	3	drive, 10² hp	40	0.01 – 200	0.84	
Concentrators:						
Heavy media circuit: Delivered	10²	capacity, Mg/hr	110	25 – 200	0.18	
Spiral gravity: Delivered	10²	capacity, Mg/hr	60	1.3 – 2500	1.0	

	Size	Unit	Cost 10³ $	Range	n	Error %
Conveyors:						
Belt: FOB excl motor	10^7	(tons/hr)(length, ft)$^{2.5}$	2	$10^5 - 10^9$	0.20	
Pneumatic, fluidizer unit: FOB air supply: FOB	10	ton/hr.	4	2 – 40	0.40	
Roller: Delivered	10	ton solids/hr.	3	2 – 20	0.30	
Screw c/s: Delivered excl motor	10^2	(length, ft)(width, in.)	0.052	10 – 500	0.90	
	10^4	(ton/hr)(length, ft)$^{1.6}$	3	$10^3 - 5 \times 10^5$	0.46	35
Cranes:						
Overhead bridge: Field erected	10	lifting capacity, ton	16	1 – 200	0.57	30
Crushers:						
Cone: FOB crusher only	10^2	drive, hp	39	30 – 300	0.92	
Gyratory: FOB excl motor	3	drive, hp	4	1 – 30	0.50	50
	300		230	120 – 1,000	1.19	40
Jaw: FOB excl motor	10	drive, hp	10	1 – 60	0.65	
	100		85	60 – 400	0.81	
Twin roll: FOB excl motor	5	drive, hp	9	1 – 20	0.94	60
Heavy duty	50		19	1 – 300	0.61	60
Pulverizer or impact: FOB excl motor	10	drive, hp	5.2	2 – 500	0.66	50
Lump breaker: FOB excl motor	10	drive, hp	1	5 – 20	1.10	
Crystallizers:						
Batch vacuum c/s: Del. incl vacuum	2	working capacity, 10^3 gal	30	0.5 – 10	0.68	
Conventional forced circulation c/s: FOB	100	crystal capacity, ton/d	85	10 – 1000	0.53	
Growth and classifying c/s: FOB	100	crystal capacity, ton/d	130	$10 - 10^4$	0.62	100
Mechanical c/s: FOB	70	cooling area, ft²	5.5	30 – 150	0.55	
Cyclones:						
Single high efficiency c/s: FOB	10	capacity, 10^3 scfm	3	1 – 80	0.56	30
Multi: FOB	10	capacity, 10^3 scfm	2	1 – 150	0.66	30
Deaerators:						
Vacuum type: FOB	200	capacity, US gpm	8.8	50 – 1000	0.43	

	Size	Unit	Cost 10^3 \$	Range	n	Error %
Forced draft type: FOB	100	capacity, US gpm	5.4	50 – 800	0.45	
Dialysis: Installed	3	membrane area, 10^3 ft^2	32	0.5 – 60	0.79	
Digester: anaerobic: Installed	$\begin{cases}10\\300\end{cases}$	volume, 10^3 ft^3	$\begin{cases}37\\480\end{cases}$	1 – 35 35 – 600	0.41 0.97	
Distillation tower; complete tower-trays: Installed	4000	$\left(\dfrac{\text{actual}}{\text{trays}}\right)\left(\dfrac{\text{feed, lb/yr}}{10^6}\right)^{0.65}$	1000	300 – 30,000	1.0	26
Drives: Gear unit: FOB excl motor	$\begin{cases}40\\500\end{cases}$	$\left(\dfrac{\text{drive,}}{\text{hp at 1800 rpm}}\right)\left(\dfrac{\text{nominal}}{\text{reduction ratio}}\right)^{0.5}$	$\begin{cases}0.58\\3.6\end{cases}$	4 – 150 150 – 2000	0.45 0.75	
V belt and pulley: FOB	10	drive, hp	0.14	2 – 30	0.88	
Sprockets and roller chain: FOB	10	drive, hp	0.055	2 – 10	0.21	
Dryers: Cone, jacketed vacuum s/s: FOB incl auxil	10	working capacity, ft^3	9.2	1 – 300	0.50	
Drum, atmos c/s: FOB excl. motor	100	surface area, ft^2	22	10 – 400	0.52	40
Fluidized bed, direct fired c/s: FOB incl auxil	10	$\left(\dfrac{\text{diam,}}{\text{ft}}\right)\left(\dfrac{\text{fluidizing}}{\text{velocity, ft/sec}}\right)^{0.35}$	45	3 – 26	0.73	
Dryers: Rotary, indirect fired c/s: FOB incl motors	4	peripheral area, 10^2 ft^2	28	1 – 20	1.00	40
Rotary, direct fired c/s: FOB incl auxil	4	peripheral area, 10^2 ft^2	18	1 – 40	0.88	30
Installed	100	solid waste, ton/d	150	40 – 600	0.84	40
Rotary, steam tube c/s: FOB incl motor	10	heating area, 10^2 ft^2	18	4 – 70	0.75	30
Rotary, vacuum c/s: FOB incl auxil	1	peripheral area, 10^2 ft^2	23	0.2 – 10	0.49	30
Roto-louvre, atmos c/s: FOB incl auxil	2	peripheral area, 10^2 ft^2	35	0.5 – 10	0.62	10
Sand bed, for sludge: Installed	$\begin{cases}20\\200\end{cases}$	surface area, 10^3 ft^2	$\begin{cases}29\\220\end{cases}$	5 – 43 43 – 1000	0.63 0.96	50
Shelf, vacuum c/s: FOB excl trays, vac. equip	1	tray area, 10^2 ft^2	5.1	0.15 – 10	0.56	
Spray $\sim 150°C$ c/s: FOB	5	water evap/hr, 10^3 lb	150	0.25 – 20	0.71	

	Size	Unit	Cost 10³ $	Range	n	Error %
Tray-Truck c/s: FOB excl trays	1	tray area, 10^2 ft²	4	0.20 – 15	0.37	
Tunnel c/s: FOB incl auxil excl motor	4	heated surface, 10^2 ft²	64	1.5 – 15	0.93	20
Transported bed c/s: FOB incl auxil	1	water evap/hr, 10^3 lb	40	0.60 – 20	0.42	30
Turbo c/s: Del incl motors	1	drying area, 10^3 ft²	48	0.20 – 20	0.66	
Ejectors:						
Single stage: 100 psig steam: FOB ejector	3	(lb/hr air)/(mm Hg abs.)	0.80	0.2 – 30	0.50	70
Two stage: FOB incl condenser, piping	1	(lb/hr air)/(mm Hg abs.)	1.9	0.2 – 10	0.43	30
Multistage: FOB incl condenser, piping	10	(lb/hr air)/(mm Hg abs.)	5.0	0.2 – 100	0.26	40
Electrodialysis:						
Membranes, spacers, electrodes: FOB	40	area, 10^3 ft²	400	20 – 80	0.70	
Unit for 4000 ppm feed: Installed	1	capacity, 10^6 US gal/d	1,600	0.02 – 100	0.82	
Electrostatic precipitators, G-S, FOB	{ 1, 20 }	gas flow, 10^4 cfm at 40°C	{ 23, 115 }	0.1 – 8, 8 – 100	0.39, 0.81	40, 40
Electrostatic separators: Del incl motor	10	capacity, 10^3 lb/hr	12	2 – 70	0.60	
Elevators, bucket: Del excl motor	10^3	(ton/h)(length, ft)$^{1.6}$	3	$10^3 - 5 \times 10^5$	0.46	35
Engines, gasoline: FOB	400	drive, hp	50	30 – 7000	0.82	70
Evaporators: Natural circulation c/s: FOB	50	heating area, ft²	10	20 – 200	0.50	
Forced external circulation c/s: FOB	1	heating area, 10^3 ft²	65	0.2 – 5	0.74	40
Internal circulation, horizontal tube c/s: FOB	5	heating area, 10^2 ft²	20	1 – 90	0.47	30
vertical basket c/s: FOB	5	heating area, 10^2 ft²	21	1 – 60	0.55	60
Vertical long tube; rising/falling film c/s: FOB	10	heating area, 10^2 ft²	23	0.1 – 1000	0.68	70
Vertical agitated film 316 s/s: FOB	{ 0.05, 1 }	heating area, 10^2 ft²	{ 10, 45 }	0.01 – 0.18, 0.18 – 2.5	0.36, 0.62	30, 30
Jacketed glass lined vessel: FOB	1	volume, 10^2 US gal	16	0.5 – 10	0.48	
Extractors: Podbielniak centrifugal: Del	{ 10, 25 }	capacity, US gpm	{ 15, 27 }	4 – 15, 15 – 40	0.37, 0.78	
Rotating disc, c/s: Del	10^2	(height, ft)(diam., ft)$^{1.5}$	3.5	3 – 2000	0.84	
Vertical agitated, s/s: Del incl motor	10^2	(height, ft)(diam., ft)	43	1 – 5000	0.81	60

	Size	Unit	Cost 10³ $	Range	n	Error %
Horizontal mixer-settler unit, rubber lined: I	10²	horiz. area, ft²	30	15 – 600	0.67	30
Extruders, c/s: FOB incl variable speed drive	10	drivepower, hp	11	2 – 200	0.59	60
Fans: Centrifugal radial: Del excl motor	30	capacity, 10³ scfm	2.3	3 – 200	0.84	40
incl motor	30		4.5	3 – 100	0.92	40
Vane axial: FOB excl motor	10	capacity, 10³ scfm	5.2	4 – 40	0.65	60
incl motor	3		6.0	1 – 10	0.35	60
Propeller: FOB package incl motor	20	capacity, 10³ scfm	0.50	1 – 100	0.40	50
Feeders:						
S, rotary star: Del excl motor	10	diam., inches	1.3	3 – 10	0.66	
Apron: Del excl hopper, motor	400	(ton/hr)(length, ft)$^{0.55}$	12	50 – 5000	0.70	
Filters:						
Plate and frame c/s: Del	1	effective area, 10² ft²	1.7	0.1 – 10	0.55	30
Pressure leaf, vertical c/s: Del	1	effective area, 10² ft²	5.1	0.3 – 15	0.57	
horizontal c/s: Del	1	effective area, 10² ft²	7.1	0.3 – 15	0.51	40
Vacuum rotary drum c/s: FOB incl motor	1	effective area, 10² ft²	19	0.1 – 15	0.48	50
Vacuum rotary disk c/s: FOB incl motor	1	effective area, 10² ft²	16	0.4 – 10	0.68	
Horizontal plate, c/s: Del filter	5	effective area, ft²	3.2	1 – 10	0.62	
Horizontal tilting pan c/s: FOB	1	effective area, 10² ft²	32	0.1 – 45	0.33	
Belt filter: s/s: FOB	200	effective area, ft²	80	100 – 350	0.58	
Microstrainer c/s: Installed	10	capacity, 10⁶ US gal/d	300	0.3 – 100	0.84	
Deep bed: Installed	100	horiz. area, ft²	72	1 – 20,000	0.63	
Flotation:						
Dissolved air for LS: Installed	1	capacity, 10⁶ US gal/d	35	0.1 – 10	0.47	
Induced draft for SS: Del	{0.4 / 2}	capacity, 100 ft³	{1.6 / 3.6}	0.21 – 1 / 1 – 3	0.37 / 0.74	
Foam separators for waste water: Installed	1	capacity, 10⁶ US gal/d	56	0.25 – 5	0.80	
Furnaces:						
Box type direct fired c/s: Del	40	heat absorbed, 10⁶ Btu/h	54	10 – 400	0.75	40
Vertical cylinder direct fired c/s: FOB	10	heat absorbed, 10⁶ Btu/h	40	0.5 – 100	0.74	50
Multiple hearth c/s: Installed	1	capacity, 10³ lb/h	430	0.15 – 4	0.59	

	Size	Unit	Cost 10³ $	Range	n	Error %
Fluid bed incinerated: Installed	{0.5, 3}	capacity, 10³ lb/h	{270, 900}	{0.4 – 1, 1 – 9}	{0.53, 0.78}	
Generators: turbine drive: FOB incl drive	10⁴	power output, kW	600	3000 – 50,000	0.73	20
Grit chamber for waste water: Installed	300	surface area, ft²	18	50 – 1500	0.37	40
Heat Exchangers:						
Shell-tube, floating head c/s: Del	1	surface area, 10³ ft²	6.5	0.02 – 20	0.59	40
Fixed tube × 0.85; U-tube × 0.87; kettle × 1.35						
Shell-tube—finned tube floating head c/s: Del	{2, 6}	total area, 10³ ft²	{6.7, 15}	{0.7 – 3, 3 – 10}	{0.57, 0.78}	{20, 20}
Air cooled, finned c/s: FOB	3	bare tube area, 10³ ft²	26	0.2 – 20	0.8	30
Plate coil c/s serpentine type: Del	{10, 30}	surface area, ft²	{0.033, 0.063}	{5 – 15, 15 – 40}	{0.36, 0.78}	
Cascade, cast iron: Del	1	surface area, 10² ft²	0.40	0.4 – 2.5	1.0	20
Double pipe, c/s internal finned: Del	20	total area, ft²	0.40	3 – 250	0.14	20
Plate 316 s/s: Del	{150, 350, 700}	surface area, ft²	{5.5, 13.0, 22.0}	{100 – 200, 200 – 500, 500 – 1000}	{0.65, 0.65, 0.90}	
Plate-fin (lamella) c/s: Del	3	surface area, ft²	3.0		1.00	100
Spiral plate (Rosenblad) c/s: Del	{1, 3, 7}	surface area, 10² ft²	{1.4, 2.2, 3.7}	{0.4 – 2, 2 – 4, 4 – 7}	{0.27, 0.48, 0.72}	
Spiral tube c/s: Del	{5, 30}	coil area, ft²	{0.12, 0.47}	{2.5 – 7.5, 7.5 – 60}	{0.43, 0.83}	
Tank suction header c/s: FOB	2	surface area, 10² ft²	1.3	0.3 – 20	0.58	
Bayonet heater c/s: Del	3	surface area, ft²	0.14	1 – 6	0.35	
Mandrel wound Al: FOB	15	surface area, 10³ ft²	180	10 – 20	0.76	80
Cubic; graphite: FOB	70	surface area, ft²	1.7	10 – 200	0.46	
Coils in a tank c/s: FOB excl tank	30	surface area, ft²	0.29	1 – 300	0.33	
Thermal screw c/s: FOB excl motor	1	surface area, 10² ft²	10	0.1 – 4	0.78	40
Electric immersion c/s: FOB	50	energy, kW	0.70	10 – 200	0.87	

Description	Size	Unit	Cost 10³ $	Range	n	Error %
Hopper, S, storage: FOB	100	volume, ft³	0.060	5 – 280	0.91	
Hydraulic Press, c/s 100 psig: Del incl motor, drive	{100}{400}	area, ft²	{50}{95}	{5 – 280}{280 – 800}	{0.23}{1.00}	40
Hydrocyclones: FOB cyclone only	6	body diam, in.	0.45	1 – 100	1.07	
Ion exchange, rubber lined tank: FOB excl resin	10^2	exchange volume, ft³	15	$3 – 10^3$	0.53	40
Complete water demineralizer: Installed	0.5	capacity, 10^6 US gal/d	330	0.25 – 1	1.00	
Jigs: Delivered incl motor and ragging	{10^2}{10^3}	capacity, Mg/d	{2.5}{8.6}	{40 – 350}{700 – 1400}	{0.17}{1.56}	
Kneaders: Double shaft sigma c/s: FOB incl motor	10	capacity, ft³	21	0.6 – 70	0.53	40
Vacuum tilting c/s: FOB incl motor	10	capacity, ft³	32	3 – 50	0.40	
Knives: Rotary: Delivered	30	drive, hp	5.5	5 – 100	0.84	
Magnetic separators: permanent:						
Dry drum: FOB incl motor	{1}{5}	$\left(\dfrac{\text{drum width}}{\text{ft}}\right)\left(\dfrac{\text{diam}}{\text{ft}}\right)^{1.25}$	{1.7}{3.5}	{0.6 – 1.7}{1.7 – 10}	{0.26}{0.66}	
Wet drum: 500 Gauss: Del incl motor	7	drum width, ft	8	3 – 10	1.00	
Pulley; tramp metal: FOB excl motor	4	$(\text{width, ft})(\text{diam, ft})^{1.65}$	1.6	0.8 – 12	0.86	20
Pulley; minerals processing: FOB excl motor	4	$(\text{width, ft})(\text{diam, ft})^{1.5}$	2.1	1 – 20	0.82	30
Double gap plate: FOB	30	width, inches	0.54	6 – 50	1.02	
Grate: 4 bank: FOB	10	pipe length, inches	2	6 – 15	0.94	
Rectangular, suspended, lift: FOB	24	length, inches	2.2	18 – 48	1.53	
Cross belted: FOB incl motor	30	belt width, inches	6.5	20 – 48	1.40	
Magnetic Separators: electromagnetic:						
Rectangular, suspended, lift: FOB in line × 1.85; cross belted × 1.87	5	power, kW	3.5	2 – 12	1.00	
Induced roll, dry: FOB	0.9	power, kW	8	0.5 – 4	0.70	40
High intensity, alternating polarity: FOB unit	{1.5}{5}	power, kW	{7.2}{13}	{1.2 – 1.7}{4 – 7}	{0.58}{0.79}	

	Size	Unit	Cost 10³ $	Range	n	Error %
Mills:						
Cage (impactor, micropulverizer) FOB excl motor	10	drive, hp	4	4 – 200	0.28	50
Swing hammer mill: FOB excl motor	{10, 100}	drive, hp	{4, 21}	3 – 75 / 75 – 400	0.75 / 0.41	50
Roller mill (twin or ring): FOB excl motor	100	drive, hp	33	10 – 600	0.62	50
Attrition: Del incl drive	30	drive, hp	3.5	5 – 1000	0.63	30
Autogenous, c/s: Del incl drive excl motor	{1, 10}	drive, 100 hp	{100, 350}	0.5 – 4 / 4 – 60	0.71 / 0.31	
Ball: FOB excl liner, motor, balls	100	drive, hp	36	5 – 6000	0.70	
Pebble: FOB incl liner, motor	10	drive, hp	5.5	3 – 2000	0.79	
Rod, FOB excl rods, motor	100	drive, hp	37	5 – 6000	0.74	
Fluid energy: FOB incl auxil	1	air jet: 10³ scfm	42	0.8 – 1.4	0.88	
Colloid: s/s: FOB incl motor	10	drive, hp	6.5	5 – 35	0.61	
Two roll mill for blending: Del incl motor	100	drive, hp	27	50 – 300	0.72	
Mill Circuits:						
Ball, open: 100 mesh: Installed unit	5	capacity, ton/h	58	1 – 200	0.65	20
Rod, open: 65 mesh: Installed unit	5	capacity, ton/h	38	1 – 200	0.65	20
Mist Eliminators: FOB excl vessel	10	capacity, 10³ scfm	12	8 – 200	0.72	
Mixers:						
Anchor, top entry, closed tank: FOB incl. motor	2	drive, hp	1.35	1 – 3	0.41	
Propeller, portable: FOB incl motor	2	drive, hp	0.6	0.25 – 7.5	0.58	30
Propeller, fixed, top entry, open: FOB incl motor	5	drive, hp	1.1	1 – 30	0.52	40
Propeller, fixed, top entry, closed: FOB incl motor	5	drive, hp	1.8	1 – 50	0.57	40
Propeller, side entry c/s: FOB incl motor	{2, 10}	drive, hp	{0.92, 1.55}	1 – 5 / 5 – 30	0.19 / 0.48	
Mixers:						
Turbine, fixed, top entry, open: FOB incl motor	10	drive, hp	2.1	2 – 30	0.45	50
fixed, top entry, closed: FOB incl motor	10	drive, hp	3.2	2 – 200	0.56	20

	Size	Unit	Cost 10^3 \$	Range	n	Error %
Planetary action mixer, c/s: Del incl motor	3	drive, hp	2.3	0.5 – 5	0.66	
Diffused air: Installed	$\begin{Bmatrix}4\\30\end{Bmatrix}$	air capacity, 10^3 scfm	$\begin{Bmatrix}46\\250\end{Bmatrix}$	0.4 – 7.5 7.5 – 50	0.66 0.93	80
Motors, electric:						
AC induction, 3 phase TEFC: FOB	1	drive, 10^2 hp	2.1	0.5 – 2000	1.10	
AC induction, wound rotor, TEFC: FOB	$\begin{Bmatrix}10\\70\end{Bmatrix}$	drive, hp	$\begin{Bmatrix}3.7\\5.8\end{Bmatrix}$	10 – 25 25 – 200	0 0.77	
AC synchronous, open: FOB	3	drive, 10^3 hp	48	0.5 – 10	0.96	
DC, open: FOB	20	drive, hp	1.1	7 – 100	0.56	
Packed towers:						
Complete s/s incl Pall® rings: Installed	190	(height, ft)(diam., ft)$^{1.85}$	90	1 – 100	1.07	
incl gauze packing: Installed	190	(height, ft)(diam., ft)$^{1.85}$	270	0.6 – 250	1.00	
Piping network: typical straight run c/s: FOB \$/ft Installed \$/ft: × 6 – 7	6	nominal diam., in	0.0028	1 – 24	1.33	
Typical complex network: FOB \$/ft: × 2 Installed \$/ft: × 13						
Pressure vessels:						
Horizontal drum c/s (150 psig): FOB	1	volume, 10^3 US gal	1.9	0.1 – 80	0.62	
Vertical towers c/s (150 psig): FOB	100	(height, ft)(diam., ft)$^{1.5}$	5	10 – 3000	0.81	40
Jacketed reactors c/s (150 psig): FOB incl mixer	1	volume, 10^2 US gal	2.8	0.1 – 40	0.53	
Pumps: liquid						
Centrifugal c/s: FOB excl motor	$\begin{Bmatrix}10\\100\end{Bmatrix}$	drive, hp	$\begin{Bmatrix}0.46\\1.3\end{Bmatrix}$	0.5 – 40 40 – 400	0.3 0.67	50 50
Mixed flow c/s: FOB incl motor	20	capacity, 10^3 US gpm	20	1 – 200	0.81	60
Axial c/s: FOB incl motor	20	capacity, 10^3 US gpm	14	1 – 300	0.75	40
Peripheral (turbine) c/s: FOB incl motor	20	drive, hp	1.7	1 – 1000	0.46	40
Reciprocating c/s: FOB excl motor	$\begin{Bmatrix}2\\20\\100\end{Bmatrix}$	drive, hp	$\begin{Bmatrix}1.9\\5.4\\14.5\end{Bmatrix}$	0.3 – 3.4 3.4 – 35 35 – 350	0.26 0.49 0.70	40 40 40

	Size	Unit	Cost 10^3 \$	Range	n	Error %
Diaphragm, s/s: FOB incl motor	10	capacity, US gpm	0.70	1 – 300	0.37	30
Rotary gear c/s: FOB incl motor	50	capacity, US gpm	0.48	10 – 1000	0.36	
Rotary moyno c/s: FOB excl motor	$\{\begin{smallmatrix}40\\200\end{smallmatrix}$	capacity, US gpm	$\{\begin{smallmatrix}0.93\\2.1\end{smallmatrix}$	10 – 100 / 100 – 400	0.46 / 0.56	50
Rotary sliding vane c/s: FOB excl motor	100	capacity, US gpm	0.85	10 – 1000	0.74	
Pump house:						
For water supply: Installed	100	drive incl standby, hp	40	10 – 20,000	0.66	40
	0.5	capacity, 10^6 US gpd	32.5	0.2 – 0.9	0.36	
For raw sewage: Installed	$\{\begin{smallmatrix}2\\50\end{smallmatrix}$		$\{\begin{smallmatrix}65\\780\end{smallmatrix}$	0.9 – 3.5 / 3.5 – 400	0.60 / 0.84	
Rectifiers: AC to DC, uni-converter: FOB	30	power, kW	5.5	10 – 80	0.61	
Screens: Single deck c/s: vibrating, std: Del incl motor	500	screen area, ft²	3.0	150 – 700	0.62	
Scrubbers:						
Wet cyclone, c/s: FOB excl fans	10	capacity, 10^3 scfm	4	0.5 – 100	0.72	50
Venturi-jet, c/s: FOB excl fans	10	capacity, 10^3 scfm	5	1 – 100	0.50	
Impingement baffle, c/s: FOB excl fans	10	capacity, 10^3 scfm	4.5	1 – 70	0.68	
Packed tower, c/s: FOB excl fans	10	capacity, 10^3 scfm	8.3	4 – 30	0.68	
Dynamic, c/s: FOB excl settler, motor	10	capacity, 10^3 scfm	3.2	1 – 18	0.61	40
Settlers:						
No central rake: Installed	10	horiz. surf. area, 10^3 ft²	120	0.7 – 30	0.38	
Central rake: Installed	$\{\begin{smallmatrix}0.4\\10\end{smallmatrix}$	horiz. surf. area, 10^3 ft²	$\{\begin{smallmatrix}14\\135\end{smallmatrix}$	0.1 – 0.8 / 0.8 – 100	0.36 / 0.78	
API oil: Installed	1	capacity, 10^6 US gal/d	64	0.3 – 3	0.84	
Silo, conical, c/s: FOB	1	volume, 10^3 ft³	0.11		0.67	
Starters:						
Single phase: FOB	3	drive, hp	0.043	1 – 8	0.26	50
Three phase: FOB	1	drive, 10^2 hp	0.70	0.1 – 20	1.0	80
Storage tanks:						
Spherical at 30 psig: Field erected	1	volume, 10^2 m³	2.8	0.4 – 15	0.70	40
Spheroids at 15 psig: Field erected	3.78	volume, 10^3 m³	90	1.2 – 5	0.73	

302

	Size	Unit	Cost 10³ $	Range	n	Error %
Underground cavity salt dome:	3	volume, 10⁴ m³	450	0.8 – 5	0.73	
mined cavern	3	volume, 10⁴ m³	1400	1.3 – 10	0.58	
Water towers: Installed	1	volume, 10³ m³	110	0.4 – 6	0.88	40
API flat bottom, cone roof: FOB	1	volume, 10⁴ US gal	6.2	0.1 – 85	0.32	30
Field erected	1	volume, 10⁴ US gal	70	0.03 – 3	0.58	40
floating roof × 1.1; lifter roof × 1.3						
Surface aerators, c/s: FOB	20	drive, hp	8.5	1 – 200	0.55	
Tanks: atmospheric: horizontal cylinder, c/s: FOB	1	volume, 10³ US gal	1.4	0.1 – 40	0.57	20
Vertical cylinder c/s: FOB	1	volume, 10² US gal	1	0.1 – 20	0.30	
Vertical, jacketed, c/s: FOB	1	volume, 10³ US gal	4.5	0.07 – 1.5	0.57	
Vertical, agitated, c/s: FOB incl motor	1	volume, 10³ US gal	3.7	0.1 – 20	0.50	
Trays:						
Sieve tray c/s: Delivered Cost/tray	10	diameter, ft	0.60	3 – 15	2.00	30
valve × 1.4; trough × 1.4; bubble cap × 2.8						
Tray unit: c/s						
Installed excl tower	10³	(height, ft)(diam., ft)¹·⁶⁵	4.5	20 – 60,000	0.88	50
Trickling filters: Installed	{ 10 / 100 }	filter volume, 10³ ft³	{ 35 / 160 }	4 – 25 / 25 – 300	0.45 / 0.79	
Turbines, c/s:						
Steam, single valve, single stage: FOB	300	energy, kW	11	10 – 4000	0.51	
Single valve, multistage: FOB	3000	energy, kW	100	1000 – 20,000	0.46	
Multivalve, multistage: FOB	3000	energy, kW	160	2000 – 20,000	0.35	
Gas driven: FOB	5	energy, 10³ kW	250	1 – 30	0.80	
Combustion gas driven: FOB incl auxil	5	energy, 10³ kW	520	0.65 – 15	0.55	
Vacuum pumps, c/s:						
Rotary vane: FOB incl motor	30	capacity, cfm	1.2	4 – 1000	0.43	50
Rotary piston oil-sealed: FOB incl motor	100	capacity, cfm	2.2	1 – 4,000	0.55	30
Rotary liquid piston: FOB excl motor	1000	capacity, cfm	4.7	200 – 10,000	0.75	
Oil diffusion pump: FOB complete	0.2	capacity, 10³ cfm	0.285	0.01 – 3.5	0.22	
	20	capacity, 10³ cfm	2.7	3.5 – 50	0.81	

Cost Correlations
for Auxiliaries

D

All prices refer to North American values for mid 1970 corresponding to a Marshall–Stevens index of 300.

More details are given by Woods (1974).

	Size	Unit	Cost 10³ $	Range	n	Error %
Steam generation:						
gas-oil fired boiler, 250 psig: Delivered & field erected	20	capacity, 10⁴ lb/hr	1,000	2 - 200	0.80	50
: Package unit del	3	capacity, 10⁴ lb/hr	50	0.05 - 20	0.71	50
steam boiled only, fired: Delivered	3	capacity, 10⁴ lb/hr	52	1 - 60	0.82	
waste heat boiler, unfired: Delivered	3	capacity, 10⁴ lb/hr	48	0.1 - 20	0.62	
Dowtherm furnace unit: Del package unit	1	heat absorbed, 10⁶ BTU/hr	13.5	0.2 - 10	0.56	
Electrical power generation:						
portable incl steam generation & turbo: package FOB	40	capacity, kW	4.3	10 - 100	0.73	20
field erected unit ex steam:	4	capacity, MW	1,600	0.5 - 1,000	0.84	30
nuclear power unit	700	capacity, MW	3.2 × 10⁵	50 - 100	0.84	20
Refrigeration:						
packaged mechanical: Installed	100	capacity, tons	40	10 ‒ 1000	0.73	30
steam vacuum: Installed	100	capacity, tons	45	20 - 1000	0.68	
low temp. Dewar: Installed	100	capacity, watts	400	9 - 1000	0.50	
Cooling tower, forced or induced draft:						
Installed	1	capacity, 10⁴ US gpm	90	0.1 - 10	0.87	
Water ex river, pumped & filtered: Installed	1	capacity, 10⁶ US gal/d	14	0.4 - 10	0.81	
ex surface water, pumped, filtered, chlorinated: Installed	1	capacity, 10⁶ US gal/d	400	0.2 - 100	0.68	
softening Installed	1	capacity, 10⁶ US gal/d	180	30 - 1000	0.44	
demineralizing, Installed	10	capacity, 10⁴ US gal/d	45	1 - 40	1.19	
Waste disposal:						
waste water, municipal, secondary treat: Installed	1	capacity, 10⁶ US gal/d	450	0.2 - 30	0.81	60
packaged extended aeration: Installed	1	capacity, 10⁴ US gal/d	35	0.1 - 100	0.63	
packaged conventional activated sludge: Installed	1	capacity, 10⁶ US gal/d	580	0.01 - 10	0.62	
packaged contact stabilization: FOB	1	capacity, 10⁴ US gal/d	12	0.1 - 100	0.40	
via membrane ultrafiltration: Installed	30	capacity, 10⁴ US gal/d	29	0.8 - 8	0.78	

	Size	Unit	Cost 10^3 \$	Range	n	Error %
septic tank and underground tile bed: Installed	4	capacity, 10^3 US gal/d	13	1 – 20	0.82	
lagoon: Installed	10	capacity, 10^4 US gal/d	28	1 – 60	0.71	
deep well disposal of liquid	1	capacity, 10^6 US gal/d	1500	0.4 – 5	0.81	
Sludge disposal						
via digestion, filtering, disposal	1	capacity, 10^6 US gal/d	80	0.2 – 4	0.62	
via digestion, filtering, furnace	18	capacity, 10^3 lb/hr	1×10^4			
Incinerators:						
municipal: Installed with recovery	300	capacity, ston/d	3700	100 – 2000	0.87	
Chimney, brick: Installed	1000	(height, ft) (diam, ft)$^{0.3}$	470	300 – 1500	1.23	
Inert gas generator unit: Package installed	1	capacity, 10^4 scfh	73	0.1 – 10	0.57	

Unit Usages

for

Different Processes

E

More details and data are given by Woods (1974) and Erskine (1969).
In the table, the various additional component usages are abbreviated
as:

F.O.	Fuel oil
R( )	Refrigerant (C)
BW	Boiler Water
PW	Process Water
CA	Compressed Air
F.G.	Fuel Gas
C	Coal

Product	Process	Feed or by-product compound	Raw material (or By-products) mt or Mg	Maintenance %	Operating Labor mh/unit	Operating Labor at capacity 10³ Mg/y	Steam Mg	Electricity MJ	Cooling water Mg	Comments
Acetaldehyde	oxidation or dehydration of ethanol	ethyl alcohol.	1.5 to 1.2 [1.05]*				3	180	500	
		hydrogen								
	single stage oxidation with O₂ Ex ethylene	ethylene	0.67 [0.64]		0.5	60	1 (3 at)	160	180	BW 0.5 Mg
		oxygen, Nm³	270				0.2 (12 at)			PW 7 Mg
		hydrogen chloride	0.015							
	two stage oxidation with air Ex ethylene	ethylene	0.67		0.4	80	1.2	1000	200	BW 0.3 Mg
		air, Nm³	1570							PW 30 Mg
		hydrogen chloride	0.040							
Acetic Acid	Ex acetylene	acetylene	0.62							
	Ex Methanol BASF	methyl alcohol	0.62			80	3.7	470		
		carbon monoxide, Nm³	63							
		(propionic acid)	(0.002)†							
		(other organics)	(0.002)							
	Ex acetaldehyde	acetaldehyde	0.76 [0.73]		0.35	50	3	470	125	
		air, Nm³	228							
		catalyst	0.003							
	Ex naphtha without catalyst	naphtha	1.27		0.7	50	10.5	5600	300	BW 35 Mg
		(formic acid)	(0.21)							
		(propionic acid)	(0.12)							
		(succinic acid)	(0.03)							
		(steam)	(10)							
	with catalyst	naphtha	1.17		0.7	50	9.2	5300	250	BW 35 Mg
		(formic acid)	(0.07)							

*Theoretical conversion requirements.
†By-product.

308

Product	Process	Feed or by-product compound	Raw material (or By-products) mt or Mg	Main-tenance %	Operating Labor mh/unit	at capacity 10³ Mg/y	Steam Mg	Electricity MJ	Cooling water Mg	Comments
Mixed 0.75 Ac₂O 0.25 AcOH	Ex acetaldehyde	(propionic acid) (succinic acid) (steam) acetaldehyde	(0.12) (0.03) (9.3) 0.875				2.7	700	300	PW 0.005 Mg
Phosphorus as P₂O₅	electrolytic furnace	air, Nm³ phosphate rock coke silica pebble matrix carbon electrodes	1700 3.7 0.6 0.66 0.0077		0.96		0.97	21600	34	
Phthalic Anhydride	Ex naphthalene classical	naphthalene (steam)	1.1 to 1.2 [0.86] (3 to 4)		0.35	100	nil.	4000 to 5500	100	PW: 4 – 7 Mg F: 4 – 12 GJ
	von Heyden	naphthalene (steam)	1.06 to 1.08 [0.86] (3 to 4)	3 to 3.5	0.44	100	nil.	4000 to 5500	100	PW: 4 – 7 Mg F: 4 – 12 GJ
	Sherwin-Williams	naphthalene (steam)	1.04 [0.86] (4 to 4.5)	2.5 to 3	0.26	100		3000 to 4500	150	PW: 5 to 6 Mg. F: 4 GJ
	Ex orthoxylene	o-xylene (steam)	1 to 1.03 [0.72] (4.5 to 5)		0.44	100		3000 to 3600	75	PW: 5 Mg. F: 4 GJ
	von Heyden	o-xylene (steam)	1.04 [0.72] (4 to 5)		1.	30		2000 to 2700	50 to 100	PW: 1 to 3 Mg. F: 3 – 4 GJ
	BASF	o-xylene (steam)	0.95 to 1.0 [0.72] (4 to 5)		1.	30		2000 to 2700	50 to 100	PW: 1 to 3 Mg. F: 3 – 4 GJ
	Progil	o-xylene (steam)	0.80 [0.72] (1)		1.4	30		2600	560	PW: F: 4 GJ

309

Product	Process	Feed or by-product compound	Raw material (or By-products) mt or Mg	Main-tenance %	Operating Labor mh/unit	Operating Labor at capacity 10³ Mg/y	Steam Mg	Elec-tricity MJ	Cooling water Mg	Comments
Polybutadiene		butadiene	1.10 [1.00]		1.5	50	8.5	2900	760	PW: 25 Mg, F: 760 m³, Nitrogen: 14 m³, R. (−10): 1.15 GJ
Polybutylene	Witco. Kaldo	butene	1.20 [1.00]		0.33	3000	2	4800	25	F: 12.5 GJ
Steel		high P. pig iron	0.753 − 0.607							
		scrap	0.323 − 0.496							
		finishing	0.006							
		iron ore	0.055 − 0							
		limestone	0.110 − 0.090							
		refractories	0.020 − 0.018							
		oxygen m³	60 − 55							
	Electric Furnace cold	low P pig iron	0.054		0.4	3000		1980		
		scrap	1.023							
		finishing	0.005							
		iron ore	0.010							
		limestone	0.025							
		refractories	0.010							
		oxygen m³	10							
		electrode	0.0055							
	direct hot charge	low P pig iron	0.723		0.35	3000		1620		
		scrap	0.31							
		finishing	0.005							
		iron ore	0.120							
		limestone	0.050							
		refractories	0.015							
		electrode	0.0045							

Product	Process	Feed or by-product compound	Raw material (or By-products) mt or Mg	Main-tenance %	Operating Labor		Steam Mg	Elec-tricity MJ	Cooling water Mg	Comments
					$\frac{mh}{unit}$	at capacity 10^3 Mg/y				
	prerefiner hot charge	low P pig iron	0.797		0.35	3000		900		C(Mg) 0.010
		scrap	0.342							
		finishing	0.005							
		iron ore	0.020							
		limestone	0.080							
		refractories	0.025							
		oxygen m³	30							
		electrode	0.003							
	direct hot and [prerefined] hot	high P pig iron	0.722 [0.791]		0.35	3000		1730 [900]	10	
		scrap	0.309 [0.339]							
		finishing	0.005 [0.005]							
		iron ore	0.140 [0.020]							
		limestone	0.080 [0.100]							
		refractories	0.020 [0.030]							
		oxygen m³	— [35]							
		electrodes	0.005 [0.003]							

Author Index

AACE Bulletin, 161
Alger, P.L., 14
Ali, A.M., 59
Allen, D.H., 115
Anderson, R.E., 93, 228
Antonacci, D.W., 172
Aries, R.S., 14, 157, 208, 220, 223
Arnold, T.H., 162, 182, 194
Association of Professional Engineers of
    Ontario, 11
Auld, J.R., 204
Austin, G.T., 217

Bach, N.G., 190
Backman, J., 67
Balfour, F.J., 184
Barish, N.H., xii
Barr, F.T., 205
Bauman, H.C., xii, 141, 145, 153, 168, 170,
    171, 172, 191, 192, 194, 196, 202, 203,
    204, 205
Beam, K.A., 92, 93
Bechtel, L.R., 205
Berenson, Conrad, xii, 51, 60, 61, 65
Billet, R., 172
Bird, R.B., 257
Black, J.H., 157, 159
Blair, A.G., 170, 173, 174
Blewitt, B.J., 100, 125
Bliss, H., 172
Blume, J.H., 241
Boffey, P.M., 16
Boodman, D.M., 59
Branscomb, L.M., 7
Braunweiler, J.R., 76
British Chemical Engineering, 160
Brown, R.G., 59

Carson, Rachel, 26
Castex, L., 217
Catry, J.P., 217
Chapman, F.S., 171
Chemical Engineering, 160
Chemical Engineering News, 57
Chemical Engineering Staff, 14
Chauvel, A., 217
Chilton, C.H., xii, 153, 160, 162, 164, 168,
    182, 194, 208, 223
Christensen, N.A., 14
Clark, D.S., 224
Clark, R.L., 216
Clerk, J., 185, 193
Commoner, B., 6
Corrigan, T.E., 156, 182, 237
Crane, B., 93
Crane Canada Ltd., 22
Crowe, C.M., 68, 109, 177, 236, 240

Dasgupta, A.K., 27
Decossas, K.M., 168
Defiece, A.N., 146, 147
De Garmo, E.P., 75, 82
Denzler, R.E., 168
Dershowitz, A.F., 224
Dickens, S.P., 201
Dicicco, R.W., 223
Dickson, R.A., 204
Diller, R.M., 169
Dinning, T.N., 204
Doig, I.D., 147
Doody, F.S., 58
Douglas, F.R., 201
Drew, J.W., 172
Dryden, C.E., 109, 160

Edge, C.G., 127
Engineering News Record, 163
Enyedy, G., Jr., 169
Erskine, M.G., 308

Faith, W.L., 216
Fabrycky, W.J., 75, 271
Federal Water Pollution Control Adminis-
    tration, 163, 184
Fiegel, L.J., 8
Fishburn, P.C., 31
Forrester, J., 34
Furlow, R.H., 109, 160

Gaboury, J.A.M., 20
Gallagher, J.T., 185, 193
Ganis, B., 60
Gershefski, G.W., 68
Ginder, A.F., 172
Glazier, E.M., 185, 192, 194
Globe and Mail, 78
Gordon Commission, 58
Grant, E.L., 75
Gregory, J.C., 76
Groggins, P.H., 216
Grosselfinger, F.B., 192
Grumer, E.L., 214
Gushee, D.E., 18
Guthrie, K.M., 168, 170, 171, 191, 194, 197,
    198, 200, 202, 203, 204, 205

Hahn, A.V., 217
Hamielec, A.E., 68, 109, 177, 236, 240
Hamilton, G.E., 146, 147
Hand, W.E., 172, 197, 199, 200
Happel, John, 81, 84, 112, 123, 125, 127, 137,
    141, 157, 194, 208
Harberger, A.C., 27
Harris, J.S., 30
Heneghan, W.F., 76, 141, 145
Herron, D.P., 141, 144
Hirsch, J.H., 185, 192, 194
Hirschmann, W.B., 76
Hodgins, J.W., 9
Hoffman, T.W., 68, 109, 177, 236, 240
Holland, F.A., 171
Hougen, O.A., 23
Hughson, R.V., 14
Hull, A.P., 7

Imperial Oil Ltd., 216
Ireson, W.G., 75

Jelen, F.C., xii, 132
Johri, H.P., 30
Johnson, A.I., 68, 109, 177, 236, 240
Jordan, D.G., 30
Jordan, W.A., 60

Kammermeyer, K., 57
Kapfer, W.H., 57, 125, 141

Kardos, G., 34
Kastens, M.L., 192
Katell, S., 184
Kazanowski, A.D., 31
Keating, C.J., 204
Keeney, R.L., 31
Kempster, J.H., 122, 127
Keyes, D.B., 216
Kharbanda, O.P., 22
Kiddoo, G., 155, 158
Kiefer, D.M., 30
Kirk, H.F., 216
Kobe, K.A., 216, 217
Koltun, S.P., 168
Konig, H., 184
Krathwohl, D., 9

Lamberton, C.H., 204
Lang, H.J., 181
Larson, C.E., 146, 147
Lear, J., 7
Leprince, P., 217
Leung, T.K.Y., 130, 131
Lewis, W.E., 237
Liebson, I., 219
Lightfoot, E.N., 257
Liptak, B.G., 204
Lurgi, 216
Luth, F.A.D., 184
Lynn, L., 155, 156

McEntree, H.R., 224
McGraw-Hill Department of Economics, 58
McKelvey, K.N., 237
McKetta, J.J., Jr., 216, 217
McNeill, T.F., 224
Magee, J.F., 59
Malloy, J.B., 61, 127
Man Made World, 6
Marchitto, M., 158
Marglin, S.A., 27
Massey, D.J., 157, 159
Merrill Lynch, Pierce, Fenner and Smith, 55
Miles, L.D., xii
Miller, C.A., 151, 162, 169, 176, 182, 184,
    186, 201, 206
Miller, D.R., 241
Mills, H.E., 171, 172, 204
Mueller, J.W., 59
Myer, J.N., 55
Myers, A.L., 68
Mylo, J., 171

Nader, R., 16
National Bureau of Economic Research, 58
National Science Foundation, 67
Nelson, W.L., 162, 163, 167, 185, 192, 205
Nenniger, E., 230, 232
Newton, R.D., 157, 208, 220, 223
Norden, R.B., 164, 167
Noyes, R., 216
Nicolai, L.A., 241

O'Donnell, J.P., 202, 203
Oliver, E.D., 172

Olmstead, S.P., 14
Olsen, R.A., 75
O'Meara, J.T., Jr., 8
Osburn, J.P., 57
Othmer, D.F., 216
Otto, E.A., 93

Packard, V., 39, 45
Page, J.S., 168, 172, 204
Papucciyan, T.L., 184
Patterson, W.H., 167
Patton, E.L., 168
Pearce, D.W., 27
Perry, J.H., 20, 23, 24, 51
Peters, M., xii, 144, 157, 172, 204, 208, 219
Popper, H., xii, 14
Popular Mechanics, 78
Powers, G.J., 219
Prater, N.H., 171, 172
Procter & Gamble, xii, 48, 50

Ragatz, R.A., 23
Raichle, L., 172
Reilly, P.M., 30
Reisman, A., 134
Reul, R.I., 127, 144
Riegel, E.R., 216, 217
Riggs, J.L., xii, 59, 93
Royal Commission on Banking and
    Financing, 92
Rudd, D.F., 59, 100, 101, 112, 219, 228

Schuman, S.C., 90, 158, 214
Schweyer, H.C., 155, 156
Science Council of Canada, 65, 66, 67
Sentance, L.C., 13, 14
Shannon, P.T., 68, 109, 177, 236, 240
Sheldrick, M.G., 16
Shreve, R.N., 216
Sieder, W.D., 68

Simmonds, W.H.C., 64
Sirrola, J.J., 219
Sittig, M., 216
Sokullu, E.S., 185
Stanford Research Institute, 158
Starr, C., 7
Stevens, R.W., 162
Stewart, W.E., 257
Street, G.L., 156, 183
Szendrovits, A.Z., 48, 134

Taylor, G.A., 75, 76, 134
Teller, A.J., 10
Thatcher, C.M., xii
Thuesen, H.G., 75, 271
Timmerhaus, K.D., xii, 144, 172, 204, 208,
    219
Toffler, A., 6
Tory, E.M., 149
Trischman, C.A., 219
Twaddle, W.W., 61

U.S. Department of Commerce, 65, 92, 93

Walas, S.M., 194
Waller, T.C., 161
Watson, C.C., 59, 100, 101, 112, 228
Watson, K.M., 23
Wayman, M., 217
Weaver, J.B., 76, 141, 145
Wessel, H.E., 90, 220, 223
West, A.S., 219
White, T.H., 25
Woods, D.R., 68, 109, 168, 177, 192, 197,
    236, 240, 288, 291, 305, 308
Wroth, W.F., 197

Zabel, H.W., 158
Zimmerman, O.T., 172, 204

Subject Index

Acceptance of jobs, ethics, 14
Accounts payable, definition, 260
Accounts receivable, definition, 260
Accuracy:
  in answers, variety of, 17
  of answers and the time constraint, 17–26
  versus time, 17–26
Acetaldehyde:
  capital cost of plant, 288
  unit usages, 231, 309
Acetic Acid:
  capital cost of plant, 288
  unit usages, 309
Acetone, capital cost of plant, 288
Acetylene:
  capital cost of plant, 288
  cost component, 214
Acrylic acid, capital cost of plant, 288
Acrylic fiber, capital cost of plant, 288
Acrylonitrile:
  capital cost of plant, 288
  cost component of, 214
Activated sludge unit, cost, 292, 306
Adipic acid, capital cost of plant, 289
Administrative costs, as a component of cost,
  223
Administrative expense, definition, 260
Adsorbers, cost, 292
Advertising, 60
Aeration tanks, cost (see Basins)
Aerators, costs (see Mixers, Diffused air, and
  Surface aerators)
Agitators, costs (see Mixers)
Air compression, cost factors for, 202
Air cyclone classifiers, costs (see Classifiers)
Algorithm for problem solving, 20
Alkylation plant, capital cost, 289
Alkyl Benzene, capital cost of plant, 289
Alloy equipment, cost of, 185, 192, 193, 194

Alum, capital cost of plant, 289
Alumina, capital cost of plant, 289
Aluminum, capital cost of plant, 289
Aluminum sulfate, capital cost of plant, 289
Ammonia, capital cost of plant, 289
Ammonium nitrate, capital cost of plant, 289
Anaerobic digester, costs (see Digester)
Annual costs, definition, 260
Annual reports of companies, 54, 55
API separators, costs, 302
Approximation, principle of successive, 18
Appurtenances, definition, 260
Apron feeders, costs, 297
Asset, definition, 260
Asset life, 79, 80
Assocation of Professional Engineers of the
  Province of Ontario, ethics, 10
Associations, professional, 9
Atmospheric vessels, costs (see Tanks)
Attitudes, of professionals, 9
Attrition mill, costs, 300
Australia:
  depreciation rate, 86
  labor effectiveness, 192
Autogenous mill, costs, 300
Automobile, depreciation of, 77
Auxiliaries:
  cost factors for, 184, 189, 191, 201, 202
  cost of, 183, 201–202
  definition of, 150
Axial compressors, costs (see Compressors)

Bag filters, cost, 292
Balance sheet in an anuual report, 54
Ball mill, costs, 300
Bare module factor method for capital cost,
  196–199

Barometric condensers, cost, 292
Base cost for the factor method, 176
Basins, cost, 292
Basis choosing for product cost estimation, 213
Battery limits, definition, 151
Belt conveyors, costs (see Conveyors)
Belt filter, cost, 297
Benefit to society criterion, 3, 7
Blenders, costs, 292
Blowers, costs, 292
Bond debt, 93
Brazil, labor effectiveness, 192
Breakeven curve, 226–228
Bridge cranes, cost (see Cranes)·
Bubble cap distillation tray costs, 172
Bubblers, costs (see Mixers, Diffused air)
Bucket elevators, costs (see Elevators)
Buildings:
    cost factors for, 184, 188, 199, 202
    estimate of the cost of, 91
Bulk buying, effect of on correlations, 170
Business outlook, predicting, 58
Byproducts, cost of, 224

Canada:
    depreciation rate, 86
    labor effectiveness, 192
    R and D expenditure, 65, 66, 67
    sales tax, 191
    tax incentives, 61
Capacities of process plants, estimates, 156
Capacity:
    and capital cost, 160
    effect of on costs, 224–228
Capital:
    cost of, 93, 94
    from plowback, 93
    required during construction period, 205
Capital cost estimation:
    correlation method, 159–175
    factor method, 175–207
    table of factors for, 184
    and the time available, 152, 153
    universal factor method, 154–159
    worksheet for, 207, 208
Capitalized cost:
    definiton and calculations, 131, 132
    comparison with other methods, 134–144
Capital ratio method (see Universal factor method)
Capital recovery factor:
    discrete and continuous, 76
    equal payment, definition, 72
    values, 272
Car, depreciation of, 77
Cash flow diagram and the cash and project position diagrams, 98
Cash on hand (see Working capital)
Cash position diagram:
    and the cash flow diagram, 98
    comparison with other methods, 134–144
CE index (see Chemical Engineering index)
Centrifugal blowers, costs (see Blowers)
Centrifugal compressors, costs (see Compressors)
Centrifuges, costs, 292
Chain drives, costs (see Drives)
Chemical Engineering Index:
    definition, 162
    values, 165, 166

Chemical Marketing Magazine, 157
Chemicals, estimating selling price of, 159
Chimney, costs, 307
Chlorination contactors (see Basins, cost)
Chlorine, unit usages for, 229
Choosing among alternatives via financial attractiveness, 97–148
Classifiers, costs, 293
Coagulation unit, costs, 293
Coal, cost of, 218
Code of ethics, example of, 10
Colloid mill, costs, 300
Columns, costs (see Distillation, Pressure vessels)
Communications, cost factors for, 202
Company:
    annual reports, 54
    cash flow diagram, 52, 53, 55, 56, 98
    example data of allocation of funds, 56
    good decisions from, viewpoint, 1
Competition:
    effect on selling price, 61
    perfect, 36
    types of, 39
Compound amount factor, definition, 71
    values, 272
Compressed air, cost of, 219
Compressor:
    costs, 293
        bare module factors for, 198, 199
    station, costs, 293
Concentrators, costs, 293
Cone crusher, costs (see Crushers)
Cone dryers, costs (see Dryers)
Constraint:
    definition, 3
    effect on correlations, 168, 169
Construction period, capital required during, cost, 205
Contact stabilization unit, costs, 306
Containers as a component of cost, 222
Contingency, 183, 203
Contractor's fees, 183, 203
Conveyors, costs, 294
Cooling towers, costs, 306
Cooling water:
    cost of, 218
    usage, quick test of, 215
Corporate ethics, 9, 15
Correlations, errors in, 167
Correlations for capital cost estimation, 159–175
    time available, 152
Cost:
    per function, 235, 236, 237
    per property, 235, 238, 239
    per unit of production, 235
Cost, distribution of, 40, 41, 42
Cost, fixed and variable, 40, 42, 43
Cost, general prediction of, 221
Cost, product, factors for, 222, 223
Cost allocation, definition, 260
Cost estimation for mechanical processing, 224
Cost increments, 235
Costing byproducts, 224
Cost of capital, 93
    accounting for, 111, 123
    definition of, 99
    values of, 100
Cost-plus policy, 61
Cost price of product, and time, 211

Cost price of product, estimation of, and time, 211
Costs:
  components of product, 212
  components of, 210–212
  list of factors, 40
  of chemicals, data, 157
Cost value, definition, 46
Cranes, costs, 294
Criteria:
  list for decision making, 3
  using to make decision, 28
Criterion, definition, 3
Crushers, costs, 294
Crystallizers, costs, 170, 294
Current ratio, definition and usual value, 57
Cutters, costs, (*see also* Knives)
  rotary, costs, 299
Cycle, life of product:
  from consumer's view, 28
  from producer's view, 29
Cyclone classifiers, costs (*see* Classifiers)
Cyclones, costs, 294

DCE (*see* Internal rate of return)
Deaerators, costs, 294
Decision making, 27, 28
Decision matrix, 31
Decisions:
  effect of general policies on, 49, 50, 51
  effect of resources on, 49
  type in a company, 47–67
Declining balance depreciation, 81, 83
Deep bed filter, costs (*see* Filter)
Deep well disposal system, costs, 307
Delumper, costs (*see* Crushers)
Demand for a commodity, 36
Demisters, costs, 300
Depletion, definition, 54
Depreciation, 77–91
  approximations in terms of interest rate, 137
  book, 87
  and the cash flow diagram, 87
  definition, 53
  methods, summary table, 86
  methods of, 80–86
  and plowback, 62, 63, 64
  as shown on the cash flow diagram, 55
  for tax purposes, 87
Dialysis unit, costs, 295
Diffused air mixers, costs, 301
Digester, costs, 295
Digesters, for sludge disposal, costs, 307
Diminishing returns, example, 40, 43
Diminishing utility, law, 36
Direct condensers, costs (*see* Barometric)
Directly attributable costs, definition, 210
Discounted cash flow (*see* Internal rate of return)
Dissolved air flotation unit, costs (*see* Flotation)
Distillation system, cost of, 174
Distillation tower, costs, 295
Distillation tray costs, 172
Distribution of resources in company, data, 50, 56
Dividends, definition, 62
  rate of, definition, 57
Double declining balance depreciation, 81
Double shaft sigma kneaders, costs, 299

Dowtherm furnace, cost, 168
Dowtherm furnace unit, costs, 306
Drives, costs, 295
Drum dryers, costs (*see* Dryers)
Drum magnet, costs, 299
Drums, process, costs (*see* Pressure vessels)
Dryers, costs, 295
Duties, estimation, 180

Earnings per share, definition, 62
  data, 63
Edge mill, costs (*see* Blenders)
Economic:
  indicators, 58, 59
  models, 35
Economic feasibility criterion, 3, 8
Economics:
  definition of, 35
  review of, 35
Effective interest rate, definition, 73
Efficiency of processes, effect of on costs, data, 61
Ejectors, costs, 296
Elasticity, 37
Electrical:
  factors, 184, 185, 186, 190, 191, 198, 199
  power generators, costs, 306
  substation and distribution, cost factors for, 202
Electrical distribution, cost factors for, 202
Electric generators, costs, 298
Electricity, cost of, 218
Electrodialysis unit, costs, 296
Electromagnetic separators, costs, 299
Electrostatic:
  precipitators, costs, 296
  separators, costs, 296
Elevators, costs, 296
EMIP:
  definition and calculations, 113–115
  method, comparison with other methods, 134–144
  and the time available, 104
  values for, 106
Employee responsibility, 11
Engineer, role of in decisions, 47, 48
Engineering expense, 183, 202
Engineering News Record index (*see* ENR index)
Engineer's method (*see* Rate of return)
Engineer's responsibilities, 10
Engines, costs, 296
England, labor effectiveness, 192
ENR index:
  definition, 163
  values, 165, 166
Environmental feasibility criterion, 6
EPA STP index:
  definition, 163
  values, 166
Equalization basins, cost (*see* Basins)
Equipment, estimating cost of, 160–175
Equipment cost for factor methods, 176
Equipment costs, 291–303
Equity, shareholders, 93
Equity capital on the cash flow diagram, 55, 87
Equivalent annual cost method, 134
Equivalent maximum investment period (*see* EMIP)
Error allowable and the time available, 17–26

Esteem value, definition, 46
Esthetics, 6, 9
Ethics, 4
    criterion, 8–16
    example interpretation of code, 12
    macro, 9
    micro, 8
Ethyl alcohol, unit usages for, 231
Evaporation ponds, costs (see Basins)
Evaporators, 296
Exchange value, definition, 46
Expansion, policy for, 64
Expenditure for R and D, 66, 67
Extended aeration treatment unit, costs, 306
Extractors, costs, 296
Extruders, costs, 297

Factor method of cost estimation, 175–204
    equipment cost for, 176
Factor methods for capital cost estimation:
    accuracy, 154
    and time available, 152
Factors, Lang for capital cost estimation,
        180–182
Factors, multiple for capital cost estimation,
        182
Factors, selection of, for cost estimation,
        185
Factors for capital cost estimation, table of,
        184
Falling film evaporators, cost
        (see Evaporators)
Fans, costs, 297
Feeders, costs, 297
Field expense, 183, 203
Field expense factors, 184, 185, 186, 190, 191,
        198, 199
Filters, bag, cost, 292
Filters, costs, 297
Financial attractiveness:
    and the time available, 102–105
    worksheet for, 143
Financial attractiveness criterion, 3, 26
Financial attractiveness methods, compari-
        son, 134–144
Financial feasibility, 91–94
Financial feasibility criterion, 3, 26
Financial objectives for a company, choice
        of, 57
Financing, as a component of cost, 223
Finished product storage, cost factors for,
        202
Fire protection, cost factors for, 202
Fixed capital investment:
    components of, 183
    estimation of, 150–209
    as part of the total investment, 150
Fixed costs, 40, 42, 43
Flocculation unit, costs (see Coagulation)
Flotation unit, costs, 297
Flow diagrams and cost estimation, 176
Flow diagrams and piping cost estimation,
        185
Fluid bed furnace, costs (see Furnace)
Fluid energy mill, costs, 300
Fluidized bed dryers, costs (see Dryers)
Fluid processing plant, 181
Foam fractionators, costs, 297
FOB, definition, 176
Forecasting the future business outlook, 58
France, labor effectiveness, 192

Freight, estimating cost, 180
Fuel gas, cost of, 218
Fuel oil, cost of, 218
Furnaces:
    alloy factors for, 193
    bare module factor for, 198, 199
    costs, 297
    Dowtherm, costs, 168
Future, anticipating, 6, 25, 27–28
Future, predicting the financial, 58
Future worth factor, definition, 71

Gas Cyclone, costs (see Cyclone)
Gasoline engines, costs, 296
Gas scrubbing equipment, costs, 302
Gas supply and distribution, cost factors for,
        202
Gauze packing, costs, 301
Gear unit, costs (see Drives)
General expense:
    definition, 210
    as fraction of the selling price, 41, 90, 214
Generators, costs, 298
Germany, labor effectiveness, 192
Goal of a company, choices of, 57
Good decisions, definition, 1
Grass roots plant, definition of, 150, 151, 153
Grate magnet, costs, 299
Grinders, costs (see Mills or Crushers)
Grit chamber, costs, 298
Gyratory crusher, costs (see Crushers)

Heat exchangers:
    alloy factors for, 193
    bare module factors for, 198, 199
    cost correction factors for, 173
    costs, 298
Heavy duty crusher, costs (see Crushers)
Heavy media concentrators, costs
        (see Concentrators)
Helical screw compressors, costs
        (see Compressors)
Home office expense, 183
Hopper, costs, 299
Horizontal plate filters, costs (see Filters)
Horizontal ribbon blenders, costs
        (see Blenders)
House, estimate of cost of, 91
Human worth and responsibility, 9
Hydraulic press, costs, 299
Hydrocyclones, costs, 299

Ideas, good and bad, 1
Ion exchange unit, costs, 299
Immersion heater, costs
        (see Heat Exchangers)
Impact crusher, costs (see Crushers)
Impact feasibility criterion, 3, 6
Impactor, costs, 300
Improvement of operations, ideas for,
        234–240
Improvement of processes, effect of on costs,
        data, 61
Improving efficiency, policy for, 64
Incinerator, fluid bed, costs, 298
Incinerators, costs, 307
Income statement in an annual report, 54
Incremental costs, 44, 45

Incremental present worth
  (*see* Present value)
Index, inflation, 161–167
India, labor effectiveness, 192
Indirect expenses, definition, 202
Indirectly distributable costs, definition, 210
Induced roll magnet, costs, 299
Inert gas, cost of, 219
Inert gas generator, costs, 307
Inflation, accounting for in costs, 161–167
Inflation indices, comparison of, 164
Information:
  ethical use of, 12
  ethics of, 14
  pressures of time, 25
Initiative, 9
Innovation:
  cost of and elements of, 65
  definition, 65
Installation, definition, 180
Installation costs, estimating, 180, 184, 186, 187, 190, 191, 198, 199
Instrument air compression and distribution, cost factors for, 202
Instrument factors, 184, 185, 186, 190, 191, 198, 199
Instruments, bare module factors for, 199
Insulation factors, 184, 185, 186, 190, 191, 198, 199
Insurance:
  as a component of cost, 222
  estimate of amount, 91
Interest:
  and risk, 100–102
  compound, 70, 71, 72
  continuous compounding, 75, 76
    definition, 73
  definition, 69
  equal payment series, 74
  present worth calculations, 74
  sample, 70, 71
Interest, rate of, definition, 70
Interest rate, effective, definition, 73
Interest rate of return (*see* Internal rate of return)
Interest recovery period (*see* IRP)
Internal rate of return, 115–118, 127–130
  comparison with other methods, 134–144
  and payback time, 130, 131
  and the time available, 104
Invention:
  definition, 65
  different aspects of, 66
Inventory:
  effect of varying, 51, 58, 59
  policies, 58, 59
Investment in shares, 93, 94
Investor's method (*see* Internal rate of return)
IRP, and the time available, 104
  definition and calculations, 113–115
  method, comparison with other methods, 134–144
  values for, 106
Italy, labor effectiveness, 192

Jacketted evaporators, costs
  (*see* Evaporators)
Jacketted reactors, costs(*see* Tanks)
Jacketted reactors, costs (*see* Evaporators)

Japan:
  labor effectiveness, 192
  R and D expenditure, 66
Jaw crusher, costs (*see* Crushers)
Jigs, costs, 299

Kettles, costs (*see* Pressure vessels)
Kneaders, costs, 299
Knives, rotary, costs, 299
Knock out pots, costs (*see* Pressure vessels)

Labor:
  as a component of cost, 222
  component of the capital cost, 194–196
  cost, 221
  cost contribution, estimation of, 220, 221
  factors for in capital cost estimation, 191
  as a fraction of the selling price, 41, 90, 214
  and production capacity, 225
  rates in different countries, 192
Lagoon, costs, 307
Land, cost of, 205
Lang factor method of capital cost estimation, 180–182
Lang factors, alloy factors for, 193
Law of diminishing utility, 36
Law of optimum sloppiness, 18
Learning, effect of on costs, 61
Life:
  of an asset, 79, 80
  design, 80
  economic, definition, 80
  tax of an asset, 80
Life cycle of products, 28
Lighting, cost factors for, 202
Limitations of cost correlations, 167–170
Liquid cyclone, costs (*see* Hydrocyclone)
Liquidity ratio, definition, 57
Living expenses, estimates of, 91
Lump breaker, costs (*see* Crushers)

Magnetic separators, costs, 299
Main plant items for costing, selecting, 176
Maintenance:
  as a component of cost, 222
  cost of, 49, 50, 60
Making decisions, 27
MAPI method, 134
Margin, definition and decay of with time, 61
Marginal cost, 44, 45
Marginal return:
  comparison with other methods, 134–144
  definition and calculations, 133, 134
Marginal revenue and demand, 44, 45
Market, economic definition of, 36
Market conditions of supply and demand, 38
Market feasibility criterion, 37
Marketing:
  as a component of cost, 223
  relative to other company activities, 48, 60
Market research, 49, 50, 60
Marshall and Stevens index:
  definition, 162
  values, 165
Marshall and Swift index
  (*see* Marshall and Stevens)

Matching accuracy with the time available, 17
Material component of the capital cost, 194–196
Materials, factors for in capital cost estimation, 191
Materials of construction, factors for different than carbon steel, 193
Maturity, need for, 9
Maximum profit, 44, 45
Maximum size, effect of on correlations, 168
Membrane ultrafiltration treatment unit, costs, 306
Men per shift converted to MH, 221
Metallurgical plant factors for the capital cost estimation, 184
Metallurgical processing equipment, costs (see App. C, 291–307)
Metals, estimating selling price of, 159
Mexico, labor effectiveness, 192
Micropulverizer, costs, 300
Microstrainer, costs (see Filter)
Mill circuits, costs, 300
Mills, costs, 300
Mined caverns, costs, 303
Mineral processing, factors to estimate the capital investment, 184
Minerals, estimating selling price of, 159
Mining equipment, costs of (see App. C, 291–307)
Mist eliminators, costs, 300
Mixers (see also Blenders)
    alloy factors for, 193
    costs, 300
Mixer settler extractor, costs (see Extractor)
Models, economic model of man's behavior, 35
Monel, cost factor for, 193
Money, sources of, 92–94
Monopoly, 39
Morals, 8
Motors, costs, 301
MPI definition, 176
M's, four (Money, Manpower, Materials, Machinery), 42, 48
MS index (see Marshall and Stevens)
Multicyclone costs (see Cyclone)
Multijet condensers, costs, 292
Multiple hearth furnace costs, 297
Municipal secondary treatment unit, costs, 306

Natural resource feasibility criterion, 3, 16
Nelson refinery index:
    definition, 162
    values, 165, 166
Nelson true cost index:
    definition, 163
    values, 165, 166
Nominal interest rate, definition, 73
Nuclear power plant, costs, 306
n scale up exponent, values of, 161, 168, 172, App. B, C, D.

Objective, financial of a company, 57
Objectives of the book, 31
Oil diffusion pump, costs, 303
Oligopoly, 39
Operating days, definition, 214

Operating ratio, definition, 57
Operating supplies as a component of cost, 222
Opportunity cost, definition of, 99
Optimum sloppiness, 18
Organizational chart of a company, 47, 48, 49
Originality feasibility criterion, 3, 6
Outline of book, 31
Outlook, business, 58
Output, effect of reduced on costs, 224–228
Oxygen, unit usage for, 229

Packed towers, costs, 301
Pan blenders, costs (see Blenders)
Patentable idea, 6
    comparison with other methods, 134–144
    definition and calculations, 105–108
Payback time:
    and internal rate of return, 130, 131
    and the time available, 104
    values for, 106
Pebble mill, costs, 300
Percent return (see Rate of return)
Personal:
    good decisions from a personal viewpoint, 1
    responsibilitiy of engineer, 11
Phosporus, unit usages, 310
PHS STP index (see EPA STP index)
Phthalic anhydride, unit usages, 310
Physical plant cost, definition, 183
Piping costs, 301
Piping factors, 184, 185, 186, 190, 191, 198, 199
Plan of the book, 31
Plowback of funds, 62–67
Pneumatic conveyors, costs (see Conveyors)
Podbielniak extractor, costs (see Extractor)
Policy:
    for distribution of profit, 61
    for distribution of resources, 57
    for inventory, 58
    overall financial, 57
Political feasibility criterion, 3, 8
Pollution control, criteria for selecting, 27
Pollution control equipment, costs (see specific items in App. C or D)
Polybutadiene, unit usages, 311
Precipitators, electrostatic, costs, 296
Premium worth (see Present value)
Present value:
    of annuity, definition, 72
    comparison with other methods, 134–144
    definition and calculations, 115–127
    and the time available, 104
Present worth (see Present value)
Present worth factor, definition, 71
    values, 272
Press, hydraulic, costs, 299
Pressure vessels, costs, 301
Pricing policies, 61
Primary settler, costs (see Settler)
Principal, definition, 69
Problem solving in the time available, 19
Process feasibility, 3–6
Process flow diagram development and costing, 176
Process vessels (see Pressure vessels, Tanks)
Process water, cost of, 219
Process water systems, cost factors for, 202
Processes, classification into solid, solid-fluid, and fluid, 181

Processing, mechanical, costing, 224
Product quality, ethics, 13, 16
Professional associations, 9
Professional engineer's responsibilities, 10
Professional ethics, 8–16
Profit:
    definitions of, 88, 89
    distribution, 52, 61–66
    distribution, as shown on the cash flow
        diagram, 53
    distribution of, policy for, 61
    equations for, 88, 89
Profitability method (see Internal rate of
    return)
Profits-worth ratio, definition and usual
    value, 57
Project position diagram and the cash flow
    diagram, 98
Propylene oxide, capital cost of plant, 289
Protein, capital cost of plant, 289
Pseudocumene, capital cost of plant, 289
Public responsibility of engineer, 10
Public service sector, decision making in, 27
Public works, criteria for selecting, 27
Pulley, magnetic, costs, 299
Pulp, capital cost of plant, 289
Pulverizer, costs (see Crushers)
Pumps:
    alloy factors for, 193
    bare module factors for, 198, 199
    centrifugal, cost, 171
    costs, 301
    house, costs, 302

Quality, ethics of product, 13
Quality, product, ethics, 16

Railroads, cost factors for, 202
R and D, expenditures, 60, 65, 66, 67
    relative to other company activities, 48,
        49, 60, 65, 66
Rake classifiers, costs (see Classifiers)
Rate of dividends, definition, 57
Rate of interest, definition, 70
Rate of return:
    comparison with other methods, 134–144
    definition and calculations, 108–110
    and the time available, 104
Ratios, to show financial performance, 57
Raw material, as a fraction of selling price,
    41, 90, 214
Raw material, cost contribution, 215
Raw material storage, cost factors for, 202
RDC extractor, costs (see Extractors)
Reaching decisions, 27
Reactors, costs (see Pressure vessels)
Reciprocating compressors, costs
    (see Compressors)
Rectifiers, costs, 302
Refinery, estimate of the cost of, 91
Refrigeration, cost factors for, 202
Refrigeration unit, costs, 306
Regulated costs, definition, 225
Rent, estimate of, 91
Research:
    as a component of cost, 223
    types of within a company, 66
Research and development (see R and D)
Resorcinal, capital cost of plant, 289

Resource:
    and economics, 35
    natural, feasibility criterion, 3, 16
Resources:
    distribution of, example of, 50, 56
    in a company, distribution of, 48–67
    natural, use of, 9
    needed for production list, 40
Return:
    definition of net, 88, 89
    expected, 61
Revenue, total, and elasticity, 37
Ribbon blenders, costs (see Blenders)
Ring roller mill, costs, 300
Risk:
    accounting for, 99–102
    definition of, 99
    and its effect on the cost of capital, 94
Risk capital, sources of, 92
Roads and sidewalks, cost factors for, 202
Rod mill, costs, 300
Roller conveyors, costs (see Conveyors)
Rootes blowers, costs (see Blowers)
Rotary blenders, costs (see Blenders)
Rotary dryers, costs (see Dryers)
Rotary knives, costs, 299
Rotary liquid piston vacuum pumps, costs,
    303
Rotary lobe blowers, costs (see Blowers)
Rotary sliding vane blowers, costs
    (see Blowers)
Rotary vacuum filter, costs (see Filter)
Rotating disc extractor, costs (see Extractor)
Roto-louvre dryers, costs (see Dryers)
Royalties as component of cost, 222
Royalty income, 55

Safety feasibility criterion, 3, 5
Sales and marketing, as a component of cost,
    223
Sales tax estimation, 180, 191
Sand bed dryers, costs (see Dryers)
Sand filter, costs (see Filter, deep bed)
Sanitary waste disposal, cost factors for, 202
Scale up exponent, values of, 161, 168, 172,
    App. B, C, D.
Scrap value, 80
Screens, costs, 302
Screw, heated processor, costs (see Heat
    exchangers, Thermal screw)
Screw conveyors, costs (see Conveyors)
Scrubbers, costs, 302
Sedimentation tanks costs, 302
Selecting alternatives when there is no
    income, 27
Selling price:
    and cost, 223
    determining, 61
    effect of competition on, 61
    estimating, 157–159
    estimation, 228, 229
    example, 41, 49, 50, 60, 61
    example of too small, 51
    fractional components of, 90
Selling price ratio method of estimating
    costs, 214
Sensitivity of financial attractiveness criteria,
    145, 148
Separators, electrostatic costs, 296
Separators, magnetic, costs, 299
Septic tank, costs, 307

Services:
  factors for the capital cost estimation of, 201
  relative to other company operations, 48, 223
Settler, 302
Settling tanks, costs, 302
Shares, as sources of income for corporations, 93
Shelf dryers, costs (see Dryers)
Short run, definition, 40
Silos, storage, costs, 302
Simple rate of return (see Rate of return)
Single factor method for capital cost estimation, 180–182
Single factors, alloy factors for, 193
Single payment:
  compound amount factor:
    continuous, 76
    discrete, 76
  present worth factor:
    continuous, 76
    discrete, 76
Sinking fund:
  deposit factor:
    definition, 71
    values, 272
  depreciation, 81, 82, 83
  depreciation rate, approximation for, 137
Site preparation factors, 184
Sloppiness, law of optimum, 18
Sludge disposal, costs, 307
Sludge storage and drying basins, costs
      (see Basins)
Soap, capital cost of plant, 290
Social feasibility criterion, 3, 8
Society, good decisions from society viewpoint, 1
Soda ash, capital cost of plant, 290
Sodium, capital cost of plant, 290
Sodium carbonate, capital cost of plant, 290
Sodium chlorate, capital cost of plant, 290
Sodium hydroxide:
  capital cost of plant, 290
  unit usages, 229
Solid–fluid processing plant, 181
Solid processing plant, 181
Solids feeders, costs, 297
Solids handling equipment, costs
      (see Conveyors and Elevators)
Solids mixers (see Blenders)
Solvent extractors, costs (see Extractors)
Solving problems in the time available, 19
Sorbitol, capital cost of plant, 290
Spain, labor effectiveness, 192
Special circumstances, effect of on correlations, 169, 170
Spiral blenders, costs (see Blenders)
Spiral classifiers, costs (see Classifiers)
Spiral gravity concentrators, costs
      (see Concentrators)
Spray dryers, costs (see Dryers)
Sprocket drives, costs (see Drives)
Stainless steel, cost factor for, 193
Starters, costs, 302
Start up, cost of, 205
Star valve feeders, costs, 297
Steam:
  cost of, 218
  distribution, cost factors for, 202
  generation, cost factors for, 202
Steam boiler, costs, 306
Steam ejectors, costs, 296

Steam tube rotary dryers (see Dryers)
  usage, quick test of, 215
Steel, capital cost of plant, 290
Steel, unit usages, 311, 312
Steel factors, 184, 185, 186, 190, 191, 198, 199
Stock shares, as sources of income for companies, 93
Storage and handling, factors for capital cost estimation, 201
Storage silos, costs, 302
Storage tanks, costs, 302
Storage vessel, cost, 169
Straight line depreciation, 80, 83
  approximation for, 137
Strategy for solving problems, 18
Stream days, definition, 214
Styrene, capital cost of plant, 290
Successive approximation:
  and capital cost estimation, 152
  and financial attractiveness, 104
  principle of, 18
  and product cost estimation, 213
Sugar, capital cost of plant, 290
Sulfuric acid, unit usages for, 231
Sum of the year's digits depreciation, 82, 83, 86
Supervision:
  as a component of cost, 222
  and production capacity, 225
Supply, 37
Surface aerators, costs, 303
Swing hammer mill, costs, 300

Tanks, bare module factors for, 198
Tanks, storage, costs, 169, 302
Tank suction header, costs
      (see Heat exchangers)
Tax, effect of on profit distribution, 61, 62
Taxation, corporate, 86–91
Technical feasibility criterion, 3, 5
Technological advances, effect of on correlations, 169
Technological changes, effect of on inflation indices, 167
Testing equipment, cost of, 205
Thermal screw, 298
Thickeners, costs, 302
Time:
  adjusting costs for, 161
  and sense of urgency, 9
  feasibility criterion, 3, 17, 26
  versus accuracy, 17–26
Time available:
  and financial attractiveness, 102–105
  fixed capital cost estimation, 152, 153
  and product cost estimation, 211
Total investment:
  comparison with other methods, 134–144
  definition, 150
Towers, costs (see Pressure vessels)
Towers, distillation, costs (see Distillation)
Tower trays, costs, 303
Transported bed dryers, costs (see Dryers)
Trays:
  cost of distillation bubble cap, 172
  costs, 303
Trickling filters, costs, 303
Truck dryers, costs (see Dryers)
Tunnel dryers, costs (see Dryers)
Turnover ratio, definition and usual value, 57

Turnover ratio method (*see* Universal factor method)
Turbines, costs, 303
Turbo dryers, costs (*see* Dryers)
Twin roll crusher, costs (*see* Crushers)
Twin roller mill, costs, 300
Twin shell blenders, costs (*see* Blenders)
Two roll blender, costs (*see* Mills)
Two roll mill, costs, 300

Ultrafiltration unit, costs, 306
Underground storage, costs, 303
Uniform series compound amount factor:
   definition, 71
   discrete and continuous, 76
Uniform series present worth factor, discrete and continuous, 76
Uniform series sinking fund deposit factor discrete and continuous, 76
Uniqueness, pricing the, 61
United Kingdom, tax incentives, 62
United States:
   depreciation rate, 86
   labor effectiveness, 192
   R and D expenditures, 66, 67
   sales tax, 191
Universal factor method:
   accuracy, 154
   definition and calculations, 154–159
   and the time available, 152
Urgency, sense of, 9
Use value, definition, 46
Utilities:
   cost of, 218
   as fraction of the selling price, 41, 90
   factors for the capital cost estimation of, 201
Utility cost contribution, estimation of, 215–220
Utility diminishing, 35, 36
Utility usage and capacity, 225

Vacuum deaerator, costs (*see* Deaerator)
Vacuum dryers, costs (*see* Dryers)
Vacuum pumps, costs, 303
Value:
   cost, definition, 46
   esteem, definition, 46
   exchange, definition, 46
   types of, 45, 46
   use, definition, 46

Variable costs, 40, 42, 43
V-belt drive, costs (*see* Drives)
Venture game, xii, 48
Venture profit:
   comparison with other methods, 134–144
   definiton and calculation, 111–113
   and the time available, 104
Venture worth (*see* Present value)
Vertical spiral blenders, costs (*see* Blenders)
Vessels:
   alloy factors for, 193
   bare module factors for, 198, 199
   pressure, costs, 301
   storage, cost correlation for, 169
   and tanks, 302
Vibrating screens, costs, 302

Waste disposal, ethics, 16
Waste heat boiler, costs, 306
Waste stabilization basins, costs (*see* Basins)
Waste treatment:
   cost of, 219
   criteria for, 27
   equipment, costs of (*see* App. C)
   plant, estimate of the cost of, 91
   units, costs, 306
Waste water treatment index (*see* EPA STP index)
Waste water treatment plants, factors for the capital cost estimation, 184
Water:
   demineralizers, costs, 306
   softeners, costs, 306
   supply, cost factors for, 202
   towers, costs (*see* Storage)
   treatment, cost factors for, 202
   treatment facility, costs, 306
Water, cost of, 218
Wiped film evaporators, costs (*see* Evaporators)
Working capital, 49, 52, 56, 64
   estimation of, 204
   as part of the total investment, 150
Worksheet:
   for estimation of the capital cost, 206, 207
   for financial attractiveness calculations, 143

Yard and fence lighting, cost factors for, 202
Yield, definition, 62

Date Due